Readings in Social Research Methods

Readings in Social Research Methods

THIRD EDITION

DIANE KHOLOS WYSOCKI
University of Nebraska at Kearney

THOMSON
WADSWORTH

Australia • Brazil • Canada • Mexico • Singapore • Spain
United Kingdom • United States

THOMSON

WADSWORTH

Readings in Social Research Methods,
Third Edition
Diane Kholos Wysocki

Acquisitions Editor: Chris Caldeira
Assistant Editor: Christina Ho
Editorial Assistant: Tali Beesley
Marketing Manager: Michelle Williams
Marketing Assistant: Emily Elrod
Marketing Communications Manager: Linda Yip
Project Manager, Editorial Production: Samen Iqbal
Creative Director: Rob Hugel
Art Director: John Walker
Print Buyer: Nora Massuda
Permissions Editor: Bob Kauser
Production Service: Aaron Downey, Matrix Productions Inc.
Copy Editor: Patricia Herbst
Cover Designer: Yvo Riezebos Design
Cover Image: Frederic Cirou/Getty Images
Compositor: Integra
Text and Cover Printer: Thomson West

Printed in the United States of America
1 2 3 4 5 6 11 10 09 08 07

Library of Congress Control Number: 2006939174

ISBN-13: 978-0-495-09337-4
ISBN-10: 0-495-09337-8

Thomson Higher Education
10 Davis Drive
Belmont, CA 94002-3098
USA

For more information about our products, contact us at:
Thomson Learning Academic Resource Center
1-800-423-0563

For permission to use material from this text or product, submit a request online at
http://www.thomsonrights.com.
Any additional questions about permissions can be submitted by e-mail to
thomsonrights@thomson.com.

To my husband Bill
Thanks for all of your love, support, and commitment.

and
To Julia Stumkat, our German host daughter
For all your help and insight into what students would want in a research methods book.

Contents

PREFACE x

PART I **An Introduction to Inquiry**

1 Here We Go! Get Ready to Find Out Why You Should Learn About Research Methods 1

1 *From* The Sociological Imagination 7
C. Wright Mills

2 *The Reality of Everyday Life* 11
Peter Berger and Thomas Luckmann

2 Research and Theory: They Go Hand in Hand 17

3 *School Tracking and Student Violence* 23
Lissa J. Yogan

4 *Murder Followed by Suicide in Australia, 1973–1992: A Research Note* 33
Jo Barnes

3 Ethics: You Must Have Ethics in Life and Especially in Research 41

5 *Taking Names: The Ethics of Indirect Recruitment in Research on Sexual Networks* 47
Lewis H. Margolis

6 *The Ethics of Conducting Social-Science Research on the Internet* 55
James C. Hamilton

7 *Code of Ethics* 58
American Sociological Association

PART II The Structuring of Inquiry

4 Research Design: Now It's Time to Plan 61

8 *Public Assistance Receipt Among Immigrants and Natives: How the Unit of Analysis Affects Research Findings* 66
Jennifer Van Hook, Jennifer E. Glick, and Frank D. Bean

9 *Consequences of Participating in a Longitudinal Study of Marriage* 74
Joseph Veroff, Shirley Hatchett, and Elizabeth Douvan

5 Conceptualization and Operationalization: We Have to Explain What We Are Studying 82

10 *An Epidemiological Survey on the Presence of Toxic Chemicals in Soaps and Cosmetics Used by Adolescent Female Students from a Nigerian University* 86
Ifeyinwa Flossy Obuekwe, Mabel Ochei Uche, and M. Pharm

11 *Conceptualization of Terrorism* 91
Jack P. Gibbs

6 Indexes and Scales: Now We Get to Measure It All! 98

12 *A Study of Differences in Business Ethical Values in Mainland China, the U.S., and Jamaica* 103
Lillian Y. Fok, Sandra J. Hartman, and Kern Kwong

13 *The Reverse Social Distance Scale* 111
Motoko Y. Lee, Stephen G. Sapp, and Melvin C. Ray

7 Sampling Made Easy 117

14 *Sex in America* 123
Robert T. Michael, John H. Gagnon, Edward O. Laumann, and Gina Kolata

15 *The Eurowinter Project: The Use of Market/Social Research Methods in an International Scientific Study* 130
Colin McDonald

PART III Methods of Observation

8 Experimental and Survey Research: Putting It All Together 138

16 *Prepaid Monetary Incentives and Data Quality in Face-to-Face Interviews: Data from the 1996 Survey of Income and Program Participation Incentive Experiment* 144
Michael Davern, Todd H. Rockwood, Randy Sherrod, and Stephen Campbell

17 *Sex in America—The Sex Survey* 151
Robert T. Michael, John H. Gagnon, Edward O. Laumann, and Gina Kolata

18 *The Internet and Opinion Measurement: Surveying Marginalized Populations* 157
Nadine S. Koch and Jolly A. Emrey

9 Field Research and Unobtrusive Measures: Fun in the Field 163

19 *Comparisons Between Thai Adolescent Voices and Thai Adolescent Health Literature* 169
Vipavee Thongpriwan and Beverly J. McElmurry

20 *Amateur Stripping and Gaming Encounters: Fun in Games or Gaming as Fun?* 176
Julie Ann Harms Cannon, Thomas C. Calhoun, and Rhonda Fisher

21 *Thinking Through the Heart* 185
Ann Goetting

10 Existing Data and Evaluation Research: Let's Find Out What Works 191

22 *What Sociologists Do and Where They Do It: The NSF Survey on Sociologists' Work Activities and Workplaces* 194
Robert J. Dotzler and Ross Koppel

23 *Professors Who Make the Grade: (Factors That Affect Students' Grades of Professors)* 202
Vicky L. Seiler and Michael J. Seiler

Pg 144

APPENDIX: Writing and Reading a Research Paper 213

24 *Construction of Masculinity: A Look into the Lives of Heterosexual Male Transvestites* 222
Diane Kholos Wysocki

GLOSSARY 227
INDEX 231

Preface

Diane and Jay in front of Mendenhall Glacier

I have been teaching research methods and working with students on their own research projects since I began teaching in 1996. I love working with undergraduates and helping them as they make sense of the world in which they live by conducting research. It's great fun to watch students think of a research question about something they see in their day-to-day lives and be able to turn that idea into a project, see their projects come alive, and help them present their projects at various conferences around the country. Whether you are a student who wants to go to graduate school or not, the research experience is priceless and most often times a lot of fun. Plus, you never know, you might decide later on, after working for a few years, that you do want to go onto graduate school. And voilà—you already have experience with research and presentations at conferences to put on your academic résumé. Maybe you have even been fortunate enough to have published your work with the help of a wonderful professor who has been mentoring you.

Five or six years ago, I had a student named Jay in some of my classes. We have kept in touch, and my husband and I even visited Jay and his wife in Alaska while we were on an Alaskan cruise. Jay is now an officer in the military. A few weeks ago, he decided to take classes to obtain his master's degree. But since he is in the military and the school he is going through is all online, he won't be able to write a master's thesis. Well, thinking ahead, he realizes that one day he is going to get out of the military and will want a Ph.D. The master's will help, and he is excited to find out that his undergraduate research methods class is coming in really handy now because he understands research design in his graduate courses. So, he has connections to me and to other people who can help him write a master's thesis and really do a good study. Jay knows that there is much more to education than taking classes and that research is an important key. Plus it is always a good idea to build a relationship with your professors. You never know when you will need them in the future.

I know that sometimes research can be difficult and that some students are even a little hesitant to take a research methods course. I worry about that. I want all of you to understand that research can be a lot of fun, and I want to help you enjoy it. There are some great textbooks available about research methods. However, it has been my experience that students like to hear not only about the concepts they need to learn but also how those concepts have been used in original studies. It has also been my experience that the more interesting a research topic is and the more closely it connects with students' lives, the easier the material is to understand.

I cannot possibly cover everything there is to know about research methods in this reader. That isn't even the point of a reader. It would be an impossible undertaking and would just replicate what you learn from a textbook. Instead, I have compiled a series of brief readings that can be used to support the terms and concepts you will learn in your research methods class. You will find that these chapters parallel Earl Babbie's *The Practice of Social Research*, 12th edition, and *The Basics of Social Research*, 4th edition, which makes this reader a perfect companion for Babbie's widely used texts. However, this reader may also be used with any other research text currently on the market because the concepts it illuminates are those central to any course in research methods.

Readings in Social Research Method, 3rd edition, is intended for undergraduate students who are taking their first research methods course. The goal is to provide an introduction to the important issues and topics while supporting those ideas with interesting original research articles.

ORGANIZATION OF THE READER

Readings in Social Research Methods, 3rd edition, is divided into three parts and has 10 chapters. This book is organized to follow the format of Earl Babbie's *The Practice of Social Research*, 12th edition, and *The Basics of Social Research*, 4th edition. The reader can be used along with his textbooks or by itself. What I have tried to do is gather articles that are relevant and that I thought would hold your interest. There are two or three articles in each chapter supporting the concepts discussed and three review questions at the end of each article. The glossary at the end of the book contains important terms that appear in bold type throughout the text.

Chapter 1, "Here We Go! Get Ready to Find Out Why You Should Learn About Research Methods," begins Part 1, covering the basics about research.

This chapter tells you that our ideas about the world around us might not be as accurate as our "commonsense" ideas would have us believe. You will learn that we all have two realities in our lives: one that is based on what we see and know to be real and the other that we believe to be real because someone else told us it is real. In this chapter you will learn how important this idea is to research.

Chapter 2, "Research and Theory: They Go Hand in Hand," focuses on how the data we collect are empty and meaningless unless they are combined with theory. You will learn about four different paradigms that can be used in your research and learn the difference between deductive and inductive theory.

Chapter 3, "Ethics: You Must Have Ethics in Life and Especially In Research," appears early in this reader. In some other textbooks, you will see it as a chapter toward the end of the book or as an appendix. This placements leads me to believe that ethics could be an afterthought. I believe that having a good grasp of the ethical problems in research is important to remember while you read this book. Thus, you will be able to think about important ethical issues as you design a project or read about someone else's. You need to understand why participation should be voluntary, why you should not deceive or harm your subjects, and what role the institutional review board plays. It is also important when you are reading the research of other people to be able to tell if they ethically conducted their research.

Part 2 begins with Chapter 4 "Research Design: Now It's Time to Plan." In this chapter, you will learn that the purpose of research is to explore, describe, and explain the phenomenon you want to study. You will also learn that units of analysis can be very confusing at times and that the most common units of analysis are the individual, the group, the organization, the social category, the social artifact, the social institution, and the society. Finally, you will learn why time plays such an important role in research. It helps to describe changes or differences in behaviors within a framework of different ages or stages across the life span.

Chapter 5, "Conceptualization and Operationalization: We Have to Explain What We Are Studying," will tell you how to take variables and put them into identifying concepts that you can ultimately measure during your project. For instance, if you are investigating religiosity, you can conceptualize that concept by giving it a definition. Let's say you define religiosity as someone who goes to his or her place of worship at least once a week. You can then operationalize that concept and measure it by asking the question: "How many times a week do you go to your place of worship?"

Once you know what you are studying, Chapter 6, "Indexes and Scales: Now We Get to Measure It All!," can help you construct a way to measure your variables. You will also learn the difference between using an index and a scale and how to determine which would be best for your particular research question.

An important topic within research methods is in Chapter 7, "Sampling Made Easy," where you will learn how you pick the group you want to conduct research on. Often, it is impossible to pick the entire population because it is much too large. Therefore, you must somehow find a sample that represents the population. You will learn various sampling techniques and how to pick the best one for your project.

In Part 3, you will learn various modes of observations. Chapter 8 is called "Experimental and Survey Research: Putting It All Together." Experiments are the easiest way to explain concepts that you need to know such as that the independent variable causes the dependent variable. This works well in controlled environments such as a lab, but when experiments are done on people, you have to think about other variables that can affect the dependent variable. Survey research is probably the most common method used in the social sciences and involves administering a questionnaire in person, through the mail, or over the Internet.

Chapter 9 is called "Field Research and Unobtrusive Measures: Fun in the Field." Field research involves going where some type of action is happening and observing it. This action can be on a street corner, at a public library, or on a grade school playground. Narrative research involves listening to people's "voices" and letting people tell their own stories. As researchers, we are sometimes so busy asking questions that we forget to just listen and may miss what our subject is trying to tell us. Regardless, interviewing is important in research, and you will learn various techniques for asking questions. In content analysis, you can analyze anything such as books, newspaper articles, pictures in magazines, or bumper stickers. For example, you might be interested in how women are portrayed in computer advertisements. What are their roles? Are they actually shown working with the computer, or are they helping a man who is working with the computer?

In Chapter 10, "Existing Data and Evaluation Research: Let's Find Out What Works," you will learn how existing data can support any type of research you are conducting. Suppose you are interested in gender differences in sixth-grade math classes. You can go to the U.S. Department of Education database where they have been surveying large numbers of students about their feelings and beliefs regarding their own math abilities. This type of existing data can support and guide your project. Evaluation research is used to find out how well programs are working to cause the desired change in either individual behaviors or programs.

The Appendix, "Writing and Reading a Research Paper," is something that you might want to read at the beginning of the semester. Most professors will want you to write a paper and will have you reading articles not only in this book but ones that you have to find in the library. Because both reading and writing are so important and students are often confused about both, I have included this appendix. It will increase your knowledge about each part of an article, how to properly use citations, and how to make sure you stay out of trouble with unintentional plagiarism.

ACKNOWLEDGMENTS

I have many people to thank who have helped me with this book. To begin, I must thank Dr. Earl Babbie for his support with every edition. It is truly an honor to have my reader paired with his textbooks. There is no better name in research methods. He is very much the research guru in my world and also a very nice man. I would like to thank Susan Badger and Sean Wakely for making sure this book went to its third edition. I really appreciate your support and help. Next, I must thank my outside reviewers, who made numerous suggestions and comments about the third edition. Having been a reviewer myself, I know that a constructive review requires time away from other activities that are very important. To Elizabeth Chute, Carroll College; Qingwen Dong, University of the Pacific; Terri Earnest, Arkansas Tech University; Mike Lacey, Colorado State University; William McDonald, Georgetown University; Angela G. Mertig, Middle Tennessee State University; Adina Nack, California Lutheran University; Ellen S. Parham, Northern Illinois University; Mary Virnoche, Humboldt State University; and Carlos E. Zeisel, Salem State College. I appreciate the time you took to make comments on the drafts of this book. I also want to thank Aaron Downey at Matrix Productions for overseeing the production of this edition, Samen Iqbal who is the production manager, and my copyeditor, Patricia Herbst. Knowing what an author wants to say and making it come alive on the pages is an amazing ability. I can't thank you enough for your help and comments. I also want to thank my husband, Bill Rasmussen, who makes sure I have everything I need when I am writing, especially under a deadline. He is my retired househusband whose willingness to clean, cook, and do laundry allows me the ability to work and write. He is truly my partner in a feminist marriage. And finally, there wouldn't be a need for a reader without students who have developed an interest in research and gone on to conduct their own projects with me over the years. Having students who love research as much as I do is what teaching is all about. So, with that said, thanks to Julia Stumkat, Laura Logan, Jennifer Thalken, Sandi Nielsen, Jessica Reinert, Jessica Seberger, Alyse Sutton, Sierra Whitney, Josh Hagel, Jena Lynch, Thomas Threlkeld, and Nathan Wragne—to name just a few—who remind me frequently why I love my job so much. I also want to personally thank Dr. Charles Frankum and Dr. Alice Luknic. Dr. Frankum said he always wanted his name in a book and who knows why he made it possible for this book to be written. Thanks and here you are, I didn't forget. Dr. Luknic, thanks for being my partner in health care for so many years. You have made such a difference in my life. I can't thank you enough.

1

Here We Go! Get Ready to Find Out Why You Should Learn About Research Methods

Anytime you read the newspaper or listen to a news report, you hear about some type of research study. So whether you like it or not, you are always going to hear about research and be around research. For example, my husband Bill reads a lot of newspapers online everyday (he is retired from Boeing and has the time to e-mail my students and me what he thinks would interest us). Over the past few weeks alone, USAToday.com published information about many research studies. For instance, it has been reported that although Americans spend billions of dollars on vitamins each year, there is not enough scientific evidence to determine whether a multivitamin/mineral supplement taken every day helps prevent chronic diseases such as heart disease and cancer (Hellmich, 2006). In another study, the human papilloma virus, or HPV, the most common sexually transmitted infection in the United States, is believed to be the cause of about 70 percent of cervical cancers and most cases of genital warts, which are spread by skin-to-skin contact. Also, patients with HIV/AIDS can receive a single pill that combines the three drugs known as the cocktail therapy (Anonymous, 2006a). Furthermore, the Food and Drug Administration is working to approve a vaccine against the HPV virus (Rubin, 2006), and it is reported that although the use of illegal drugs has dropped, about 4.5 million teens have tried prescription drug painkillers such as Vicodin and OxyContin to get high because they believe that using prescription drugs is safer than using illegal drugs (Anonymous, 2006b).

Readings in Social Methods Research, 3rd edition, is designed to help students learn about scientific research methods and know how to decipher the studies that you hear about every day in the newspaper, on TV, and on the radio.

Although you will be learning about research methods to reach your goal of completing this course, you will find that the things you learn, the way you will be taught to think, your ability to gather information, and your capacity to draw your own conclusions will go far beyond this class. I find that many students are quite fearful of taking a research methods course and have preconceived ideas about how difficult the course will be. Sometimes they even dig their heels in, making it difficult for me to teach and difficult for them to learn. (Did you put off taking this course until the end of your college career?) I believe it is best to take the methods causes early in your college career because then you can possibly find some topic you are really interested in researching and present it at conferences or even get it published with the help of your professor.

Some textbooks are overwhelming and lack strong examples, primary sources, and exciting readings. My desire is to make research methods as fun to learn as they are for me to teach. So *Readings in Social Methods Research,* 3rd edition, is designed as a reader with basic information and brief, stimulating, readings that will capture your attention, along with a variety of questions to help you incorporate what you have learned with what you have read.

This book is suitable for students in basic research methodology classes who are just beginning to learn about research. The process of reading research is important because most of us read much more research than we actually conduct. However, knowing how to read a research paper and understand it is a skill that must be learned and practiced, and this reader will help you. This takes us back to the beginning of the chapter where we started out with examples of research that my husband found on USAToday.com. You, too, hear about these kinds of research projects all the time. But how do you know if what you hear on the news, in the newspapers, and even from your friends is accurate and should be believed? What you are going to learn from this book is how to tell the difference between good and bad science.

WHY ARE YOU TAKING THIS CLASS?

Why are you taking this class? Are you interested in social research methods? Are you required to take the course? Do you want to understand certain types of articles that you have read for your school courses or for your job? Whether you are taking this class for any of those reasons or for any number of your own reasons, an important part of learning about research is understanding how the research is conducted and how the conclusions are reached. The only way for you to understand the conclusions, however, is to learn how researchers plan and conduct their research projects.

Just think about it. What types of questions do you have about the world in which you live? In May 2006, Anthony Bell, 25, of Baton Rouge walked into the

Ministry of Jesus Christ Church and shot five people before fleeing with his wife and three children. Leaving his children unharmed, Bell killed his wife before being captured by police. "This is going to be one of the worst days in the history of our city," Police Chief Jeff Leduff said after Bell was captured (Simpson, 2006). As a budding researcher, you might wonder about Bell's motives and about the effects of this disaster on society. Why would a man carry a gun into a church, kill five people, and then kill the mother of his children? What conditions were these children and their parents living in before this tragedy? Could those conditions in any way influence the rest of the children's lives? Why did Bell think that shooting people was the way to handle his problems? Did he learn this strategy at home? Did he learn it from television? Was that day in May 2006 really one of the "worst days" in Baton Rouge's history as the police chief suggested? How would you go about finding answers to some of these questions? We are all curious about one thing or another, and the key to satisfying our curiosity is to find out if our ideas are correct, to learn which ideas are not, and to make recommendations for change.

Here is another important reason to learn about research methods. We often see TV sales pitches that say things like "75 percent of doctors interviewed prescribed drug X for relief of arthritic pain." Would you believe this claim? Would it make you want to purchase drug X? What questions might you ask about this claim? An understanding of research methods will help you figure out what questions you should ask. For instance, how many doctors were interviewed? What if there were only four interviews? Would you feel confident about a drug that three doctors said they liked? What kinds of questions were the doctors asked about prescribing drug X? If they were asked, "Have you ever prescribed drug X?," were they just as likely to have prescribed drugs A, B, C, or D? Who interviewed the doctors? If the manufacturers of drug X did the interviewing, were the doctors compensated for their participation in the study? Could compensation have swayed their responses? You might think you have received correct answers to your questions from those who conducted the study, but the answers might be to encourage you to buy the product and have nothing to do with reality or truth.

DIFFERENT REALITIES

Research[1] is a series of steps, techniques, exercises, and events that can be applied to every sphere of life to help you understand the world in which you live. If you want to actually conduct research on doctors to determine how likely

1 Words in **boldface** are defined in the glossary at the back of the book.

they are to prescribe drug X to their patients, you need to come up with some sort of plan to help guide your research. Your plan of action can also be called **research methods** because the methods you use are an essential set of skills, insights, and tools needed to answer any kinds of questions. If you still think about the drug X study, you might ask some questions about the types of methods that were used to conclude that 75 percent of the doctors prescribed drug X. Who did the researchers actually talk to? How did they find the doctors to interview? If, before conducting the study, the researchers had a plan about how they were going to do their research, you could actually go back and look at their methods if you had a question or a doubt. The methods the researchers used could help you decide if the findings were reliable and could be trusted.

Why do you think methods sections are so important to research? One problem in research is that it is easy for any of us to be uncertain about what is real and what is not. How do you view the world? What kinds of practices, thoughts, values, and insights do you have about the world based on where you came from? Would they be different for someone who grew up in a different situation or a different culture? Where do you get your ideas about different cultures, people, and countries?

In 1999, I spent four weeks traveling through Singapore, Malaysia, and Thailand with my youngest son Jonathan, who was 19 years old at the time and had been backpacking around the world by himself. By the time I met up with him in Singapore, he had already been in numerous countries over a seven-month span. As you can imagine, I was worried sick about him. Some countries that he planned on going to concerned me because my notions about those countries were based on movies I had seen in the past.

Years earlier, I had seen *Midnight Express* (1978), in which Turkish authorities arrest a young American tourist after he tries to smuggle hashish out of the country. This young man is sentenced to 30 years in prison, where his realities are pretty harsh, and his parents are unable to get him out and back into the United States. The things done to him in the prison were so terrible I had to leave the theater and couldn't watch the rest of the movie, but the memory stayed with me as my reality of a foreign country. In another film, *Return to Paradise* (1998), one American is arrested in Malaysia for a prankish misdemeanor. Although he and his friends all shared in the prank, he takes the rap for all of them, and is sentenced to be hanged as a drug trafficker, and is held for years in a terrible Malaysian prison. In a more recent movie of this type, *The Beach* (2000), Richard (Leonardo DiCaprio) travels to Thailand and end's up in grave danger on an island with some friends. We actually visited this island and it is very beautiful. Even though I am a sociologist and understand there are different types of realities, movies like these heightened my concern about my son going to Asia. This would be my **agreement reality** because the things I considered real were real only because I had learned about them through the media and people around me. This agreement reality took precedence over anything else.

Not until I actually went to Asia with my son and traveled all around, met the people, ate their food, and learned about the culture did I develop my **experimental reality**, where the things I knew were a function of my own direct experiences rather than the experiences of others. I found that the things I had been concerned about originally were not as real as I had thought. The people were wonderful, they were helpful, I learned about lifestyles different from my own, and my concerns were unfounded. When I left my son in Thailand and came back to Nebraska, I wasn't as worried as I had been before I experienced the realities of these countries myself and saw that the people were not out to capture young Americans and throw them into prisons never to be seen again. This doesn't mean, however, that you can break the law in these countries and get away with it. The real reality is that if you do something illegal in another country, you are subject to that country's laws and punishments.

How would two different realities affect the outcomes of research? Preconceived ideas about the situations you are studying can blind you to things that are right in front of you. You might be looking at something from only one point of view and be completely unaware of other points of view. What do you think? Do you believe that your agreement reality and your experimental reality could affect the outcome of the research you are conducting? The methods a researcher uses give us an idea about the researcher's perspective and the way data were gathered and help us to understand the methods and to interpret the findings accurately.

HUMAN INQUIRY

Although your own realities play a big part in the type of research you are interested in and the conclusions you come up with, one thing you need to know is that you don't need to reinvent the wheel when you begin a research project. Furthermore, your topic doesn't have to be something no one else has ever thought about. You already know some things for sure about the world around you—for instance, that the world is round and that if you drop something it will fall. Such ideas are based on **tradition**. So if you accept what everyone "knows" to be true, then you don't have to start from scratch. You can look at research reports to see what other researchers have found, because their findings may provide a basis for your own research.

Tradition is good; it saves some time and energy. But be aware that it also can be bad. There is a good chance that the findings are inaccurate and that you do not look far enough to find another "truth." Similarly, judgment errors can be made because all of us tend to believe people who are in positions of **authority**. Suppose you go to the doctor's office for a checkup and you are told that something might be wrong and you need major surgery. Would you question the doctor, who seems to be an authority on the subject? Or would you believe you must have the surgery regardless of how you feel about it because the doctor is an authority figure and you believe that doctors' suggestions are legitimate?

STEPPING BACK

If you are reading about research, how can you see beyond your personal realities and tradition and the authority of those who have conducted research previously? In *The Sociological Imagination* (1956), the theorist C. Wright Mills distinguishes between **personal troubles** and **public issues** and stresses the difference between them. Personal troubles occur within all of us and within our immediate relationships with others. Public issues, in contrast, have to do with the environments in which we live. If you get a job after graduating from college but you aren't earning enough money to support your children and pay the rent, you have a personal trouble. If you believe that you might have been tracked in school to take home economics or shop classes rather than math and science and that this tracking happened not only to you but to many other young people, who like you today lack the skills needed for a better paying job, then your earning ability is a public issue (Claus, 1999).

How can you know the difference between personal troubles and public issues in your own research? Mills (1916–1962) describes five basic steps to follow. First, you must *distance yourself.* Often, you are so immersed in your everyday life that it is difficult to see things that are right in front of you. You need to think yourself "out of the immediacy." Second, you must *engage in a systematic examination of empirical methods and observations.* This means you must conduct research to help you find answers to your questions. To do this, however, you must work within your own experiences. Third, you must *eliminate ethnocentrism.* **Ethnocentrism** is the feeling and belief that your group's attitudes, customs, and behaviors are superior to those of other groups. Let's say you grew up in a rural area and your sociology assignment is to observe gang members in the inner city. Would the fact that you have never been to an inner city and have never seen a gang member, except in movies, influence the conclusions you might draw about their behaviors? Fourth, you must *analyze the data* that you collect. An analysis of your data may tell you that your commonsense ideas about a topic are actually incorrect. Fifth, you should *take action.* If you know something is amiss, you must do something about it. Improvements in society depend on action. Whether you take action by publishing your results in an academic journal or by standing on a picket line, your research can help to transform society.

REFERENCES

Anonymous. 2006a, July 12. HIV/AIDS patients get first once-daily, 3-in-1 pill. *USA Today*. Retrieved July 12, 2006, from http://www.usatoday.com

Anonymous. 2006b, May 16. Teen abuse of prescription drugs grows. *USA Today*. Retrieved from http://www.usatoday.com

Claus, J. 1999. You can't avoid the politics: Lessons for teacher education from a case study of teacher-initiated tracking reform. *Journal of Teacher Education*, 50(1): 5.

Hellmich, N. 2006, May 17. Panel neutral on multivitamins. *USA Today*. Retrieved from http://www.usatoday.com

Mills, C. Wright. 1956. *The sociological imagination*. New York: Oxford University Press.

Rubin, R. 2006, May 17. Cervical cancer vaccine up for FDA review. *USA Today*. Retrived from http://www.usatoday.com

Simpson, D. 2006, May 21. Suspect captured after 5 killed in Louisiana. Retrieved May 21, 2006, from http://news.yahoo.com/s/ap/20060521/ap_on_re_us/church_shooting;_ylt=AiDrk0m9b4J3whBnqpbS8KOs0NUE;_ylu=X3oDMTA2Z2szazkxBHNlYwN0bQ–

SUGGESTED FILMS

Tribute to C. Wright Mills (T. Hayden et al., 2001) (119 min.). Washington, DC: National Cable Satellite Corp. Friends and colleagues read from the book *C. Wright Mills: Letters and Autobiographical Writings*, published by the University of California Press. They also talk about their connections with Mills and about the inspiration of his writings on their lives. Mills was a sociologist and teacher whose anti-establishment writings influenced the reformist social thinking of the 1960s.

Research Methods for the Social Sciences (V. Dalli, B.K. Lary, M. Gunn, M. Swift, and M. Fortunato, 1996) (33 min). Austin, TX: Horizon Film and Video. Describes the research methods used in the social sciences and the steps used to apply the scientific method. Ethical research methods are discussed.

1

From *The Sociological Imagination*

C. WRIGHT MILLS

It is important to start a research course by learning about C. Wright Mills, who argues that although the social sciences are filled with what researchers have done in the past, the questions and conclusions that are found can be constructed differently depending on who conducts the research. You must remember that your own reality may influence the ways in which you look at life and may blind you to other possibilities. By using your sociological

SOURCE: From Mills, C. Wright. 1959. The promise. In *The Sociological Imagination*. New York: Oxford University Press, pp. 3–8. Reprinted by permission of the publisher.

imagination, you can understand the larger context and how it affects individual lives. As you read this selection, think about how your life is affected by the bigger picture that Mills writes about.

Nowadays men often feel that their private lives are a series of traps. They sense that within their everyday worlds, they cannot overcome their troubles, and in this feeling, they are often quite correct: What ordinary men are directly aware of and what they try to do are bounded by the private orbits in which they live; their visions and their powers are limited to the close-up scenes of job, family, neighborhood; in other milieus, they move vicariously and remain spectators. And the more aware they become, however vaguely, of ambitions and of threats which transcend their mediate locales, the more trapped they seem to feel.

Underlying this sense of being trapped are seemingly impersonal changes in the very structure of continent-wide societies. The facts of contemporary history are also facts about the success and the failure of individual men and women. When a society is industrialized, a peasant becomes a worker; a feudal lord is liquidated or becomes a businessman. When classes rise or fall, a man is employed or unemployed; when the rate of investment goes up or down, a man takes new heart or goes broke. When wars happen, an insurance salesman becomes a rocket launcher; a store clerk, a radar man; a wife lives alone; a child grows up without a father. Neither the life of an individual nor the history of a society can be understood without understanding both.

Yet men do not usually define the troubles they endure in terms of historical change and institutional contradiction. The well-being they enjoy, they do not usually impute to the big ups and downs of the societies in which they live. Seldom aware of the intricate connection between the patterns of their own lives and the course of world history, ordinary men do not usually know what this connection means for the kinds of men they are becoming and for the kinds of history-making in which they might take part. They do not possess the quality of mind essential to grasp the interplay of man and society, of biography and history, of self and world. They cannot cope with their personal troubles in such ways as to control the structural transformations that usually lie behind them. Surely it is no wonder. In what period have so many men been so totally exposed at so fast a pace to such earthquakes of change? That Americans have not known such catastrophic changes as have the men and women of other societies is due to historical facts that are now quickly becoming "merely history." The history that now affects every man is world history. Within this scene and this period, in the course of a single generation, one sixth of mankind is transformed from all that is feudal and backward into all that is modern, advanced, and fearful. Political colonies are freed; new and less visible forms of imperialism installed. Revolutions occur; men feel the intimate grip of new kinds of authority. Totalitarian societies rise, and are smashed to bits—or succeed fabulously. After two centuries of ascendancy, capitalism is shown up as only one way to make society into an industrial apparatus. After two centuries of hope, even formal democracy is restricted to a quite small portion of mankind. Everywhere in the underdeveloped world, ancient ways of life are broken up and vague expectations become urgent demands. Everywhere in the overdeveloped world, the means of authority and of violence become total in scope and bureaucratic in form. Humanity itself now lies before us, the super-nation at either pole concentrating its most coordinated and massive efforts upon the preparation of World War Three.

The very shaping of history now outpaces the ability of men to orient themselves in accordance with cherished values. And which values? Even when they do not panic, men often sense that older ways of feeling and thinking have collapsed and that newer beginnings are ambiguous to the point of moral stasis. Is it any wonder that ordinary men feel they cannot cope with the larger worlds with which they are so suddenly confronted? That they cannot understand the meaning of their epoch for their own lives? That—in defense of selfhood—they become morally insensible, trying to remain altogether private men? Is it any wonder that they come to be possessed by a sense of the trap? It is not only information that they need—in this Age of Fact, information often dominates their attention and overwhelms their capacities to assimilate it. It is not only the skills of reason that they need—although their struggles to acquire these often exhaust their limited moral energy.

What they need, and what they feel they need, is a quality of mind that will help them to use information and to develop reason in order to achieve lucid summations of what is going on in the world and of what may be happening within themselves. It is this quality, I am going to contend, that journalists and scholars, artists and publics, scientists and editors are coming to expect of what may be called the sociological imagination. The sociological imagination enables its possessor to understand the larger historical scene in terms of its meaning for the inner life and the external career of a variety of individuals. It enables him to take into account how individuals, in the welter of their daily experience, often become falsely conscious of their positions. Within that welter, the framework of modern society is sought, and within that framework the psychologies of a variety of men and women are formulated. By such means the personal uneasiness of individuals is focused upon explicit troubles and the indifference of publics is transformed into involvement with public issues.

The first fruit of this imagination—and the first lesson of the social science that embodies it—is the idea that the individual can understand his own experience and gauge his own fate only by locating himself within his period, that he can know his own chances in life only by becoming aware of those of all individuals in his circumstances. In many ways it is a terrible lesson; in many ways a magnificent one. We do not know the limits of man's capacities for supreme effort or willing degradation, for agony or glee, for pleasurable brutality or the sweetness of reason. But in our time we have come to know that the limits of human nature are frighteningly broad. We have come to know that every individual lives, from one generation to the next, in some society; that he lives out a biography, and that he lives it out within some historical sequence. By the fact of his living he contributes, however minutely, to the shaping of this society and to the course of its history, even as he is made by society and by its historical push and shove.

The sociological imagination enables us to grasp history and biography and the relations between the two within society. That is its task and its promise. And it is the signal of what is best in contemporary studies of man and society. No social study that does not come back to the problems of biography, of history and of their intersections within a society has completed its intellectual journey. Whatever the specific problems of the classic social analysts, however limited or however broad the features of social reality they have examined, those who have been imaginatively aware of the promise of their work have consistently asked three sorts of questions:

1. What is the structure of this particular society as a whole? What are its essential components, and how are they related to one another? How does it differ from other varieties of social order? Within it, what is the meaning of any particular feature for its continuance and for its change?
2. Where does this society stand in human history? What are the mechanics by which it is changing? What is its place within and its meaning for the development of humanity as a whole? How does any particular feature we are examining affect, and how is it affected by, the historical period in which it moves? And this period—what are its essential features? How does it differ from other periods? What are its characteristic ways of history-making?
3. What varieties of men and women now prevail in this society and in this period? And what varieties are coming to prevail? In what ways are they selected and formed, liberated and repressed, made sensitive and blunted? What kinds of "human nature" are revealed in the conduct and character we observe in this society in this period? And what is the meaning for "human nature" of each and every feature of the society we are examining?

Whether the point of interest is a great power state or a minor literary mood, a family, a prison, a creed—these are the kinds of questions the best social analysts have asked. They are the intellectual pivots of classic studies of man in society—and they are the questions inevitably raised by any mind possessing the sociological imagination. For that imagination is the capacity to shift from one perspective to another—from the political to the psychological; from examination of a single family to comparative assessment of the national budgets of the world; from the theological school to the military establishment; from considerations of an industry to studies of contemporary poetry. It is the capacity to range from the most impersonal and remote transformations to the most intimate features of the human self—and to see the relations between the two. Back of its use there is always the urge to know the social and historical meaning of the individual in the society and in the period in which he has his quality and his being.

That, in brief, is why it is by means of the sociological imagination that men now hope to grasp what is going on in the world, and to understand what is happening in themselves as minute points of the intersections of biography and history within society. In large part, contemporary man's self-conscious view of himself as at least an outsider, if not a permanent stranger, rests upon an absorbed realization of social relativity and of the transformative power of history. The sociological imagination is the most fruitful form of this self-consciousness. By its use men whose mentalities have swept only a series of limited orbits often come to feel as if suddenly awakened in a house with which they had only supposed themselves to be familiar. Correctly or incorrectly, they often come to feel that they can now provide themselves with adequate summations, cohesive assessments, comprehensive orientations. Older decisions that once appeared sound now seem to them products of a mind unaccountably dense. Their capacity for astonishment is made lively again. They acquire a new way of thinking, they experience a transvaluation of values: in a word, by their reflection and by their sensibility, they realize the cultural meaning of the social sciences.

Perhaps the most fruitful distinction with which the sociological imagination works is between "the personal troubles of milieu" and "the public issues of social structure." This distinction is an essential tool of the sociological imagination and a feature of all classic work in social science.

What we experience in various and specific milieus, I have noted, is often caused by structural changes. Accordingly, to understand the changes of many personal milieus we are required to look beyond them. And the number and variety of such structural changes increase as the institutions within which we live become more embracing and more intricately connected with one another. To be aware of the idea of social structure and to use it with sensibility is to be capable of tracing such linkages among a great variety of milieus. To be able to do that is to possess the sociological imagination.

REVIEW QUESTIONS

1. What does C. Wright Mills mean when he says, "in this Age of Fact, information often dominates their attention and overwhelms their capacities to assimilate it"?
2. How does Mills's belief that individuals can understand their own experiences and gauge their own fate by locating themselves within their respective periods affect the outcomes of research?
3. Mills states, "No social study that does not come back to the problems of biography, of history and of their intersections within a society has completed its intellectual journey." Apply Mills's statement to a topic that might be of interest to you to research.

2

The Reality of Everyday Life

PETER BERGER AND THOMAS LUCKMANN

treatise - formal and systematic discourse in a subject; generally longer then an essay

Peter Berger and Thomas Luckmann tell us that sociology and research tap into the desire to understand the everyday social reality around us. The difficult part is that we must understand the differences between our commonsense ideas about life and the "truth." Although reality is interpreted by each individual and adds meaning to his or her world, the reality of everyday life is often taken for granted and can influence our research questions and conclusions, because we have preconceived ideas and judgments. While reading this article, think about how your commonsense reality might be different from actual reality and how the things that have happened in your life add to your commonsense ideas about the world.

Since our purpose in this treatise is a sociological analysis of the reality of everyday life, more precisely, of knowledge that guides conduct in everyday life, and we are only tangentially interested in how this reality may appear in various theoretical perspectives to intellectuals, we must begin by a clarification of that reality as it is available to the commonsense of the ordinary members of society. How that commonsense reality may be influenced by the theoretical constructions of intellectuals and other merchants of ideas is a further question. Ours is thus an enterprise that, although theoretical in character, is geared to the understanding of a reality that forms the subject matter of the empirical science of sociology, that is, the world of everyday life.

It should be evident, then, that our purpose is not to engage in philosophy. All the same, if the reality of everyday life is to be understood, account must be taken of its intrinsic character before we can proceed with sociological analysis proper. Everyday life presents itself as a reality interpreted by men and subjectively meaningful to them as a coherent world. As sociologists we take this reality as the object of our analyses. Within the frame of reference of sociology as an empirical science it is possible to take this reality as given, to take as data particular phenomena arising within it, without further inquiring about the foundations of this reality, which is a philosophical task. However, given the particular purpose of the present treatise, we cannot completely bypass the philosophical problem.

The world of everyday life is not only taken for granted as reality by the ordinary members of society in the subjectively meaningful conduct of their lives. It is a world that originates in their thoughts and actions, and is maintained as real by these. Before turning to our main task we must, therefore, attempt to clarify the foundations of knowledge in everyday life, to wit, the *objectivations* of subjective processes (and meanings) by which the *intersubjective* commonsense world is constructed.

For the purpose at hand, this is a preliminary task, and we can do no more than sketch the main features of what we believe to be an adequate

SOURCE: From Berger, P., & Luckmann, T. 1966. The reality of everyday life. In *The Social Construction of Reality: A Treatise in the Sociology of Knowledge*, pp. 19–28. Garden City, NY: Doubleday.

phenomenological sociology- study of the formal structures of concrete social experience

solution to the philosophical problem—adequate, let us hasten to add, only in the sense that it can serve as a starting point for sociological analysis. The considerations immediately following are, therefore, of the nature of philosophical prolegomena and, in themselves, presociological. The method we consider best suited to clarify the foundations of knowledge in everyday life is that of phenomenological analysis, a purely descriptive method and, as such, "empirical" but not "scientific"—as we understand the nature of the empirical sciences.

The phenomenological analysis of everyday life, or rather of the subjective experience of everyday life, refrains from any causal or genetic hypotheses, as well as from assertions about the ontological status of the phenomena analyzed. It is important to remember this. Commonsense contains innumerable pre- and quasi-scientific interpretations about everyday reality, which it takes for granted. If we are to describe the reality of commonsense we must refer to these interpretations, just as we must take account of its taken-for-granted character—but we do so within phenomenological brackets.

Consciousness is always intentional; it always intends or is directed toward objects. We can never apprehend some putative substratum of consciousness as such, only consciousness of something or other. This is so regardless of whether the object of consciousness is experienced as belonging to an external physical world or apprehended as an element of an inward subjective reality. Whether I (the first person singular, here as in the following illustrations, standing for ordinary self-consciousness in everyday life) am viewing the panorama of New York City or whether I become conscious of an inner anxiety, the processes of consciousness involved are intentional in both instances. The point need not be belabored that the consciousness of the Empire State Building differs from the awareness of anxiety. A detailed phenomenological analysis would uncover the various layers of experience, and the different structures of meaning involved in, say, being bitten by a dog, remembering having been bitten by a dog, having a phobia about all dogs, and so forth. What interests us here is the common intentional character of all consciousness.

Different objects present themselves to consciousness as constituents of different spheres of reality. I recognize the fellowmen I must deal with in the course of everyday life as pertaining to a reality quite different from the disembodied figures that appear in my dreams. The two sets of objects introduce quite different tensions into my consciousness and I am attentive to them in quite different ways. My consciousness, then, is capable of moving through different spheres of reality. Put differently, I am conscious of the world as consisting of multiple realities. As I move from one reality to another, I experience the transition as a kind of shock. This shock is to be understood as caused by the shift in attentiveness that the transition entails. Waking up from a dream illustrates this shift most simply.

Among the multiple realities there is one that presents itself as the reality par excellence. This is the reality of everyday life. Its privileged position entitles it to the designation of paramount reality. The tension of consciousness is highest in everyday life, that is, the latter imposes itself upon consciousness in the most massive, urgent and intense manner. It is impossible to ignore, difficult even to weaken in its imperative presence. Consequently, it forces me to be attentive to it in the fullest way. I experience everyday life in the state of being wide-awake. This wide-awake state of existing in and apprehending the reality of everyday life is taken by me to be normal and self-evident, that is, it constitutes my natural attitude.

I apprehend the reality of everyday life as an ordered reality. Its phenomena are prearranged in patterns that seem to be independent of my apprehension of them and that impose themselves upon the latter. The reality of everyday life appears already objectified, that is, constituted by an order of objects that have been designated as objects before my appearance on the scene. The language used in everyday life continuously provides me with the necessary objectifications and posits the order within which these make sense and within which everyday life has meaning for me. I live in a place that is geographically designated; I employ tools, from can openers to sports cars, which are realissimum: A term for God, reflecting the belief that reality, like goodness, comes in degrees, and that there must be a limiting ultimately real entity

CHAPTER 1 WHY YOU SHOULD LEARN ABOUT RESEARCH METHODS 13

designated in the technical vocabulary of my society; I live within a web of human relationships, from my chess club to the United States of America, which are also ordered by means of vocabulary. In this manner language marks the coordinates of my life in society and fills that life with meaningful objects.

The reality of everyday life is organized around the "here" of my body and the "now" of my present. This "here and now" is the focus of my attention to the reality of everyday life. What is "here and now" presented to me in everyday life is the *realissimum* of my consciousness. The reality of everyday life is not, however, exhausted by these immediate presences, but embraces phenomena that are not present "here and now." This means that I experience everyday life in terms of differing degrees of closeness and remoteness, both spatially and temporally. Closest to me is the zone of everyday life that is directly accessible to my bodily manipulation. This zone contains the world within my reach, the world in which I act so as to modify its reality, or the world in which I work. In this world of working my consciousness is dominated by the pragmatic motive, that is, my attention to this world is mainly determined by what I am doing, have done or plan to do in it. In this way it is my world par excellence. I know, of course, that the reality of everyday life contains zones that are not accessible to me in this manner. But either I have no pragmatic interest in these zones or my interest in them is indirect insofar as they may be, potentially, manipulative zones for me. Typically, my interest in the far zones is less intense and certainly less urgent. I am intensely interested in the cluster of objects involved in my daily occupation— say, the world of the garage, if I am a mechanic. I am interested, though less directly, in what goes on in the testing laboratories of the automobile industry in Detroit—I am unlikely ever to be in one of these laboratories, but the work done there will eventually affect my everyday life. I may also be interested in what goes on at Cape Kennedy or in outer space, but this interest is a matter of private, "leisure-time" choice rather than an urgent necessity of my everyday life.

The reality of everyday life further presents itself to me as an intersubjective world, a world that I share with others. This intersubjectivity sharply differentiates everyday life from other realities of which I am conscious. I am alone in the world of my dreams, but I know that the world of everyday life is as real to others as it is to myself. Indeed, I cannot exist in everyday life without continually interacting and communicating with others. I know that my natural attitude to this world corresponds to the natural attitude of others, that they also comprehend the objectifications by which this world is ordered, that they also organize this world around the "here and now" of their being in it and have projects for working in it. I also know, of course, that the others have a perspective on this common world that is not identical with mine. My "here" is their "there." My "now" does not fully overlap with theirs. My projects differ from and may even conflict with theirs. All the same, I know that I live with them in a common world. Most importantly, I know that there is an ongoing correspondence between my meanings and their meanings in this world, that we share a common sense about its reality. The natural attitude is the attitude of commonsense consciousness precisely because it refers to a world that is common to many men. Commonsense knowledge is the knowledge I share with others in the normal, self-evident routines of everyday life.

The reality of everyday life is taken for granted as reality. It does not require additional verification over and beyond its simple presence. It is simply there, as self-evident and compelling facticity. I know that it is real. While I am capable of engaging in doubt about its reality, I am obliged to suspend such doubt as I routinely exist in everyday life. This suspension of doubt is so firm that to abandon it, as I might want to do, say, in theoretical or religious contemplation, I have to make an extreme transition. The world of everyday life proclaims itself and, when I want to challenge the proclamation, I must engage in a deliberate, by no means easy effort. The transition from the natural attitude to the theoretical attitude of the philosopher or scientist illustrates this point. But not all aspects of this reality are equally unproblematic. Everyday life is divided into sectors that are apprehended routinely, and others that present me with problems of one kind or another. Suppose that I am an automobile mechanic who is highly knowledgeable about all American-made cars. Everything that pertains to the latter is a routine, unproblematic facet of my everyday life. But one day someone appears in the garage and asks me to repair his Volkswagen. I am now compelled to enter the problematic world of foreign-made cars. I may do so reluctantly or with professional curiosity, but in either case I am now faced with problems that I have not yet routinized. At the same time, of course, I do not leave the reality of everyday life. Indeed, the latter becomes enriched as I begin to incorporate into it the knowledge and skills required for the repair of foreign-made cars. The reality of everyday life encompasses both kinds of sectors, as long as what appears as a problem does not pertain to a different reality altogether (say, the reality of theoretical physics, or of nightmares). As long as the routines of everyday life continue without interruption they are apprehended as unproblematic.

But even the unproblematic sector of everyday reality is so only until further notice, that is, until its continuity is interrupted by the appearance of a problem. When this happens, the reality of everyday life seeks to integrate the problematic sector into what is already unproblematic. Commonsense knowledge contains a variety of instructions as to how this is to be done. For instance, the others with whom I work are unproblematic to me as long as they perform their familiar, taken-for-granted routines—say, typing away at desks next to mine in my office. They become problematic if they interrupt these routines—say, huddling together in a corner and talking in whispers. As I inquire about the meaning of this unusual activity, there is a variety of possibilities that my commonsense knowledge is capable of reintegrating into the unproblematic routines of everyday life: they may be consulting on how to fix a broken typewriter, or one of them may have some urgent instructions from the boss, and so on. On the other hand, I may find that they are discussing a union directive to go on strike, something as yet outside my experience but still well within the range of problems with which my commonsense knowledge can deal. It will deal with it, though, as a problem, rather than simply reintegrating it into the unproblematic sector of everyday life. If, however, I come to the conclusion that my colleagues have gone collectively mad, the problem that presents itself is of yet another kind. I am now faced with a problem that transcends the boundaries of the reality of everyday life and points to an altogether different reality. Indeed, my conclusion that my colleagues have gone mad implies ipso facto that they have gone off into a world that is no longer the common world of everyday life.

Compared to the reality of everyday life, other realities appear as finite provinces of meaning, enclaves within the paramount reality marked by circumscribed meanings and modes of experience. The paramount reality envelops them on all sides, as it were, and consciousness always returns to the paramount reality as from an excursion. This is evident from the illustrations already given, as in the reality of dreams or that of theoretical thought. Similar "commutations" take place between the world of everyday life and the world of play, both the playing of children and, even more sharply, of adults. The theater provides an excellent illustration of such playing on the part of adults. The transition between realities is marked by the rising and falling of the curtain. As the curtain rises, the spectator is "transported to another world," with its own meanings and an order that may or may not have much to do with the order of everyday life. As the curtain falls, the spectator "returns to reality," that is, to the paramount reality of everyday life by comparison with which the reality presented on the stage now appears tenuous and ephemeral, however vivid the presentation may have been a few moments previously. Aesthetic and religious experience is rich in producing transitions of this kind, in as much as art and religion are endemic producers of finite provinces of meaning.

All finite provinces of meaning are characterized by a turning away of attention from the reality of everyday life. While there are, of course, shifts in attention within everyday life, the shift to a finite province of meaning is of a much more radical kind. A radical change takes place in the tension of consciousness. In the context of religious experience this has been aptly called "leaping." It is important to stress, however, that the reality of everyday life retains its paramount status even as such "leaps" take place. If nothing else, language makes sure of this. The common language available to me for the objectification of my experiences is grounded in everyday life and keeps pointing back to it even as I employ it to interpret experiences in finite provinces of meaning. Typically, therefore, I "distort" the reality of the latter as soon as I begin to use the common language in interpreting them, that is, I "translate" the non-everyday experiences back into the paramount reality of everyday life. This may be readily seen in terms of dreams, but is also typical of those trying to report about theoretical, aesthetic or religious worlds of meaning. The theoretical physicist tells us that his concept of space cannot be conveyed linguistically, just as the artist does with regard to the meaning of his creations and the mystic with regard to his encounters with the divine. Yet all these—dreamer, physicist, artist and mystic—also live in the reality of everyday life. Indeed, one of their important problems is to interpret the coexistence of this reality with the reality enclaves into which they have ventured.

The world of everyday life is structured both spatially and temporally. The spatial structure is quite peripheral to our present considerations. Suffice it to point out that it, too, has a social dimension by virtue of the fact that my manipulatory zone intersects with that of others. More important for our present purpose is the temporal structure of everyday life.

Temporality is an intrinsic property of consciousness. The stream of consciousness is always ordered temporally. It is possible to differentiate between different levels of this temporality, as it is intrasubjectively available. Every individual is conscious of an inner flow of time, which in turn is rounded on the physiological rhythm of the organism though it is not identical with these. It would greatly exceed the scope of these prolegomena to enter into a detailed analysis of these levels of intrasubjective temporality. As we have indicated, however, intersubjectivity in everyday life also has a temporal dimension. The world of everyday life has its own standard time, which is intersubjectively available. This standard time may be understood as the intersection between cosmic time and its socially established calendar, based on the temporal sequences of nature, and inner time, in its aforementioned differentiations.

There can never be full simultaneity between these various levels of temporality, as the experience of waiting indicates most clearly. Both my organism and my society impose upon me, and upon my inner time, certain sequences of events that involve waiting. I may want to take part in a sports event, but I must wait for my bruised knee to heal. Or again, I must wait until certain papers are processed so that my qualification for the event may be officially established. It may readily be seen that the temporal structure of everyday life is exceedingly complex, because the different levels of empirically present temporality must be ongoingly correlated.

The temporal structure of everyday life confronts me as a facticity with which I must reckon, that is, with which I must try to synchronize my own projects. I encounter time in everyday reality as continuous and finite. All my existence in this world is continuously ordered by its time, is indeed enveloped by it. My own life is an episode in the externally factitious stream of time. It was there before I was born and it will be there after I die. The knowledge of my inevitable death makes this time finite for me. I have only a certain amount of time available for the realization of my projects and the knowledge of this affects my attitude to these projects. Also, since I do not want to die, this knowledge injects an underlying anxiety into my projects. Thus I cannot endlessly repeat my participation in sports events. I know that I am getting older. It may even be that this is the last occasion on which I have the chance to participate. My waiting will be anxious to the degree in which the finitude of time impinges upon the project.

The same temporal structure, as has already been indicated, is coercive. I cannot reverse at will the sequences imposed by it—"first things first" is an essential element of my knowledge of everyday life. Thus I cannot take a certain examination before I have passed through certain educational programs, I cannot practice my profession before I have taken this examination, and so on. Also, the same temporal structure provides the historicity that determines my situation in the world of everyday life. I was born on a certain date, entered school on another, started working as a professional on another, and so on. These dates, however, are all "located" within a much more comprehensive history, and this "location" decisively shapes my situation. Thus I was born in the year of the great bank crash in which my father lost his wealth, I entered school just before the revolution, I began to work just after the great war broke out, and so forth. The temporal structure of everyday life not only imposes prearranged sequences upon the "agenda" of any single day but also imposes itself upon my biography as a whole. Within the coordinates set by this temporal structure I apprehend both daily "agenda" and overall biography. Clock and calendar ensure that, indeed, I am a "man of my time." Only within this temporal structure does everyday life retain for me its accent of reality. Thus in cases where I may be "disoriented" for one reason or another (say, I have been in an automobile accident in which I was knocked unconscious), I feel an almost instinctive urge to "reorient" myself within the temporal structure of everyday life. I look at my watch and try to recall what day it is. By these acts alone I re-enter the reality of everyday life.

REVIEW QUESTIONS

1. What is the social construction of reality?
2. How can your social construction of reality influence your research?
3. What does it take to step back from your own reality in research? Can you do this completely? Must you?

(Coercive- pesuade (an unwilling person) to do something by using forces or threats

2

Research and Theory: They Go Hand in Hand

Why is research conducted? The main reason is that researchers hope their findings will contribute to the discipline while enhancing the various ways we all have of knowing about life and the world. I have found that *theory* is one of the least understood and most difficult terms for students who are learning about social science research. Regardless, it seems to me that it is most important for you to understand theories, to be able to describe various theories, and to know how to use theories in your own research. A **theory** is basically nothing more than a system of ideas that help explain various patterns in the world. Let's say it is finals time and you believe that you learn more if you study for a few hours the night before the test rather than for an hour or two every night during the semester. That belief is a theory. Theories guide you and give you clues about the direction in which to conduct research (Babbie, 2007).

Let me give you an example of how combining theories with research actually works. While I was in graduate school, I conducted a research project on transvestites (Wysocki, 1993). A transvestite is a person who wears the clothing of the opposite sex. I was investigating males who considered themselves to be heterosexual but who liked to wear women's clothing. At the beginning of the project I thought I would just describe what they were telling me about their lives: when they started cross-dressing, why they cross-dressed, and how they cross-dressed. That would have been **descriptive research**, but that type of research had already been done by other researchers. I realized (and my thesis committee did as well) that a descriptive study would not add much to the literature on transvestism. So I went looking through the literature and found many different perspectives—or theories—that I could draw from for this project. For instance, I could have used the medical model, which states that a genetic problem that can be cured by medicine makes some men want to cross-dress (Rubenstein & Engel, 1996).

Or I could have used the literature on deviance, which states that any behavior outside of the norm is considered deviant (Thio & Calhoun, 2001), and that a man who wears women's clothing is deviant because society does not considered cross-dressing normal. However, I consider myself a feminist sociologist, so I wanted to investigate transvestism from the perspective of the social construction of sex, gender, and sexuality, which states that we all have been taught how to portray ourselves based on what we have seen in the culture in which we live (Berger & Luckmann, 1966). When I used this theory as my guide, the focus of my project changed. Instead of using a descriptive, medical, or deviance perspective, I explored the aspects of femininity that my respondents wanted to take on and the aspects of masculinity that they wanted to get rid of (Wysocki, 1993).

LEVELS OF ANALYSIS AND THEORIES

There are many different ways to make sense of our social world, and each way has resulted in different explanations. In 1970, Thomas Kuhn stated that scientists work within **paradigms**—models or frameworks that help us observe and understand what we are studying. Paradigms are ways of viewing the world that dictate the type of scientific work that should be conducted and the kinds of theories that are acceptable. Because nothing stays the same, old paradigms over time are replaced by new ones (Kuhn, 1970).

As I stated earlier, theories involve constructing abstract interpretations that can be used to explain a wide variety of situations in the social world from various levels. Let me give you an example. Sagy, Stern, and Krakover (1996) examined factors that influenced the development of a sense of community in Israel. They looked at two different populations: 242 immigrants from the former USSR and 60 Israeli veterans who lived in five different temporary neighborhoods. First the researchers used a **macrolevel analysis**, which looks at large-scale social systems such as the government or economys and they examined population size, population density, number of dwelling units in the site, urbanity of the area, ethnic heterogeneity, and peripheriality of the region. Then they used a **microlevel analysis**, which looks at everyday behavior in face-to-face interactions such as how people decide whom to marry or how children communicate on a playground. The Sagy team used three kinds of variables to accomplish their goals: (1) personal attitudes: evaluation of the dwelling unit and satisfaction with public services; (2) social networks; and (3) sociodemographic characteristics. As a result of using both macro and micro analysis, they found some differences. In the veteran sample only one macrolevel variable (the number of dwelling units in the site), and in the immigrant sample three microlevel factors (evaluation of the dwelling unit, external network, and age), played a part in the underlying sense of community for different groups of people.

Even though the Sagy (1996) study didn't mention it, between the macro and micro levels would be a **mesolevel analysis** focusing on social groups and organizations such as classrooms or offices. If the Sagy team had conducted a mesolevel analysis, reseachers might have looked at the two different groups to see how they interacted with each other.

Here is another example. Let's say you have an interest in researching education. If you investigated education from the *macro* level, you could ask the question "How does college A differ from college B?" From the *micro* level, you could ask "How do women interact differently from men in the classroom?" From a *meso* level, you could ask, "How do computer science classes differ from sociology classes?"

Although you can use many different theories in your research, I am going to briefly describe the four types of theory that you are most likely to come across in your reading. They are conflict theory, functionalist theory, symbolic interactionism, and feminist theory.

Conflict theory can be traced back to the writings of Karl Marx (1818–1883), who stated that power, ideology, and conflict are closely connected and that individuals are always in competition for resources or advantages. Those who hold the most power maintain their dominance over those with less power. If you want to study domestic violence, you might use conflict theory to suggest that one person in the relationship has more power than the other and therefore has more control over some of the household situations, which could lead to violence.

Functionalist theory was pioneered by Auguste Comte (1798–1857), who believed society is similar to an organism because it is made up of various parts that contribute to keep society functioning as a whole. If everything in society has a function, then society maintains equilibrium because everyone, and every social institution, has a job or a specific role to play. Think about your own family and how each member probably has his or her own job to do. One person might be responsible for taking out the trash, another for cooking dinner, and another for paying the bills. Everyone in the family has a function, and therefore, the home retains its equilibrium if everyone does his or her part. This is the way to use functionalist theory in your day-to-day life.

Symbolic interactionism is a theory that has been influenced by the work of George Herbert Mead (1863–1931), who believed that language allows us to become self-conscious beings and that the key element in this process is the symbol. Social life actually depends on our ability to imagine ourselves in other social roles and on our ability to communicate with others. One way to communicate is by using symbols and gestures. Having a common understanding of symbols and gestures help us to make decisions about what is going on and how to respond in each situation. Have you recently told someone that you love him or her? Did you need to say this with words, or did you use symbols to convey the message? If you sent a dozen long-stemmed roses to this person at work, were the roses a symbol of your feelings? What about religious symbols worn on necklaces? What does the symbol tell you about the person? If you meet someone who is wearing a Star of David, you might assume that the person is Jewish without the person ever telling you so. Could that symbol influence your behavior toward that person? How? Could it change or influence your research?

Feminist theory has greatly influenced the way in which some researchers analyze women's positions in society (Ollenburger & Moore, 1998). With origins in the women's movement of the 1960s and 1970s, feminist theory explores the variables of sex, gender, race, and sexuality and focuses on inequality in all areas of life. In other words, feminist theory poses questions about *identity* and *differences* (Reinharz, 1992). Research on gender differences will help you understand why men and women tend to work in different areas of a production plant and usually don't work side by side (Bielby and Bielby, 1987), why women on average make less money than men who have the same amount of education (U.S. Department of Labor, 2005), and why the division of labor within the household is not equal (Berk, 1985). In my own work on various bleeding disorders (Wysocki, 1999, 2001, 2003), I focus on how women have been underdiagnosed and misdiagnosed when they show symptoms of a specific illness. I ask questions about the power differential between doctors and patients, and I explore whether or not women's complaints are minimized because they are women. Keep in mind that you don't have to be female to consider yourself a feminist or to use a feminist perspective.

RESEARCH METHODS 101

Although we are going to spend more time on these concepts in later chapters, I think it will be helpful for you as you read some of the selectious in this book to understand some of the key terms used in research. We have already talked about theories that guide us as we discover the ins and outs of the subject we are studying. We accomplish this task through the use of **concepts**, mental images that summarize a set of similar observations, feelings, or ideas used to explain exactly what is meant by the term we are using. Consider the term *social class*, and assume that I ask you the question "What social class are you in?" What does this term mean to you? Does it mean the same thing to you as it does to me? According to WordNet (2003), social class is "people who have the same social or economic status." But how do we really know for sure what your social class is? Do your parents ever say, "We are lower class"? Or do you assume that you are in a lower social class because your parents are not paying for your college education and you have to work to pay for your tuition?

To be able to measure social class, we need a **variable**—a characteristic that can change from one subject to another and must have at least two aspects. The variable "social class" could have three aspects: "upper class," "middle class," and "lower class." Suppose we believe that the higher a person's social class is, the higher the person's GPA will be, as shown in Figure 2.1. This means that we have an expectation of what we will find when the research is completed. This expectation is stated in the form of a **hypothesis,** which is a statement about how

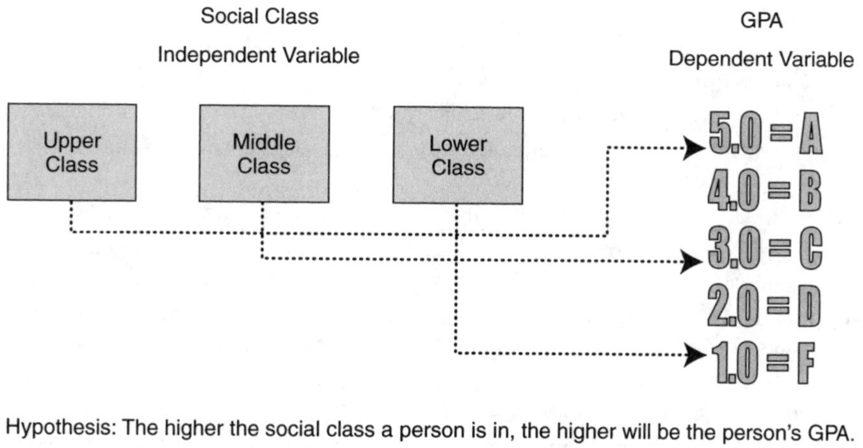

FIGURE 2.1 The Relationship Between Social Class and GPA

two or more variables are expected to relate to each other. Notice that our hypothesis has two variables: an **independent variable** and a **dependent variable.** The independent variable causally affects the dependent variable and the dependent variable is causally influenced by the independent variable. Which is which in our hypothesis? Social class is the independent variable, and GPA is the dependent variable. As you read selections 3 and 4, see if you can identify the hypothesis, the independent variable, and the dependent variable. We will go into greater detail about this in future chapters.

REFERENCES

Babbie, E. 2007. *The practice of social research* (11th ed.). Belmont, CA: Wadsworth.

Berger, P., & Luckmann, T. 1966. *The social construction of reality: A treatise in the sociology of knowledge.* Garden City, NY: Doubleday.

Berk, S. F. 1985. *The gender factory: The apportionment of work in American households.* New York: Plenum.

Bielby, D., & Bielby, W. 1987. *Sex difference in the allocation of work effort among professionals and managers.* Los Angeles: University of California, Institute for Social Science Research.

Kuhn, T. 1970. *The structure of scientific revolutions.* Chicago: University of Chicago Press.

Ollenburger, J. C., & Moore, H. A. 1998. *A sociology of women* (2nd ed.). Upper Saddle River, NJ: Prentice Hall.

Reinharz, S. 1992. *Feminist methods in social research.* New York: Oxford University Press.

Rubenstein, E. B., & Engel, N. L. 1996. Successful treatment of transvestic fetishism with sertraline and lithium. *Journal of Clinical Psychiatry*, 57(2): 92.

Sagy, S., Stern, E., & Krakover, S. 1996. Macro- and microlevel factors related to sense of community: The case of temporary neighborhoods in Israel. *American Journal of Community Psychology*, 24(5): 657–677.

Thio, A., & Calhoun, T. 2001. *Readings in deviant behavior* (2nd ed.). Boston: Allyn and Bacon.

U.S. Department of Labor. 2005. Highlights of womens' earnings in 2005. http://www.bls.gov/cps/cpswom2005.pdf.

WordNet. 2003. Social class. http://wordnet.princeton.edu/perl/webwn

Wysocki, D. K. 1993. Construction of masculinity: A look into the lives of heterosexual male transvestites. *Feminism and Psychology*, 3(2): 374–380.

Wysocki, D. K. 1999. The psychosocial and gynecological issues of women with bleeding disorders. *The Female Patient*, 24(5): 15–27.

Wysocki, D. K. 2001. Inherited bleeding disorders: Gynecologic and obstetric complications. *The Female Patient*, 26(2): 20–27.

Wysocki, D. K. 2003, January/February. You must be a mutant: Only men can have bleeding disorders—not women. *Off Our Backs—Special Women and Disability Issue*, 48–51.

SUGGESTED FILMS

Gender Dynamics in Intimate Environments: Feminist Insights for Families (Constance L. Shehan, Michael P. Johnson, 1994) (32 min.). Minneapolis, MN: National Council on Family Relations. This film briefly discusses recent, broad shifts in the basic paradigms of feminist scholarship, then uses domestic violence, household labor, and the labor market to explain recent feminist research.

Jacqui's Story: Reflections on the Doing of Feminist Research (Fran Crawford, Kisane Slaney, Jacqui Wyatt, 1998) (22 min.). Perth: Media Productions, Centre for Educational Advancement, Curtin University. Kisane Slaney, a feminist researcher who produced a video in 1990 called *Mum's the Word*, about mothers whose children were sexually abused, converses some years later with Jacqui Wyatt, one of the subjects of the video. Jacqui Wyatt reflects on her experience of having been a subject of research and on the relationship between researcher and subject.

The History of Sociology (Banning K. Lary, Anna Carlton, Michael Westin, Dax Xenos, 2004) (32 min.). New York, NY: Promedion Productions. This is an introductory exploration of the history of sociology and sociologists from premodern times to the present, covering a broad spectrum of the world's cultures. This film also talks about social conflict paradigm, structural functional paradigm, and symbolic interactionism.

Ethnomethodology as a Topic (Mike Emmison interviews Rod Watson, 1984) (50 min.). Brisbane: University of Queensland DAVS TV Unit. Mike Emmison interviews Rod Watson from the University of Manchester about the difference between ethnomethodology and symbolic interactionism.

How to Conduct an Experiment (Educational Video Network, 2004) (20 min.). Huntsville, TX: Educational Video Network. Although this film is about experiments described later in this book, it also shows students how every experiment that's conducted adds to our collective knowledge of the world and shows why experimentation is crucial to scientific discovery, how to use the scientific method, and how to distinguish between an independent variable and a dependent variable.

The Scientific Method (Robert Willgoos, Don Hall, Charlotte Angel, Jim Wolfe, Alice Look, 1999) (25 min.). Charleston, WV: Cambridge Educational. You will explore the basic steps in scientific methodology: defining the problem and forming a hypothesis, experiments and observations, analyzing data, forming conclusions, and communicating results.

3

School Tracking and Student Violence

LISSA J. YOGAN

There has been much attention in the media recently regarding violence in schools, especially since the Columbine High School shootings in April 1999. It is important to find ways to curb this type of violence. Yogan uses the theory of symbolic interactionism to explain the moral development children share with their teachers, how that moral development is affected by school practices, how these changes affect peer group interaction, and how schools can positively influence and channel group formation and ultimately reduce violence in schools. Do you think that the explanations that Yogan uses in her research decrease the violence in schools?

During the late 1990s, parents and educators alike became increasingly worried about the safety of schools. Their concern was warranted. The U.S. Department of Education reports that while the overall incidence of school crime had not greatly changed in recent years, there had been an increase in some types of school crime. School crime became more violent. Since 1992, there had been more than 211 school deaths associated with violence (Wolf, 1998). A few of these killings made the national news. When the suspects and victims were identified as small-town, white, middle-class children, the nation became alarmed. Over the past two years, there have been numerous cries to form national, state, and local task forces to confront the growing problem of school violence. Many of these task forces began to examine school security systems, specifically the school's measures of crime prevention and control. Were there enough metal detectors? Were the entrances locked? Were there enough security guards in place? While these security measures might prevent some incidents of violence, they do nothing to help us understand why violent crime within schools has increased. In particular, they ignore the structure of the organization of schooling.

This article will focus on one aspect of school organizational structure: the effects that tracking (placing students in ability-based groups) has had on students' interactions with peers and adults. Looking at how and why students are tracked and how track placement affects their sense of self is one

SOURCE: From Yogan, L. J. 2000. School tracking and student violence. *Annals of the American Academy of Political and Social Science*, 567: 108–122.

way of understanding the increase in school violence, and it can suggest organizational changes as a way to combat it. I will begin by reviewing several theories and concepts that underlie the process of self-development. Understanding how a person grows and develops and understanding how a school's structure may influence a person's self-development toward violent behavior can suggest organizational changes that will ultimately result in decreased use of violence.

SYMBOLIC INTERACTIONIST THEORY AND STUDENT-TEACHER INTERACTION

Social interaction, or, specifically, the interaction of students with peers and adults, is the subject matter of symbolic interactionism, one of the main branches of sociological theory. Symbolic interactionism is based on the assumption that meaning and learning (education) are gained through interaction with others. How a person understands others, how others come to understand that person, and how the person comes to understand and identify himself or herself are part of the symbolic interaction process. It is through symbolic interaction that an individual develops a sense of self; who we are is partly a reflection of how others see us, as Charles Horton Cooley (1909) first pointed out. He called this idea the "looking glass self." In particular, we are shaped by our interactions with people who are significant to us. What is different for each of us is the group of people we consider to be significant; thus each of us undergoes a similar process to develop a unique self. Symbolic interactionism also delves into the role that perception and meaning play in these significant interactions.

We can use symbolic interactionism to understand the role of shared meaning in student-teacher interaction. Herbert Blumer (1969) states that symbolic interactionism rests on three simple premises. The first is that human beings act toward things on the basis of the meanings that the things have for them. The second premise is that the meaning of these things is derived from or arises out of the social interaction that one has with one's social counterparts. The third premise is that these meanings are handled and modified through an interpretive process used by the person in dealing with the things he or she encounters.

Using these three premises to look at teachers, it can be hypothesized that teachers will act toward students based on the meanings that students (as objects) have for them. This hypothesis was supported by the classic studies of Rosenthal and Jacobson (1968) and Rubovitz and Maehr (1971, 1975). In the Rosenthal and Jacobson study, the meaning that students had for teachers was controlled by the researchers. The researchers told the teachers that some of the students were likely to do well that year. In reality, the researchers randomly selected the students they labeled as likely to do well, yet the teachers acted toward the students based on the meanings that were given by the researchers (not by any actual measure of ability).

The second premise, that the meaning that students have for the teachers will be based on the social interaction that teachers have with their self-identified social counterparts, was also shown in the Rosenthal and Jacobson study. Teachers identified the researchers as their social counterparts and adopted their meanings rather than developing meanings independently.

The third premise, that the meanings given to students by the teacher's social counterparts will be modified through an interpretive process of the teacher, suggests that it is possible to change socially constructed meanings rather than simply adopt them. The changing of socially constructed meanings can be seen in the story of Jaime Escalante (Mathews, 1988). Escalante was the subject of the movie *Stand and Deliver* (1988). Escalante's social counterparts (other teachers) had decided that the Hispanic youths in their school would not be capable of learning, could not achieve at a college level, and would be doing well simply to graduate. He modified this interpretation and arrived at a new meaning. His new meaning of students was that these students could work college mathematical problems, could simultaneously manage school and home lives, and could succeed in high school. Escalante was able to modify the beliefs of his counterparts through the ideas he held about his abilities (self-evaluation) and through his beliefs about the barriers produced by racism and school ability groupings.

Understanding these three basic tenets of symbolic interaction is therefore helpful in formulating ideas about successful teacher-student interactions, but it does not completely address the process through which the three tenets are filtered. Two important questions that affect student-teacher interaction are (1) From where do groups of social counterparts (that is, teachers) derive their meanings of others? And (2) what are the interpretive processes that teachers use in modifying students' meanings?

George Herbert Mead (1934) provides one answer to the first question. He states that we each belong to a number of different socially functioning groups. Teachers and students may identify themselves as members of many different groups, including professional teachers' organizations, neighborhood communities, families, athletic organizations, and ethnic and religious groups. An individual identifies with a group or groups because he or she is able to understand the behaviors of members of these groups and integrate his or her own behavior with the behavior of the members. When individuals find it difficult to understand and integrate their behaviors with the behaviors of others, as sometimes happens in social interactions between students and teachers, it is likely that difficulty arises because the individuals are acting as members of two or more different social groups. In his description of social organization and the ideal of human society, Mead states, "We often find the existence of castes in a community which make it impossible for persons to enter into the attitude of other people although they are actually affecting and are affected by these other people. The ideal of human society is one which does bring people so closely together in their interrelationships, so fully develops the necessary system of communication, that the individuals who exercise their own peculiar functions can take the attitude of those whom they affect. Remember that what is essential to a significant symbol is that the gesture which affects others should affect the individual himself in the same way. Human communication takes place through such significant symbols, and the problem is one of organizing a community which makes this possible."

This passage outlines two significant points that should be considered in teacher-student interactions. The first is that castes exist in communities and affect both members of the caste group and outsiders. Castes also exist in schools.[1] There are several ways castes at school are generated and affected, not least through race, class, and gender stereotypes in the wider society. However, one way these social forces come together to produce school castes that are found to be "virtually irreversible" is through tracking (Lawrence, 1998, 52; see also Schafer, Olexa, and Polk, 1972). Tracking is the placement of students into groups based on perceived intellectual ability or readiness to learn. However, because schools are not pure caste societies, it is assumed that the shared meaning described in Mead's ideal human society can be approximated within a carefully structured classroom environment.

The creation of this special classroom environment is the second key point of Mead's passage for the present analysis. For the creation of such an environment, it is necessary that the teacher (one who initiates interaction for the purpose of education) understand how his or her significant symbols of communication affect students differently. In addition, the teacher must understand when and why students are using different symbols to communicate. Thus knowledge of a student's primary social reference group and how that group differs from other students' reference groups and the teacher's social reference group is necessary for socially congruent instruction. If the instruction is not socially congruent, students are not likely to understand their teacher, and they are less likely to engage in the learning process.

The point is that current interactions are complicated by past interactions. Just as the literature on HIV and AIDS warns that when one has sexual intercourse with someone, one is, in effect, making sexual contact with all the previous partners of that person, the theory on social interaction tells us that we bring aspects of our past interactions into our present ones. It is precisely because of this link between the past and the present that interactions become both the problem of and the solution to school violence.

Students who enter the classroom with a history of exposure to violence may carry that violence and the ways of thinking that rationalize violence into all their interactions. They may interpret some actions through this way of thinking. A teacher, who typically is not living in a violence-filled community, may not understand how students interpret his or her actions, may not understand how students resolve and make sense of their own interactions, and may draw on stereotypes as a reference for meaning. Unless we change the organizational structure of schools to break down castes and create a more heterogeneous grouping of people, students who do not share the teacher's background are not likely to be influenced by that teacher or the institution that the teacher represents. A lack of bonding with an important societal institution such as school can lead to deviant behavior and to more serious forms of rule violation involving violence.

Violence that results in death is an extreme form of deviance. Deviance or delinquency among youths has been studied for many years. Hirschi's social control theory (1969) says that delinquency occurs when youths fail to bond with conventional social institutions. Within society, there are several conventional institutions; one of these is the institution of education represented by schools and schoolteachers. Strong bonds with school, described by Hirschi as the individual's relationship with school or teachers, and the amount of time spent on school-related activities compared to the amount of time spent on non-school-related activities contribute to an individual's willingness to conform to societal conventions. When individuals are bonded to conventional institutions, they are less likely to act in deviant ways. Thus one of the keys to reducing violence within schools is to increase the bonds that students feel to the school or to conventional others within the school.However, one of the aspects of school organization that reduces bonding for certain groups is tracking.

TRACKING

Increasing the bonds that students form to school through teachers is made more difficult by the process of tracking. "Tracking" is a word that is used to describe the ability groups established by the schools. Theoretically, these ability groups are supposed to enable more effective education because students with similar ability levels and readiness to learn will be taught together to their optimum level of academic performance. Teachers can concentrate on just one type of student instead of having to prepare lesson plans that account for more than one type, such as advanced, average, and remedial students.

In reality, however, tracking has not made education more effective. Instead, it has created and perpetuated many of society's problems. The institutional practice of tracking that is now common in most public schools has numerous effects on both teachers and students. It has been found to affect how students view themselves (self-identity), how they evaluate themselves (self-image), and how others view them (public identity) (Kelly and Pink, 1982, 55; Lawrence, 1998, 52). It has been criticized for the following reasons:

> More minority and lower income students are in the basic or low-ability tracks; placement in the track tends to be permanent, with little movement up or down in spite of students' learning and progress; and tracking has a labeling and stigmatizing effect so that teachers expect less of lower tracked students and frequently their expectations are correct.
>
> (LAWRENCE, 1998, 52)

Many of these effects can be related to self-development and social bonding. Tracking affects teachers' expectations of students' performance (Oakes, 1985; Kelly and Pink, 1982; Rosenthal and Jacobson, 1968). The concept of self-fulfilling prophecy tells us that if students are labeled as educationally inferior or superior, that is how they will perform. Thus tracking sends messages to students about inferiority and superiority.

Tracking also separates students on variables other than intellectual ability (Alexander, Cook, and McDill, 1978), including race, class, father's occupation, misconduct, and past academic record rather than IQ (Kelly and Grove, 1981). This means that students are denied the opportunity to interact in the classroom with a heterogeneous group of students. The odds are good that those in their classes will mirror their socioeconomic and minority or majority status.

Tracking also has produced qualitative and quantitative instructional differences (Gamoran, 1986; Karweit, 1987). For those at the top, the belief is that their way is best, and their educational achievement provides all the evidence of success they need. For those at the bottom, school becomes yet another hurdle to achieving self-esteem and developing a positive sense of self. Studies have documented the harmful effects of tracking on the academic achievement of those students in the lower tracks (Oakes, 1985, 1990). Tracking has also created a structure in which students do not receive equal knowledge, skills, or credentials for success beyond high school. Those in the upper tracks usually receive an education that prepares them for college, while those in the bottom tracks receive an education that focuses on remedial skills, or what Willis (1993) described as "learning to labor."

In addition to the inequality in educational outcome associated with tracking, studies show that placement in tracks reflects a student's race and socioeconomic status. Low-income, African American, and Latino children are more frequently placed in low-level classes (regardless of achievement) than Euro-American children with higher family incomes (Oakes and Guiton, 1995; Welner and Oakes, 1996). Indeed, evidence suggests that, even controlling for IQ and previous ability, "blacks and low income students were still more likely to be found in the basic or low ability tracks" (Lawrence, 1998, 52; see also Schafer, Olexa, and Polk, 1972). Because tracking favors the students in the upper tracks over those in the lower tracks, it is easy to hypothesize that those in the lower tracks will be less likely to bond with the institution of school. It is still likely, however, that the students will bond with other students within their ability group, or track, especially those of similar racial, ethnic, gender, or class background. This is one of the problems of interaction: it is an ongoing process that can produce negative as well as positive outcomes, if organizational arrangements do not take account of its existence.

If students form bonds with other students who are similar to them, they are not as likely to diversify and expand their thinking as are students who bond with students who are dissimilar to them. Our knowledge grows as our range of experiences, both vicarious and real, grow. Each new experience or new way of thinking to which we are exposed may cause us to reevaluate that which we thought we knew (Perry, 1970). When we receive more supports than challenges, our thinking becomes stagnant. Thus students who are surrounded by students who share their social, ethnic, and class position in society (a support) are less likely to be challenged in their thinking. Stagnant thinking is not the goal of education.

One possible way to remedy this situation is for the students to form bonds with the teacher, who can then challenge their ways of thinking and help them grow. However, this option is complicated by reality. As discussed earlier, often the teacher is different from the student in age—sometimes by many years—as well as in other demographic characteristics. Not only are these differences magnified by tracking; they also may reflect differences in socioeconomic status and race. Even though the majority of students in many urban schools belong to a minority group, teachers continue to be predominantly white (U.S. Department of Education, 1993). Also, teachers belong to the middle class, but many students (particularly those in lower tracks) belong to the lower class. Thus it takes great effort and desire on the part of the student and the teacher to form a common bond. It is more likely that students will initially bond with other students. If we are to change thinking processes, students have to be given more opportunities to bond with other students who are both similar and dissimilar to them. The opinions of other students matter. How others see us affects our development of self. How others view us also affects our self-esteem.

SELF-ESTEEM

Social interactions and the development of self are linked to self-esteem and the process of self-development described earlier. The concept of self-esteem is embedded in the theory of symbolic interaction. Self-esteem is also a conceptual component of the more inclusive process of self-conception. The process of self-conception is considered a key element in the relationship between individual behavior and the social organization of which the individual is a part. Linkages have been made between self--esteem and racial bias (Ashmore and Del Boca, 1976; Harding et al., 1969) and between self-esteem and teacher effectiveness (Edeburn and Landry, 1976). In both instances, the link between a person's self-evaluation and subsequent behavior can be seen.

At an individual level, needs for self-esteem and superior status are considered to be among the major causes and perpetuators of prejudice and racial discrimination (Allport, 1954; Ashmore and Del Boca, 1976; Harding et al., 1969; Tajfel and Turner, 1979). Self-esteem works through group identification to produce discriminatory behaviors in some individuals. All people desire positive evaluation by others and self. Tajfel and Turner (1979) have shown that people who have low self-esteem tend to seek positive evaluation by identifying a uniqueness (positive specialness) for their in-group over an identified out-group. In the United States, this often takes the form of (perceived) positive white in-group norms compared to (perceived) negative black out-group norms.

However, this identification can also take the reverse form. In the reverse form, minority students perceive or declare their culture and its norms as superior to those of their white, middle-class teacher. This need for positive distinctiveness leads to perceived intergroup competition and motivates prejudice and discriminatory behaviors. Within school, the need for positive distinctiveness may lead students and teachers in upper-level tracks to perceive the tracks as a form of competition and thus develop a prejudice against those in lower-level tracks. This phenomenon was demonstrated by Finley (1984), who noted that a competition existed between teachers for high-level or high-status students.

It has also been noted that a particular anti-achievement culture has developed among African American students, who are typically placed in lower tracks (Suskind, 1998; Fordham, 1988). The ideology within this culture says that to succeed academically is to become "white." Thus, within some groups that are typically relegated to the lower tracks, the need for positive distinctiveness leads to the formation of a culture that is the antithesis of the culture of the teacher, the educational process, and the school's perceived culture of academic success (Cohen, 1955).

Self-esteem has also been linked to achievement and performance. Research has shown a positive correlation between self-esteem and school achievement (Stevens, 1956; Fink, 1962; Williams and Cole, 1968; Simon and Simon, 1975). Additional studies have shown that teacher-student interaction is an important variable in the student's self-esteem and achievement. Edeburn and Landry (1976) state that teachers who themselves have a positive self-image affect their students more positively than do teachers who have a low or negative self-image. Davidson and Lang (1960) found that the more that children perceive their teachers' feelings toward themselves as positive, the better the academic achievement of the children. Thus positive teacher self-esteem is an important variable in reducing culturally induced prejudicial attitudes and is important in the successful educational interaction of teachers and students.

Unfortunately, tracking sends a message to those in the lower tracks that they are not as good as other students. Teachers all too often support this message as they talk down to students or dumb down the course requirements. Power (1993) found that track level does have a direct effect on self-esteem; as track level increases, so does self-esteem. Her analyses also indicate that a student's self-esteem is susceptible to the effects of track placement even years after the placement occurred. Students who were placed in the lower tracks in elementary school still showed decreased self-esteem in high school. This tells us that, although students age, they rarely are able to overcome the negative effects of tracking.

What has been described so far is theory and research evidence on self-formation, an explanation of why some students become deviant, and the relationship of tracking to the development of self and to the development of bonds with schools or with individuals in schools. I would now like to discuss how these processes can lead to both the expression of violence and the elimination of violence by linking theory and research with the reality of life in today's society.

SCHOOLS, SOCIETY, AND VIOLENCE

During the 1990s, many people pointed to the change in the family as the cause of violence.[2] They suggested that the increase in one-parent households and two-income families had led to decreased attention to what our youths were doing. Of course, this change in family structure is linked to both political and economic changes in society. Through the implementation of no-fault divorce laws, the political system has made it easier for men and women to end marriages. The increased divorce rate has led to an increase in one-parent households. Our economic structure has increased opportunities for women to become employed outside the home, and downsizing and technological advances have made two incomes in a family more of a necessity than in the past. Thus the change in adult family members' ability to spend time with children reflects more than just a change in the institution of the family. It reflects much broader changes in society.

From their beginnings, schools have mirrored society. The school model still commonly used is one that is based on the structure of factories. Students enter at a set time (similar to punching a time clock); they move down the assembly line of reading, writing, and arithmetic; and they emerge at graduation as a finished product. Through tracking, schools reflect the economic and racial segregation of society. School districts are tied to place of residence, and school funds are commonly tied to property taxes. Both districts and their property taxes reflect the extreme residential segregation common in the United States. What is intriguing is why schools mirror society when they do not have to do so.

One of the American school's early tasks was to socialize immigrants. In other words, early in the history of public education, schools were seen as the institution most able to change individuals. Schools could socialize and make those deemed inferior (immigrants) into model citizens who would understand and support the norms and values (such as democracy and equality for all) of their new culture. Somewhere along the way, schools quit socializing into model citizens those deemed inferior and instead instituted processes that maintained the inferior student's entering status. Today, when students graduate, their master status is still likely to be their race or socioeconomic status. In the past, an immigrant's ethnicity or socioeconomic status became less important if he or she were educated. In large part, society's acceptance of an immigrant was due to the fact that the immigrant had been socialized through heterogeneous interaction. That interaction took place in schools where there were no tracks. There was simply a heterogeneous group of students who interacted with and learned about each other over the course of several years. Both immigrant and native born were changed by the experience. Values and norms merged, and, at the end, both immigrant and native born had roughly the same status in society.

Remember that symbolic interactionists tell us that who we are is determined by our social interactions with significant others. If I have a family and friends who are moral, law-abiding, happy people who tell me consistently good things about myself, I am probably a person who is moral, law abiding, and happy. But if I have family, friends, or a society that tells me I am worthless, that breaking some laws is acceptable, and that others' lives are not worth much, then I am likely to become a person that is angry, disobedient, and potentially dangerous. What happens if I am isolated? I get the message that society does not want to be with me, and I might interpret that in such a way as to become jealous of or angry with society. Insofar as tracking contributes to this separation and isolation, it also contributes to the general level of school violence, although evidence of a direct relationship between tracking and delinquency remains unclear (Lawrence, 1998). Schools are the one institution that have in the past proved themselves successful at transforming individuals' place in society. They did this through carefully structured interactions between students and teachers. Today, instead of mirroring society's faults, schools should use the opportunity and time given to them to model a more positive society.

They can and should help create a society in which students from all different educational, racial, and economic backgrounds interact. Tracking does not do this. Currently tracking reinforces social class and racial segregation patterns. Moreover, it does not just separate; it tells one group that it is better than another. One of the most common ways that peer groups and friendships are formed is through classroom formation and shared experiences. It is critical to the development of self and to cognitive growth that individuals are exposed to diverse ways of thinking. Good teachers can make this happen.

Clearly, there is also a strong need for leadership within schools and, specifically, within classrooms. In recent years, the teaching profession has not attracted the nation's best and brightest. This is a serious problem. Teachers may be one of the few adults whom children have in their lives on any consistent basis. The economic demand on parents, particularly mothers, has decreased the amount of time they have to spend with their children. Thus the responsibility of teachers to be role models and moral guides is increased. Teachers need to take time to talk about what is right and wrong. They need to help teach citizenship, civility, respect, and compassion for others. They need to offer thoughtful critiques of society and the media and thought-provoking questions about how to handle difficult situations without resorting to violence. As a society, we cannot afford for teachers to be moral relativists. Too many children do not have enough adults willing or present to offer solid moral teaching and guidance. If students are taught problem-solving skills by watching action films or by other teens who see multiple reasons why it is acceptable to use violence against someone else, they are more likely to resort to violence when they face a problem. Students today need more than heterogeneous groupings within their schools. They need strong teachers who know how to connect with them and how to simultaneously build their self-esteem and challenge their ways of thinking and problem solving.

NOTES

1. Castes might also operate in subgroups at schools, such as jocks, preppies, skaters, thespians, gangstas, goths, and so on.
2. In a nonscientific survey of Internet users, a CNN (1999) poll reported that parents were seen as the leading cause of school violence by 29 percent of the 59,698 respondents, followed by access to guns and the media.

REFERENCES

Alexander, Karl L., Martha Cook, & Edward L. McDill. 1978. Curriculum tracking and educational stratification: Some further evidence. *American Sociological Review*, 43: 47–66.

Allport, Gordon W. 1954. *The nature of prejudice*. Reading, MA: Addison-Wesley.

Ashmore, Richard D., & Frances K. Del Boca. 1976. Psychological approaches to understanding intergroup conflicts. In *Towards the elimination of racism*, ed. Phyllis A. Katz. New York: Pergamon.

Blumer, Herbert. 1969. *Symbolic interactionism: Perspective and method*. Berkeley: University of California Press.

CNN. 1999. CNN Interactive Quickvote. Available http://www.cnn.com/.

Cohen, Albert. K. 1955. *Delinquent boys: The culture of the gang*. New York: Free Press.

Cooley, Charles Horton. 1909. *Social organization*. New York: Scribner.

Davidson, Helen H., & Gerhard Lang. 1960. Children's perceptions of their teachers' feelings toward them related to self-perception, school achievement, and behavior. *Journal of Experiential Education*, 29: 107–118.

Edeburn, Carl E., & Richard G. Landry. 1976. Teacher self-concept and student self-concept in grades three, four, and five. *Journal of Educational Research*, 69: 372–375.

Fink, Martin B. 1962. Self-concept as it relates to academic underachievement. *California Journal of Education Research*, 13: 57–62.

Finley, Merrilee K. 1984. Teachers and tracking in a comprehensive high school. *Sociology of Education*, 57: 233–243.

Fordham, Signithia. 1988. Racelessness as a factor in Black students' school success: Pragmatic strategy or pyrrhic victory? *Harvard Educational Review*, 58: 54–84.

Gamoran, Adam. 1986. Instructional and institutional effects of ability grouping. *Sociology of Education*, 59: 185–198.

Harding, John, Harold Prochansky, Bernard Kutner, & Isidor Chein. 1969. Prejudice and ethnic relations. In *Handbook of social psychology*, ed. Lindzay Gardner & Elliot Aronson, 2nd ed., vol. 5. Reading, MA: Addison-Wesley.

Hirschi, Travis. 1969. *Causes of delinquency*. Berkeley: University of California Press.

Karweit, Nancy. 1987. Diversity, equity, and classroom processes. In *The social organization of schools*, ed. Maureen T. Hallinan. New York: Plenum.

Kelly, Delos H., & Winthrop D. Grove. 1981. Teachers' nominations and the production of academic "misfits." *Education*, 101: 246–263.

Kelly, Delos H., & William T. Pink. 1982. School crime and individual responsibility: The perpetuation of a myth? *Urban Review*, 14(1): 47–63.

Lareau, Annette. 1989. *Home advantage: Social class and parental intervention in elementary education*. Washington, DC: Falmer.

Lawrence, Richard. 1998. *School crime and juvenile justice*. New York: Oxford University Press.

Lee, Valerie E., & Julia B. Smith. 1995. Effects of high school restructuring and size on early gains in achievement and engagement for early secondary school students. *Sociology of Education*, 68: 241–270.

Mathews, Jay. 1988. *Escalante: The best teacher in America*. New York: Henry Holt.

Mead, George Herbert. 1934. *Mind, self, and society: From the standpoint of a social behaviorist*. Chicago: University of Chicago Press.

Oakes, Jeannie. 1985. *Keeping track: How schools structure inequality*. New Haven, CT: Yale University Press.

Oakes, Jeannie 1990. *Multiplying inequalities: The effects of race, social class, and tracking on opportunities to learn math and science*. Santa Monica, CA: Rand.

Oakes, Jeannie, & Gretchen Guiton. 1995. Matchmaking: The dynamics of high school tracking decision. *American Educational Research Journal*, 32(1): 3–33.

Perry, William, Jr.1970. *Intellectual and ethical development in the college years*. New York: Holt, Rinehart & Winston.

Power, Ann Marie R. 1993. *The effects of tracking on high school students' self-esteem*. Master's thesis, University of Notre Dame.

Ray, Karen. 1995. *Grant High School case report*. Los Angeles: University of California at Los Angeles, Center for Research for Democratic School Communities.

Rosenthal, Robert, & Lenore Jacobson. 1968. *Pygmalion in the classroom: Teacher expectation and pupils' intellectual development*. New York: Holt, Rinehart & Winston.

Rubovitz, Pamela C., & Martin L. Maehr. 1971. Pygmalion analyzed: Toward an explanation of the Rosenthal-Jacobson findings. *Journal of Personality and Social Psychology*, 19: 197–203.

Rubovitz, Pamela C., & Martin L. Maehr. 1975. Teacher expectations: A special problem for Black children with White teachers? In *Culture, child, and school: Sociocultural influences on learning*, ed. Martin L. Maehr and William M. Stallings. Monterey, CA: Brooks/Cole.

Schafer, Walter, Carol Olexa, & Kenneth Polk. 1972. Programmed for social class: Tracking in high school. In *Schools and delinquency*, ed. Kenneth Polk & Walter Schafer. Englewood Cliffs, NJ: Prentice Hall.

Simon, William E., & Marilyn G. Simon. 1975. Self-esteem, intelligence, and standardized academic achievement. *Psychology in the Schools*, 12: 97–100.

Stand and Deliver. 1988. An *American Playhouse* Theatrical Film, Menendez/Musca & Olmos Production. Burbank, CA: Warner Brothers.

Stevens, Peter H. 1956. *An investigation of the relationship between certain aspects of self-concept and student's academic achievement*. Ph.D. dissertation, New York University, 1956. Abstract in *Dissertation Abstracts*, 16: 2531–2532.

Suskind, Ron. 1998. *A hope in the unseen: An American odyssey from the inner city to the Ivy League*. New York: Broadway Books.

Tajfel, Henri, & John C. Turner. 1979. An integrative theory of intergroup conflict. In *The social psychology of intergroup relations*, ed. William G. Austin & Stephen Worchel. Monterey, CA: Brooks/Cole.

U.S. Department of Education. National Center for Education Statistics. 1993. *Digest of education statistics*. Washington, DC: Government Printing Office.

Van Galen, Jane. 1987. Maintaining control: The structuring of parent involvement. *In schooling in social context: Qualitative studies*, ed. G. W. Noblit & W. T. Pink. Norwood, NJ: Ablex.

Wells, Amy Stuart, & Jeannie Oakes. 1998. Tracking, detracking, and the politics of educational reform: A sociological perspective. In *Sociology of education: Emerging perspectives*, ed. Carlos Alberto Torres & Theodore R. Mitchell. Albany: State University of New York Press.

Welner, Kevin G., & Jeannie Oakes. 1996. (Li)ability grouping: The new susceptibility of school tracking systems to legal challenges. *Harvard Educational Review*, 66(3): 451–470.

Williams, Robert L., & Spurgeon Cole. 1968. Self-concept and school adjustment. *Personnel and Guidance Journal*, 46: 478–481.

Willis, Paul E. 1993. *Learning to labour: How working class kids get working class jobs*. Aldershot, United Kingdom: Ashgate.

Wolf, Stephen M. 1998. Curbing school violence: Our youth, and our schools, need support before an incident occurs—not after. *Attache (U.S. Airways)* Sept. 9.

REVIEW QUESTIONS

1. How does Yogan use the theory of symbolic interactionism in this paper? What would have been different if the author used some other theory?
2. What does the author mean when she hypothesizes that "teachers will act toward students based on the meanings that students (as objects) have for them"?
3. Can you come up with your own questions and thoughts about a study you might consider on school violence? What theory would you use and why?

4

Murder Followed by Suicide in Australia, 1973–1992

A research note

JO BARNES

Barnes reports on the findings of a study of murder-suicide in Australia from a feminist perspective. The study is based on the analysis of 188 events in four states of Australia spread over a period of 20 years from 1973 to 1992. It focuses on two types of murder-suicide—events in which a male offender kills his female partner and events in which a parent kills his or her child or children. The motivations of men and women who commit murder and then kill themselves are qualitatively different. Suicide is often studied from criminal justice and a mental health perspective; in addition, some studies are purely descriptive. Notice how the focus changes when muder-suicide is studied from a feminist perspective.

INTRODUCTION

Murder-suicide has been a somewhat neglected topic of study in sociology and has mainly been the domain of mental health and epidemiology studies. As a consequence, the conclusions drawn have concentrated on the occurrence of murder-suicide as a rare event that is perpetrated by a mentally unstable person who has finally lost control. This has meant that the social circumstances that surround the event have been ignored or accepted as a given. This study focuses on intimate and familial murder-suicide and places these types of murder-suicide in a feminist framework in order to add an extra dimension to existing explanations.

A general overview of the literature reveals three distinct approaches to the study of murder followed by suicide. The first approach is the comparison of murder-suicide with the separate acts of murder and suicide (e.g. Wolfgang 1958; West 1965; Mackenzie 1961; Wallace 1986). The second approach is that which accounts for murder-suicide in terms of mental illness (e.g. Berman 1979; Goldney 1977; Rosenbaum 1990). And finally, there have been a number of empirical studies which seek to describe murder-suicide in terms of the profiles of offender and victim, the relationship of the offender to the victim, and the context in which the murder-suicide took place (e.g. Palmer and Humphrey 1980; Allen 1983; Easteal 1994).

SOURCE: From Barnes, J. 2000. Murder followed by suicide in Australia, 1973–1992: A research note. *Journal of Sociology*, 36(1): 1–12.

The various studies have been useful in identifying the actors involved in murder-suicide and in describing the relationships and circumstances that surround many of the events. Murder-suicide is a gendered activity—in the majority of cases men are the instigators of murder-suicide and women and children are the victims. It is also familial—the victims are predominantly intimately involved with the offender or they are the children of the offender. Expressions of jealousy, frustration and hostility that culminate in violence, which is often an ongoing factor within the relationship, are also recognized as important components in the murder-suicide event. Yet previous researchers have taken their existence for granted and have failed to question why men should feel jealous or hostile towards their wives or lovers. Why is it that men, in particular, are so determined not to allow their partner to leave? Why do the male offenders feel jealous and hostile to such an extent that they would rather kill the one they love and die themselves than accept that their partner no longer wishes to be part of their lives? The social context within which notions of ownership and control have developed and the use of violence to enforce them is an important element which needs to be addressed in relation to the murder-suicide event.

There has generally been a lack of gender differentiation in the studies of murder-suicide. The lack of concentration on women as offenders is understandable because of the much smaller incidence of women offenders in the murder-suicide event. However, the omission of a discussion around gender from the descriptions of murder-suicide results in two outcomes. First, an assumption is made that the conditions of women's lives are essentially the same as those of men and therefore an analysis that reflects men's experience is basis enough to describe the role of men and women in the murder-suicide event. Second, although the conditions of women's lives may differ from those of men, these differences are not seen as pertinent to the murder-suicide event.

While some studies acknowledge that children are often the victims in murder-suicides, most researchers have concentrated on the intimate relationship between offender and victim. This has meant that general descriptions of murder-suicide have tended to include male and female offenders as one category with only passing reference to the fact that while male offenders tend to murder adult females and sometimes their own children, female offenders are much more likely to kill only their children. Although the question of why women who kill their intimate partners rarely kill themselves is beyond the scope of the present study, we need to ask why in the majority of female initiated murder-suicides the victims are children. Why is it that women take such positive steps to kill their own children—an act that is contrary to the strong emphasis on the mothering role that is inherent in a modern capitalist society such as Australia?

METHOD

Although the definition of murder-suicide appears to be a simple one in which one person kills one or more people and then kills himself or herself, it is still problematic. Murder-suicide is a not a monolithic act. The event itself has many dimensions and it is the varying conditions within murder-suicide that confound the attempt to understand all murder-suicides within a single explanation. Indeed what is defined as murder-suicide, often by those who investigate the crime, can also be seen variously as murder and suicide as separate events; murder that is followed by the suicide of the offender in an act of remorse; double suicide in which one persons kills another and himself or herself in collusion with that person; or murder-suicide as an entity in itself, in which both the murder and the suicide are planned and carried out. It is with this latter definition of murder-suicide that this research is concerned.

Data for this project were collected on each event classified by the State Coroner as a murder-suicide. A function of the Coroner is to investigate every aspect of any death that is reported to him or her in order to ascertain and confirm the deceased's identity, the circumstances surrounding the death, the clinical cause of death, and the identity of any person who may have contributed to that death. In order to do this, the Coroner is assisted by specialist investigators such as police experts, scientists, forensic pathologists and other specialists who may be needed. In each state the Coroner collects information on both the offender and victim which usually consists of personal details such as age, gender and other demographic details, a detailed account of the discovery of the bodies, accounts by witnesses and relatives that may offer some background information, as well as copies of suicide notes and autopsy reports.

Using the Coroner's records, demographic details such as age, gender, occupation and nationality were examined. In addition, background information such as accounts from witnesses and relatives, copies of suicide notes and autopsy reports were also studied. Problems related to the data must be acknowledged when using them for purposes other than that for which they were collected. The information is collected by police officers in order to ensure that no prosecuting actions need to be taken and it is these officials whose decisions impact on what information is collected. At the same time, researchers are totally reliant on the objectivity of those collecting the information initially. It is these officials who make decisions as to which information is important in terms of what they require. Additionally, many of the witness statements are written in language that is stilted and concise, reflecting police procedure, rather than the emotive language that can be assumed to have been exhibited so shortly after such a traumatic event. Nevertheless, in most cases statements by relatives and friends often give detailed information on relationships and circumstances which, at least in the police and Coroner's minds, contexualize the event so that he or she is able to conclude that a verdict of murder-suicide is appropriate.

FINDINGS

As can be seen from Table 1, a total of 405 known murder-suicides were recorded as such between the years 1973 and 1992 in five states. The number of incidents ranged from 13 in 1974 to 34 in 1987, with an average of 20 per year. It is apparent that NSW (average 8.6) and Victoria (average 7.4) have the greatest number of murder-suicides each year while South Australia averages two murder-suicides per year. Because of the lack of complete figures for Western Australia and Tasmania it would be unwise to calculate statistics for these states; however, if the available figures are extrapolated to those missing periods, one could estimate that Western Australia averages approximately two murder-suicides per year and Tasmania one per year. While overall the number of murder-suicides remains fairly consistent each year, 1987 inexplicably stands out as having an abnormally high number of reported murder-suicide events in Victoria and NSW. Of the 188 cases in the present sample there were 188 offenders (those who murdered and subsequently committed suicide) and 250 murdered victims. The most distinctive feature overall was that 90 percent (170) of the offenders were male while 70 percent (177) of the victims were female. Male offenders were older than female offenders—the mean age of male offenders being around 43 years ($n = 169$), while the mean age of female offenders was about 32 years ($n = 17$). The majority of male offenders (53 percent) were in the 30–49 age group, while the majority (82 percent) of female offenders were in the 20–39 age group. Male victims, too, were generally older than female victims. The mean age of male adult victims was 43 years ($n = 37$), while the mean age of female adult victims was 39 years. Around 28 percent of the victims were aged 15 years or less.

Of the 250 victims in this sample, 50.4 percent were or had been in an intimate relationship with the offender (intimates are defined as present and past spouses, defactos and lovers). The second largest category (29 percent) was that of "own child." An interesting observation arising out of the data is that the victim of a male offender is more likely to be an intimate of the offender (54 percent), while the victim of a female offender is more likely to be her own child (75 percent). Those victims in an existing relationship with the offender accounted for 40 percent of all victims, while victims who had terminated their

TABLE 1 Number of Known Murder-Suicide Events in Each State, 1973–1992

Year	South Australia	Victoria	Western Australia	Tasmania	New South Wales	Total
1973	0	6	N/A	N/A	10	16
1974	2	6	N/A	N/A	5	13
1975	3	6	1 (#)	N/A	5	15
1976	5	8	1 (#)	N/A	13	27
1977	1	7	0 (#)	N/A	6	14
1978	3	3	1 (#)	1	7	15
1979	3	11	1 (#)	1	8	24
1980	0	9	1 (#)	1	11	22
1981	1	5	1 (#)	1	11	19
1982	2	7	1 (#)	1	8	19
1983	3	8	2 (#)	N/A	5	18
1984	2	10	1 (#)	N/A	12	25
1985	1	6	2 (#)	N/A	14	23
1986	2	11	0 (#)	2	7	22
1987	3	14	2	3	12	34
1988	2	11	1	N/A	5	19
1989	2	6	2	1	8	19
1990	0	6	3	1	7	17
1991	3	5	4	1	11	24
1992	3	3	5	2	7	20
Total	41	148	29	15	172	405

(#) Perth only—country areas not available

SOURCE: Data collected by author from Coroners' records in each state except NSW where it was collected by the NSW Bureau of Crime Statistics and Research.

relationship with the offender totaled 10 percent of all victims. About 29 percent of all victims were the child of the offender and 7 percent of all victims were related to the offender either by blood or marriage. In four cases the victim was a son or daughter of a partner or ex-partner. In addition, there were six cases in which the victim was a perceived sexual rival of the offender. In 16 cases both the partner or ex-partner and at least one child were murdered by the offender, while in 14 cases the offender killed two or more of his own children. There were only six cases in which the victim was a stranger.

The data indicated that the mode of death differed according to the gender of the offender. Male offenders were more likely to use what are considered to be more violent ways of committing both murder and suicide. For male offenders, a firearm was the favored weapon for both murder (73 percent) and suicide (74 percent). This contrasts with female offenders who were less likely to use firearms for the murder (15 percent) or the suicide (17 percent). A more "passive" mode of murder and suicide was favored by female offenders—carbon monoxide poisoning or suffocation accounted for 39 percent of murders and 28 percent of suicides.

Murder-suicide is essentially a domestic event and this is reflected in the number of murder-suicides which take place in the home (69 percent). Both the murder and the suicide occurred in most cases away from public gaze or at least in close proximity to the offenders' and/or victims' homes. Many of the events (43 percent) took place in the home where both the victim and the offender were living at the time; 14 percent took place in the victim's home, often following the victim's departure from the family home and 10 percent took place at the offender's home. Often in these cases the victims had returned to collect their belongings from the family home or perhaps to discuss the break-up of the relationship. The nature of murder-suicide is reflected in the location of its occurrence.

As in studies on domestic violence, the privacy of the home makes it difficult to research the circumstances in which murder-suicide takes place. Previous violence is a feature of some murder-suicides (37 percent) and can be categorized into two types—that which was a characteristic of the relationship generally and that which preceded the murder-suicide. In some cases both types of violence were present while in others the violence could be seen as part of the process of the murder-suicide. Studies of domestic violence have persistently agreed that it is impossible to know precisely how much violence actually exists. Alternatively, while the actual murder-suicide cannot be ultimately hidden it is impossible to gauge how close domestic violence becomes to being murder and perhaps suicide. As Rod (1980) argues, it is often a matter of luck that intimate violence does not become murder.

The over-consumption of alcohol has often been used in our culture as an excuse for a loss of self-control but there is no scientific evidence that alcohol is the cause of violent behavior—the popular notion that alcohol transforms the male into a violent brute has not been substantiated. According to MaxAndrew and Edgerton (1969), alcohol intoxication affects the sensor motor abilities but its effects on behavior are determined by socialization. There are very few cases in which it can be said that alcohol or drugs were the "cause" of murder-suicide. This is not to say that alcohol does not play some part in some murder-suicides but it seems that alcohol in most cases is a facilitator, that is, it enables the offender to act in a way which may not have occurred at that time had the offender not been drinking.

Mental and physical illness, despite earlier studies that argue to the contrary, did not appear to be prevalent in the majority of murder-suicides in the Australian sample. Reference to the offender's mental condition occurred in only 25 percent of the cases in this study. In only 13 percent of cases the offender had been treated by a doctor prior to the murder-suicide. Diagnoses ranged from "nerves" and depression to paranoid schizophrenia. In a number of cases the "nerves" and depression had been reported as being the outcome of circumstances such as relationship breakup, unemployment or child custody battles.

Above all else, murder-suicide is gendered. In the current study male offenders numerically account for 90 percent of all murder-suicides while females make up 71 percent of victims in the event. The relationship between the offender and victim has been seen as an important issue in this study because in the majority of cases murder-suicide involves couples who are in an intimate relationship. Murder-suicide as a single act seems to be most prevalent in circumstances where the offender kills his spouse and/or children and shortly after, as part of that same motivation, kills himself.

Daly and Wilson's (1988) account of the masculine and intimate features of homicide can usefully be applied to murder-suicide. Developing a conceptual framework that describes the masculine element of homicide, Daly and Wilson argue that women are viewed by their partners in proprietary terms and as such are regarded as men's exclusive property. They argue that sexual jealousy and rivalry are the dominant motives in homicides in which men are the offenders and women the victims, and deaths are often prompted by separation or the threat of separation. Masculine proprietariness, often founded on violence, pervades the stories of intimate murder-suicide in this study—the female partner becomes a possession that must be taken along on the journey to death.

An ingredient of the masculine possessiveness of female victims by their male partners is jealousy. Often reported in the accounts of murder-suicide is a statement such as, "He was very jealous about her and he told me if he could not have her no one else would." At the same time, in many cases the victim has left the relationship or announced an intention to leave. Broken relationships in murder-suicide are predominant and in many cases the victim had left or was threatening to leave the offender. In 35 percent of cases the main factor in the murder-suicide event was the fact that the victim had left the relationship or was threatening to leave. Despite other factors being present (such as jealousy, the threat of violence, etc.), it is the departing threat or action that triggers the sequence of events. There are several reasons (and these are not necessarily mutually exclusive) why the victim has resolved to leave her partner—it may be that the relationship has broken down, it may be because of violence shown towards the victim, or it may be that the victim has begun a relationship with another man.

The following selected case studies illustrate the points made above.

Case 1 A 19-year-old male offender and his 18-year-old female victim had known each other for approximately 12 months and had been engaged to be married for three months. For a short time they lived together. However, following repeated arguments and fights which included physical abuse by the male partner, the female victim broke off the engagement and the offender left their apartment to return to his parents' home. Over the following month the offender made repeated attempts to contact his ex-fiancée who shunned his approaches and sought to avoid him. Finally the offender approached his victim outside her home and an argument took place during which the offender put a rifle to his victim's head and fired causing fatal head injuries. He then turned the gun on himself. In a letter written earlier in the day to his parents the offender wrote: "I was going to ask her one more time [to come back to him] and if she didn't it was the only way out because I wasn't having no other guy handling my [victim]."

Case 2 A 39-year-old female forced her 47-year-old husband to leave the home and an abusive marriage. Three weeks later the husband returned and shot his wife. He later rang the police and said "I just had to do it. We've been separated you know. I just couldn't stand it." He then shot himself.

Although it would appear that murder-suicides involving children as the victims of male and female parents have similar qualities, there are nevertheless some important differences. Men appear to plan the murder and the suicide as a single act so that they will retain possession of their children and, in some cases, purposefully act out of spite towards the partner they can no longer have. The notion of possession and/or control flows through into murder-suicides involving child victims. Like the intimate murder-suicide, men who kill their children in murder-suicide cases often do so as a reaction to the loss of those children. The children are often the objects of a custody battle that the men are losing or have lost. Again, the concepts of possession and jealousy are primary here and the idea of "If we cannot live together, we will die together" has significant strength.

Case 3 The offender's wife had left him approximately 12 months before the murder-suicide took place and the couple had recently attended the Family Court in which custody of their three children had been awarded to the wife. The couple exhibited bitter feelings towards each other concerning which the family court judge wrote:

> The hearing virtually turned into a forum for each party involved to participate in character assassination, and despite the real purpose of the case, the continuing welfare of the children, they made bitter accusations against one another with almost no thought of the children in mind.

In what was apparently a pre-arranged plan when he failed to gain custody, the offender took his three children aged five, three and two years old for a drive (under the custody arrangements) and did not return. The offender and his children were found dead approximately a week later, the offender having administered sleeping tablets to the children and himself and then asphyxiating them all in the car in a state forest. He wrote to his mother: "If A, B and C and I cannot be together in life we are together in peace."

According to earlier research (Wolfgang 1958; Wallace 1986), women who kill their adult male partners rarely commit suicide and this is confirmed by this study, in which there are only four cases in which a female offender killed her male partner. Rather, it is young children who are the victims of female initiated murder-suicides. In this study 69 victims (28 percent) were aged 15 years or less and female offenders were responsible for the deaths of 18 (26 percent) of these young people.

For women, it would seem that it is suicide that is the prime objective of a female initiated murder-suicide but in her quest to end her own life she does not relinquish her responsibility for the welfare of her children. Because children are the most likely victims of female offenders in murder-suicide cases, the general belief has been that women who kill their own children must by definition be somehow mentally unfit. I would argue that although the motivations of men and women who kill their children and then themselves are qualitatively different, they both occur within a context of patriarchal norms. Chodorow's (1978) thesis of object relations—in which qualities for successful nurturing become embedded in personality based on gender identity, coupled with a basic theory of socialisation—allows the construction of a scenario in which women have suicide as their ultimate aim, and in order to protect their children they take them out of this life. Women who kill their own children are acting out their mothering role to its consummate level.

CONCLUSION

This research has been an attempt to "step back" and determine why offenders should feel the need to cling to ideas of dominance, possession and protection of their partners and children. Although in the final analysis it is still necessary to consider why individuals should commit murder-suicide in preference to any alternative course of action, it is argued that the patriarchal nature of our society provides the fertile context for an individual to kill a loved one and then commit suicide. For a more complete understanding of this tragic phenomenon of murder-suicide, the empirical analysis needs to be placed in a combined psychological and sociological framework.

REFERENCES

Allen, N. H. (1983) "Homicide Followed by Suicide; Los Angeles, 1970–1979." *Suicide and Life Threatening Behavior* 13(3): 55–165.

Berman, A. L. (1979) "Dyadic Death: Murder-Suicide." *Suicide and Life Threatening Behavior* 9(1): 15–23.

Chodorow, N. (1978) *The Reproduction of Mothering: Psychoanalysis and the Sociology of Gender.* Berkeley: University of California.

Daly, M., and M. Wilson (1988) *Homicide.* New York: Aldine de Gruyter.

Easteal, P. (1994) "Homicide-Suicides Between Adult Sexual Intimates: An Australian Study." *Suicide and Life Threatening Behaviour* 24(2): 140–151.

Goldney, R. D. (1977) "Family Murder Followed by Suicide." *Forensic Science* 9: 219–228.

Mackenzie, R. W. (1961) *Murder and the Social Process in New South Wales 1933–1957.* Unpublished Doctoral Thesis, Sydney: University of Sydney.

MaxAndrew, C., and R. B. Edgerton (1969) *Drunken Comportment: A Social Explanation.* Chicago: Aldine.

Palmer, S., and J. A. Humphrey (1980) "Offender-Victim Relationship in Criminal Homicide Followed by Offender's Suicide, North Carolina 1972–1977." *Suicide and Life Threatening Behaviour* 10(2): 106–118.

Rod, T. (1980) "Marital Murder" in J. Scutt (ed.) *Violence in the Family: A Collection of Conference Papers*. Canberra: Australian Institute of Criminology.

Rosenbaum, M. (1990) "The Role of Depression in Couples Involved in Murder-Suicide and Homicide." *American Journal of Psychiatry* 147(8): 1036–1039.

Wallace, A. (1986) *Homicide: The Social Reality*. Sydney: NSW Bureau of Crime Statistics and Research, Attorney General's Department.

West, D. J. (1965) *Murder Followed by Suicide*. London: Tavistock Publications.

Wolfgang, M. E. (1958) "An Analysis of Homicide-Suicide." *Journal of Clinical and Experimental Psychopathology* xix(3): 208–218.

REVIEW QUESTIONS

1. Barnes's research is based on feminist theory. However, the researcher states that murder-suicides could be investigated from other perspectives. What are those perspectives?
2. If you were to conduct a similar study using perspectives other than feminism, what types of questions would you ask? To whom would you pose the questions? What kind of results do you think you would get?
3. What methods are described in this study? If you had to design a similar study, how would you do it?

3

Ethics: You Must Have Ethics in Life and Especially in Research

I believe that a discussion about ethics is very important and must occur before you begin learning about the different steps in research design. It is imperative that you understand why research must be conducted ethically, what kind of research is unethical, and how to know the difference.

Ethics are a set of common values on which researchers ground their professional and scientific work (American Sociological Association, 2005). Ethics tell us what is good and bad, right and wrong. Often, however, the ethics underlying research projects seem to be connected to the researchers' personal values—a connection that can be problematic.

Recall from Chapter 1 that C. Wright Mills said you must step out of your own world and work within your limited experiences to *really* understand how other people live, how they think, and how they feel. If you can't do this, there might be a problem if your own values and ethics keep you from conducting research ethically. Furthermore, values and ethics are always open to negotiation and change. What is ethical for one person might not be ethical for another, and what is considered ethical in some societies might not be ethical in others. Your discipline has its own **code of ethics**, set up to help guide your research. You can find the code of ethics by looking up your national organization on the Internet.[1] Ethical considerations in research developed as a direct result of unethical experimentation on humans.

1 For instance, if you are a sociologist, you can find your code of ethics at http://www.asanet.org/members/ecoderev.html. If you are a social worker, you can find your code of ethics at http://www.socialworkers.org/pubs/code/code.asp.

RESEARCHERS WHO HAD NO ETHICS

During World War II, many unethical experiments were conducted by the Nazis, who used people in their experiments because "the guinea pigs, were, of course, the prisoners" (Aroneanu, 1996:(85). Experiments were often done on people without anesthetic and were intended to maim or kill. For instance, air was injected into the veins of people who were in concentration camps to see exactly how much compressed air could be injected into a person without causing an embolism (Aroneanu, 1996). In another experiment, paddles were placed on either the temple or the forehead and the neck; then an electric current was applied to test which method of electric shock worked best (Aroneanu, 1996). In the Nuremberg war crimes trials after World War II, an international military tribunal tried high-ranking Nazi officials for their actions toward humans during the war (Aly, Chroust, & Pross, 1994). Twenty-one officials who went to trial were sentenced to death (Foner & Garraty, 1991).

The Nuremberg trials took place in the mid-1940s, so the ethical issues that came up then should have made later researchers aware of the need to keep subjects safe and free from harm. However, since that time many experiments have had devastating consequences with little regard for human life, even in the United States.

One individual who believed strongly in experimentation on humans was Andrew C. Ivy, an eminent researcher and vice president of the University of Illinois Medical School. He had been asked by the American Medical Association to be its representative at the Nuremberg doctors' trial, and he was the prosecution's key witness on American medical ethics. Ivy testified to the high ethical standards of American researchers during the war, including those working in penal institutions. However, Ivy believed that prisoners were good subjects to use in experiments because official coercion was unnecessary in a prison environment and prisoners in the United States were available and easily "handled." Prisoners ended up as subjects of experiments for studies of athlete's foot, infectious hepatitis, syphilis, malaria, influenza, and flash burns (Hornblum, 1997).

The list of experiments conducted on people without their knowledge or consent is amazingly long. During the 1940s and 1950s, 40 people were injected with radioactive isotopes, including plutonium and uranium, so researchers could investigate the occupational dangers that nuclear workers faced (Gordon, 1996). In another case in 1945, a black male cement worker involved in a car accident in Tennessee was taken to the Manhattan Project Army Medical Center to have his bones set. He stayed in the hospital for a few weeks, and during his time there, he became the first of 18 unsuspecting patients in various distinguished American medical institutions to be injected with plutonium in an effort to investigate plutonium's health effects on the body (Moreno, 2000; Welsome, 1999). Similarly, in the "Green Run Study," radioactive gas was deliberately and secretly discharged over Washington State from a government nuclear plant. Local vegetation and animals absorbed high levels of radiation, and it is believed that the radiation increased the incidence of cancer (Gordon, 1996).

One of the most famous studies in the United States was the "Tuskegee Syphilis Study," begun in 1932 by the U.S. Public Health Service. Without their knowledge or consent, 399 poor, mostly illiterate African American sharecroppers in Alabama became part of an experiment. When the study began, these men were in the later stages of syphilis, but they were told they had "bad blood." They did not consent to be in the study; they didn't even know there was a study. Researchers kept track of the men over the next 40 years. The men received no treatment but were given diagnostic spinal taps, aspirin, and even free lunches so researchers could observe the cource of untreated syphilis in black men (Reverby, 2000). This study was exposed to the public in 1972. In 1997 President Bill Clinton gave an official apology to the eight participants who were still alive.

In India, from 1976 to 1988, a researcher attempted to study rates of progression of uterine cervical dysplasia to malignancy in 1,158 Indian women. The lesions progressed to invasive cancer in 9 of the women, and 62 women developed carcinoma of the cervix before they were treated. It has been alleged that the researcher neither informed the women that their lesions were known to progress to cancer nor offered them treatment at the outset (Mudur, 1997). Many more studies that are considered unethical are going on all over the world. I chose these examples to give you some sense of what is considered unethical research.

ETHICAL ISSUES IN RESEARCH

The first goal of ethical researchers is to secure the **voluntary participation** of all human participants. Subjects should be asked to participate in a study and *must* give their consent. Because participants may be asked to reveal personal information or may be given something that could have long-lasting physical or mental effects, it is crucial that they know they are part of a study.

Is it ethical to go into an Internet chat room and collect conversations between individuals without telling them that you are watching them? Some researchers are doing this. Others believe that if you are watching or participating as a researcher, you must tell your subjects that you are watching what they do and what they say and ask them for their permission (Wysocki, 1999). Participants can give their **informed consent** only *after* they have been informed about the purpose of the study, who the researchers are and who they work for, and exactly what will be done during the study. Informed consent didn't become a reality until 1947, after those who were involved in the Manhattan Project wanted to declassify some of their secret reports (Moreno, 2000). As a result, a new policy stated that no "substance, known to be, or suspected of being, poisonous or harmful should be used in human subjects unless all of the following were met: (a) that a reasonable hope exists that the administration of such a substance will improve the condition of the patient, (b) that the patient give his complete and informed consent in writing, and (c) that the responsible next of kin give in writing a similarly complete and informed consent, revocable at any time during the course of the treatment" (Moreno, 2000: 141).

The second goal of ethical researchers is to *do no harm* to their respondents, either physically or psychologically. In 1971, Philip Zimbardo began the "Prison Experiment." College-age men who were willing subjects were picked up at their homes, charged with a crime, spread-eagled against a police car, and handcuffed before being placed in a makeshift "jail" in a basement at Stanford University. The young men were randomly assigned to be guards or inmates so researchers could study the psychological effects of prison life. Then the trouble began, and "in less than 36 hours into the experiment, Prisoner #8612 began suffering from acute emotional disturbance, disorganized thinking, uncontrollable crying, and rage" (Zimbardo, 1999). Critics of the study disagree about whether any true harm was done to the participants.

The third goal of ethical researchers is to *protect the identity* of their subjects. As a researcher, you must make sure that while information is gathered and data are collected, you as the researcher can provide research subjects with either **anonymity** or **confidentiality.** It is important for you to understand the distinction between these two terms.

Anonymity is ensured when no one, not even the researcher, knows the identity of the respondents. A survey conducted on the Internet could be anonymous. Respondents complete the survey and return it via e-mail not to the researcher but to a third party who removes any identifying information and then forwards the e-mail to the researcher. This is all done electronically; no person comes in contact with the data until they reach the researcher.

Confidentiality, in contrasts, is ensured when the researcher knows who the respondents are but does not reveal their identities. Confidentiality can be safeguarded in a number of ways. Remember my transvestite study mentioned in Chapter 2? My respondents were not concerned that I knew their identities. The surveys were not anonymous, but I had assured the participants confidentiality. When they submitted their surveys, I gave each survey a number and removed the respondent's name. I kept a computer file of the numbers and the names and other identifying information. Once the study was complete, I deleted that information from my computer, placed it on a disk, and locked it away so no one else could have access to it.

The fourth goal of ethical researchers is to *not deceive subjects*. Do you have the right to lie about who you are and to engage in research without the knowledge of the respondents? Deceiving people is unethical. Stanley Milgram (1969) conducted a study on obedience. The subject was told to obey a set of increasingly callous orders to shock another individual when the wrong answer to a question was given. Milgram deceived the subjects by not telling them the true purpose of the experiment, which was to guage their willingness to follow orders to inflict pain. Although the findings in this study proved valuable for society, the subjects were deceived and showed signs of psychological harm.

The fifth goal of ethical researchers involves *analysis and reporting*. As a researcher, you have ethical obligations to your subjects and to your colleagues to report both positive and negative findings (Babbie, 2007).

In 1995, Marty Rimm, a Carnegie Mellon undergraduate, published in the *Georgetown Law Journal* the results of his study about pornography on the Internet. Rimm's findings, however, were found to be both misleading and meaningless. Rimm had inflated the amount of pornographic images stored on the Internet, and his methodology was in question (Elmer-Dewitt, 1995). Unfortunately, Rimm's "findings" were cited in congressional hearings as evidence that the Internet should be controlled to reduce the amount of "indecent" material it made available, and Rimm was invited to speak as an "expert" during congressional hearings in support of the Communications Decency Act. The consequences of Rimm's flawed analysis and inaccurate reporting for the research, the researcher, the journal, and the institution were severe.

To help ensure that research is conducted in an ethical manners, **institutional review boards** (IRBs) have been established at every agency that receives federal research support. IRB members, usually faculty, review all research proposals to make sure that the rights and interests of the subjects are protected, that the research is ethical, and that no harm will be done to the subjects.

Now that you know a little about ethics, be sure to think about the needs of others as you plan your research projects. Ask yourself if you would want to be part of your study. If your answer is no, then you need to rethink it.

REFERENCES

Aly, G., Chroust, P., & Pross, C. 1994. *Cleansing the fatherland: Nazi medicine and racial hygiene.* Baltimore, MD: The Johns Hopkins University Press.

American Sociological Association. 2005. *Code of ethics* [Electronic version]. Retrieved June 3, 2006, from http://www.asanet.org/page.ww?section=Ethics&name=Code+of+Ethics+Introduction

Aroneanu, E. 1996. *Inside the concentration camps: Eyewitness accounts of life in Hitler's death camps.* Westport, CT: Praeger.

Babbie, E. 2007. *The practice of social research* (11th ed.). Belmont, CA: Wadsworth.

Elmer-Dewitt, P. 1995, July 3. On a screen near you: Cyberporn. *Time*, pp. 38–43.

Foner, E., & Garraty, J. A. (eds.). 1991. Nuremberg trials (1945–1946 trials of Nazi officials). *The reader's guide to American history.* Boston: Houghton Mifflin.

Gordon, D. 1996. The verdict: No harm, no foul. *Bulletin of the Atomic Scientists*, 52(1): 33–41.

Hornblum, A. 1997. They were cheap and available: Prisoners as research subjects in twentieth century America. *British Medical Journal*, 315(7120): 1437–1442.

Milgram, S. 1969. *Obedience to authority.* New York: Harper & Row.

Moreno, J. D. 2000. *Undue risk: Secret state experiments on humans.* New York: W. H. Freeman.

Mudur, G. 1997. Indian study of women with cervical lesions called unethical. *British Medical Journal*, 314(7087): 1065–1067.

Reverby, S. 2000. *Tuskegee's truths: Rethinking the Tuskegee Syphilis Study*. Chapel Hill, NC: University of North Carolina Press.

Rimm, M. 1995. Marketing pornography on the information highway: A survey of 917,410 images, descriptions, short stories, and animations downloaded 8.5 million times by consumers in over 2000 cities and territories. *Georgetown Law Journal*, 83:1849–1934.

Welsome, E. 1999. *The plutonium files: America's secret medical experiments in the cold war.* New York: Dial Press.

Wysocki, D. K. 1999. Virtual sociology: Using computers in research. *Iowa Journal of Communication*, 31(1): 59–67.

Zimbardo, P. 1999. *The Stanford prison experiment.* Retrieved from http://www.prisonexp.org/slide-22.htm

SUGGESTED FILMS

Miss. Evers' Boys (Joseph Sargent, 1997) (118 min.). New York: Home Box Office, Anasazi Productions. In 1932, Nurse Eunice Evers is invited to work with doctors on the "Tuskegee experiment" to study the effects of syphilis. She faces a terrible dilemma when she learns the patients are denied treatment that could cure them.

The Deadly Deception (Films for the Humanities, 1993) (60 min.). Boston: WGBH Educational Foundation. This program investigates the Tuskegee Study of Untreated Syphilis in the Negro Male. African American men in Macon County, Alabama, believed they were receiving free treatment for syphilis. They were, instead, given medicines that were worthless against the disease. The experiment continued from 1932 until 1972 and was periodically written up in mainstream medical journals. The program outlines the history of the study, offers testimony from survivors and from doctors who administered it, and looks at what many consider the perversion of medical ethics and the doctor/patient relationship involved in carrying out such an experiment.

Body Doubles: The Twin Experience (Antony Thomas, 1998, 1997) (50 min.). Princeton, NJ : Films for the Humanities and Sciences. The issue of whether character and intelligence are genetically predetermined is addressed through interviews with several identical twins, including a survivor of Nazi experiments under Joseph Mengele, a set of conjoined twins, and a pair of brothers reunited after being reared apart. Also briefly presented are a gathering of twins from around the world at Twinsburg, Ohio, and twin research at the University of Minnesota.

Quiet Rage: The Stanford Prison Study (Philip G. Zimbardo, Ken Musen, John Polito, 1992, © 1991) (50 min.). Stanford, CA : Stanford University (distributor). This film discusses a prison simulation experiment conducted in 1971 with students at Stanford University and considers the causes and effects that make prisons such an emotional issue. Documentary includes new film, flashback editing, follow-ups 20 years later, and an original music score. It reveals the chronology of the transition of good into evil, of normal into the abnormal.

5

Taking Names

The Ethics of Indirect Recruitment in Research on Sexual Networks

LEWIS H. MARGOLIS

Margolis argues that indirect recruitment breaches the basic ethical principles of beneficence, nonmalfeasance, respect for autonomy, and justice. He first describes an indirect recruitment strategy in which researchers ask consenting respondents to provide the names and locating information of partners and friends with whom they may have engaged in a range of social activities from talking to sexual intercourse. Then he uses the ethical principles articulated in research guidelines, such as the Nuremberg Code[1] and the Helsinki Declaration,[2] to analyze the consequences of this invasion of privacy. Finally, he analyzes the relationship of the anticipated harms to the benefits to argue against the acceptability of the strategy of indirect recruitment.

Evaluating the risks and anticipated benefits of medical, behavioral, and social research is a central function of institutional review boards (IRBs). The calculation that IRBs undertake ultimately determines whether a particular research project involving human participants is permitted to proceed. In medical research the physical harms and even the anticipated benefits of a new procedure or drug are often apparent and quantifiable. In contrast, for social/behavioral research that may involve probing the most intimate feelings, thoughts, and actions of participants, the weighing of risks and anticipated benefits, the calculation of possible harms, and the acceptability of that harm, require a more intense level of scrutiny.

Even the early step of identifying and recruiting participants for a research endeavor may potentially cause harm, making participant selection a focus of IRB analysis. The usual recruitment strategy involves a sampling of households, random telephone dialing, or other mechanisms of direct invitation that allow the potential respondents to decide whether to participate before they share private information. For some studies, an intermediary, such as a physician already familiar with the desired characteristics of a potential respondent (e.g., patients with a particular disease), may be asked to make the direct contact. This offers the respondent the opportunity to participate before any private information is communicated outside of that confidential relationship with the physician.

For studies of intimate behavior, however, individuals may be reluctant to participate if they are asked to recount what may have been casual partners or if their identities are revealed to those partners. An alternative recruitment strategy, therefore, uses private information solicited indirectly

SOURCE: From Margolis, L. H. 2000. Taking names: The ethics of indirect recruitment in research on sexual networks. *Journal of Law, Medicine and Ethics*, 20(2): 159–166.

from acquaintances, medical records (where made available), and increasingly available commercial data sets to identify individuals as potential participants. Researchers then use this information to recruit potential participants. Unlike direct recruitment where the researchers are blinded to personal characteristics of potential participants before the participants consent, for indirect recruitment researchers use private information that they would not ordinarily have in order to recruit participants. Individuals who are the object of indirect recruitment strategies must, of course, still give their consent to proceed with the proposed research project.

The emergence of the AIDS epidemic in the early 1980s has caused resurgence in research on sexual behavior, because sexual relations are one of the primary mechanisms for the transmission of HIV. Both to gain an understanding of the epidemic and to develop strategies to counter it, researchers have sought to quantify sexual contacts and understand risk factors for unsafe sexual practices.[3] While conventional surveys in which respondents are asked to describe and perhaps quantify their own behavior may provide information about sexual behavior, the validity and utility of such methods have been questioned for several reasons. First, the private nature of sexual behavior, as well as the taboos associated with it, may lead respondents to censor or otherwise alter their responses.[4] Second, in a social context where sexual relationships may be ephemeral, the perceptions of each partner in the pair are necessary to understand the potential effects of these relationships on the health concerns that have prompted this research.[5] Each member of a given pair can have relationships with other individuals constituting a sexual network that would not be captured in interviews that do not solicit the identities of partners.

In order to create a sample of sexual network members or partners, consenting respondents are asked to nominate some number of people whom they consider close friends, including their most recent romantic or sexual partners. In order to assure that the sample has sufficient individuals who have engaged in sexual intercourse, respondents may be asked to list additional people with whom they have had sexual intercourse during a recent time frame. The respondent then indicates with which partners he or she has engaged in a range of social activities from talking on the telephone, to dining out, to sexual intercourse. In order to maximize the number of activities for study, the interviewer totals the activities for each partner to find those with whom the social contacts have been most frequent. The interviewer then informs the respondent that the research project would like to have the opportunity to interview those individuals and asks for their names and locating information.

Ideally, a different interviewer (blinded to the respondent's identity) will contact and interview some or all of the nominated partners, and that friend or partner may or may not participate in the study on a voluntary basis. In order to preserve the privacy of the respondent, the partner would be told only that an acquaintance nominated them because they had engaged in some type of social activity.

THE IRB ISSUE

According to the federal Office for Protection of Research Risks (OPRR), charged with interpreting and overseeing implementation of the regulations regarding the Protection of Human Subjects Act,[6] "evaluation of the risk/benefit ratio is the major ethical judgment that IRBs must make in reviewing research proposals. . . ." For research "where no direct benefits to the participant are anticipated, the IRB must evaluate whether the risks presented by procedures performed solely to obtain generalizable knowledge are ethically acceptable. There should be a limit to the risks society asks individuals to accept for the benefit of others, but IRBs should not be overprotective."[7]

The IRB faces the following questions:

1. What are the risks of harm and anticipated benefits of indirect recruitment in studies of sexual networks?
2. Is the ratio of anticipated risks to benefits for indirect recruitment reasonable and acceptable?

ANALYSIS OF THE RISKS OF HARM AND THE ANTICIPATED BENEFITS

Principles of bioethics guide the interaction between health professionals and patients. Health researchers are similarly obligated to uphold these principles, as espoused in such fundamental documents as the Nuremberg Code[8] and the Helsinki Declaration.[9] As defined by Beauchamp,[10] these duties are: (1) beneficence; (2) non-maleficence; (3) respect for autonomy; and, (4) justice.

Beneficence

Beneficence or the obligation to do good or provide benefits, guides the balance of benefits against risks. Obtaining benefits for individuals, or in the case of research, for society at-large, is basic. The Helsinki Declaration underscores, however, that "in research on man, the interest of science and society should never take precedence over considerations related to the well-being of the subject."[11]

In research on sexual networks, there is only one possible benefit to potential participants themselves. Study protocols may collect saliva and urine to determine whether participants have sexually transmitted diseases. Maintaining anonymity, the researchers not only provide the opportunity for participants to learn their disease status, but also attempt to reach individuals with positive results who fail to obtain that information on their own initiative. It is important to point out, however, that the generally accepted public health procedure for STD surveillance involves active case-finding only with the contacts or partners of individuals known to be infected.[12]

Non-maleficence

The second duty is to minimize the risk of harm. In the context of research, however, the fundamental question that IRBs consider is whether the risk of harm is justified by the anticipated benefits to the participants and society. OPRR has classified harms as physical, psychological, social, and economic[13] and defines minimal risks as those "where the probability and magnitude of harm or discomfort anticipated in the proposed research are not greater, in and of themselves, than those ordinarily encountered in daily life or during the performance of routine physical or psychological examinations or tests."[14]

Psychological harm involves two dimensions. One dimension is the stress associated with guilt, embarrassment, sorrow, anger, fear, or other emotions arising from a reported behavior. The second aspect of psychological harm involves the feelings associated with the invasion of privacy. Kelman defines privacy as "the freedom of the individual to pick and choose for himself the time and circumstances under which, and most importantly, the extent to which, his attitudes, beliefs, behavior and opinions are to be shared with or withheld from others."[15] Kelman suggests that private space is crucial to a secure identity. Researchers that violate that space "must be especially meticulous in obtaining fully informed consent."[16] Drawing on social science research,[17] Caplan further argues that privacy is a basic need, tantamount to food and shelter.[18] Individuals and communities cannot function without respect for limits on sharing private information. According to Caplan, harm comes from the very invasion of privacy, even if that violation does not cause overt detrimental stress.

Breach of confidentiality is closely related to invasion of privacy. Confidentiality refers to the duty to protect privacy and is built upon the value of trust, "the expectation that individuals and institutions will meet their responsibilities to us."[19] The belief that a physician, for example, will not reveal private information, is fundamental to the practice of medicine. Similarly, confidentiality is a basic component of marriage, friendship, and other intimate social relationships, although not guided by the same formal expectations as occur in a professional setting. Extending Caplan's argument, harm results from the knowledge that the trust that has been placed in others to assure one's privacy has been violated.

The OPRR expects IRBs to answer two primary questions regarding the potential harms associated with privacy invasions: "(1) is the invasion of privacy involved acceptable in the light of the participants' reasonable expectations of privacy in the situation under study?; and (2) is the research question of sufficient importance to justify the intrusion?"[20] IRBs should also consider whether the study can be modified so it can be conducted without invading the individual privacy of subjects.[21]

Indirect recruitment violates the basic need for privacy. As Caplan argued,[22] the ability to decide upon one's personal boundaries is a fundamental need. This means that the use of private information about individuals, without their consent, harms them. Information, such as the intimate nature of social relationships, particularly sexual encounters, which is used for recruitment, certainly falls within the domain of information for which potential participants are entitled to give their consent.

It is possible that potential partners would not feel harmed by the knowledge that acquaintances or sexual partners have undermined the confidentiality that is part of a relationship. Sorenson et al. obtained permission to contact family members from only 53.7% of a sample of individuals with cystic fibrosis.[23] Although the investigators did not explicitly ask whether probands believed that this method was a harmful breach of confidentiality, they report that none volunteered that reaction. Further, they report that only 3 of 548 relatives contacted objected to the method of contact.

Two points, however, diminish the relevance of this type of study to the issue of the context of sexual relationships. First, nearly half of the probands refused to provide the contact information, raising serious questions about potential bias in the sample. It is entirely possible that those who declined to participate did so because of their own concerns and those of their relatives about confidentiality. It would have been valuable to know, for example, if the 46.4% who declined to give contact information would have been willing to contact their relatives directly. The second point is that the investigators in this clinical study had an explicit benefit to offer the relatives, that is, testing and information about their own carrier status for cystic fibrosis. Studies of sexual networks often offer to screen for sexually transmitted diseases.

An additional harm results from the potential breach of confidentiality associated with deductive disclosure.[24] In theory, a nominated partner could figure out who had referred the project to them, but the fact that a partner would have to recall all of the people with whom they had participated in any of the social activities during the study period diminishes the risk that such a deduction would be successful. To state the obvious, if the nominating respondent recruited his or her partner directly, it would be self-disclosure. The other breach of confidentiality stemming from deductive disclosure arises from the statistical ability to determine the identity of an individual based on key demographic and other descriptors, even though conventional identifiers have been removed from the data.

In addition to the potential harm associated with deductive disclosure is the more conventional breach of confidentiality, which involves the release of private information on intimate or illegal behavior. Excellent data security systems and high standards of professional interviewers can virtually eliminate that source of harm.

Another set of harms resulting from indirect recruitment relates to the undermining of trust. Relationships between individuals are based on trust. Similar to the physician-patient relationship where the effectiveness is diminished in the absence of trust, friends and partners need to believe that their confidences will be honored. Indirect recruitment asks friends to place their trust in the hands of researchers and recruiters whom they do not know and with whom they may have established little basis for trust.

Although the charge to IRBs is the protection of individual participants, it is worth noting the potential harms to society from the violation of privacy. Warwick, for example, has argued that "disregard for trust in social research may undermine the trust necessary for a decent social order."[25] Since researchers are putatively bound to adhere to the standards set forth in various codes of research ethics,[26] individuals are entitled to a reasonable expectation of respect for those codes.

A final set of potential harms related to the violation of trust affects the community of researchers. Potential participants in future studies may demur because of their knowledge that researchers call upon participants to violate trust. Even if individuals do agree to participate, knowledge that the violation of trust is the "norm" may diminish the truthfulness of their responses, leading to untoward consequences should interventions be based on these findings. Finally, researchers may face legal or administrative restrictions, if the political perception is that basic tenets of interpersonal relationships are violated.[27]

As described by Appelbaum and Lawton, respect for autonomy, minimally, is the obligation to allow individuals the freedom to act without coercion.[28] At another level, autonomy implies respect for the means, such as information or other resources, to enable an individual to act. A third level of autonomy, building upon the absence of coercion and the provision of the means to act, is respect for the deliberative reasoning that an individual undergoes in deciding to act. Kant argued for a fourth level of autonomy, involving rational decision-making grounded in an ethical or moral framework. Autonomy at this level would involve a self-imposed restriction on behavior because of the recognition that the behavior in question violates elements of the moral order, such as respect for the autonomy of another individual. While a right to privacy is often derived from respect for autonomy, Caplan, as indicated above, has argued the reverse. Respect for autonomy is subsumed under or grounded in the belief that individuals have a basic need to define their private spaces. In response to the basic need for privacy, societies have developed respect for autonomy.

In addition to the harm resulting from the violation of the basic need for privacy, indirect recruitment infringes upon the right to autonomy. This infringement does not occur at the basic level of autonomy, absence of coercion, but indirect recruitment does affect the autonomy of individuals in the other three domains described above. In particular, indirect recruitment is based on a lack of respect for the role of privacy in the moral framework of society. This right is nearly absolute in the context of research that seeks to recruit individuals who otherwise have no established relationship with investigators, as they might in the use of disease registries or vital records. The usually extensive procedures to guarantee the anonymity of participants who have consented to participate in studies of sexual networks underscore the sensitive nature of the issues and argue for extending that respect to the recruitment process.

Distributive justice, defined as the obligation to allocate burdens and benefits fairly, entails the obligations associated with the allocation of scarce resources. There are at least two aspects of distributive justice that are relevant to recruitment. First, IRBs are obliged to assure that the potential costs and benefits of research are shared fairly among individuals, instead of only those who are readily accessible to the researcher. In underscoring respect for persons, all contemporary ethical codes of research obligate researchers to develop recruitment procedures that do not unfairly encourage or discourage individuals from participation or particular treatments. Second, concern for justice also supports the composition of a robust sample that will allow generalizable results. It would be unfair to ask individuals to participate in a study when there are no discernible benefits. The Nuremberg Code states that "the experiment should be such as to yield fruitful results for the good of society, unprocurable by other methods or means of study, and not random and unnecessary in nature."[29]

Indirect recruitment violates the principle of justice. As stated in the Nuremberg Code, researchers should assure that the information sought is unobtainable by other means. If the information is otherwise available, the study places an unfair burden on participants. Investigators in the field of research on sexual relationships have grappled with determining ethical and scientifically sound methods for many years, suggesting, at a minimum, an obligation to explore alternative methods.[30] Indirect recruitment is unjust in a second way. It is unfair that respondents are given the opportunity to consent to the release of private information, but their partners are denied that right. Partners are recruited because the project already knows that they have engaged in private behaviors with respondents.

In addition to the justice-driven aspects of developing a rigorous sample, an improper sample may violate the principle of non-malfeasance. If a sample is biased in its construction, misleading conclusions may result, leading to harms associated with interventions on behalf of the sample or the population at-large.

There are two approaches to determining the ratio of risks to benefits for the strategy of indirect recruitment. One strategy involves assessment based solely on fundamental principles. The second involves a utilitarian analysis. Whatever approach is taken, the use of information elicited without the consent of the participant should face even stricter scrutiny when used for recruitment than for analysis, because any possible threats to privacy can theoretically be removed for analysis to minimize, if not eliminate, risks to participants.

The principle-based analysis of the risks and benefits stems from two arguments. As Caplan has argued, the need for privacy is fundamental. Recognition of this need provides the foundation for the right of autonomy. Absent a conflicting need or right, much less an overriding right, the risk associated with indirect recruitment is absolute.

A second principle-based argument responds directly to the OPRR question of whether "the invasion of privacy is acceptable in the light of the subjects' reasonable expectations of privacy." In other words, the OPRR has a somewhat lower standard than Caplan for the absolute value of privacy, but does acknowledge that the individual should be entitled to determine whether the invasion of privacy is substantial. Presumably, if a partner believed that the invasion of privacy did not exceed his or her expectations, the harm would be minimal or even non-existent. The problem with this argument is that although partners may willingly enter into social relationships with the knowledge that the frailty of humans in relationships may result in the breach of confidentiality, they have a reasonable expectation that professionals, such as researchers, would respect their right of autonomy. Instead, indirect recruitment exploits the breach of confidentiality by the respondent, using this knowledge to recruit the partner.

The alternative analysis requires a weighing of the harms resulting from the invasion of privacy and balancing them against potential benefits, giving appropriate attention to the severity of the harms. On a daily basis, individuals engage in a broad range of social interactions. Since normal human interaction involves violations of confidentiality, both intentional and unintentional, one could argue that the breach of confidentiality through indirect recruitment meets the definition of minimal risk. In the words of the OPRR, does this breach fall within "subjects' reasonable expectations of privacy"? A research protocol differs, however, from the encounters of everyday life, because the intent of the interaction by the project with the respondent is to obtain information that invades the private space of the partner and violates his or her confidentiality. In addition, in the spirit of the Nuremberg Code and the Helsinki Declaration, researchers have an obligation to set and uphold a higher standard with respect to the dignity of potential research participants. One way to modify or balance this breach of confidentiality by the respondent would be to require that the respondent obtain permission from the partner, that is, use direct recruitment. Investigators tend to oppose this because it would possibly result in non-compliance by respondents who are unwilling to disclose to their partners that they have revealed sensitive information about them.

Since elaborate procedures have been designed to guarantee the confidentiality of respondents, one could argue that partners are not harmed by indirect recruitment. Partners are free to refuse to participate, knowing only that some acquaintance had nominated them because of any of a range of possible social encounters. Considering project interviewers under a broad definition of health professionals, how does this differ from sharing confidential information with a physician who maintains confidentiality? Physicians obtain confidential information after securing the free consent of their patients. The only reason that a physician would act on the confidential information provided about a partner would be where legal or ethical reporting requirements, motivated by the harm principle, mandate such action. Even though the interviewers in the study are pledged to maintain confidentiality, the fact remains that they have been given private information about the partner as a potential interviewee without first securing consent.

Even where indirect recruitment results in the harm of the loss of privacy and the right of autonomy, there may be justifications for limiting autonomy. Ethicists have proposed at least four justifications for limiting the autonomy of individuals,[31] the most relevant of which is the harm principle. The legal system also suggests it is acceptable to limit the actions of individuals which harm. Since there is no indication of partners having committed harm, using private information to recruit them cannot be justified by the harm principle. In fact, it is conceivable that a partner would use violence to ascertain who had violated their confidentiality. The importance to society of undertaking research to understand young adult risk-taking does not outweigh the respect that should be accorded to individuals in performing the research. Ironically, two issues that provoke much societal concern—pregnancy among teenagers and crime—have declined during the past 7 years, which may alter the sense of urgency and thus the risk/benefit ratio.[32]

Indirect recruitment then requires balancing the welfare principle and the harm principle. The welfare of others is both theoretical and limited to some future time. Society in general and individual young adults in particular may benefit from what is learned through this research. In contrast, indirect recruitment does nothing to diminish harm caused by partners, while at the same time harms partners through diminishing their privacy and violating their autonomy.

NOTES

1. "Trials of War Criminals Before the Nuremberg Military Tribunals Under Control Council Law," 2, no. 10 (Washington, D.C.: U.S. Government Printing Office, 1949): 181–82.
2. 18th World Medical Assembly, "World Medical Association Declaration of Helsinki," *JAMA*, 277 (1997): 925–26.
3. D. W. Seal, F. R. Bloom, and A. M. Somlai, "Conducting Qualitative Sex Research in Applied Field Settings: Real-Life Dilemmas," *Health Education and Behavior*, 27 (2000): 10–23.
4. Id.
5. J. R. Udry and P. S. Bearman, "New Methods for New Research on Adolescent Sexual Behavior," in *New Perspectives on Adolescent Risk Behavior* (Cambridge: Cambridge University Press, 1998).
6. 45 C.F.R. [sections] 46.101–46.409 (1999).
7. Office for Protection from Research Risks, *Protecting Human Research Subjects* (Washington, DC: USDHHS, 1993): at 3–8.
8. Supra note 1.
9. Supra note 2.
10. T. L. Beauchamp and J. F. Children, *Principles of Biomedical Ethics* (New York: Oxford University Press, 1994).
11. Supra note 2 at 926.
12. R. Bayer and K. E. Toomey, "HIV Prevention and the Two Faces of Partner Notification," *American Journal of Public Health*, 82 (1992): 1158–64.
13. Supra note 5.
14. Id. at 3–1.

15. H. C. Kelman, "Privacy and Research with Human Beings," *Journal of Social Issues*, 33 (1977): at 169.
16. Id. at 193.
17. See, for example, J. M. Roberts and T. Gregor, "Privacy: A Cultural View," *Nomos*, 13 (1971): 199–225; M. Mead, "Neighborhoods and Human Needs," *Ekistics*, 123 (1966): 124–26; K. Greenwalt, "Privacy," in W. Reich, ed., *Encyclopedia of Bioethics*, no. 3 (New York: Free Press, 1978): 1356–64.
18. A. L. Caplan, "On Privacy and Confidentiality in Social Science Research," in T. L. Beauchamp et al., eds., *Ethical Issues in Social Science Research* (Baltimore: Johns Hopkins University Press, 1982).
19. D. Mechanic, "The Functions and Limitations of Trust in the Provision of Medical Care," *Journal of Health Politics, Policy and Law*, 23 (1998): at 662.
20. Supra note 6, at 3–4.
21. Supra note 6.
22. Supra note 18.
23. J. R. Sorenson et al., "Proband and Parent Assistance in Identifying Relatives for Cystic Fibrosis Carrier Testing," *American Journal of Medical Genetics*, 63 (1996): 419–25.
24. R. F. Boruch and J. S. Cecil, *Assuring the Confidentiality of Social Research Data* (Philadelphia: University of Pennsylvania Press, 1979).
25. D. P Warwick, "Types of Harm in Social Research," in Beauchamp, supra note 18, at 111.
26. Supra notes 1 and 2.
27. Supra note 25.
28. D. Appelbaum and S. V. Lawton, *Ethics and the Professions* (Englewood Cliffs: Prentice Hall, 1990).
29. R. J. Levine, *Ethics of Regulation and Clinical Research*, 2nd ed. (Baltimore: Urban & Schwarzenberg, 1986): at 426.
30. Supra note 3.
31. J. Feinberg, *Social Philosophy* (Englewood Cliffs: Prentice Hall, 1973).
32. See, for example, S. J. Ventura, T. J. Mathews, and S. C. Curtin, "Declines in Teenage Birth Rates, 1991–97: National and State Patterns," *National Vital Statistics Reports*, 47, no. 12 (Hyattsville: National Center for Health Statistics, 1998); D. C. Anderson, "The Mystery of the Falling Crime Rate," *American Prospect*, 8, no. 32 (1997): 49–55.

REVIEW QUESTIONS

1. What does Lewis Margolis think about indirect recruitment? Why?
2. Do you think there is another way besides indirect recruitment to obtain respondents for sensitive studies such as those on sexuality?
3. Do you think researchers should be studying the sexual patterns of people they don't know?

6

The Ethics of Conducting Social-Science Research on the Internet

JAMES C. HAMILTON

The Internet and the World Wide Web have advanced our ability to gain information at an amazing rate. Each year, more and more individuals either have their own personal computers or have access to computers in their schools, libraries, or places of work. With technological advances comes the possibility for researchers to connect with people who otherwise might be difficult to reach because of proximity to the researcher or because of the desire to remain anonymous. Even though more and more researchers are using the Internet to gather data, change doesn't happen without the possibility of the problems that Hamilton addresses in this article. If the things individuals write on the Internet are available to the public, should a researcher really have to be concerned with ethics on the Internet?

Over the past four or five years, the amount of social-science research conducted on the Internet has increased exponentially. More than 100 World Wide Web sites now invite visitors to participate in a wide variety of scientific research, or in activities that resemble scientific research, including personality tests, intelligence tests, and opinion surveys.

Other sites bear a superficial resemblance to those used for legitimate research, but are designed solely for entertainment purposes. For instance, visitors to the Free Internet Love Test site (http://www.lovetest.com) can provide information—including astrological signs—about themselves and their partners, and receive feedback about their compatibility.

The growth of research on the Internet has outpaced the efforts of researchers—and advocates for the ethical treatment of research participants—to understand the implications of this new methodology and to develop guidelines for its responsible use. The Internet clearly is a very powerful research tool, and its benefits—such as the ability to reach large numbers of people, at very low cost—are alluring. But like all powerful tools, it can be destructive if it is not used properly, or if it falls into the wrong hands.

An Internet search that I conducted suggests that on-line researchers are not consistently employing the safeguards that are used to protect participants in traditional research. For example, in studies not conducted on line, participants must read and sign a statement that describes the research and explains their rights. Although on-line researchers could easily convey the same type of information on a Web page, many on-line research sites dispense with that important safeguard.

Complicated studies often require that researchers give participants additional information, beyond the informed-consent statement. In practice, many studies are so complex that it is impossible to give participants a full explanation of the research before they participate, without running the risk

SOURCE: From Hamilton, James C. 1999, December 3. The ethics of conducting social-science research on the Internet. *Chronicle of Higher Education*, 46 (15): B6(2). Used with permission.

of skewing the results. As an example, participants who are told that a study concerns how the race of a defendant influences jurors' decisions are likely to alter their responses to appear unprejudiced. Therefore, many researchers give participants a post-experimental debriefing—that is, they provide a full explanation of the research only after the participants have completed the experiment. On-line researchers could design their Web sites to send participants to a debriefing page after they are finished, but many do not.

What's more, even if researchers include a debriefing page, they cannot make participants read it. That problem highlights some of the ethical issues raised by the fact that researchers have so little control over the nature of participants' experiences in on-line research. In face-to-face studies, researchers can see if participants have an adverse reaction to the study and can take steps to assist them—perhaps by terminating their participation and debriefing them with extra care. In on-line studies, it is not possible for researchers to safeguard the emotional well-being of participants in the same way. Many researchers have opted to address that limitation by providing disclaimers, which state that people should not participate if they feel that they cannot handle the emotional impact of the procedure or of any feedback they might receive.

Although that might seem to be a sensible way to deal with the problem, current ethical guidelines prohibit the use of such disclaimers. Federal agencies that support research—as well as scientists' professional organizations—assert that researchers must protect the rights of their participants, and that they cannot simply ask people to sign away those rights.

Another ethical risk posed by on-line research has to do with the confidentiality of data collected over the Internet. In general, most Internet users enjoy complete anonymity. Unless someone provides personal information voluntarily, there is almost no practical way to determine the identity of a visitor to a given Web site. Although it is possible to identify the Internet address from which a particular message was sent, that address rarely belongs to a single identifiable individual. Even at academic institutions in which professors' computers are connected directly to the Internet, a machine might well use a different address each time the professor turns it on.

The anonymity that is common on line makes it possible for individuals to submit data on multiple occasions—either accidentally or intentionally—with virtually no chance of being detected. Because such multiple responses on a wide scale can invalidate a study, researchers may ask participants for identifying information, such as e-mail addresses. Or a researcher might use something called a cookie to identify the computer from which each participant submitted his or her response. However, both of those methods compromise the researcher's ability to guarantee the confidentiality of the data.

Even worse, computer hackers can easily intercept participants' responses to on-line studies. If they also intercept identifying information, the results for the participants could be disastrous—particularly if the study deals with sensitive issues, such as criminal or sexual behavior.

Usually institutional review boards—which work to insure that all research involving human subjects complies with applicable legal and ethical standards—save researchers from any breaches of confidentiality and other ethical lapses. However, some on-line research is being conducted without the required approval of an IRB. Recently, a doctoral student at a major U.S. university confided to me that neither he nor his dissertation chairman had thought to secure IRB approval for his on-line dissertation research. Even when IRBs are consulted about on-line research, they may be ill-equipped to evaluate the studies.

Based on my correspondence with members of IRBs around the country, I estimate that roughly half of the members have received proposals for on-line research, while only a few of the members have reported that their IRB had developed guidelines for evaluating ethical risks and safeguards in such research.

Careful evaluation of proposals for online research requires considerable expertise in the area of Internet hardware and software. To properly evaluate those proposals, IRB members need to know who will run the Web site: the researcher, from his or her own computer; the staff of a university's computer center; or a third party. If the researcher does not have complete control of the computer serving the site, the IRB must know the identities of everyone who will have access to the data, and how confidentiality will be maintained.

Beyond those general issues, IRB members need to deal with specific technical questions. These include whether data are collected only when the participant hits the "submit" button, or before the participant decides that he or she is finished; whether the participant is automatically referred to a debriefing page if he or she quits in the middle of the study; and whether participants can delete their data after they learn the purpose of the study. It takes considerable technical savvy to know enough to ask such questions, let alone to evaluate the answers.

As technology becomes increasingly sophisticated, more experimenters will be able to have on-line research sites, but the danger is that fewer will have adequate knowledge of how their sites work, in order to insure the well-being of the participants. As a result, IRBs will also have to begin evaluating the technical credentials of on-line researchers, to insure that they—or their technological consultants—have sufficient expertise to implement the appropriate technical safeguards.

Perhaps the greatest threat to on-line research is the danger to its credibility posed by data-collection sites established primarily for commercial or entertainment purposes. Those Web sites far outnumber academic-research sites, and in many cases, it is not easy to sort out which is which.

Although many commercial data-collection sites are forthcoming about who is sponsoring the research and how the data will be used, several such sites attempt to make money by deceiving participants. For example, several commercial sites appear to offer free personality or intelligence testing—but after completing the tests, participants are informed that they need to pay for a full report of their performance. Other commercial sites promise more-elaborate feedback to visitors who provide identifying information for the sponsor's database. Sites that employ such deceptive tactics may make the public suspicious of all data-collection sites, including those that serve legitimate scientific purposes.

Data-collection sites that are designed primarily for entertainment (such as the Pooh-Piglet Psychometric Personality Profiler, at http://home. rochester.rr.com/jbxroads/pooh/ [URL updated –Ed.], where you can discover whether you are more like Pooh, Piglet, Tigger, or Eeyore) might have an equally damaging effect on the public's attitude toward on-line scientific research. Most of the entertainment sites are operated by private individuals for their own amusement, and are designed to provide feedback to visitors, not data for the site's owner. It is likely that visitors might fill out the forms several times, with different data, to see what kinds of feedback they get—about whether they're introverted or extroverted, say, or what kind of person they should marry.

Such sites may not lead Web surfers to believe that it is important to respond accurately or honestly to on-line tests, questionnaires, or surveys—or even to respond only once. Were participants in on-line scientific experiments to take the same approach, the data they provided would be of no use. Rather than trying to enforce higher standards on such sites, academic researchers should put their efforts into doing a better job of identifying the scholarly nature of their sites. Few researchers make use of design elements that would help reassure potential participants about the legitimacy of their research. Those elements include the prominent display of the name and logo of the researcher's university, information allowing participants to contact the researcher, and links to other sites with information about the researcher's credentials, such as the Web page of his or her department and the site of the IRB that approved the study.

We need guidelines to help researchers and members of IRBs alike insure that online research is both scientifically and ethically sound. Professional and governmental organizations that advocate support for science, such as the American Association for the Advancement of Science and the National Science Foundation, as well as groups that promote research in the social sciences, such as the American Psychological Society, should work together to establish such guidelines.

At a minimum, the guidelines should require all on-line researchers to provide information that would permit participants to contact the researcher, a means for obtaining participants' fully informed consent, full disclosure of any risks to their confidentiality, a post-experimental debriefing page, and a way for the participants to learn about the results of the study. The guidelines also should include up-to-date information on the technologies used to conduct on-line research and a set of criteria for evaluating the technical aspects of proposed on-line studies.

Ideally, the guidelines would standardize on-line research in a way that would help Internet users to distinguish academic-research sites from other kinds. It would also be useful for IRBs to maintain a list—on line, of course—of on-line studies that they have approved.

Once the guidelines have been put into practice, we will need to educate the public about them, and about making well-informed decisions on participating in online research. The organizations that created the guidelines could set up a Web site for the public that would explain the risks and benefits of on-line research, and make potential participants aware of ways to distinguish legitimate, scientific-research sites from commercial or entertainment sites. Researchers could provide a link from their sites to that public-education site.

On-line research holds much promise for many academic disciplines. However, we will not serve the interests of science if we do not make sure that such research is conducted ethically. We must not forget our responsibilities to our participants, even when we meet them only in cyberspace.

REVIEW QUESTIONS

1. Find a survey on the Internet. Can you tell whether the survey is from an academic institution? Was it approved by an IRB? How can you tell?
2. Can research on the Internet be anonymous? Does it need to be? Explain your reasoning in detail.
3. Do you think observing behaviors in an Internet chat room should have IRB approval before the observations begin? Why or why not?

7

Code of Ethics

American Sociological Association

The American Sociological Association's (ASA's) Code of Ethics sets forth the principles and ethical standards that underlie sociologists' professional responsibilities and conduct. These principles and standards should be used as guidelines when examining everyday professional activities. They

SOURCE: From American Sociological Association, 2005. Code of ethics, Retrieved from http://www.asanet.org/page.in?section=Ethics&name=Ethics

constitute normative statements for sociologists and provide guidance on issues that sociologists may encounter in their professional work.

ASA's Code of Ethics consists of an Introduction, a Preamble, five General Principles, and specific Ethical Standards. This Code is also accompanied by the Rules and Procedures of the ASA Committee on Professional Ethics which describe the procedures for filing, investigating, and resolving complaints of unethical conduct.

The Preamble and General Principles of the Code are aspirational goals to guide sociologists toward the highest ideals of sociology. Although the Preamble and General Principles are not enforceable rules, they should be considered by sociologists in arriving at an ethical course of action and may be considered by ethics bodies in interpreting the Ethical Standards.

The Ethical Standards set forth enforceable rules for conduct by sociologists. Most of the Ethical Standards are written broadly in order to apply to sociologists in varied roles, and the application of an Ethical Standard may vary depending on the context. The Ethical Standards are not exhaustive. Any conduct that is not specifically addressed by this Code of Ethics is not necessarily ethical or unethical.

Membership in the ASA commits members to adhere to the ASA Code of Ethics and to the Policies and Procedures of the ASA Committee on Professional Ethics. Members are advised of this obligation upon joining the Association and that violations of the Code may lead to the imposition of sanctions, including termination of membership. ASA members subject to the Code of Ethics may be reviewed under these Ethical Standards only if the activity is part of or affects their work-related functions, or if the activity is sociological in nature. Personal activities having no connection to or effect on sociologists' performance of their professional roles are not subject to the Code of Ethics.

PREAMBLE

This Code of Ethics articulates a common set of values upon which sociologists build their professional and scientific work. The Code is intended to provide both the general principles and the rules to cover professional situations encountered by sociologists. It has as its primary goal the welfare and protection of the individuals and groups with whom sociologists work. It is the individual responsibility of each sociologist to aspire to the highest possible standards of conduct in research, teaching, practice, and service.

The development of a dynamic set of ethical standards for a sociologist's work-related conduct requires a personal commitment to a lifelong effort to act ethically; to encourage ethical behavior by students, supervisors, supervisees, employers, employees, and colleagues; and to consult with others as needed concerning ethical problems. Each sociologist supplements, but does not violate, the values and rules specified in the Code of Ethics based on guidance drawn from personal values, culture, and experience.

GENERAL PRINCIPLES

The following General Principles are aspirational and serve as a guide for sociologists in determining ethical courses of action in various contexts. They exemplify the highest ideals of professional conduct.

Principle A: Professional Competence

Sociologists strive to maintain the highest levels of competence in their work; they recognize the limitations of their expertise; and they undertake only those tasks for which they are qualified by education, training, or experience. They recognize the need for ongoing education in order to remain professionally competent; and they utilize the appropriate scientific, professional, technical, and administrative resources needed to ensure competence in their professional activities. They consult with other professionals when necessary for the benefit of their students, research participants, and clients.

Principle B: Integrity

Sociologists are honest, fair, and respectful of others in their professional activities—in research, teaching, practice, and service. Sociologists do not knowingly act in ways that jeopardize either their own or others' professional welfare. Sociologists conduct their affairs in ways that inspire trust and confidence; they do not knowingly make statements that are false, misleading, or deceptive.

Principle C: Professional and Scientific Responsibility

Sociologists adhere to the highest scientific and professional standards and accept responsibility for their work. Sociologists understand that they form a community and show respect for other sociologists even when they disagree on theoretical, methodological, or personal approaches to professional activities. Sociologists value the public trust in sociology and are concerned about their ethical behavior and that of other sociologists that might compromise that trust. While endeavoring always to be collegial, sociologists must never let the desire to be collegial outweigh their shared responsibility for ethical behavior. When appropriate, they consult with colleagues in order to prevent or avoid unethical conduct.

Principle D: Respect for People's Rights, Dignity, and Diversity

Sociologists respect the rights, dignity, and worth of all people. They strive to eliminate bias in their professional activities, and they do not tolerate any forms of discrimination based on age; gender; race; ethnicity; national origin; religion; sexual orientation; disability; health conditions; or marital, domestic, or parental status.

They are sensitive to cultural, individual, and role differences in serving, teaching, and studying groups of people with distinctive characteristics. In all of their work-related activities, sociologists acknowledge the rights of others to hold values, attitudes, and opinions that differ from their own.

Principle E: Social Responsibility

Sociologists are aware of their professional and scientific responsibility to the communities and societies in which they live and work. They apply and make public their knowledge in order to contribute to the public good. When undertaking research, they strive to advance the science of sociology and to serve the public good.

REVIEW QUESTIONS

1. What are the "Preamble" and "General Principles" sections of the Code about?
2. Why must a sociologist be concerned with social responsibility?
3. How does the Code of Ethics influence our research agenda?

4

Research Design: Now It's Time to Plan

Before you actually begin learning about specific research designs, it is important for you to understand some of the terms that you will hear throughout your research methods class. There are numerous reasons to conduct research—almost as many reasons as there are researchers. Furthermore, research studies may have multiple purposes. The most common reasons for conducting research, however, are to explore, describe, and explain the phenomenon that is being studied (Babbie, 2007).

REASONS FOR RESEARCH

Exploratory research may be the first stage of a research project. Its purpose is to give the researchers new knowledge about a phenomenon so that they can design an in-depth secondary study. For instance, one exploratory study investigated children who presented with symptoms of attention-deficit/hyperactivity disorder (ADHD). The aim of the study was to find out (1) how advanced practice registered nurses (APRNs) recognized and diagnosed children suspected of having ADHD, (2) their comfort levels in treating these children, and (3) the accuracy rates of the methods they used. This study used **questionnaires** as a way of exploring and gathering information about the APRNs and their perceived abilities in working with children with ADHD (Vlam, 2006). An exploratory study allows the researchers to make recommendations for providers and design new studies to see which recommendations are most helpful.

In another exploratory studies, the researchers focused on undergraduate social work students who were working a half-time job while pursuing a full-time course load. They examined relationships among the average number of hours the students worked, perceived interference of work with studies, and the students' overall grade point averages (Hawkins, Smith, Hawkins, and Grant, 2005). The lower grade point averages that were found might suggest that it is very difficult for students who are working to have enough time for study.

Descriptive research allows the researcher to develop ideas about a well-defined topic and then describe the phenomenon in question. For instance, Swinyard and Smith (2003) were interested in the lifestyle characteristics of online shoppers. They mailed questionnaires to 4,000 U.S. households that were connected to the Internet. Fifty percent of the questionnaires were addressed to women and 50 percent to men. Over 1,700 questionnaires were returned. After analyzing the data, Swinyard and Smith found that online shoppers are younger, better educated, wealthier, and have greater computer literacy.

In another study, Robbins and Fredendall (2001) looked at the similarity between variables resulting in team success in higher education and variables resulting in team accomplishments in other environments. Upper-class undergraduate students at a southeastern U.S. university participated in a longitudinal survey filling out four questionnaires in the course of a semester. The students worked together in project teams in various courses. The researchers used variables such as cohesiveness, composition, and climate. They found that team cohesiveness and a collaborative team climate had significant positive impacts on team members' motivation and satisfaction. The study also showed that teams whose members had similar traits and characteristics reached a higher level of performance. Members of a diverse team, in contrast, had to overcome challenges to harmony and cohesion. The researchers pointed out, however, that nowadays diverse backgrounds and viewpoints are common and actually enrich teamwork.

Explanatory research seeks to identify the causes or effects of some phenomenon. After you explore a topic and have a fairly good description of it, you might begin to wonder about it. You might want to know why it happens in the way it does. Does it really always happen in the way you think it will? If something else were around, would the results be different? Recall the researchers who studied the lifestyle characteristics of online shoppers. Now they might want to explain why some people prefer shopping online. Could it be that online shopping is easier or more entertaining for them? Could it be that online shoppers try to avoid socializing with others at the stores? Explanatory research might provide answers to those questions.

UNITS OF ANALYSIS

When measuring variables, researchers use **units of analysis** to describe variables and explain the differences among them. The most common units of analysis in social science research are the individual, the group, the organization, the social category, the social artifact, the social institution, and the society.

The most typical unit of analysis is the *individual,* such as university students who are asked in a survey to rate their teachers. In another example, Johnson

(2000) investigated a randomly selected group of individuals living in Indiana to find out what types of people supported the Promise Keepers, a conservative, nondenominational evangelical Christian organization for men. The results of this study suggested that for men with lower education levels, the self-esteem they gained from being Promise Keepers was important, and for men with higher education levels, the political nature of the organization was important.

Using *groups* as the unit of analysis, Winfree, Bernat, and Esbensen (2001) conducted a systematic comparison of gang-related attitudes and behavior of Hispanic and Anglo youths living in two southwestern cities. The researchers explored the attitudes and orientations of both gang and nongang eighth-grade students. Even though the statistical comparisons supported the position that the children in one city expressed higher levels of pro-gang attitudes, there did not appear to be significant differences in self-reported gang membership. Hispanic youths in both cities, however, were more pro-gang in their attitudes and orientations and reported higher levels of gang membership.

The use of *organizations* as the unit of analysis can provide interesting comparisons in many different areas. One of those areas is health care. The rapid growth of health maintenance organizations (HMOs) in recent years has raised concerns about the quality of care, access to care, and patient satisfaction that big organizations provide. Because it is believed that there are widespread variations in patient care between HMOs and fee-for-service health care providers, Riley, Potosky, Klabunde, Warren, and Ballard-Barbash (1999) compared the care older women with breast cancer received from both types of organizations. The researchers found no difference in the diagnosis of the disease but a difference in the treatment plans.

Using *social artifacts* as the unit of analysis is always fun. Social artifacts can include bumper stickers, newspapers, books, and the news media. For instance, Scharrer (2001) studied more than 300 male characters in police and detective television dramas from 1970 to 1990 to examine their levels of hypermasculinity and antisocial behavior. The results of this study indicated for all male characters a strong association between physical aggression/antisocial behaviors and hypermasculinity.

In another example, using textbooks as the social artifacts, Zittleman and Sadker (2002) investigated the treatment of gender in 23 teacher education textbooks published between 1998 and 2001. They found that progress was minimal, that introductory/foundation texts devoted slightly more than 7 percent of their content to gender issues, and that coverage in methods texts averaged little more than 1 percent. The researchers found that a commitment to gender fairness was expressed in several of the textbooks. They also noticed that specific resources and strategies to achieve that goal were often absent, and that inadequate, stereotypic, and inaccurate treatment of gender was commonplace. The use of textbooks as a unit of analysis in this study suggests that although student teachers may learn that gender equity in the classroom is important, the textbooks they use do not explain how to make it a reality.

Using the correct unit of analysis in your research is very important. Two types of problems are associated with using the wrong unit of analysis. The

ecological fallacy is the fallacy that occurs when an inference about individuals is made from data that actually came from observations of groups. **Reductionism** is a problem that occurs when a single, narrow concept is used to explain a complex phenomenon, thus *reducing* to a simple explanation something that is actually quite complex. Here is an example. Let's say you want to compare the blood pressure of two groups of patients, so you take the blood pressure on each arm of each patient. The unit of analysis is the patient. If you use each of the blood pressures taken on, say, 50 patients, you would have 100 blood pressures. What would the 100 blood pressures do to the analysis? It can lead to problems of interpretations. It might, in fact, be better and more accurate, to analyze the average of the two blood pressures for each patient (Bland & Altman, 1995). Knowing your unit of analysis is most important to your results.

THE TIME DIMENSION

Time plays an important role in research. Researchers often describe changes or differences in behaviors within a framework of different ages or stages across the life span. You might want to know if marriage is the same now as it was 90 years ago. Maybe you found a study describing how individuals picked their mates during the 1920s. You could use that study to see if the way individuals pick their mates has changed in the past 80-plus years.

A **longitudinal study** allows you to assess a change in the behavior of one group of subjects at more than one point in time. Let's say that in 2008 you decide to track a group of 10-year-olds who live with parents who smoke to see if the children themselves eventually start to smoke. You plan to contact them again in 2010, 2012, 2014, and so on, until they are 21 years old. This research is longitudinal because you are examining changes in smoking habits over an extended period. The advantage of this type of study is that provides information about changes over a long period of time. The main disadvantage to this type of study is its cost: Keeping track of the subjects for the duration of the study is expensive. Furthermore, the dropout rate for this type of study may be high because people move and don't leave forwarding addresses or change their minds about participating.

A **cross-sectional study** allows you to examine several groups of people at one point in time. For a cross-sectional study of smoking habits in the year 2008, you might contact 10-year-olds, 12-year-olds, 14-year-olds, all the way up to 21-year-olds. If all your subjects grew up in households where people smoked, you might be able to find out when the children themselves made a decision to smoke or not smoke. The major advantages of this type of study are that it is inexpensive, it involves a short time span, and the dropout rate is low. The disadvantages are that it reveals nothing about the continuity of the phenomenon on a person-by-person case, the subjects may be the same chronological age but may be of different maturational ages, and it gives no information about the direction of change within the group.

REFERENCES

Babbie, E. 2007. *The practice of social research*, 9th ed. Belmont, CA: Wadsworth/Thomson Learning.

Bland, M., & Altman, D. G. 1995. Comparing methods of measurement: Why plotting difference against standard method is misleading. *Lancet,* 346(8982): 1085–1087.

Hawkins, C. A., Smith, M. L., Hawkins, R. C., & Grant, D. 2005. The relationships among hours employed, perceived work interference, and grades as reported by undergraduate social work students. *Journal of Social Work Education*, 41(1): 13–28.

Johnson, S. 2000. Who supports the Promise Keepers? *Sociology of Religion*, 61(1): 93–104.

Marcenko, M. O., & Samost, L. 1999. Living with HIV/AIDS: The voices of HIV-positive mothers. *Social Work*, 44(1): 36–45.

Masheter, C. 1998. Friendships between former spouses: Lessons in doing case-study research. *Journal of Divorce and Remarriage*, 28(3–4): 73–97.

Riley, G. F., Potosky, A. L., Klabunde, C. N., Warren, J. L., & Ballard-Barbash, R. 1999. Stage at diagnosis and treatment patterns among older women with breast cancer: An HMO and fee-for-service comparison. *Journal of the American Medical Association*, 281 (8): 720–733.

Robbins, Tina L., & Fredendall, Lawrence D. 2001. Correlates of team success in higher education. *Journal of Social Psychology*, 141(1): 135–136.

Scharrer, E. 2001. Tough guys: The portrayal of hypermasculinity and aggression in televised police dramas. *Journal of Broadcasting and Electronic Media*, 45(4): 615–635.

Swinyard, William R., & Smith, Scott M. 2003. Why people (don't) shop online: A lifestyle study of the Internet consumer. *Psychology and Marketing*, 20(7): 567–597.

Vlam, S. L. 2006. Attention-deficit/hyperactivity disorder: Diagnostic assessment methods used by advanced practice registered nurses. *Pediatric Nursing*, 32(1): 18–25.

Winfree, T. L., Bernat, F. P., & Esbensen, F. 2001. Hispanic and Anglo gang membership in two southwestern cities. *Social Science Journal*, 38(1): 105–117.

Zittleman, K., & Sadker, D. 2002. Gender bias in teacher education texts: New (and old) lessons. *Journal of Teacher Education*, 53(2): 168–181.

SUGGESTED FILMS

Improving Research Quality (Edith Cowan University, 1993) (26 min.). Perth: Media Production Unit, Edith Cowan University. This film describes checks that can be utilized to evaluate qualitative research. Some strategies are suggested for implementation before, during, and after entering the field. The film concludes with a discussion on the descriptive and interpretational goals of qualitative research.

Searching for Hawa's Secret (National Film Board of Canada, 1999) (47 min.). New York: First Run/Icarus Films. Canadian scientist Frank Plummer discovers that a small group of sex workers in a Nairobi shantytown seem to be immune from HIV. He uses an exploratory research method to show that he believes a vaccine for HIV might come from duplicating whatever it was that makes this group of women immune.

High/Scope Perry Preschool Study Through Age 27 (David P. Weikart, L. J. Schweinhart, 1993) (30 min.). Ypsilanti, Mi: High/Scope Educational Research Foundation. This video contains footage of principal investigators David P. Weikart and Lawrence J. Schweinhart describing the most recent project findings in their longitudinal study on children.

Joan Kessner Austin: Identifying Family Variables Influencing Behavioral Problems in Children with Epilepsy (Joan Kessner Austin, Linda Cronenwett, 1993) (25 min.). St. Louis, MO: Mosby–Year Book. The focus of Dr. Austin's research is psychosocial adaptation of children and adolescents with epilepsy and their families. Her current longitudinal research, which is based on family stress theory, identifies factors that predict adaptation to epilepsy and compares them with factors that predict adaptation to asthma.

8

Public Assistance Receipt Among Immigrants and Natives: How the Unit of Analysis Affects Research Findings

JENNIFER VAN HOOK, JENNIFER E. GLICK, AND FRANK D. BEAN

For this article, Van Hook, Glick, and Bean studied the differences in rates of public assistance between immigrant and native households. Using the 1990 and 1991 panels of the U.S. Census Bureau's Survey of Income and Program Participation, the researchers found the differences were significant only at the level of larger units of analysis. Therefore, the way the Census Bureau defined the unit of analysis could have played a major role in the results of the study and the lives of people. Notice how the authors describe the units of analysis that they used.

Why choose one unit of analysis or presentation over another? In analyzing data or presenting results on welfare usage, a researcher might select individuals or a unit that involves the collection of individuals in some more aggregate form, such as families or households. Most studies that compare immigrants' and natives' welfare use rely on such aggregate-level units. In these studies, if one or more individuals within the unit receive public assistance income, the entire unit is classified

SOURCE: From Van Hook, J., Glick, J. E., & Bean, F. D. 1999. Public assistance receipt among immigrants and natives: How the unit of analysis affects research findings. *Demography*, 36(1): 111–120.

as a welfare-receiving unit. There are several reasons for selecting such aggregates as the unit of analysis and presentation. First, household and resident family members often share resources and amenities (Greenhalgh, 1982; Lloyd, 1995) and are often grouped together for determining eligibility for welfare. Second, for administrative purposes, public officials may require statistics that use aggregate-level units such as families because these units better approximate eligibility units. Third, researchers and advocates of the poor may find statistics that use aggregate units particularly meaningful for assessing the determinants of public assistance receipt. This is because welfare use arguably derives from the characteristics of the units of eligibility (i.e., the circumstances of the family and the ability of potential earners in the family to support their dependents), not necessarily from the characteristics of each of the individuals, particularly the children.

Four kinds of aggregate-level units that have been or can be used for presenting statistics on welfare receipt are the household, family household, family, and minimal household unit. The household has been the most frequently used unit for analyzing and presenting data on immigrants' welfare receipt. Research on household recipiency clearly shows that receipt among immigrant households has increased over the last two decades (Bean, Van Hook, & Glick, 1997; Borjas, 1994; Borjas & Trejo, 1991; Trejo, 1992). By 1980, immigrants' recipiency had surpassed natives', a trend that has continued during the 1980–1990 decade. A disadvantage of comparisons involving all households is that some contain unrelated individuals who may not share resources or participate in decisions relating to long-term resource consumption or production (Greenhalgh, 1982; Kuznets, 1978). One solution is to present results for family households, or households containing individuals related through blood, marriage, or adoption (Kuznets, 1978). The presentation of results for family households typically excludes single-person households and households containing unrelated individuals (Blau, 1984; Jensen, 1988; Tienda & Jensen, 1986). Compared with studies based on households, studies based on family households report similar patterns but smaller immigrant-native differences (Jensen, 1988; Tienda & Jensen, 1986).

The presentation of results at the household or even the family household level, however, may misrepresent the level of recipiency, both because multiple sources of recipiency can exist within the same household or family household and because unrelated individuals are excluded. For example, most analyses simply examine whether any member of a household receives welfare without considering the number of welfare grants going to the household. A single-recipient household may contain one recipient or several, depending upon the complexity of the household. Further, samples restricted to family households could omit some types of welfare receipt. Because samples restricted to family households do not include single individuals (who may be eligible for SSI but not AFDC), they may be more likely to detect recipiency of AFDC than of SSI.

The family (or subfamily) has been considered an appropriate unit of analysis and presentation because families, rather than individuals or households, are used to determine eligibility for AFDC (Simon, 1984). Families are defined as co-residential units containing the family head, spouse (if present), and dependent children. Multiple-family units may reside within the same household. Welfare eligibility is based on the resources of one family regardless of the potential recipients' access to the resources of co-residential or nonresidential extended family members. Therefore, it may be more accurate to consider the characteristics of spouses, partners, and dependent children than to consider those of the entire household or family household when examining welfare use. As with samples of family households, however, samples of families do not include single or unrelated individuals and therefore exclude many SSI recipients.

An alternative is to use the minimal household unit. The minimal household unit, often relied on in research on extended family households, refers to the smallest identifiable unit within a household that has the potential to reside independently of others (Biddlecom, 1994; Ermisch & Overton,

1985; Glick, Bean, & Van Hook, 1997). Families as well as single individuals are counted as separate units. Presenting results for minimal household units offers the advantage of using families (i.e., they approximate the unit used to determine eligibility) while including data for single, unrelated individuals.

As the preceding discussion implies, the goal among many researchers studying immigrants' welfare receipt has been to focus on units that approximate co-residential groups that share resources or that are considered as a single unit when applying for welfare (e.g., Bean et al., 1997). This goal, however, may not be appropriate for addressing some kinds of research questions. For instance, researchers attempting to compare the per capita costs of welfare recipiency between immigrants and natives might be best served by presenting results for samples of individuals. Because welfare grants to families and couples increase with the number of dependents (U.S. House of Representatives, 1994), researchers presenting results for households or families in order to compare the "welfare burden" of two groups may reach erroneous conclusions to the degree that household or family size and recipient density differ appreciably between the two groups. Further, in analyses of the fiscal implications of immigration, the National Research Council recommends relying on individuals (Smith & Edmonston, 1997) because aggregate-level units are temporally unstable. Researchers using longitudinal analyses of welfare use may have difficulty tracking families or households over time when they break apart and re-form (Citro & Michael, 1995; Lloyd, 1995).

More important for present purposes, not all persons grouped together in aggregate-level units are identical with respect to welfare receipt and other important social indicators such as nativity status. In many cases, a welfare-receiving household is counted as one household no matter how many recipients it contains, and immigrant households are counted as receiving welfare even if no immigrant household members received welfare (i.e., if U.S.-born household members received welfare). Such heterogeneity within households is no small issue. Although most immigrants live in households headed by immigrants and most natives live in households headed by natives (over 95% in both cases), 25% of adults and 80% of children living in households headed by immigrants are U.S.-born citizens (estimated from the 1990 U.S. Public Use Micro-data Sample). The extent to which unit nativity composition is problematic largely depends on how researchers treat U.S.-born children living in immigrant households. If researchers adopt the household (or other aggregate units) as the unit of analysis and define its nativity based on the nativity of the householder (e.g., Borjas, 1994) or the nativity of the householder or the householder's spouse (e.g., Bean et al., 1997), they assume, intentionally or not, that native-born children are immigrants. Because nativity-related eligibility criteria for AFDC and other public assistance for children are based on children's place of birth, not the nativity of parents, and because immigrant parents are not eligible for AFDC benefits in their first five years of residence in the United States, some immigrant households can be classified as households receiving welfare only because of the presence of a native-born child.

DATA AND MEASURES

To examine the extent to which comparisons of immigrant and native recipiency are affected by the unit of presentation, we use data from the 1990 and 1991 panels of the Survey of Income and Program Participation (SIPP). One major reason for using the SIPP, as opposed to the CPS or U.S. census data, to study the consequences of presenting results for individual, family, and/or household-level units is that it is the only large data source that contains detail regarding which children and other dependents are covered by public assistance payments. We combine the 1990 and 1991 panels to obtain enough cases to allow the calculation of reliable estimates for immigrants by type of assistance received.

The unit of analysis is the individual because welfare recipiency is determined from SIPP data for each person. For the presentation of results, we construct samples of individuals, family members (individuals residing with relatives), minimal household units, families, households, and family households. We group individuals into units according to their living arrangements and familial relationships as of January 1990 or 1991 (depending on the year of the SIPP panel). Minimal household units are co-residential family units and single individuals. Thus, the primary family unit (containing the householder; spouse; and any single, dependent children under age 25), additional family units in the household (married couples with or without dependent children, single parents with a child or children), and single adults aged 25 or older are all counted as separate units. Each single adult, including unmarried parents living in the homes of their adult children, is classified as a separate unit. Families are defined as minimal household units that contain two or more related individuals. The household sample contains all households as defined by the U.S. Census Bureau. Family households are the subset of households that contain two or more individuals related to the household head. Finally, family members are individuals who reside with relatives. The family, family household, and family member samples differ from the others in that the units in the family samples are composed of family members, not the full set of persons interviewed in the SIPP as are the units in the individual, minimal household unit, and household samples. Hereafter, we refer to the samples of family members, families, and family households as the family samples.

Immigrants are broadly defined as foreign-born persons living in the United States, and natives are defined as U.S.-born persons. Individuals born abroad of American parents and those born in U.S. outlying areas (e.g., Puerto Rico) are counted as native born. Unfortunately, the SIPP does not collect country-of-birth information for children under age 15. For most of these children, we use mother's, and in some cases, father's, place of birth as a proxy: If the child's natural mother is foreign born and immigrated after the child was born, then the child is classified as foreign born; otherwise, the child is classified as U.S. born. We are unable to match 12% of the children with their natural mothers. For this group, we use the natural father's or a guardian's nativity as a proxy. Using these procedures, we classify 98% of children as either foreign born or U.S. born. The remaining 2% of children are classified as having the same nativity as the head of their family unit. The weighted percentage of children classified as foreign born following these procedures is 3.3 percent, a figure that is larger than the percentage calculated from 1990 U.S. census data (2.7 percent; the two estimates are significantly different at $p < 0.05$). Units in which the head or the spouse of the head is foreign born are classified as immigrant, and the remaining units are defined as native. Units in which the head or spouse was born in an outlying area or is a foreign-born post-secondary student are excluded from the sample, and persons living in such units are excluded from the individual-level samples. Hence, even though persons born in U.S. Outlying Areas are initially classified as native born, most are eventually excluded from the samples of individuals. The number of cases in each of the samples are presented separately by nativity in Table 1.

The SIPP collects monthly data on who in each household receives various types of cash public assistance benefits and which dependents, if any, are covered by the welfare payments. We define recipients as those who report receiving, or are reported as having received, at least one type of public assistance income during the month of January 1990 or 1991 (depending on year of the SIPP panel). The types of public assistance that we count as welfare are the three primary cash assistance programs: AFDC, SSI, and General Assistance. Recipient units are defined as those in which at least one member is a recipient. We differentiate between recipients of the two major types of cash assistance, AFDC and SSI, because the two programs serve different populations and involve different types of policy responses. We define AFDC and SSI recipients and recipient units in the same way as described previously for recipiency of any type of public assistance. For example, AFDC

TABLE 1 Unweighed Numbers of Cases in Each Sample, by Nativity

Sample	Immigrants	Natives
Households	3,268	26,643
Minimal household units	4,017	31,624
Individuals	6,463	71,138
Family households	2,680	18,608
Families	2,670	18,067
Family members	5,509	59,841

SOURCE: [U.S. Bureau of the Census, 1993] Survey of Income and Program Participation, 1990 and 1991 panels.

recipients are those who are reported as having received or as having been covered by AFDC in January and AFDC recipient units are those containing at least one AFDC recipient.

RESULTS

Rates of public assistance receipt among immigrants and natives are presented in Table 2 for households, minimal household units, individuals, family households, and families. In the case of the individual-level statistics presented in Table 2, we treat children as immigrant or native based on their estimated place of birth, not the birthplace of their parents or household head. As shown in the top panel of the table, use of any type of public assistance among immigrants exceeds that among natives when larger units of aggregation are used. In both the household-based comparisons (i.e., households, minimal household units, and individuals) and the family-based comparisons (i.e., family households, families, and family members), the level of welfare receipt for immigrants is significantly higher than that for natives only in the cases of the most aggregated units (household or family households). Welfare receipt is not significantly higher among immigrants than among natives in the cases of the smaller units. Thus, research comparing welfare receipt of immigrants and natives can reach divergent conclusions based solely on the use of different units of analysis or presentation.

Does this finding hold up when we examine different types of welfare receipt? When all sources of welfare are separated into cash assistance received from AFDC, from SSI, or from other sources (not examined here), the patterns observed for "any type of public assistance" are generally replicated, especially in the case of SSI: The use of larger-sized units makes immigrants' receipt appear higher relative to natives' than does the use of smaller-sized units. When nativity differences are examined, the differences involving AFDC are not statistically significant for any of the units, although in each of the three aggregate units involving families, AFDC receipt of natives exceeds that of immigrants. In the case of SSI, however, immigrants' receipt exceeds natives' receipt, irrespective of the unit examined. Thus, as we have argued elsewhere (Bean et al. 1997), the findings of research based on immigrant-native comparisons of welfare receipt also depend on the type of welfare receipt examined. We cannot determine why immigrant-native comparisons are affected by using different units of presentation from simple examinations of units. For the sake of brevity, we focus only on how assessments of immigrant levels of receipt vary depending on whether household-level versus individual-level units are used. To estimate the magnitude of the contribution of nativity differences in household size, in the average number of recipients per receiving unit, and in household nativity composition to household-level differences in welfare receipt, we decompose the differences following the procedure outlined by Das Gupta (1993). Although the overall nativity differences in

TABLE 2 Public Assistance Recipiency Among Immigrants and Natives, by Unit of Presentation and Public Assistance Program, January 1990/1992

	Percentage Who Received Public Assistance Benefits			
	Immigrants	Natives	Immigrants minus Natives	Standard Error of the Difference
Any Type of Public Assistance				
Households	8.30	6.62	1.68*	.536
Minimal household units	6.85	6.19	.66	.439
Individuals	6.52	5.75	.77	.527
Family households	8.56	7.02	1.54*	.610
Families	6.86	6.41	.45	.553
Family members	6.60	5.85	.75	.575
AFDC				
Households	3.38	3.06	.32	.353
Minimal household units	2.79	2.70	.09	.287
Individuals	3.42	3.75	−.33	.391
Family households	4.15	4.31	−.16	.440
Families	4.29	4.67	−.38	.447
Family members	4.03	4.44	−.41	.459
SSI				
Households	4.78	3.48	1.30*	.413
Minimal household units	3.88	3.23	.65*	.334
Individuals	2.79	1.66	1.13*	.348
Family households	4.42	2.83	1.59*	.443
Families	2.61	1.74	.86*	.343
Family members	2.30	1.12	1.18*	.342

*Difference is statistically significant ($p < .05$).

SOURCE: [U.S. Bureau of the Census, 1993] Survey of Income and Program Participation, 1990 and 1991 panels.

AFDC receipt are not statistically significant, some of the separate components might be. Hence, we repeat the decomposition analyses for each of the three welfare measures: overall welfare, AFDC, and SSI receipt. Because age is important in different ways for AFDC and SSI receipt, we examine children and adults separately.

The difference in overall welfare recipiency between immigrants and natives measured at the household level is 1.68 percentage points, a gap that is statistically significant. Much of the difference in welfare is due to (a) differences in rates measured at the individual level, (b) differences in household size, (c) differences in recipient clustering, (d) differences in household nativity composition, and (e) differences in recipient nativity composition. Because households contain both adults and children, each of the components (except the individual-rate component) is further broken down into a part due to adults and a part due to children. The numbers in the far right-hand column of the table can be interpreted as the amount and direction of the immigrant-minus-native difference if immigrants and natives were identical on each of the other variables examined. The other factors also contribute to the immigrant-native difference, some operating to increase it and others to reduce it. For example, the higher recipient clustering within immigrant households reduces the household differential by nearly three fourths of a percentage point (0.70), indicating that the household-level differences would be even larger if welfare receipt were not more concentrated within immigrant households. Similarly, if the lower homogeneity of households (i.e., lower proportions of immigrants in immigrant households than of natives in native households) were the only factor at work, the direction of the difference between immigrants and natives would be reversed.

SUMMARY AND DISCUSSION

The results show that immigrant-native comparisons of welfare recipiency depend on the unit chosen for the analysis and presentation of data. When welfare receipt is evaluated at the level of larger units, such as households or families, immigrants exceed natives in the extent to which they receive welfare. In the cases of smaller units, however, there are no differences between immigrants and natives in overall welfare receipt. However, immigrants exceed natives in SSI but not AFDC receipt, irrespective of the unit of analysis or presentation used. The findings also indicate that if immigrants and natives had identical living arrangements, immigrants' receipt would not significantly exceed natives' receipt in the case of AFDC, but it would exceed natives' receipt more in the case of SSI. The nativity difference in AFDC receipt would even reverse direction (although the difference would not be statistically significant) if immigrants and natives had identical living arrangements. Aggregate-level comparisons of welfare receipt by nativity thus tend to overstate use of AFDC but to understate use of SSI among immigrants in comparison with natives. However, nativity differences are also affected by group differences in children's nativity. When native-born children in households headed by immigrants are treated as foreign born, AFDC receipt of immigrant households is statistically significantly lower than that of native households.

Broadly speaking, the work presented here illustrates a set of problems that can occur in many research situations. Group comparisons of rates can be sensitive to the choice of unit of analysis or presentation, and discrepancies in results between studies using different units of analysis or presentation can arise from group differences in living arrangements.

Moreover, multivariate analyses do not adjust for the confounding influences of group differences in characteristic clustering or aggregate unit size. For instance, one may use a sample of households to estimate models that control for household size and composition and that adjust the independent variable to take into account multiple recipients per receiving household. Estimates of the group differentials produced by such models, however, fail to replicate the standardized differentials estimated by the method used in this paper (e.g., see Das Gupta, 1993). The reason is that, unlike the standardized differentials, multivariate models do not hold the individual-level rate constant. Rather than treat only the aggregate unit size as a measure of the dispersion of a population of persons and characteristics across households, multivariate models treat covariates, such as household size, as determinants of the probability that one or more individuals in a household display a given characteristic. The predicted prevalence rates differ from those observed because different aggregate unit sizes have different levels of association with the rates, not because a fixed number of persons and recipients are redistributed across households. Hence, rather than rely only on multivariate modeling to fix the problems associated with using a particular unit of analysis, researchers should be selective about their choices of the units of analysis and presentation.

REFERENCES

Bean, F. D., J. V. W. Van Hook, & J. E. Glick. 1997. Country-of-origin, type of public assistance and patterns of welfare recipiency among U.S. immigrants and natives. *Social Science Quarterly*, 78: 432–451.

Biddlecom, A. E. 1994. *Immigration and co-residence in the United States since 1960.* Paper presented at the annual meeting of the Population Association of America, Miami.

Blau, F. 1984. The use of transfer payments by immigrants. *Industrial and Labor Relations Review*, 37(2): 222–239.

Borjas, G. J. 1994. The economics of immigration. *Journal of Economic Literature*, 32: 1667–1717.

Borjas, G. J., & S. J. Trejo. 1991. Immigrant participation in the welfare system. *Industrial and Labor Relations Review*, 44(2): 195–211.

Citro, C. F. & R. T. Michael, eds. 1995. *Measuring poverty: A new approach.* Washington, DC: National Academy Press.

Das Gupta, P. 1993. *Standardization and decomposition of rates: A User's Manual.* U.S. Bureau of the Census, Current Population Reports, Series P23–186. Washington, DC: U.S. Government Printing Office.

Ermisch, J. F., & E. Overton. 1985. Minimal household units: A new approach to the analysis of household formation. *Population Studies*, 39: 33–54.

Fix, M., & J. S. Passel. 1994. Perspective on immigration: A series of three op-ed articles. *Los Angeles Times*, August 1–3.

Glick, J. E., F. D. Bean, & J. V. W. Van Hook. 1997. Immigration and changing patterns of extended household/family structure in the United States: 1970–1990. *Journal of Marriage and the Family*, 59: 177–191.

Goldscheider, F. K., & L. J. Waite. 1991. *New families, no families? The transformation of the American home.* Berkeley/Los Angeles: University of California Press.

Greenhalgh, S. 1982. Income units: The ethnographic alternative to standardization. *Population and Development Review*, 8(Supplement): 70–91.

Jensen, L. 1988. Patterns of immigration and public assistance utilization, 1970–1980. *International Migration Review*, 22(1): 51–83.

King, M., & S. H. Preston. 1990. Who lives with whom? Individual versus household measures. *Journal of Family History*, 15(2): 117–132.

Kuznets, S. 1978. Size and age structure of family households: Exploratory comparisons. *Population and Development Review*, 4(2): 187–223.

Levitan, S. A. 1985. *Programs in aid of the poor* (5th ed.). Baltimore: Johns Hopkins University Press.

Lloyd, C. B. 1995. *Household structure and poverty: What are the connections?* Population Council, Social Science Research, Research Division Working Papers, No. 74.

Ruggles, P. 1990. *Drawing the line: Alternative poverty measures and their implications for public policy.* Washington, DC: Urban Institute Press.

Simon, J. 1984. Immigrants, taxes, and welfare in the United States. *Population and Development Review*, 10(1): 55–69.

Smith, J. P., & B. Edmonston, eds. 1997. *The New Americans: Economic, demographic, and fiscal effects of immigration.* Washington, DC: National Academy Press.

Tienda, M., & L. Jensen. 1986. Immigration and public assistance participation: Dispelling the myth of dependency. *Social Science Research*, 15: 372–400.

Trejo, S. J. 1992. Immigrant welfare recipiency: Recent trends and future implications. *Contemporary Policy Issues*, 10(2): 44–53.

U.S. Bureau of the Census. 1993. *Survey of income and program participation (SIPP) 1990 waves 1–8 longitudinal microdata file technical documentation.* Washington, DC: U.S. Bureau of the Census.

U.S. Commission on Immigration Reform. 1994. *U.S. immigration policy: Restoring credibility, report to Congress.* Washington, DC: U.S. Commission on Immigration Reform.

U.S. Commission on Immigration Reform. 1997. *Becoming an American: Immigration and immigrant policy, report to Congress.* Washington, DC: U.S. Commission on Immigration Reform.

U.S. House of Representatives, Committee on Ways and Means. 1994. *1994 Green Book: Background material and data on programs within the jurisdiction of the Committee on Ways and Means.* Washington, DC: U.S. Government Printing Office.

REVIEW QUESTIONS

1. What units of analysis were used for this study?
2. What were the differences in the results based on the units of analysis used?
3. Could the researchers have used some other unit of analysis? What would it have been? Do you think it would have shown different results?

9

Consequences of Participating in a Longitudinal Study of Marriage

JOSEPH VEROFF, SHIRLEY HATCHETT, AND ELIZABETH DOUVAN

Veroff, Hatchett, and Douvan suggest there might be some consequences to conducting longitudinal studies. Using the data from a four-year study of black and white newlyweds, the researchers randomly selected couples to be in either the large, main study group or a smaller control group. Subjects in the main study group received more frequent and intense interviewing during the study. Notice how more interaction over a longer period could affect the outcome of the study.

There are some issues that researchers who use survey methodology would like to repress. Perhaps the most disturbing of these is the possibility that the methods they use may actually cause a short- or long-term change in the very phenomenon they are trying to measure—in other words, that certain survey research designs, particularly longitudinal ones, may comprise an unintentional intervention that changes attitudes or behavior or both, Here we present research from an experimental manipulation in a 4-year longitudinal study of marital adjustment and stability among black and white urban newlyweds that suggests that such effects may occur.

We incorporated this experimental design in response to a concern raised by human subjects review boards at both the University of Michigan and the National Institute of Mental Health. Both groups wondered whether long-term, in-depth inquiry into the bases of affection, conflict, difficulties and problems in a marriage, perceptions of each other, attitudes toward gender roles, general levels of well-being in the marriage, and the like could raise concerns in a married couple about each other that would not have been considered had we not asked about them.

In research directly relevant to the question, Wilson et al. (1984) found that having undergraduates

SOURCE: From Veroff, J., Hatchett, S., & Douvan, E. 1992. Consequences of participating in a longitudinal study of marriage. *Public Opinion Quarterly*, 56: 325–327.

explain their dating relationships (i.e., telling them to "list all the reasons you can think of why your relationship . . . is going the way it is") had a disruptive effect on attitude-behavior consistency—that is, the relationship between feelings toward their partners and whether the couple is dating several months later, as compared to a control group. Wilson, Kraft, and Dunn (1989) have reanalyzed the data and have found that the disruptive effect occurs only for couples who had been dating a short amount of time. Various explanations are offered. The ones given greatest credence focus on the assumption that people in longer relationships probably have more consistent schemas about the relationship and hence are less likely to generate new material about the relationship in the interview that would disrupt the connection between present attitude and future behavior. This should be less true for the shorter relationships. The implication of these results for our study is that interviewing newlyweds who had known each other a long time might be less disruptive of their ongoing relationship than interviewing newlyweds who have been in shorter relationships. One might have similar expectations with regard to whether or not the couples lived together before marriage. We might assume that cohabitation would give the couples broader experiences to develop schemas that are more resistant than those of couples who did not live together.

Wilson et al. (1989) are doing parallel research on other attitude objects besides dating partners—particularly political figures. In that context, they find that there is a bidirectional attitude change when subjects are asked to generate explanations for their attitudes. Some become more positive over time; some more negative. Following Wilson's lead, we would expect an increased variance on measures of marital well-being over time for couples we intensively interviewed at more points than for a control group interviewed less intensively and for a shorter period of time.

Thus, there is some evidence to suggest that the kind of effect that concerned the human subjects board might result from our 4-year prospective study of newlyweds in first marriages. Little is known about attitudinal or behavioral change resulting from data collection. However, we generated two general hypotheses about what types of effects we might find when we examine marital adjustment and well-being among randomly sampled couples in our main study and control groups. First, following Wilson et al.'s (1989) lead, we explored whether there was greater variance in marital quality measures in the second year among the study group compared to the control group. Second, we felt that the general effect of more frequent and intensive interviews would be positive by the fourth year, with the main study group having better marital adjustment and stability than the control group. We felt that both of these effects would be smaller for couples who had considered themselves a couple for a longer period of time as Wilson, Kraft, and Dunn's (1989) research suggested.

METHOD

Two samples—a main study group and a control group—were each randomly selected from a sampling frame of eligible couples applying for marriage licenses in Wayne County, MI, during a 3-month period (April–June 1986). To be eligible, the marriage had to be the first for both, and the wife had to be 35 or younger. In the first and third years of the study, both spouses in the main study group were first interviewed using standard structured questionnaires containing both open and fixed response questions. These face-to-face interviews averaged 80 minutes. Later, on another day, they were interviewed together using two innovative techniques. They were first asked to construct a joint narrative, to "tell the story" of their relationship, and then they participated in a revealed differences task (explained further below). These interviews were audiotaped and averaged 30 minutes. In years 2 and 4, spouses were interviewed separately by telephone for an average of 15 minutes, again using structured questionnaires.[1] Race of interviewer and respondent were matched for the face-to-face interviews.

In comparison, the control group was interviewed minimally over the 4-year period. In order

TABLE 1 Attrition for Study and Control Respondents (by Year)

	Number of Respondents in Eligible Sample[a]	Responded %	Refused %	Not Located or Interviewed
Year 1				
Study	1,148	65	22	13
Control	172[b]	69	9	22
Year 2				
Study	746	92	3	4
Control	114	92	0	7
Year 3				
Study	681	85	8	7
Control[c]				
Year 4				
Study	559	90	5	5
Control	102	86	7	7

[a] In year 1, this was the original listed sample minus all those respondents who turned out not to be married or not living in Wayne County; in years 2–4, this represented the number of people who were interviewed in the prior year and were still married.
[b] Only the wives in the couples listed were interviewed; the response rate, noninterviews, and refusals are based on the wives only.
[c] The control sample not interviewed in year 3.

to get baseline data for the control group, wives received a short structured interview averaging 7 minutes in the first year. In years 2 and 4, the control couples were contacted by phone using the same method as for the main study group. However, in year 2, the controls were asked only a subset of the questions (all closed-ended) with the interviews averaging 5 minutes, compared to the 15 minutes for the main study. Between waves, study group couples were sent an anniversary card with an enclosed postcard to be returned if they had moved or changed phone numbers. No contact was made with the control group between waves.

In the first year of the study, 373 main study couples—199 black and 174 white—were interviewed in their homes 3–7 months after they were married. The overall response rate for the study was 66 percent,[2] which is high given that the cooperation of both spouses was needed for inclusion in the study. Fifty-nine wives in the control group, 36 percent of them black, were interviewed during the same period in the first year. Table 1 presents, for the study group and the control group separately, the eligible sample of respondents[3] for that year; response rate (the number interviewed/the number of eligible respondents); percent refusals; and percent not interviewed, which could be for a variety of reasons (sickness, impossible to locate, moved too far away for interviewing). There were no significant differences in response rates in black and white study samples, but the black control sample responded at a significantly lower rate than the white control sample. Within race, the response rates for study and control samples are comparable.

The topics in the structured questionnaires in years 1 and 3 for the main study included the following: the quality and density of couples' networks; the way they interact with each other, with considerable focus on how they handle conflicts; their feelings about their relationship, including irritations, sexual tensions, and ways they care for each other; how they assign household chores and their attitudes toward these arrangements; their perceptions of themselves and each other, and their ideals for themselves and each other; their general well-being and specific marital well-being; and much more. The questionnaires in years 2 and 4 contained mostly closed format questions, which represented replications of items included in main marital well-being measures, significant life events, and selected other topics.

As noted earlier, the couple interview included two novel procedures. In the narrative, the couple told an open-ended story of their relationship using only a storyboard with topical markers cuing coverage of their first meeting, their courtship, the wedding, life after the wedding, and hopes for the future. This was a difficult task for some couples, who gave less involved or merely descriptive stories. However, most couples became involved in the storytelling task, which for them presented a chance to pull together many strands of their relationship. Some spouses were surprised to hear each other's version of their experience as a couple. In the second procedure, husbands and wives separately rated the importance of a number of marital ideals (e.g., "If you're fighting, cool off before you say too much") and then had to resolve their differences. This procedure often elicited large differences in attitudes toward marriage. We were interested in the way the couples resolved their differences, but the couples were clearly interested in how they differed on important marital issues and ideals.

RESULTS

We evaluated our general hypotheses using two approaches. First, we examined the variance on overall attitudinal indicators of marital well-being for the study and control group to see if, like Wilson et al. (1989), we found bi-directional changes between the first and second year. Next, we looked at the effects of being in the main study or the control group on marital stability and on several indicators of marital adjustment or well-being.

The first approach yielded some evidence supporting Wilson et al.'s (1989) findings that explaining an attitude can enhance that attitude in some people but disrupt it in others and hence induce an increased variance in that attitude. Whereas there were no study group-control group differences in the variances on a measure of marital satisfaction in the first year, by the second year the variance on that measure was significantly higher in three of the four gender × race groups. And again by year 4 there were no significant study group–control group differences in variance. These results thus gave us some indirect evidence that our main study methodology may have had disruptive effects on the marital well-being of some respondents. Although it was plausible to think that the amount of time a couple lived together as a couple would be a moderating factor in affecting this pattern (the variance effect should be minimal for long-term couples and clearest for couples who had not lived together before marriage), an analysis testing this hypothesis using a question asked of the couples about their cohabitation history yielded no significant findings.

Our second approach yielded non-significant results with regard to marital stability over the 4 years but did yield some provocative results using attitudinal assessments of marital experience in the fourth year. When we compared the separation and divorce rates of couples at the end of the study, we found that the main study couples appeared to have fared worse than the control couples. We found that 9 percent of the original control sample and 15 percent of the original study sample were known to be divorced or separated at the end of the study. This difference proved to be non-significant in a logit analysis of the divorced/separated versus married status of couples at year 4, which included two other variables known to be significantly related to both the couple's study status and fourth-year marital status: race (black couples were more likely to become divorced and were proportionally more represented in the study sample); and wives' initial feelings about the ease of talking with their husbands (lower in the divorced couples and higher in the control sample). Even if we included those respondents who are nonascertained on marital status as part of the divorced/separated group,[4] the predictive power of study status is not significant, although the trend becomes stronger. Testing a model that includes race as a factor interacting with study status also yields no significant results, nor does a model that includes how long a couple lived together before marriage as an interacting factor. Thus, the initial study status difference in marital stability washes out with proper controls.

A different picture emerges when we compare the attitudes that study versus control status couples express about their marital quality the fourth year. Many of couples not interviewed at the end of the study were those who were non-respondents or who were not followed because they separated or divorced over the first 3 years. Admittedly, this would leave us with couples who are on the whole better off. However, there still could be differences in the marital quality of study and control group couples that could speak to our overall hypothesized effect.

How to measure marital quality in the fourth year? We had many options, since the control sample was given more attitudinal questions in the fourth year than they were given in previous panels. Crohan and Veroff (1989) distinguished four factors for the overall perceptions and feelings about marriage measured in our study. These reflect (1) the couple's general happiness; (2) the sense of competence each spouse feels in the spouse role; (3) perceptions of equity in the relationship; and (4) the sense of control each spouse feels to make things right in the relationship. The following presents one prototypic item for each dimension of marital well-being:

Marital happiness (five items). "Taking things altogether, how would you describe your marriage?" Would you say your marriage is very happy, a little happier than average or not too happy?"

Marital competence (two items). "Since you have been married, how often have you felt you were not as good a (wife/husband) as you would like to be—often, sometimes, rarely or never?"

Marital equity (two items). "All in all, considering how much each of you put into your marriage, who would you say gets more out of being married—you, your (wife/ husband) or both of you equally?"

Marital control (two items). "Every (wife/ husband) experiences times when things between (herself/himself) and (her husband/his wife) are not going as well as (she/he) would like. When such times come up for you, how often do you feel that you can do or say something to make things better—most of the time, sometimes or hardly ever?"

To evaluate our hypothesis of better marital quality as the result of being involved in the study group versus the control group, we used these four measures of overall marital quality and two measures tapping specific aspects of the relationship—the sexual aspect and an index of marital tension.

These two indices were two of five factors emerging from a factor analysis of all specific marital qualities not assessed in the Crohan and Veroff (1989) indices. These were the only two significantly correlated with the central measure of marital happiness and, hence, relevant to assessing well-being. Prototypic items for each of these scales are listed below.

Negative aspects of sexual life (three items). "How often in the past month did you feel upset about the way the two of you were getting along in the sexual part of your relationship—often, sometimes, rarely, or never?"

Marital tension (four items). "During the past month, how often did you feel irritated or resentful about things your (wife/husband) did or didn't do—often, sometimes, rarely or never?"

When certain aspects of marital quality or well-being were assessed, the study group marriages appear to have fared better than those of the control group. For marital equity, we found a significant main effect for study status and a significant interaction effect of gender, race, and study status. Study group couples perceived more equity in their marriages at the end of the study than did control couples. The significant interaction comes from the fact that the main effect was particularly true for black wives. Also, wives and husbands in the study group felt more competent in their spousal roles than those in the control. The other results suggest that marital tensions are higher in control couples and that black study group wives are less likely than black control wives to perceive their sex life as negative. All in all, these results suggest that better-adjusted marriages may have developed among study couples as a result of the more frequent and more involved interviewing.

SUMMARY AND DISCUSSION

Apart from trying to assess whether our marriage study design had negative or positive effects on the marriages we were monitoring, we were also attempting to address a more general question of whether longitudinal survey studies of social phenomena can inadvertently effect short- or long-term changes in the natural course of things.

Our evidence suggests that being part of an intensive, longitudinal study focused on feelings one has about his or her marriage, and perceptions of the feelings of one's spouse, may result in both attitudinal and behavioral changes among newlywed couples. Similar to Wilson et al. (1989), we found some significant results that suggest negative effects on the natural life course of the marriages of our respondents. Although we realize the negative effect (the greater variance in marital satisfaction expressed by the study group compared to the control group) is merely suggestive, we think it is important to consider. We also found clear evidence of positive effects of being in the study. The marriages of study group couples after 4 years seem more adjusted. Perhaps the study group interviewing experience caused couples to focus on a number of issues earlier in their marriage than they would have done naturally. We had no control over spouses talking after the interviewers left. And it may be that the marriages of couples that remained intact to the end of the study were better off as a consequence of their having reflected on these issues. While Wilson's research suggested that those who had been in relationships for shorter time periods were more susceptible to either positive or negative changes, we found no such evidence.

Using how long the couple lived together before marriage as an indicator of length of intimate association, we found no significant results or even marginal trends for relationship length as a moderator on the effects of study status on increased variance in satisfaction, stability, or fourth year marital quality.

Whether results of this study would generalize to less extensive and intensive surveys of marriage or other interpersonal relationships is an open question. Nevertheless, the results should alert survey researchers, who have become increasingly interested in asking respondents complex questions about significant people, that the topics they probe may linger as issues in their respondents' lives.

This study may also alert researchers to parallel effects that may occur when surveys inquire in depth about any topic that has not been well considered prior to the survey. Wilson and his colleagues have evidence that asking people about their reasons for supporting certain political figures can disrupt their original attitudes. Although their work has been primarily with undergraduate students, similar results could be found in the general population. Their research strongly suggests that political voting preferences, not just voting behavior, may be affected by a survey interviewer asking respondents why they have a particular view. More than a quarter of our marriage study was composed of similar open-ended questions.

Although the results presented here are tentative, researchers should consider the possibility that their studies, especially if they use in-depth interviews about personal matters, may unintentionally trigger new perspectives in respondents and subsequently change their lives. We are too tempted to see respondents as passive beings dutifully conforming to their role in the survey interview. They may be more reactive than we think.

NOTES

1. Because the telephone interviewing staff was almost all white, an experiment was conducted in the second year to detect race of interviewer effects among blacks interviewed over the phone. The black sample was randomly split into two groups, one done by white telephone interviewers and the other by black field interviewers using their home telephones. No race of interviewer effects were found.
2. This couple response rate is larger than one would expect if an 80 percent response rate was obtained for each spouse separately. The joint probability of getting the couple given this individual rate would be 0.64 or 64 percent.
3. In the first year, this figure excluded those who, in the original listing obtained from the county clerk office, did not get married or whose address at time of interviewing was not in Wayne County; in subsequent years it excluded those from whom there was no interview in the prior year or having been interviewed in the prior year said they were separated or divorced or that their spouse had died.
4. There would be reason to believe that there were numerous unhappy, if not divorced and separated, couples among those who were not interviewed because we could not contact them or they refused to be interviewed. Evidence for this assertion comes from an analysis of whether an index of expressed marital happiness in a preceding year differentiates those who were and were not interviewed in the subsequent year. For years 2–4, consistent results, most of them significant at the 0.05 level: compared to those who were interviewed, those not interviewed reported being less happy in the preceding year when they were interviewed.

REFERENCES

Anderson, Barbara A., Brian D. Silver, & Paul R. Abramson. 1988. The effects of the race of the interviewer on measures of electoral participation by Blacks in SRC national election studies. *Public Opinion Quarterly*, 52: 53–83.

Clausen, Aage. 1968. Response validity: Vote report. *Public Opinion Quarterly*, 41: 56–61.

Crohan, Susan E., & Joseph Veroff. 1989. Dimensions of marital well-being among White and Black newlyweds. *Journal of Marriage and the Family*, 51: 373–384.

Kraut, Robert E., & John B. McConahey. 1973. How being interviewed affects voting: An experiment. *Public Opinion Quarterly*, 37: 381–398.

Traugott, Michael W., & John P. Katosh. 1979. Response validity in surveys of voting behavior. *Public Opinion Quarterly*, 43: 359–377.

Yalch, Richard F. 1976. Pre-election interview effects on voter turnout. *Public Opinion Quarterly*, 40: 331–336.

Wilson, Timothy D., Dana S. Dunn, Jane A. Bybee, Diane B. Hyrnan, & John A. Roloado. 1984. Effects of analyzing reasons on attitude-behavior consistency. *Journal of Personality and Social Psychology*, 47: 5–16

Wilson, Timothy D., Dana S. Dunn, Dolores Kraft, & Douglas J. Lisle. 1989. Introspection, attitude change and attitude-behavior consistency: The disruptive effects of explaining why we feel the way we do. In *Advances in Experimental Social Psychology*, ed. L. Berkowitz, 22: 287–343. Orlando, FL: Academic Press.

Wilson, Timothy D., Dolores Kraft, & Dana S. Dunn. 1989. The disruptive effects of explaining attitudes: The moderating effect of knowledge about the attitude object. *Journal of Experimental Social Psychology*, 25: 379–400.

REVIEW QUESTIONS

1. What did the researchers find that was problematic with this longitudinal study?
2. What was the difference between the control group and the research group? How did that difference affect the outcome of the project?
3. Would it have been better to use a cross-sectional design? Why or why not?

5

Conceptualization and Operationalization: We Have to Explain What We Are Studying

QUALITATIVE VERSUS QUANTITATIVE RESEARCH

Any data that you collect will be *raw* data—data that have not been processed in any way. It is pretty nearly impossible to do much with raw data.

Suppose you have a class and have some basic information about class members such as this:

Student #	Name	Student's Feelings About the Class	GPA	Final Grade
1	Sam	Hated it	2.5	54
2	Lucy	Bored by it	3.8	87
3	Wilbur	Love the class	4.0	100
4	Fran	Hated it	4.0	98
5	Craig	Bored by it	2.9	76

The table contains raw data. You really don't know what any of it means, and you must find out.

In **quantitative research**, raw data must be converted into some type of numerical equivalents before you can do any type of analysis and statistical testing. The numerical equivalents are necessary to describe the data and to explain whether or not the data support your hypothesis (which we discuss a little later). For instance, referring to the preceding table, you can convert the GPAs of all the students to find the class GPA average.

In **qualitative research**, data are collected from notes, observations, and interviews and usually are not summarized by numbers or analyzed with statistics.

In this chapter, we focus on how to begin to define a concept so you can gather the raw data you will need for your project. Suppose you heard a news report that said, "Students who are more religious are less likely to get caught for MIPs (minor in possession of alcohol)." Would you be curious and want to know if it is true? What kind of questions could you ask to find out? You would first need to come up with a **hypothesis**—a tentative statement about the empirical relationship between two or more **variables.** The variable is a characteristic or property that can vary by taking on different values. The **independent variable** is the variable hypothesized to cause, or lead to, a variation in the dependent variable. The **dependent variable** is the variable whose variation is hypothesized to depend on or be influenced by the independent variable.

Forming a research question involves defining the **concept**, or mental image, that summarizes a set of similar observations, feelings, or ideas. How will you know exactly how to design your research project unless you understand exactly what you are going to measure? Research questions tend to revolve around concepts and variables that often are not easy to differentiate and thus must be carefully defined so others will understand precisely what you mean and what you are measuring.

Let's say that your hypothesis is as follows: "Students who are more religious are less likely to get caught for MIPs." In this case, your dependent variable is MIP, which you believe will be influenced by your independent variable, which is religiosity. You can use an arrow to visualize this relationship:

Independent variable		Dependent variable
Religiosity	⟶	MIP

The term *religiosity* is very abstract. What do you think it means? Before defining it, you first need to conceptualize *religiosity*. **Conceptualization** means that you identify and define the concept so you can study it. You can conceptualize religiosity as the behavior of someone who goes to a house of prayer at least one time a week, says prayers every night before going to bed, follows the Ten Commandments exactly, and believes in a Higher Power. With those ideas in mind, you have a working notion about what the term *religiosity* means. Having conceptualized *religiosity,* you are able to indicate the presence or absence of religiosity by specifying one or more indicators. An **indicator** is what you choose to be a characteristic of the variable you are studying. Thus, praying every night would be an indicator of religiosity. Suppose you and your classmates have different ideas about religiosity. You might want distinguish between "feelings of religiosity" and "actions of religiosity." These specific aspects of the concept are called **dimensions.**

Now that you have your independent variable figured out, you have to decide how you are going to **operationalize** it for your particular study. To operationalize a variable, you must say exactly how you will measure the variable. To find out how religious a person really is, you could ask the following questions:

1. How many times have you been to a place of worship within the last month?
2. Do you pray every night before you go to bed?

When you operationalize a variable, you go from thinking abstractly about a term that you want to research to figuring out exactly what you want to know about the term and what measure you will use to find out if your hypothesis is correct.

Another aspect that is important to the research process is the **validity** of your measurements. This means that validity is the strength of our conclusions, inferences, or propositions and lets us know if our data is correct. To measure validity, you must be sure that what you are using to operationalize your variable is actually measuring the variable you are studying. You need to be sure that the measurement you use is measuring the entire variable, not just part of it.

Let's say you want to study the rate of success of the students in your research methods class. Would you ask each student to answer the question, "What grade did you receive in research methods?" Will that really tell you how successful students are in the class? Can you measure their success by asking only about their grade, and would this give you a valid answer? No, it wouldn't because there are other questions you are missing and a number of ways to measure student's success; grades provide only one way. Other indicators of success in the class might include: How involved a student is in the class, whether a student is doing independent research with a professor, and how often a student actually comes to class. Can you think of other indicators?

Reliability is the consistency of your measurement, or the degree to which an instrument measures the same way each time it is used under the same condition with the same subjects. In other words, it is the repeatability of your measurement. A measure is considered reliable if a person's score on the same test given twice is similar. In our example of student's success, we would want to measure our variable a few times to see if there is a change. For instance, does the entire class get better grades on the final than they did on the midterm?

CONSTRUCTING QUESTIONS

You might think it is easy to ask people questions. In fact, you probably ask questions all the time. However, when you are writing questions for a research project, you must consider certain things. For instance, you wouldn't want to ask the question "Are you religious?" Why wouldn't you? What types of answers would you receive? Would the responses really answer the question you want to ask?

There are many kinds of questions. **Open-ended questions** allow respondents to answer in any way they want. **Close-ended questions** require respondents to select an answer from a list of possible answers. Some questions are very good; others are not useful. It is important for you to know the difference. Questions should be relevant to your hypothesis and variables. A question that has nothing to do with either shouldn't be in your **questionnaire.** Questions should be clear and straightforward, such as "What grade did you receive on your last methods test?"

What about this question: "Do you know how to design a questionnaire, and what grade did you receive on your methods test?" That is a **double-barreled question.** A double-barreled question is a single survey item that asks two questions but allows only one answer; making it difficult for respondents to reply.

How would you answer this question: "Do you never not want chocolate for dinner?" This is a **double negative question**—a question in which the two negative words *never* and *not* pave the way for misinterpretation.

You also need to consider the **social desirability** of your question. Do you think anyone would actually answer "yes" to the question. "Do you beat your animals?"

SUGGESTED FILMS

The Standardized Field Sobriety Test: A New Weapon Against Drunk Drivers (American Bar Association, Kemper National Insurance Companies,1991) (15 min.). Chicago: American Bar Association. This film uses dramatizations and interviews to demonstrate and discuss the validity of sobriety tests as probable cause and evidence in DWI cases.

Standardized Tests: What Contributes to Native American Low Performance (Carlon Ami, 2005) (43 min.). North Amherst, MA: Microtraining Associates. In this film the directors discuss how and why the use of research and evaluation in educational contexts (e.g., standardized testing) have been used inappropriately with Native Americans and other ethnic minority children, thereby leading to incorrect assumptions about students' educational gains and achievement in grades K–12 and higher education.

Stress and Aggression in the Workplace (Michelle Y. Blakely, 2002) (1 hr., 54 min., 50 sec.). Washington, DC: Department of Veterans Affairs. This program involves all three of the VA's agencies: the VHA, the VBA, and the NCA. It discusses a research project that was developed and a survey that was conducted at VA sites. Project team members and participants share and reflect on some of the things they discovered.

NOW with Bill Moyers: Daniel Yankelovich on Public Opinion Research (Daniel Yankelovich, Bill D. Moyers, Mark Ganguzza, Larry Goldfine, 2004) (36 min.). Princeton, NJ: Films for the Humanities and Sciences. Bill Moyers talks with the survey pioneer recently named one of the twentieth century's 10 most influential people in the area of public policy. From his vast experience in the field, Daniel Yankelovich explains the agendas behind public opinion research, homing in on its uses and abuses by special interest groups. He also discusses the integral link between the economy and education, as well as what Americans can do to become poll-savvy.

10

An Epidemiological Survey on the Presence of Toxic Chemicals in Soaps and Cosmetics Used by Adolescent Female Students from a Nigerian University

IFEYINWA FLOSSY OBUEKWE, MABEL OCHEI UCHE, AND M. PHARM

The authors used an epidemiological survey that investigated the presence of toxic chemicals in creams, lotions, and soaps used by 200 female students between 17 and 26 years of age from a Nigerian university. Most of these cosmetics and soaps, which were imported from Europe, contained hydroquinone and mercuric iodide, previously banned worldwide in cosmetics and soaps. The authors designed a survey to find out how many students were using the products and whether they knew they should be concerned about the health implications of using them.

INTRODUCTION

In Nigeria today, the cosmetic use of bleaching agents by women is widespread. Hydroquinone, a common bleacher, is a white crystalline powder which darkens upon exposure to light and air. It may cause transient erythema and a mild burning sensation as well as undesirable pigmentation changes (1).

Occasionally, hypersensitivity occurs and so some sources recommend skin testing before use. Hydroquinone also may have caused conjunctiva changes, so contact with the eyes must be avoided.

SOURCE: From Obuekwe, Ifeyinwa Flossy, Ochei Uche, Mabel & Pharm, M. 2004. An epidemiological survey on the presence of toxic chemicals in soaps and cosmetics used by adolescent female students from a Nigerian university. *Journal of International Women's Studies*, 5(5): 85–90. Reprinted by permission.

A report of patchy de-pigmentation of the palm, forefinger and base of the neck in a West Indian woman after using a cosmetic containing hydroquinone was documented (2). An epidemiological survey on the use of bleaching agents by the women of Bamako (Mali) has been studied (3). It was observed from the study of 210 subjects, that 21% of the cosmetics used were hydroquinone-containing products and 11% mercuric derivatives. The study also observed some dermatological effects, which did not hinder the use of these agents, and that bleaching was particularly frequent in unmarried women. Localized exogenous ochronosis (blue-black hyper-pigmentation) of the face developed in a fifty-year-old black woman who had used a proprietary bleaching cream containing 2% hydroquinone up to six times daily for about two and half years. Eighteen months after discontinuing the use of the cream, the hyper-pigmentation cleared, except for some residual changes in the periorbital areas (4). Brown discoloration of the nails developed in two women after the use of hydroquinone-containing cosmetic skin-lightening creams for actinic lentingines of the hands (5).

Hydroquinone increases melanin excretion from melanocytes and may also prevent its production. It is topically used as a de-pigmenting agent for the skin, which should be protected from sunlight to reduce re-pigmentation. It is also used as an antioxidant from ether. In the United Kingdom, [the law states a limit of 2%] maximum concentration of hydroquinone in hair dyes and cosmetic products for localized skin lightening. Analysis of forty-one skin-lightening creams available over the counter in the UK revealed that 8 contained more than 2% hydroquinone (6). An analytical study of the cosmetic products used and artificial de-pigmentation practice of the skin in women of Dakar, Senegal, were evaluated (7). They established that those products were essentially corticoids and hydroquinone-base products and could induce serious dermatological trouble to users and suggested emergency actions to be taken for eradication.

Soaps are the sodium and potassium salts of fatty acids or similar products formed by the saponification or neutralization of fats or oils with organic or inorganic bases. They may irritate the skin by removing natural oils and may produce redness, soreness, cracking and scaling and papular dermatitis. There may be some irritation of the eyes and mucous membranes. Ingestion of some soap may cause gastro-intestinal irritation and occasionally vomiting. Treatment is usually symptomatic. A severe allergic reaction occurred in a thirty-three-year-old pregnant woman soon after being given an enema consisting of a proprietary brand of soap flakes in about 2 pints of water. She developed swelling of the mouth, numbness in the limbs, tightness in the chest, bronchospasm and generalized ulticaria and subsequently collapsed and became unconscious. She soon recovered with oxygen therapy, adrenaline and chlorpheniramine and delivered a baby without any untoward effects (8).

Meningitis in 3 women who had received spinal anesthesia was also attributed to the use of detergent solution (Alconox) in the cleansing of syringes (9). Small amounts of residue were found in syringes subjected to the procedure. A soap enema prepared inaccurately and concentrated soap solution in a liter produced inflammation of the colonic mucosa, with hypertension, nausea and vomiting and fever in a woman in active labor. The baby was stillborn (10). Such enemas were hazardous and of questionable value. There is an evidence of strong association between dysuria (painful or difficult urination) and the use of soap. Of 22 women with dysuria who stopped (16) or reduced (6) their use of soap on the sexual organs, dysuria disappeared completely in 17 women; 4 out of 6 whose use of soap was unchanged still had dysuria on follow-up (11). It must be noted that the National Agency for Food and Drugs Administration and Control (NAFDAC)—a regulatory body in Nigeria—stipulates that all active ingredients used in the manufacture of drugs, soaps and cosmetics must be printed on the packaging materials.

This study therefore evaluates the presence of toxic chemicals (hydoquinone and mercuric iodide) in cosmetics and soaps used by adolescent female students from a Nigerian university and its health implications.

TABLE 1 Questionnaire Used in the Study

i.	Age;
ii.	sex; kind of cosmetics do you use (creams, lotion, jelly, etc.);
iii.	the active ingredients contained in the cream (please check the label on the cream, lotion, etc.);
iv.	ever used a bleaching cream before and for how long;
v.	type of reaction after application of products;
vi.	whether the cosmetic in use was made locally or imported;
vii.	kind of bathing soap in use (medicated, antiseptic, mild, etc.);
viii.	type of active ingredients contained in the soap (please check the accompanying package);
ix.	how long the soap has been in use;
x.	if the soap was made locally or imported;
xi.	whether a mixture of different soaps and creams have been used and;
xii.	finally if there was any advice on the use of cosmetics and soaps?

METHODOLOGY

The method used in this survey was questionnaire-based. Well-structured, in-depth and open-ended questionnaires were given out to respondents who were adolescent female students of the University of Benin, Benin City, Nigeria.

The aim of this survey was to identify the presence of these toxic chemicals banned world wide in cosmetics and soaps (as indicated on packaging labels by manufacturers of such products), used by adolescent female students from a Nigerian university—the University of Benin, Benin City. The length of time the products have been in use, as well as the contraindications on the users, were the main criteria on which this study was based.

Questionnaires were given out to respondents, who could all read and write, and included the questions in Table 1. The questionnaires were distributed amongst 300 adolescent female students of the University of Benin, Benin City, Nigeria. The female students were selected from their halls of residence. An estimated 1000 female students live in the halls of residence at the University of Benin. Three hundred students who make up to about 30% of the female student population were randomly sampled and used for the study.

RESULTS

Of the 300 questionnaires distributed, 200 students returned them. Table 2 shows the age distribution of the 200 respondents who used cosmetics and soap containing toxic chemicals. Age was actually no barrier to the use of these pharmaceutical products because it spanned from 17 to 26 years with 40 (20%) of the respondents in the age bracket of 25 years. Eight (4%) of the respondents who were younger (17 years) also used the bleaching creams. Tables 3 and 4 also show the duration of the use of the bleaching creams and soaps among the respondents. Some have used these cosmetics for more than five years and continued despite the side effects.

DISCUSSION

The packaging materials results of the labels of the products show that hydroquinone and mercuric derivatives are active ingredients used in the manufacture of cosmetics and soaps respectively imported into Nigeria. Occasionally, hypersensitivity has occurred and some sources recommend

TABLE 2 Age Distribution of the 200 Respondents

Age	Number of Respondents	% Distribution
17	8	4
18	22	11
19	26	13
20	28	14
21	18	9
22	22	11
23	18	9
24	10	5
25	40	20
26	8	4

TABLE 3 The Duration of Use and Effects of the Bleaching Creams Among the Respondents

Duration of Use	No. of Respondents	%
1–2 weeks	26	13
2 months–2½ years	14	7
Had skin irritation	5	2.5
Lightened their skin	20	10
No effect on skin	135	67.5

TABLE 4 The Duration of Use of the Soap Among the Respondents

Duration of Use	No. of Respondents	%
2–6 months	45	22.5
1 year	35	17.5
2 years	58	27
3 years	12	6
4 years	10	5
5 years	30	15
> 5 years	13	6.5

"skin testing" before use. This was observed in 5 (2.5%) of the respondents in this study who claimed that they had irritation and some burning sensations during use of the creams containing hydroquinone. Hydroquinone has caused conjunctiva changes, so contact with the eyes should be avoided. In this study, 17% of the creams and 35% of the soaps contained potassium mercuric iodide respectively. This should be viewed with great concern especially when most of the users claimed that they were ignorant of the health implications involved in the use of such toxic pharmaceutical products.

Black women have been known to bleach their skin using hydroquinone-based products (3, 4, 5 and 7). Even when dermatological side effects were observed, they did not hinder the use of these agents. In the present study, about 13% (26) of the respondents claimed that they used the bleaching creams briefly (1–2 weeks); 7% (14) used them for so long (2 months –21½ years); 2.5% (5) had irritation during use and another 10% (20) had their skin lightened by the bleaching agents (Table 2). This phenomenon is facilitated by easy access to skin bleaching products available in the town market places and it affects an important part of the female population of all ages (educated, illiterate, married and single).

Sodium lauryl sulphate (SLS) is an anionic emulsifying agent. It is a detergent and wetting agent used in medicated shampoos and as a skin cleanser. SLS is known to penetrate the skin and cause cutaneous irritation. Epidermal concentrations of SLS after application of 1% (34mm) aqueous SLS solution for 24 hours were above the threshold levels, which are known to evoke typical skin irritation responses. Traces of SLS were observed in tissues 7 days after single 24 hours application of SLS (12). Cumulative treatment of SLS significantly increased the concentration of this compound in the underlying epidermis. This has actually shown that traces of these toxic chemicals—hydroquinone and the mercuric derivatives—could be detected in increased concentrations in the underlying epidermis of the skin, days or even months after they have been applied. This again calls for serious health concern on the part of the users.

CONCLUSIONS AND RECOMMENDATIONS

The results of this study have shown that hydroquinone and mercuric derivatives are still being used in cosmetics and soaps in the Nigerian market despite the worldwide ban of such chemicals. This is a very serious health concern, especially since most of the respondents claimed that they were ignorant of the health implications involved. Nigeria should not be a dumping ground for pharmaceutical products manufactured with such chemicals.

This study recommends that Government Regulating Agencies (Standards Organization of Nigeria—SON—and NAFDAC), in control of the regulations and importation of these pharmaceutical products, should ensure that such undesirable products are not registered or allowed entry into the country. Also, a follow-up action to educate young girls on the implications of using these toxic products, which could be injurious to their health, is highly recommended. "Skin testing" before use of these pharmaceutical products is also recommended, as hypersensitivity has been known to occur in some cases during use. The use of soaps for enema should also be discouraged. Stiff penalties/sanctions should be imposed on importers and local manufacturers who produce and import into Nigeria those cosmetics products containing toxic chemicals (hydroquinone and mercuric derivatives) which have been banned worldwide.

REFERENCES

1. *Martindale—The Extra Pharmacopoeia*. 29th Edition (Ed. by James, E. F. Reynolds). The Pharmaceutical Press, London, 1989.
2. Ridley C. M. (1984). A report of patchy depigmentation of the palm, fore finger and the base of the neck in a West-Indian woman after using a cosmetic cream containing hydroquinone. *Br. Med. J.* 288: 1537.
3. Mahe, A., Blanc, L., Halna, J. M., Keita, S., Sanago, T. and Bobin, P. (1993). An epidemiological survey on the cosmetic use of bleaching agents by the women of Bamako (Mali). *Ann. Dermatol. Venereol.* 120(12): 870–3.
4. Cullison, D. et al. (1983). Localized exogenous ochronosis (blue-black hyper pigmentation) of the face. *J. Am. Acad. Derm.* 8: 882.
5. Mann, R. J. and R. R. M. Harman. (1983). *Br. J. Derm.* 108: 363.
6. Boyle, J. and C. T. C. Kennedy. (1986). Analysis of 41 skin lightening creams available over the counter in the UK. *Br. J. Derm.* 114: 501.
7. Sylla, R., A. Diouf, B. Niane, B. Ndiaye, M. B. Guisse., A. Diop., M. Ciss and D. Ba. (1994). Artificial depigmentation practice of the skin in women of Dakar and analytical study of the cosmetic products used. *Dakar. Med.* 39(2): 223–6.
8. Smith, D. (1967). *Br. Med. J.* 4: 215.
9. Gibbons, R. B. (1969). Meningitis in 3 women who had received spinal anesthesia. *J. Am. Med. Ass.* 210: 900.
10. Pike, B. F. et al. (1971). *New Eng. J. Med.* 285: 217.
11. Ravnskov, U. (1984). Evidence of a strong association between dysuria and the use of soap. *Lancet.* 1: 1027.
12. Patil, S., Singh, P., K. Sarasour and H. Maibach. (1995). Quantification of sodium lauryl sulphate penetration into the skin and underlying tissue after topical application—pharmacological and toxicological implications. *J. Pharm. Sc.* 84(10): 1240–4.

REVIEW QUESTIONS

1. What is the hypothesis?
2. What are the independent and dependent variables?
3. How did the researchers distribute the questionnaire?

11

Conceptualization of Terrorism

JACK P. GIBBS

Conceptualizing a variable is not always easy to do. There are many different ways to conceptualize the same term. Therefore, it is important to state how you are using the concept in the project you are conducting. In this article, Gibbs discusses the issues and problems that surround the conceptualization of terrorism. *Most definitions are based on purely personal opinions, but Gibbs goes beyond a personal definition of* terrorism *by emphasizing the definition's bearing on five major conceptual questions, each of which introduces a major issue or problem.*

Definitions of terrorism are controversial for reasons other than conceptual issues and problems. Because labeling actions as "terrorism" promotes condemnation of the actors, a definition may reflect ideological or political bias (for lengthy elaboration, see Rubenstein, 1987). Given such considerations, all of which discourage attempts to define terrorism, it is not surprising that Laqueur (1977, p. 5) argued that

> *A comprehensive definition of terrorism does not exist nor will it be found in the foreseeable future. To argue that terrorism cannot be studied without such a definition is manifestly absurd.*

Even granting what Laqueur implies—that terrorism is somehow out there awaiting definition—it is no less "manifestly absurd" to pretend to study terrorism without at least some kind of definition of it. Leaving the definition implicit is the road to obscurantism.

Even if sociologists should overcome their ostensible reluctance to study terrorism (for a rare exception, see Lee, 1983), they are unlikely to contribute to its conceptualization. The situation has been described succinctly by Tallman (1984, p. 1121): "Efforts to explicate key concepts in sociology have been met with stifling indifference by members of our discipline."

There are at least two reasons why sociologists commonly appear indifferent to conceptualizations. First, Weber [1978] and Parsons [1951] gave the work a bad name in the eyes of those sociologists who insist (rightly) on a distinction between substantive theory and conceptual analysis. Second, conclusive resolutions of conceptual issues are improbable because the *ultimate* justification of any definition is an impressive theory that incorporates the definition. Nonetheless, it is crippling to assume that productive research and impressive theories are possible without confronting conceptual issues and problems. The argument is not just that theorizing without definitions is sterile, nor merely recognition that theory construction and conceptualization should go hand in hand. Additionally, one can assess definitions without descending to purely personal opinion, even when not guided by a theory.

SOURCE: From Gibbs, J. P. 1989. Conceptualization of terrorism. *American Sociological Review,* 54(3): 329–334.
Reprinted by permission.

Systematic tests of a theory require definitions of at least *some* of the theory's constituent terms; but test findings, even those based on the same units of comparison, will diverge if each definition's empirical applicability is negligible, meaning if independent observers disagree when applying the definitions to identify events or things. To illustrate, contemplate a question about any definitions of terrorism: How much do independent observers agree in judging whether or not President Kennedy's assassination was terrorism in light of the definitions? As subsequent illustrations show, simple definitions may promote agreement in answers to the Kennedy question and yet be objectionable for theoretical reasons; but the immediate point is that an empirically applicable definition does not require a theory. By contrast, given evidence that a definition promises negligible empirical applicability, no theory can justify that definition.

Still another "atheoretical" criterion is the definition's consistency with convention. That criterion cannot be decisive, because it would preclude novel definitions; but it is important when the field's professionals must rely on outsiders for data and, hence, presume appreciable congruence between their definitions and those of the outsiders. That consideration is particularly relevant here, because in analyzing terrorism social scientists often rely on reports of government officials, journalists, and historians.

Conceptual issues and problems haunt virtually all major terms in the social and behavioral sciences, and any definition is ambiguous if it does not answer questions bearing on those issues and problems. There are at least five such questions about terrorism. First, is terrorism *necessarily* illegal (a crime)? Second, is terrorism *necessarily* undertaken to realize some particular type of goal and, if so, what is it? Third, how does terrorism *necessarily* differ from conventional military operations in a war, a civil war, or so-called guerrilla warfare? Fourth, is it *necessarily* the case that only opponents of the government engage in terrorism? Fifth, is terrorism *necessarily* a distinctive strategy in the use of violence and, if so, what is that strategy?

The questions are answered in light of a subsequent definition of terrorism, but more than a definition is needed. The pursuit of a theory about terrorism will be furthered by describing and thinking about terrorism and all other sociological phenomena in terms of one particular notion, thereby promoting the recognition of logical and empirical associations. The most appropriate notion is identified subsequently as "control," but a defense of that identification requires a definition of terrorism (*not* of "terror").

A DEFINITION OF TERRORISM

Terrorism is illegal violence or threatened violence directed against human or nonhuman objects, provided that it:

1. was undertaken or ordered with a view to altering or maintaining at least one putative norm in at least one particular territorial unit or population;
2. had secretive, furtive, and/or clandestine features that were expected by the participants to conceal their personal identity and/or their future location;
3. was not undertaken or ordered to further the permanent defense of some area;
4. was not conventional warfare and because of their concealed personal identity, concealment of their future location, their threats, and/or their spatial mobility, the participants perceived themselves as less vulnerable to conventional military action; *and*
5. was perceived by the participants as contributing to the normative goal previously described (*supra*) by inculcating fear of violence in persons (perhaps an indefinite category of them) other than the immediate target of the actual or threatened violence and/or by publicizing some cause.

CLARIFICATION, ISSUES, AND PROBLEMS

In keeping with a social science tradition, most definitions of terrorism are set forth in a fairly brief sentence (see, e.g., surveys by Oots, 1986, pp. 5–8, and Schmid & Jongman, 1988, pp. 32–38). Such definitions do not tax the reader's intellect or patience, but it is inconsistent to grant that human behavior is complex and then demand simple definitions of behavioral types.

The Illegality of Terrorism

Rubenstein's definitions (1987, p. 31) is noteworthy if only because it makes no reference to crime or illegality: "I use the term 'terrorism'. . . to denote *acts of small-group violence for which arguable claims of mass representation can be made.*" However, even granting that terrorism is an illegal action, there are two contending conceptions of crime, one emphasizing the *reactions* of officials as the criterion and the other emphasizing normative considerations (e.g., statutory law). Because of space limitations, it is not feasible to go much beyond recognizing the two contending conceptions. It must suffice to point out that an action may be illegal or criminal (in light of statutes and/or reactions by state officials) because of (1) where it was planned; (2) where it commenced; and/or (3) where it continued, especially in connection with crossing a political boundary. Such distinctions are relevant even when contemplating the incidence of terrorism.

One likely reaction: But why is terrorism *necessarily* a crime? The question suggests that *classes* of events or things exist independently of definitions. Thus, it may appear that "stones" and "humans" denote ontologically *given* classes, but in the context of gravitational theory, stones and humans are *not* different. However, to insist that all definitions are *nominal* is not to imply that conventional usage should be ignored; and, again, the point takes on special significance when defining terrorism. The initial (unnumbered) part of the present definition is consistent with most other definitions and also with this claim: most journalists, officials, and historians who label an action as "terrorism" evidently regard the action as illegal or criminal. However, it is not denied that two populations may differ sharply as to whether or not a particular action was a crime. As a *necessary* condition for an action to be terrorism, only the statutes and/or reactions of officials in the political unit where the action was planned or took place (in whole or in part) need identify the action as criminal or illegal.

Violence and Terrorism

Something like the phrase "violence or threatened violence" appears in most definitions of terrorism (see Schmid & Jongman, 1988, p. 5). As in those definitions, the phrase's key terms are here left as primitives; and whether they must be defined to realize sufficient empirical applicability can be determined only by actual attempts to apply the definitions.

Despite consensus about violence as a *necessary* feature of terrorism, there is a related issue. Writers often suggest that only humans can be targets of violence, but many journalists, officials, and historians have identified instances of destruction or damage of nonhuman objects (e.g., buildings, domesticated animals, crops) as terrorism. Moreover, terrorists pursue their ultimate goal through inculcation of fear and humans do fear damage or destruction of particular nonhuman objects.

The Ultimate Goal of Terrorists

The present definition indicates that terrorists *necessarily* have a goal. Even though it is difficult to think of a human action that is not goal oriented, the consideration is controversial for two reasons. One reason is the allegation that terrorists are irrational or mentally ill (see, e.g., Livingston, 1978, pp. 224–239; and Livingstone's commentary, 1982, p. 31, on Parry), which raises doubts as to whether terrorists have identifiable goals. The second reason why part 1 of the definition is controversial: many sociologists, especially Durkheimians, do not emphasize the purposive quality of human behavior, perhaps because they view the emphasis as reductionism. In any case, a defensible definition of virtually any term in sociology's vocabulary requires recognition of the relevance of internal behavior (e.g., perception, beliefs, purpose). Thus, without part 1 of the present definition, the distinction between terrorism and the *typical* robbery becomes obscure. The typical robber does not threaten violence to maintain or alter a putative norm; he or she is concerned only with behavioral control in a particular situation.

A defensible definition of a norm is not presumed (see Gibbs, 1981, pp. 9–18, for a litany of difficulties). Rather, it is necessary only that at least one of the participants (those who undertake the violent action or order it) view the action as contributing to the maintenance or alteration of some law, policy, arrangement, practice, institution, or shared belief.

Part 1 of the definition is unconventional only in that goals of terrorists are *not* necessarily political. Many definitions create the impression that all terrorism is political (for a contrary view, see Wilkinson, 1986, p. 51), but the very term "political terrorism" suggests at least two types. The concern of social scientists with terrorism typologies is premature (see, e.g., the commentary by Oots [1986, pp. 11, 301], on Mickolus's notions of international, transnational, domestic, and interstate terrorism). No terrorism typology amounts to a *generic* definition (see the survey in Schmid & Jongman, 1988, pp. 39–59), and without the latter the former is bound to be unsatisfactory.

Military Operations and Terrorism

To repeat a previous question: How does terrorism *necessarily* differ, if at all, from conventional military operations in a war, civil war, or so-called guerrilla warfare? The question cannot be answered readily because there are no clearly accepted definitions of conventional military operation, war, civil war, and guerrilla warfare. "Guerrilla" is especially troublesome because journalists are prone to use the word without defining it but such as to suggest that it is synonymous with terrorism (a usage emphatically rejected by Laqueur, 1987, and Wilkinson, 1986).

Conventional military operations differ from terrorism along the lines indicated by parts 2, 3, and 4 of the definition. However, the definition does not preclude the possibility of a transition from terrorism to civil war. One tragic instance was the Easter Rising in Ireland (1916), when rather than perpetuate the terrorism tradition, a small group of Irish seized and attempted a permanent defense of government buildings in Dublin, vainly hoping that the populace would join them in open warfare. Today, it is terrorism rather than civil war that haunts Northern Ireland, and the term "guerrilla warfare" has no descriptive utility in that context.

Terrorism as a Special Strategy

One feature of terrorism that makes it a distinctive (though not unique) strategy is violence. That feature is described in part 5 of the definition.

Part 5 is controversial primarily because it would exclude action such as this threat: "Senator, if you vote for that bill, it will be your death warrant." Why would such a threat not be terrorism? A more theoretically significant answer is given subsequently. Here it must suffice to point out that scores of writers have emphasized "third-party" or "general" intimidation as an essential feature of terrorism; and journalists, officials, or historians only rarely identify "dyadic intimidation" (X acts violently toward Y but *not* to control Y's behavior) as terrorism.

"State Terrorism" as a Special Issue

Zinam's definition (1978, pp. 244–45) illustrates one of many reasons why definitions of terrorism are so disputable: "[Terrorism is] the use or threat of violence by individuals or organized groups to evoke fear and submission to obtain some economic, political, sociopsychological, ideological, or other objective." Because the definition would extend to the imposition of legal punishments by government officials to prevent crimes through *general* deterrence, in virtually all jurisdictions (see Morris, 1966, p. 631) some aspects of criminal justice would qualify as terrorism; and Zinam's definition provides no basis for denying that it would be "state terrorism." Even granting that a state agent or employee acts for the state only when acting at the direction or with the consent of a superordinate, there is still no ostensible difference between the use or threat of violence in law enforcement and Zinam's terrorism.

Had Zinam defined terrorism as being *necessarily* illegal or criminal, then many instances of violence by a state agent or employee at the direction or with the consent of a superordinate would not be terrorism. However, think of the numerous killings in Nazi Germany (Ernst Roehm, the Storm Troop head being a well-known victim) during the Night of the Long Knives (June 30, 1934). Hitler ordered the slaughter, and *at the time* the killings were illegal in light of German statues; but Hitler publicly acknowledged responsibility, and the only concealment was that perceived as necessary to surprise the victims. Surely there is a significant difference between such open, blatant use of coercion by a state official (dictator or not) and the situation where regime opponents are assassinated but officials disavow responsibility and the murders are so secretive that official complicity is difficult to prove. The "rule of terror" of Shaka, the famous Zulu chief, is also relevant. Shaka frequently ordered the execution of tribal members on a seemingly whimsical basis, but the orders were glaringly public (see Walter, 1969). Shaka's regime illustrates another point: in some social units there may be no obvious "law" other than the will of a despot, in which case there is no basis to describe the despot's violence as illegal. The general point: because various aspects of government may be *public* violence, to label all of those aspects "terrorism" is to deny that terrorism has any secretive, furtive, or clandestine features.

Given the conceptual issues and problems that haunt the notion of state terrorism, it is hardly surprising that some writers attribute great significance to the notion, while others (e.g., Laqueur, 1987, pp. 145–146) seem to reject it. The notion is not rejected here, and the following definition does not make it an extremely rare phenomenon. State terrorism occurs when and only when a government official (or agent or employee) engages in terrorism, as previously defined, at the direction or with the consent of a superordinate, but one who does *not* publicly acknowledge such direction or consent.

The foregoing notwithstanding, for theoretical reasons it may prove desirable to limit the proposed definition of terrorism *(supra)* to *nonstate* terrorism and to seek a quite different definition of *state* terrorism. Even so, it will not do to presume that all violence by state agents is terrorism. The immediate reason is that the presumption blurs the distinction between terrorism and various kinds or aspects of law enforcement. Moreover, it is grossly unrealistic to assume that all instances of genocide or persecution along racial, ethnic, religious, or class lines by state agents (including the military) are terrorism regardless of the means, goals, or circumstances. Nor is it defensible to speak of particular regimes (e.g., Stalin's, Hitler's, Pol Pot's) as though all of the related violence must have been state terrorism. For that matter, granted that the regimes were monstrous bloodbaths, it does not follow that the state agents in question made no effort whatever to conceal any of their activities and/or their identity. Readers who reject the argument should confer with American journalists who attempted to cover Stalin's Soviet Union, Hitler's Germany, or Pol Pot's Cambodia. Similarly, it is pointless to deny that secretive, clandestine, or furtive actions have been characteristic of "death squads" (many allegedly "state") in numerous Latin American countries over recent decades. It is commonly very difficult to prove that such groups murder with the knowledge and/or consent of state officials; but the difficulty is one justification for identifying the murders as terrorism, even though the state-nonstate distinction may be debatable in particular instances.

DIFFICULTIES IN EMPIRICAL APPLICATION

One likely objection to the present definition of terrorism is its complexity; but, again, demands for simplicity are inconsistent with human behavior's complexity. Nonetheless, application of the definition does call for kinds of information that may not be readily available. Reconsider a previous question: Was President Kennedy's assassination terrorism? The present definition does not permit an unequivocal answer, largely because there are doubts about the goals of the assassination and whether or not it was intimidation. If terrorism were defined as simply "the illegal use or threat of violence," an affirmative answer to the Kennedy question could be given; but the definition would also admit *(interalia)* all robberies and many child abuses. Similarly, the phrase "for political purposes" would justify an affirmative answer to the Kennedy question; but the implication would be a tacit denial of *apolitical* terrorism, and divergent interpretations of "political" are legion. Finally, although a definition that specifically includes "murder of a state official" would maximize confidence in an affirmative answer to the Kennedy question, there must be doubts about the feasibility of such an "enumerative" definition of terrorism. And what would one make of the murder of a sheriff by his or her spouse?

The general point is that a *simple* definition of terrorism tends to delimit a class of events so broad as to defy valid generalizations about it (reconsider mixing presidential assassinations, robberies, and child abuses) or so vague that its empirical applicability is negligible. In the latter connection, the Kennedy illustration indicates the need to grant this methodological principle: the congruence dimension (but not the feasibility dimension) of a definition's empirical applicability is enhanced when independent observers agree that the definition cannot be applied in a particular instance because requisite information is not available. If that principle is not granted, sociologists will try to make do with simple definitions and whatever data are readily available.

Presumptive and Possible Terrorism

Comparative research on terrorism commonly is based on the use of the term "terrorism" by journalists or officials. Hence, insofar as the use of data on *presumptive* terrorism can be justified, a definition's utility is enhanced by its correspondence with the use of the term "terrorism" by journalists and officials. Although only potentially demonstrable, my claim is that the present definition corresponds more with such use of the term than does any simpler definition, such as: terrorism is illegal violence.

Even when terrorism research is based on *descriptions* of violent events, as in newspaper stories, there may be cases that can be designated as *possible* terrorism even though the information is not complete; and a definition's empirical applicability can be assessed in terms of agreement among independent observers in such designations. In that connection, the present definition points to the kind of information needed for truly defensible research on terrorism, which is not the case when investigators try to make do with a much simpler definition, or no definition at all.

REFERENCES

Durkheim, Émile. 1949. *The division of labor in society.* New York: Free Press.

Gibbs, Jack P. 1981. *Norms, deviance, and social control.* New York: Elsevier.

Harris, Marvin. 1979. *Cultural materialism.* New York: Random House.

Laqueur, Walter. 1977. *Terrorism.* London: Weidenfeld and Nicolson.

Laqueur, Walter, 1987. *The age of terrorism*. London: Weidenfeld and Nicolson.

Lee, Alfred M. 1983. *Terrorism in Northern Ireland*. Bayside, NY: General Hall.

Livingston, Marius H., ed. 1978. *International terrorism in the contemporary world*. Westport, CT: Greenwood.

Livingstone, Neil C. 1982. *The war against terrorism*. Lexington, MA: Heath.

Morris. Norval. 1966. Impediments of penal reform. *University of Chicago Law Review*, 33: 627–656.

Noakes, Jeremy. 1986. The origins, structure and function of Nazi terror. Pp. 67–87 in *Terrorism, ideology, and revolution*, edited by Noel O'Sullivan. Brighton, England: Harvester.

Oots, Kent L. 1986. *A political organization approach to transnational terrorism*. Westport, CT: Greenwood.

Parsons, Talcott. 1951. *The social system*. New York: Free Press.

Rubenstein, Richard E. 1987. *Alchemists of revolution*. London: I. B. Tauris.

Schmid, Alex P., and Albert J. Jongman. 1988. *Political terrorism*. Rev. ed. Amsterdam: North-Holland.

Skocpol, Theda. 1979. *States and social revolution*. London: Cambridge University Press.

Tallman, Irving. 1984. Book review. *Social Forces* 62: 1121–1122.

Walter, Eugene V. 1969. *Terror and resistance*. New York: Oxford University Press.

Weber, Max. 1978. *Economy and society*. 2 vols., continuous pagination. Berkeley: University of California Press.

Wilkinson, Paul. 1986. *Terrorism and the liberal state*. 2nd ed. New York: New York University Press

Zinam, Oleg. 1978. Terrorism and violence in light of a theory of discontent and frustration. Pp. 240–268 in *International terrorism in the contemporary world*, edited by Marius H. Livingston. Westport, CT: Greenwood.

REVIEW QUESTIONS

1. What are some of the problems and issues that occur with personal definitions of *terrorism*?
2. How does Gibbs finally conceptualize *terrorism*?
3. What type of research can be done based on the new definitions of *terrorism*?

6

Indexes and Scales: Now We Get to Measure It All!

In Chapter 5, you learned some of the foundations for **quantitative research**. Quantitative research uses numerical representation and the manipulation of variables to describe and explain the topic being studied. In this chapter, you will learn how to create reliable **measurement techniques**, so you can transform your concepts into variables. You already know that nearly any social phenomenon you can think about can be studied. The key to designing a research project, however is to make sure that you can accurately measure the **variables**, either directly or indirectly.

A FEW MORE THINGS TO THINK ABOUT

Before we begin, a few terms and concepts need to be explained. Not all variables have **mutually exclusive attributes**. This means that at *most* only one of the events may occur. For instance, let's say you are flipping a coin. The chances of coming up heads and tails on the same coin at the same time is not possible because they are mutually exclusive events. Here is another example. In a study of children aged 6–16, researchers wanted to determine if there is a difference in risk factors and measures of children with severe asthma (Kelley, Mannin, Homa, Savage-Brown and Holguin, 2005). The researchers used both a questionnaire and a skin prick test in order to separate the children into the following mutually exclusive categories: atopic asthma, nonatopic asthma, resolved asthma, frequent respiratory symptoms with no asthma diagnosis, and normal. So the children fit into only one of the categories. They found that the asthma risk factors and the measures of severity varied between children with different types of asthma.

What happens, however, if the variable you are measuring isn't as easy to measure as "marital status" and "religion"? Let me give you an example. Many of my students are very concerned about their grades. Some don't want to take a research methods course and put off taking it until their senior years because they don't want the low grade that they think they'll receive to hurt their grade point average (GPA). (I try to make the subject matter fun, but it still is a difficult course!) I always ask them how they define "success" in a class. How do you define it? Is success based only on your GPA? It might be. Maybe you are stressed because you are afraid your perfect GPA might go down if you take a difficult course.

I **operationalize** the abstract concept of "success" in other ways as well. I operationalize "success" as a student who understands the definitions taught in class and knows how to put those concepts to use in a research project. I also think success is what else you do in school, how involved you are in activities and research projects, and whether a student spends time asking me questions. What kinds of response would I get if I asked my students, "Are you successful in college?" Unless I have operationalized success for them, their definitions might be different from each other's and from my definition. Based on my definition of success, I might ask them questions such as these: "What was your last test grade in the class?" "Define an independent variable and a dependent variable." "Design an experiment, and state the hypothesis and the variables that you would use." Students who can do all of these things fit into my definition of the concept of "success." But there is more to think about than just asking a few questions.

SCALES AND INDEXES

Scales and indexes give researchers information about the variables they are studying and make it possible to assess the quality of the measurement. Scales and indexes tend to increase reliability and validity, while they condense and simplify the data that are collected. An **index** is a composite numerical score that is obtained when various parts of a construct are each measured and the measurements are combined into a single score. For example, *U.S. News and World Report* evaluates Ph.D. programs in five major disciplines almost every year. Objective measures such as the test scores of entering students, faculty/student ratios, and reputation ratings from both inside and outside of academia are used to rank the programs. Various people also judge the overall academic quality of the programs on a scale ranging from 1 ("marginal") to 5 ("outstanding"). Then experts rescale the final score to rank each program (Morse and Flanigan, 2005). If you visit the *U.S. News and World Report* Web site—www.usnews.com/usnews/edu/grad/rankings/phdhum/brief/socrank_brief.php—you will see that in 2005 the top three Ph.D. programs in sociology were as follows:

University of Wisconsin—Madison	4.9
University of California—Berkeley	4.8
University of Michigan—Ann Arbor	4.7

A **scale** is a composite measurement in which numbers assigned to specific positions indicate degrees of the variable being considered. Scales can measure the intensity or pattern of a response along a continuum and are often used when the researcher wants to measure respondents' feelings about something. For instance, in a study to assess the associations between quality of life and attitudes toward sexual activities in adolescence, researchers used the Comprehensive Quality of Life Scale. This scale measures students' objective and subjective quality of life in seven areas: material well-being (possessions), health, productivity, intimacy, safety, place in the community, and emotional well-being. Subjective quality of life was assessed on two **dimensions**: satisfaction (responses were made on a seven-point scale ranging from "delighted" to "terrible") and importance (responses were made on a 5-point Likert Scale ranging from "could not be more important" to "not at all important").

The **Likert Scale** was developed in the 1930's by Rensis Likert. This is one type of closed-ended question where the respondents' state their feelings or attitudes about the issue being studied. In a Likert Scale your respondents must indicate how closely their feelings match the question or statement on a rating scale. The number at one end of the scale represents least agreement, or "Strongly Disagree," and the number at the other end of the scale represents most agreement, or "Strongly Agree." For example, you may have completed a student evaluation in which you rate your professor at the end of the semester. The evaluations at my school look like this:

Overall, how would you rate the teachings in this course?
(circle one number):

Superior	Above average	Average	Below average	Unsatisfactory
A	B	C	D	E

The **Bogardus Social Distance Scale** measures perceptions of the social distance separating groups from one another. Emory Bogardus developed the scale in the 1920s to measure the willingness of members of one ethnic group to associate with members of another ethnic group. The scale can be used with other groups, including religious, political, and deviant groups. This scale assumes that a person who refuses contact or is uncomfortable around a person from the group in question will answer negatively as the items move closer to what the person is uncomfortable with.

If you ask the question "Do you like getting to know people from other cultures?" the individual you ask might simply answer "no." If you use the Bogardus Social Distance Scale, you can ask a series of questions:

Please state yes or no to the following statements about how comfortable you would be having a person from (another country):

—As a student enrolled in your college
—As a student in your class
—As a student sitting next to you in class
—As a student living in the same dorm as you do
—As your roommate

If you find your respondents begin answering "no" as the questions become closer in proximity to the group or person you are asking them about, then you might see that the respondents would be uncomfortable with people from other countries if they were to live in closer proximity to them.

The **semantic differential scale** is similar to the Likert Scale because it asks the respondents to choose between two opposite positions. For instance, LaRocca and Kromrey (1999) investigated the perceptions of sexual harassment of 296 students as well as their perceptions of the character traits of perpetrators and victims of harassment. The students were asked to read a scenario and to use a seven-point semantic differential scale to describe the behavior and the character traits of the perpetrator and the victim. An example of some of the researchers' opposites follows:

	Very Much	Somewhat	Neither	Somewhat	Very Much	
Weak	☐	☐	☐	☐	☐	Strong
Naïve	☐	☐	☐	☐	☐	Sophisticated
Powerful	☐	☐	☐	☐	☐	Powerless
Insincere	☐	☐	☐	☐	☐	Sincere
Hostile	☐	☐	☐	☐	☐	Friendly

The students' ratings showed that female students perceived the scenario as more sexually harassing than did male students, even though both men and women judged female perpetrators less harshly than they judged male perpetrators. LaRocca and Kromrey also found that both men and women were influenced by the perpetrator's attractiveness and perceived an attractive opposite-gender perpetrator as less harassing than a same-gender attractive perpetrator.

COMPUTERS TO ANALYZE DATA

Many computer programs are available for both qualitative and quantitative analysis. Some of the programs might already be on your computer, if you have Microsoft Office, such as Word, Excel, and PowerPoint. Storing large quantities of verbal and quantitative data, these programs can do some simple calculations and allow you to work with text and graphics. However, moving beyond the capabilities of these programs, you might need to learn to use some programs specifically designed for data analysis, such as MicroCase, SAS, STATA, or Statistical Package for the Social Sciences (SPSS), which is the most popular. To get a better idea about using statistical programs in social science research, take a look at some of these books:

- *Adventures in Social Research: Data Analysis Using SPSS for Windows 95/98,* by Earl Babbie, Fred Halley, and Jeanne Zaino. 2000. Thousand Oaks, CA: Pine Forge Press.

- *SPSS for Windows Step by Step: A Simple Guide and Reference, 11.0 update,* by Darren George and Paul Mallery. 2003. Boston: Allyn and Bacon.
- *Data Analysis Using SPSS for Windows: A Beginner's Guide,* by Jeremy J. Foster. 1998. Thousand Oaks, CA: Sage.
- *Using SPSS for Windows and Macintosh: Analyzing and Understanding Data,* by Samual Green and Neil Salkind. 2003. Upper Saddle River, NJ: Prentice Hall.

REFERENCES

LaRocca, M. A., & Kromrey, J. D. 1999. The perception of sexual harassment in higher education: Impact of gender and attractiveness. *Sex Roles: A Journal of Research,* 40(11): 921.

Morse, R. J., & Flanigan, S. M. 2005. The ranking methodology. *U.S. News and World Report.* Retrieved from http://www.usnews.com/usnews/edu/grad/rankings/about/07method_brief.php

SUGGESTED FILMS

An Interview with Rensis Likert (Rensis Likert, Morton Cotlar, 1979) (20 min.). Fort Collins, CO: Colorado State University. Professor Likert discusses with students his management system for achieving high performance goals, the importance of supportive relationships in management practice, and specialized survey methods.

Free Time Boredom Measurement (Mounir G. Ragheb, Scott P. Merydith, Joan Burlingame, 1995) (28 min.). Ravensdale, WA: Idyll Arbor. This film discusses how a Likert Scale was used to help therapists measure the components of boredom experienced by patients in health care services so that appropriate intervention could be made. The scale measures the degree to which the patient finds satisfying arousal in his or her life. It measures four aspects of boredom: (1) meaningfulness (the patient has a focus or purpose during his or her free time); (2) mental involvement (the patient has enough time to think about their thoughts and finds these thoughts emotionally satisfying); (3) speed of time (the patient has enough purposeful and satisfying activity to fill his or her time); and (4) physical involvement (the patient has enough physical movement to satisfy him or her).

Reliability and Validity in Testing (Leonard H. Kreit, 1969) (22 min.). San Francisco: U.S. Department of Health, Education and Welfare, National Institute of Health. The author provides the dental teacher with an understanding of the criteria by which to judge the adequacy of tests or any other measuring instrument.

Employee Selection (Lansford Publishing, 1974) (32 min.). In this film you will learn about the nature of reliability and its essential nature in interview validity, tests, references, and employment applications.

12

A Study of Differences in Business Ethical Values in Mainland China, the U.S., and Jamaica

LILLIAN Y. FOK, SANDRA J. HARTMAN, AND KERN KWONG

The research presented in this paper continues the examination of the transition of the values and ethics that underlie business decisions in the United States, China and Jamaica by revisiting a survey process begun 10 years ago. Five business scenarios calling for decision choices were given to Jamaican, Chinese, and U.S. professionals. The researchers used a Likert Scale. Differences and similarities among the choices of the three groups are compared in this study, and the results are compared to those derived in the study conducted 10 years earlier.

INTRODUCTION

Significant changes are occurring in many parts of what has been considered the "Third World." In this study we examine possible perceptual/ethical changes over a 10-year period in two very emerging countries, Jamaica and China, and consider how they compare to the U.S., a "developed" country. The contrasts are notable. In recent years in China, the rapid growth of the Chinese economy, the participation of China in the World Trade Organization and the significant involvement of Chinese firms in the global investment community indicate emergence into major power status. In Jamaica, after independence, there has been a continuing struggle to build the economy and the infrastructure and to emerge from colonial status. In China, there has been the need to reconcile a Confucian and communist heritage with the demands of 21st century business. In Jamaica, capitalist influences are primary but lack of development leads to frustration of those aims. Under such circumstances, the increasing relevance of studies of the norms and values that are the basis for business decisions may become apparent as a basis for understanding decisions which are made in very different cultures. This study seeks to continue a longitudinal study of ethical decision-making that was begun 10 years ago, to gain a clearer understanding of the progress of the transition of two very different cultures to the free market.

We describe a methodology and results of a scenario-based survey conducted among Jamaican, Chinese and American participants. Both quantitative and qualitative results are put forth and discussed. The discussion includes considerations of historical and cultural influences that impact Jamaican and Chinese values including, in Jamaica, openness to change and the influence of capitalism and, in China, Confucianism, Maoism, market influences and differences in institutional environments.

SOURCE: From Fok, Lillian Y., Hartman, Sandra J., & Kwong; Kern, 2005. A study of differences in business ethical values in Mainland China, the U.S., and Jamaica. *Review of Business*, 26(1): 21–27.

We note that the empirical research in business ethics has traditionally focused on the U.S. and single country studies conducted in Australia [21], Britain [7, 17], India [6], Italy [9] and Russia [13]. It should be noted that, at that time and even today, the major studies from this group are conducted by researchers from Western traditional cultures and conducted in Western countries. The work of the research institute at Hong Kong Baptist University and the China European International Business School efforts appear to be extending these single country studies to China. In this research, we compare across three different cultures: Jamaica (which has not received previous study), China and the U.S.

THE CHANGES IMPACTING CHINA AND JAMAICA

China

The Chinese opening to the West and the dissolution of the former Soviet Union have fueled interest in the process of economic transition. Interest in the changes in types and methods of management decision-making was also aroused. Notable in this body of literature are the works of Byrd [5] and Lee [14]. The role of soft-technology transfer, which includes free market management skills, has been studied empirically by Levitt [15, 16] and by Shi [20]. The transition toward free market operations offers strategic windows of opportunity as one set of rules of the game replaces another [12, 20]. Reform in economic systems redefines corporate sources of legitimacy and substantively alters the business, government and society relationship [1, 22]. The overall sense is of a stable culture, but one founded upon Confucian and Maoist, rather than capitalist, social/ethical systems confronting a need to take its place in the 21st century marketplace. What will be the impact upon ethical decision making, given these pressures?

Jamaica

In understanding the situation in Jamaica, of importance is Hofstede's [10] finding that Jamaica is notably low in uncertainty avoidance. Ronen [19], compiling the results of several of Hofstede's studies, points out that Jamaica is the second lowest country in uncertainty avoidance, with Singapore ranked in the lowest position. Given the openness to change implied by low uncertainty avoidance, it may be that Jamaicans will be more open to pressures to industrialize than cultures such as China. This point has recently been underscored by Bissessar [3, 4], who has studied social services reforms and "pay for performance" appraisal reforms in several Caribbean nations, including Jamaica. Bissessar points out that the reforms studied failed in Trinidad, Tobago and Guyana, the other countries studied, but succeeded in Jamaica. As Bissessar notes, the countries have in common their colonial past and "third world" status, but differences in Jamaica permitted it to succeed where the other countries failed. One factor in Jamaica's success, he notes, was its embrace of the changes and its willingness to change whatever related systems had to change for the reforms to be effective.

In Jamaica, adoption of "capitalist" ethical systems should be far less challenging than is the case with China, in that Jamaica's heritage is capitalist and it has enjoyed a close relationship with the U.S. However, Jamaica is emerging from a colonial heritage, as noted, and is confronted with bringing together the diverse heritages of the many peoples who have contributed to its culture, notably Arawak Indians/Tainos, English, Africans, Jamaican, Indians and Jews [11]. Note, however, that these groups do not share similar ethical backgrounds or capitalist heritages, and, given Jamaica's struggles to emerge from its colonial past and to build an appropriate infrastructure for business, its openness and capitalist, Western, orientation may be less controlling than it may initially appear.

METHODOLOGY

Method and Design

The current study replicates the method and design used in previous studies in this series, continuing the vein of management and business ethics literature that uses vignettes to present various kinds of real life ethical dilemmas [8, 18]. In an effort to facilitate wider generalization and comparison with previous studies, the vignette set developed by Fritzsche and Becker [8] was used. Instrument and hypotheses replicate those used in similar studies beginning in 1993. Similar subject groups were selected to aid the comparison.

Instrument

The instrument was derived from the Becker and Fritzsche instrument and presents five vignettes. For each vignette, two responses were solicited. First, subjects were asked to indicate on a 0 to 10 point Likert Scale what their own decision would be to the scenario issue. Second, they were asked to indicate the reasoning behind their decision. Options were presented in multiple-choice format, including an open-ended option.

Hypotheses

Two hypotheses were tested for each vignette.

> Hypothesis 1: Chinese, Jamaican and U.S. subjects will select the same behavioral choice when faced with the same ethical dilemma.
>
> Hypothesis 2: Chinese, Jamaican and U.S. subjects will select the same rationales to justify their behavioral choices.

Subjects in the Current Study

- Subjects in the Chinese sample were approximately 49 managers from primarily government organizations (93.9%). The managers were roughly 90% male, and the age range was from the late 20's to early 40's, with an average age of 35.2.
- Subjects in the Jamaican sample were approximately 39 managers from a wide variety of manufacturing and service organizations. The managers were roughly 50% males, and the age range was from mid 20's to early 50's, with an average of 35.1.
- Subjects in the U.S. sample were approximately 81 managers from a wide variety of primarily service organizations (83%, with 21% of them in health care). The managers were roughly 53% male. The age range was from the late 20's to early 70's, with an average age of 34.6.

All respondents were attending graduate level management training.

- The U.S. sample was from two universities, with one in a large Southern city and one from the West Coast.
- The Jamaican sample was from a U.S.-based university.
- The Chinese sample was from two different provinces in China.

RESULTS

The findings from all three samples are summarized in Exhibits 1 through 7. The average scores and standard deviation of the likelihood of taking the action in each vignette are summarized by country in Exhibit 1. A "0" means "definitely would not" take the action and a "10" means "definitely would." For each vignette, ANOVA (Analysis of Variance) was used to see if the average scores from the Chinese, the Jamaican and the U.S. samples were significantly different from each other. The ANOVA results are summarized in Exhibit 2.

Hypothesis 1 suggested that there would be no difference in the selection of behavioral choice when faced with an ethical dilemma among the subjects from China, Jamaica and the U.S. As shown in Exhibit 2, Vignette 3 is the only one that has significant ANOVA results among the 5

EXHIBIT 1 Descriptive Statistics of Likelihood to Take Action

		N	Mean	Std. Deviation
Vignette 1	U.S.A.	81	4.84	3.11
	China	49	5.69	3.34
	Jamaica	39	5.44	3.44
Vignette 2	U.S.A.	81	3.49	3.23
	China	49	3.43	2.71
	Jamaica	39	3.18	2.57
Vignette 3	U.S.A.	81	1.83	2.16
	China	49	1.71	2.65
	Jamaica	39	3.26	3.35
Vignette 4	U.S.A.	81	2.67	2.91
	China	49	1.57	2.59
	Jamaica	39	1.92	2.95
Vignette 5	U.S.A.	81	7.89	2.76
	China	49	7.92	2.98
	Jamaica	39	8.23	2.60

vignettes. Vignette 3 describes a situation where a new technology can give the company a competitive edge but will produce excess air pollutants. With significance in the ANOVA, this finding implies that the average scores for some of countries are statistically different in Vignette 3. All three sample means were on the low side but the Jamaican sample (3.26) is significantly higher than the Chinese sample (1.71) and the U.S. sample (1.83) (see Exhibit 1). In other words, all respondents were inclined not to use the new technology that exceeded pollution limits, but those in the Chinese and the American samples were much less likely to do so than the Jamaicans. As for the other four vignettes, the data does not support significant difference among the three nations.

The findings in this study are consistent with the Whitcomb, Erdener, and Li study [22] in four out of the five vignettes. The only inconsistency is in Vignette 1. In this study, there was no significant difference in two countries, but it was found that the Chinese gave a significantly higher action score than the Americans.

Hypothesis 2 suggested that Chinese, Jamaican, and American respondents would select the same rationales to justify their behavioral choices in each case. A chi-square test of independence was used to test this hypothesis. The results are summarized in Exhibits 3 to 7. Among the five vignettes, Vignettes 1, 3 and 5 reported p-value less than 0.05. This finding implies that certain of the rationales used to justify their behavioral choices are different in the three countries.

The first vignette [Exhibit 3] concerns a bicycle company. It must make a payment to a foreign country businessman if it wants to gain access to his country's market. After making this payment, the resulting new business will yield $5 million in annual profit for the company. From Exhibit 3, the biggest discrepancy between the three countries is found in Rationales C, E, and F. 23.5% of the American respondents and 17.9% of the Jamaican respondents believed that a bribe would be unethical (Rationale C), while only 8.2% of the Chinese respondents shared this belief. Additionally, 28.4% of the American respondents, 23.1% of the Jamaican respondents versus 10.2% of the Chinese respondents justified their decision by claiming that it is an acceptable practice in other counties (Rationale E). However, 46.9% of the Chinese respondents and 30.8% of the Jamaican respondents rationalized their decision by stating that making such a payment is not unethical and is just the price paid to do business (Rationale F), when only 13.6% of the American respondents agreed.

Vignette 3 [Exhibit 5] concerns an adoption of a new technology that will give the company a competitive edge and yet will produce exceptionally high levels of air pollutants.

Rationales A and B are the two top choices among all three nations, and yet the levels of agreement are significantly different. 37% of the American respondents and 46.9% of the Chinese respondents believed that it would be illegal to adopt the new technology (Rationale A), while only 15.4% of the Jamaicans shared the same view. However, 30.9% of the American respondents and 48.7% of the Jamaican respondents indicated a concern for the environment

EXHIBIT 2 Summary of Anova Results

		ANOVA				
		Sum of Squares	df	Mean Square	F	Sig.
V11	Between Groups	24.544	2	12.272	1.158	0.317
	Within Groups	1758.911	166	10.596		
	Total	1783.456	168			
V21	Between Groups	2.649	2	1.324	0.153	0.858
	Within Groups	1437.991	166	8.663		
	Total	1440.639	168			
V31	Between Groups	65.374	2	32.687	4.781	0.010
	Within Groups	1135.016	166	6.837		
	Total	1200.391	168			
V41	Between Groups	39.905	2	19.953	2.493	0.086
	Within Groups	1328.769	166	8.005		
	Total	1368.675	168			
V51	Between Groups	3.309	2	1.654	0.212	0.809
	Within Groups	1292.597	166	7.787		
	Total	1295.905	168			

EXHIBIT 3 Vignette #1

	Reasons for Decisions (Frequency Distributions)			
Choice	Reason	U.S.	China	Jamaica
A	Against company policy	4.9%	8.2%	2.6%
B	Illegal	9.9	6.1	5.1
C	Bribe; unethical	23.5	8.2	17.9
D	No one is hurt	4.9	2.0	7.7
E	Is an acceptable practice in other counties	28.4	10.2	23.1
F	Is not unethical, just the price paid to do business	13.6	46.9	30.8
G	Other	14.8	18.4	12.8

Chi-Square Tests	Value	df	Significance Level
Chi-Square	25.649	12	0.012

(Rationale B) in their decision making process, while only 18.4% of the Chinese respondents have this concern.

Vignette 5 [Exhibit 7] concerns the issue that an auto parts contractor will face bankruptcy if its buyer finds out that a part sold by the contractor is defective. From Exhibit 7, the major difference in the reason for the selection is in Rationales C and E. The Chinese respondents predominantly (69.4%) chose Rationale C: The company has a responsibility

EXHIBIT 4 Vignette #2

Choice	Reason	U.S.	China	Jamaica
A	Unethical for Smith to provide, and unethical for employer to ask	30.9%	30.6%	20.5%
B	Unethical for employer to mislead Smith when he was hired	11.1	10.2	25.6
C	Protect Smith's reputation	2.5	4.1	7.7
D	Provide some but not all information	14.8	10.2	12.8
E	Decision based on whether security agreement is in force.	28.4	42.9	23.1
F	To keep job; loyalty to new employer	4.9	0	7.7
G	Other	7.4	2	2.6

Chi-Square Tests	Value	df	Significance Level
Chi-Square	16.884	12	0.154

EXHIBIT 5 Vignette #3

Choice	Reason	U.S.	China	Jamaica
A	It would be illegal	37.0%	46.9%	15.4%
B	Concern for the environment/life	30.9	18.4	48.7
C	Risk of getting caught with resulting negative consequences too great	18.5	20.4	10.3
D	Not their fault; equipment would be installed if available	3.7	4.1	2.6
E	The pollution would not really hurt the environment	1.2	8.2	5.1
F	Large potential with low risk	4.9	2.0	12.8
G	Other	3.7	0	5.1

Chi-Square Tests	Value	df	Significance Level
Chi-Square	24.805	12	0.016

to the public; it is criminal and dishonest to remain silent, while only 38.3% of the American respondents and 30.8% of the Jamaican respondents shared this belief. On the other hand, 38.3% of the American respondents and 41% of the Jamaican respondents versus 4.1% of the Chinese respondents reported Rationale E: Chances of causing injury or death are too great to remain silent.

The results for Hypothesis 2 are slightly different from the Whitcomb [22] study. While Vignettes 1, 3 and 5 have shown significant results in this study, Whitcomb et al. had significance in all five vignettes.

CONCLUSIONS, SUMMARY AND AFTERTHOUGHTS

Two hypotheses were tested in the current study of cross-cultural, ethical decision-making. The results of this current study were then tested against the results of the same survey administered 10 years ago as reported in the Whitcomb et al. paper [22]. The findings for the first hypothesis indicate that the decisions made by the respondents of the three nations—China, Jamaica and U.S.—were not significantly different in four out of five scenarios and are

EXHIBIT 6 Vignette #4

Choice	Reason	U.S.	China	Jamaica
A	Too dangerous to world safety	58.0%	61.2%	79.5%
B	May create image detrimental for company	9.9	6.1	7.7
C	Concerned with legal ramifications	6.2	20.4	5.1
D	Don't see responsibility as theirs to make choice	4.9	2.0	0
E	Those who want the information can get it now from other sources	12.3	8.2	5.1
F	Other	8.6	2.0	2.6

Chi-Square Tests	Value	df	Significance Level
Chi-Square	17.055	12	0.073

EXHIBIT 7 Vignette #5

Choice	Reason	U.S.	China	Jamaica
A	Ward has no additional responsibility; loyalty will keep him quiet	3.7%	12.2%	0%
B	Risk of injury or death too low to halt sale	4.9	2.0	2.6
C	The company has a responsibility to the public; criminal and dishonest to remain silent	38.3	69.4	30.8
D	Risk to firm's image, profitability and long run potential too great to remain silent	14.8	10.2	15.4
E	Chances of causing injury or death too great to remain silent	38.3	4.1	41.0
F	Other	0	2.0	10.3

Chi-Square Tests	Value	df	Significance Level
Chi-Square	41.657	12	0.000

consistent with the findings of the earlier study. Note, however, that the differences we report suggest that Jamaica, perhaps in its concern for rebuilding its economy, is willing to tolerate more violations of pollution standards than are the other countries. The flexibility implied in openness to change may be a factor, as well.

The second hypothesis deals with the rationales underlying the decisions. Results of the current study indicate significant cross-cultural differences in the decision-making rationale for three out of five scenarios. It is interesting to note the inconsistencies in alignments. At times, Jamaican rationales appear similar to those in the U.S., while at other points, China and the U.S. seem better aligned. What may be suggested is that the countries are using utilitarian approaches and are selecting the issues they will support based upon country/economic necessities rather than upon ethical concerns alone.

An encouraging note is that the previous study found significance for all five scenarios, rather than the three in this study. This finding suggests that, perhaps, the cultural gap is narrowing and that critical thought patterns are becoming increasingly similar. Further study would be required to connect this narrowing of the cultural gap to the economic transition and the changes in institutional environments.

The potential implications for firms seeking to do business in China, Jamaica and the U.S. are encouraging in that these findings suggest that the bases for cross-cultural understanding are improving, albeit slowly and incrementally. The implications for future research in this vein are rich in possibility, calling for continuing studies including examinations of regional differences within and among the three countries, exploration of alternative scenarios and the development of alternative hypotheses.

REFERENCES

1. Ansoff, H. I. 1966. *The New Corporate Strategy.* New York: Wiley.
2. Becker, H. and D. J. Fritzsche. 1987. "A Comparison of the Ethical Behavior of American, French and German Managers," *Columbia Journal of World Business*, inter, 87–95.
3. Bissessar, A. M. 2000. "The Introduction of New Appraisals Systems in the Public Services of the Commonwealth Caribbean," *Public Personnel Management*, 29, 277–292.
4. Bissessar, A. M. 2001. "Differential Approaches to Human Resource Management Reform in the Public Services of Jamaica and Trinidad and Tobago," *Public Personnel Management*, 30, 531–547.
5. Byrde, W. (Ed.) 1992. *Chinese Industrial Firms under Reforms*. Oxford: Oxford University Press.
6. Cyriac, K. and R. Dharmarj. 1984. "Machiavellianism in Indian Management," *Journal of Business Ethics*, 13, 281–286.
7. Davis, P. and S. Worthington. 1993. "Cooperative Values, Change and Continuity in Capital Accumulation: The Case of the British Cooperative Bank," *Journal of Business Ethics*, 12(11), 849–860.
8. Fritzsche, D. J. and H. Becker. 1984. "Linking Management Behavior to Ethical Behavior–An Empirical Investigation," *Academy of Management Journal* 27(1), 166–175.
9. Hinterhueber, H. H. 1991. "Die Ethik in der Unternehmung Probleme, Prinzipen and Einstellungen der Italienischen Fuehrungskraefte." In H. Steinmann and A. Loehr (eds.), *Unternehmensethik* (Stuttgart: Poeschel), 471–479.
10. Hofstede, G. 1983. *Culture's Consequences: International Differences in Work-Related Values.* London: Sage.
11. Jamaica's Culture. 2003. http://www.jis.gov.jm/information/culture.htm
12. Kao, R. W. Y. 1996. *Entrepreneurship: A Wealth Creation and Value Adding Process.* Singapore: Prentice Hall.
13. Kolosov, M. A., D. W. Martin and J. H. Peterson. 1993. "Ethics and Behavior on the Russian Commodity Exchange," *Journal of Business Ethics*, 12(9), 741–744.
14. Lee, K. 1991. *Chinese Firms and the State of Transition: Property Rights and Agency Problems in the Reform Era.* Armonk: M. E. Sharpe.
15. Levitt, C. 1997. Acquisition and Assimilation of Management Skills in Chinese Light Industrial Firms: Soft Technology Transfer to a Transitional Economy. San Diego: working paper.
16. Levitt, C. 2000. "*Agency Factors in the Successful Transfer of Soft Technology Transfer in Domestically Owned Enterprises in the PRC,*" UNESCO Conference Proceedings, Guangdong.
17. Mitchell, A., T. Puxry, P. Sikka and H. Willmott. 1994. "Ethical Statements as Smokescreens for Sectional Interests," *Journal of Business Ethics*, 13, 39–51.
18. Premeaux, S. R., and R. W. Mondy. 1993. "Linking Management Behavior to Ethical Philosophy," *Journal of Business Ethics*, 12, 349–357.
19. Ronen, S. 1986. *Comparative and Multinational Management.* New York: John Wiley & Sons.
20. Shi, Y. W. 1996. "Selecting Strategic Windows When There Are Too Many: Strategic Management in Emerging Markets," *China Business Review*. Shanghai: Fudan University.
21. Soutar, G. M., M. McNeil and C. Molster. 1994. "Impact of the Work Environment on Ethical Decision-making: Some Australian Evidence," *Journal of Business Ethics* 13(5), 327–340.
22. Whitcomb, L.L., C.B. Erdener and C. Li. 1998. "Business Ethical Values in China and the U.S.," *Journal of Business Ethics*, 17, 839–852.

REVIEW QUESTIONS

1. What is a Likert Scale? Why was a Likert Scale used in this study?
2. Why was this study done again when it was originally done 10 years earlier?
3. Describe the vinegettes. What were they for?

13

The Reverse Social Distance Scale

MOTOKO Y. LEE, STEPHEN G. SAPP, AND MELVIN C. RAY

These researchers created a "reverse" Social Distance Scale by modifying Bogardus's Social Distance Scale to measure minority groups' perceptions of the social distance established by the majority group between itself and minority groups. As you read this article, notice the reasons why using a "reverse" Social Distance Scale can affect the number of respondents who are willing to answer a survey.

The social distance between a minority group and the majority group—the most powerful group, but not necessarily the largest—has been postulated by the present authors to be based on the minority group's reaction to its perceived rejection or acceptance by the majority group, rather than on the majority group's reaction to the minority group. Thus, Bogardus's Social Distance Scale (1925), which was created from the perspective of the majority group, cannot be used to explain the nature of this type of social distance. To assess a minority group's perceptions of the distance established by the majority group between itself and the minority group (rather than the distance a minority group has established between itself and the majority group), researchers need a different type of measure.

The literature contains no mention of such a scale, and although numerous accounts of minority perceptions of prejudice appear in the writings of W. E. B. Du Bois (Weinberg, 1992) and others (e.g., Cleaver, 1967; Finkenstaedt, 1994; Grier, 1968; Silberman, 1964; West, 1993), such accounts tend to be qualitative. A review of the following studies provides additional evidence of the need for a "reverse" Social Distance Scale.

Netting (1991) reported that Chinese immigrants in Canada tended to reject Whites and other groups instead of seeking acceptance from them. "Anglos would accept Poles, the only white minority represented in the study, and Chinese. However, Chinese would not accept Anglos" (p. 101). If the goal is understanding a minority viewpoint, then it is more important to assess the distance perceived by the

SOURCE: From Lee, M. Y., Sapp, S., & Ray, M. 1996. The reverse social distance scale. *Journal of Social Psychology*, 136(1): 17–25. Reprinted by permission.

Chinese immigrants as having been created by the White Canadians than it is to assess the actual social distance between the two groups, because the former perspective is that of the minority group. Left unanswered by Netting's study was the question of whether the Chinese and the Polish immigrants' perceptions of acceptance by the Anglos were the same or similar.

Muir and Muir (1988) used Bogardus's Social Distance Scale in their study of White and Black middle-school children from the Deep South. These researchers found that, by their early teens, most of the White children had adopted an adult pattern of relating to Blacks, consisting of civil acceptance and social rejection, whereas a majority of Black children accepted Whites socially as well as publicly. The Black middle-school students were found to be more tolerant of the White middle-school students than the White students were of the Black students. The Black children's perception of the extent of their social acceptance by the White children—a factor that would have provided more information about the Black children's acceptance of the White children—was not examined.

McAllister and Moore (1991) used Bogardus's Social Distance Scale in Australia to measure majority and minority groups' perceptions of social distance from each other. McAllister and Moore attempted to explain the variation in the groups' perceptions without considering the conditional nature of the social distance established by the minority groups between themselves and the majority group. The factors that were considered by McAllister and Moore accounted for very little of the variation in social distance that was created by the two immigrant minority groups—far less than the amount of variation that was accounted for in relation to the Australian majority group ([R.sup.2] = 0.02 for the combined European immigrant group and 0.01 for the Southeast Asian group vs. 11 for the Australians, 1991, p. 100).

Tuch (1988, p. 184) tried to account for the variation in social distance among Blacks and Whites toward each other's groups, using several socioeconomic predictors. As in McAllister and Moore's study, the variables that were selected explained considerably less about the Blacks' social distance from the Whites (7%) than about the Whites' social distance from the Blacks (27%).

Wilson (1986) observed that studies addressing the correlates of Blacks' racial distance preferences have been few, and their results, inconsistent. In addition, Wilson observed that social variables predicted the social distance preferred by Blacks much more poorly than they predicted the social distance preferred by Whites.

The common finding in these studies—that the selected variables explained Blacks' preference for social distance toward Whites more poorly than they explained Whites' preference for social distance toward Blacks—suggests that important explanatory variables that would account for the social distance preferences of minority groups toward the majority group were lacking in this research. To explain the minority variation in social distance, researchers need a measure of the minority's perception of the social distance established by the majority group between itself and the minority group, because this perception is assumed to be the basis upon which minorities will establish their preferred social distance from the majority group. Even Bogardus (1959, p. 77), in his study of factors that would determine the distance between nations, called people of other nations' friendliness and open-heartedness the "nearness factors."

METHOD

Our objectives in the present study were to assess the feasibility of a "reverse" Social Distance Scale, to determine whether such a scale would differentiate among different minority groups, and to revise the scale, if necessary, based on participants' responses. We mailed a questionnaire to approximately 1,000 minority students (U.S. citizens and permanent residents) at a state university in the spring of 1993. We received 108 completed and usable questionnaires. The present results, although not generalizable, were satisfactory in light of our objectives.

The extremely low return rate for the questionnaire was probably a reflection of indifference to or avoidance of the topic of rejection/acceptance by the majority group. Responding to our Reverse Social Distance Scale may have been difficult for certain minorities. Several students, all of whom were Black, returned the questionnaire without having answered the Reverse Social Distance Scale question. These students wrote comments such as, "Do not ask these questions. I am an American" or "This type of question perpetuates the division between whites and blacks." If, as we suspect, this type of reaction was common among those who did not return their questionnaires, then the non-participants' perceptions about rejection/acception by the majority group may have differed from those of the participants. This possibility was not explored in the present study but should be investigated.

We created the Reverse Social Distance Scale by modifying the items on Bogardus's Racial Distance Scale (Miller, 1991, p. 382). The proposed scale items (distance criteria) were as similar as possible to those on Bogardus's scale, but we did make some modifications so that the items would appear realistic to college students. In contrast to Bogardus's scale, which assesses respondents' willingness to accept members of other groups in various roles (e.g., as a fellow citizen, as a neighbor), the Reverse Social Distance Scale assesses respondents' perceptions of how other groups accept them in these roles.

Items that were likely to have been experienced by college students were phrased "Do they mind . . . ?," and the other items as "Would they . . . ?" The items and the instructions for the Reverse Social Distance Scale were as follows:

Considering typical Caucasian Americans you have known, not any specific person nor the worst or the best, circle Y or N to express your opinion.

Y N 5. Do they mind your being a citizen in this country?

Y N 4. Do they mind your living in the same neighborhood?

Y N 3. Would they mind your living next to them?

Y N 2. Would they mind your becoming a close friend to them?

Y N 1. Would they mind your becoming their kin by marriage?

We did not include Bogardus's Social Distance Scale in the present study because we wanted to avoid any contamination that might result from the use of Bogardus's scale and the Reverse Social Distance Scale on the same questionnaire. We did include the Twenty Statements Test (TST; Kuhn & McPartland, 1954), however; the respondents were asked to write 20 responses (at most) to the question "Who am I?"

RESULTS

The aggregated data for the three groups are reported in Table 1. The category entitled Other Minorities included diverse groups, such as Japanese Americans, Chinese Americans, Native Americans, and other Americans, whose ancestors had immigrated from countries such as India, Sri Lanka, Vietnam, and Laos. These groups were combined into one because none of them was large enough to be considered individually in the analysis.

The results indicated that there was a significant difference among the three means. The African American students' mean score was significantly higher than those of the other two groups, indicating that, on average, the African American students perceived the distance established by the Caucasian Americans to be greater than the other two groups did. The latter two groups did not differ significantly from each other. The reason we conducted these tests of significance was to determine the magnitude of the differences in the sample, not to make generalizations about the results.

Although the scale's coefficient was high enough to be acceptable, we examined a few cases in which the responses seemed contradictory and used the respondents' comments to revise the

TABLE 1 Analysis of Variance Results

Group	N	M	SD
African Americans	48	3.65	1.74
Hispanic Americans	25	1.60	1.12
Other minorities*	35	1.80	1.80

Between groups: $F(2, 105) = 23.8$, $p = 0.001$
Note: Means with different subscripts differ significantly at 0.05.
*This category included Japanese Americans, Chinese Americans, Native Americans, and Americans whose ancestors had come from India, Sri Lanka, Vietnam, and Laos.

instructions for the scale and the wording of some items. The original version of the instructions contained the adjective "typical" (Bogardus used "stereotypic"), but one respondent criticized this term as stereotyping. Because the purpose of the scale is to assess perceptions of the distance associated with the collective majority group, or the generalized other of that group, not perceptions of the distance associated with specific individuals in that group, we recommend that future researchers use the word "most," instead of "typical" or "stereotypic," in the instructions to the scale.

There were also some contradictions with regard to the responses for the citizenship item. A few persons perceived that Caucasian Americans minded having them as fellow citizens even though the Caucasian Americans did not mind them living in the same neighborhood. These participants may have equated the concept of citizenship with rights and duties and, therefore, have viewed it as encompassing more than living in the same community. Although the citizenship item was included in Bogardus's scale, future researchers would do better to replace this item with one that pertains to a simpler concept, such as living in the same community.

We examined TST responses for the students whose scores were at either end of our scale: strong acceptance (1) or strong rejection (6). Eleven of the 48 African American students received a score of 6; of these 11 students, 6 used "African" or "Black" as their first identifier, 1 used this type of label as his or her 19th identifier, and 4 did not use a racial identifier. Six African American students received a score of 1; of these 6 students, 3 used a racial identifier in their first response to the TST, and the other 3 did not use a racial identifier at all.

None of the 25 Hispanic students received a score of 6, but 17 received a score of 1. Of these 17 students, 4 used an ethnic identifier in their 2nd, 5th, 6th, or 15th response, and the remaining 13 did not use an ethnic identifier.

Of the 35 (predominantly Asian) students in the Other Minorities group, only 1 received a score of 6. This participant used a racial identifier in his or her fourth response. Eighteen of the students in the Other Minorities group scored 1; of these students, 10 did not use a racial/ethnic identifier, 6 used a racial/ethnic identifier in their first response, 1 used a racial/ethnic identifier in his or her second response, and 1 used a racial/ethnic identifier in his or her ninth response.

DISCUSSION

The Reverse Social Distance Scale assesses minority groups' perceptions of the social distance established by the majority group between itself and minority groups. The scale differentiated between the African American students and the other two minority groups, Hispanics and Other Minorities, in the present study, but not between the latter two groups.

Researchers (McAllister & Moore, 1991, pp. 96–97) have discussed several alternatives that might account for social distance, including social learning theory (Allport, 1954), theory focusing on social experience of education (Harding, Proshansky, Kutner, & Chein, 1969), economic competition theory (Baker, 1978), contact theory (Tajfel, 1982), and the theory of authoritarian personality (Adorno, Frenkel-Brunswik, Levinson, & Sanford, 1950). However, these theories seem to be more applicable to majority group prejudice toward minority groups than to minority group prejudice toward the majority group.

Researchers have tended to ignore the influence of minority group perceptions regarding their acceptance or rejection by the majority group on the degree of social distance minority groups establish between themselves and the majority group. As Walsh (1990) indicated, researchers (e.g., Griffitt & Veitch, 1974; Van den Berghe, 1981) have recognized the role of the majority group's acceptance or rejection of minority groups on the social distance between the majority and minorities; nevertheless, Bogardus's Social Distance Scale has continued to be researchers' (e.g., Walsh's) major tool.

We assumed that minority groups in multiethnic or multiracial societies do not isolate themselves by choice, but prefer to be accepted by the majority group and to have equal access to resources and rewards. We also assumed that minority group members perceive a social distance that has been established by the majority group, between their own group and the majority group, even though minority groups' perception of this distance may differ from that of the majority group. The social distance minority groups perceive as having been established by the majority group influences the degree of social distance the minority group will establish between itself and the majority group; therefore, we expected the relationship between the Reverse Social Distance Scale and Bogardus's Social Distance Scale to be positive. We did not explore this relationship, however, because we did not include Bogardus's Social Distance Scale in the present study, to avoid any contamination of the results.

Tajfel and Turner (1986) suggested that self-identification with one's own-group is dependent upon one's evaluation of the comparisons between one's own-group and outgroups, regarding the attributes and characteristics that are valued by one's own-group. These researchers posited that members of a group whose social identity is not satisfactory will either try to improve their group's identity or leave their present group to join a group whose identify is more positive. Thus, the member of a minority group's perceived rejection or acceptance by the majority group is likely to affect the way this individual feels about the social identity of his or her own-group.

In line with Tajfel and Turner's reasoning, we examined the responses of the highest and lowest scorers on the Reverse Social Distance Scale. Six of the 11 respondents who received a score of 6 (strongest perceived rejection) used a racial/ethnic identifier in their 1st response to the TST. These participants (the first category described by Tajfel and Turner, 1986) would be likely to distance themselves from the majority and to try to establish their own separate identities. The participants who used a racial identifier in their 19th TST response and the 4 participants who did not use a racial identifier at all would be likely to try to establish their own separate self-identity or to find another group to identify with (Tajfel and Turner's second category).

The 41 respondents who received a score of 1 (strongest perceived acceptance) would be unlikely to distance themselves from the majority. Four respondents used a racial/ethnic identifier in their 5th, 6th, 9th, or 15th response on the TST, and 26 did not use a racial/ethnic identifier at all. The 14 respondents who used a racial/ethnic identifier in their 1st or 2nd response to the TST might distance themselves from the majority group to the extent that they would prefer to limit intimate relationships (i.e., mate, kin) to members of their own-groups. The relationship between the participants' scores on the Reverse Social Distance Scale and their choices of self-identifiers provided some insight about the possible effect of minority groups' perceptions of the social distance established by the majority group on minority group members' self-concept. More research is needed, however, to explore the consequences of minority groups' perceptions of social distance for the degree of social distance minority groups establish between themselves and the majority group, as well as the consequences of these perceptions for minority groups' self-concept.

REFERENCES

Adorno, T. W., Frenkel-Brunswik, E., Levinson, D. J., & Sanford, R. N. (1950). *The authoritarian personality*. New York: Harper.

Allport, G. W. (1954). *The nature of prejudice*. Reading, MA: Addison-Wesley.

Baker, D. (1978). Race and power: Comparative approaches to the analysis of race relations. *Ethnic and Racial Studies*, 1, 316–335.

Bogardus, E. S. (1925). Measuring social distance. *Journal of Applied Sociology*, 9, 299–308.

Bogardus, E. S. (1959). *Social distance*. Yellow Spring, OH: Artichild.

Cleaver, E. (1967). *Soul on ice*. New York: McGraw-Hill.

Finkenstaedt, R. L. H. (1994). *Face-to-face: Blacks in America, White perceptions and Black realities*. New York: William Morrow.

Grier, W. H. (1968). *Black rage*. New York: Basic Books.

Griffitt, W., & Veitch, R. (1974). Preacquaintance attitude similarity and attraction revisited: Ten days in a fallout shelter. *Sociometry*, 37, 163–178.

Harding, J., Proshansky, H., Kutner, B., & Chein, I. (1969). Prejudice and ethnic relations. In G. Lindzey & E. Aronson (Eds.) *Handbook of social psychology* (2nd ed., Vol. 5, pp. 1–76). Reading, MA: Addison-Wesley.

Kelley, C. F., Mannino, D. M., Homa, D. M., Savage-Brown, A., & Holguin, F. (2005). Asthma phenotypes, risk factors, and measures of severity in a national sample of U.S. children. *Pediatrics*, March 115(3), 726–732.

Kuhn, M. H., & McPartland, T. S. (1954). An empirical investigation of self-attitudes. *American Sociological Review*, 19, 68–76.

McAllister, I., & Moore, R. (1991). Social distance among Australian ethnic groups. *Sociology and Social Research*, 75, 95–100.

Miller, D. C. (1991). *Handbook of research design and social measurement* (5th ed.). Newbury Park, CA: Sage.

Muir, D. E., & Muir, L. W. (1988). Social distance between Deep-South middle-school Whites and Blacks. *Sociology and Social Research*, 72, 177–180.

Netting, N. S. (1991). Chinese aloofness from other groups: Social distance data from a city in British Columbia. *Sociology and Social Research*, 75, 101–103.

Silberman, C. E. (1964). *Crisis in Black and White*. New York: Random House.

Tajfel, H. (1982). *Social identity and intergroup relations*. Cambridge: Cambridge University Press.

Tajfel, H., & Turner, J. C. (1986). The social identify theory of intergroup behavior. In S. Worchel & W. G. Austin (eds.) *Psychology of intergroup relations* (pp. 7–24). Chicago: Nelson-Hall.

Tuch, S. A. (1988). Race differences in the antecedents of social distance attitudes. *Sociology and Social Research*, 72, 181–184.

Van den Berghe, P. (1981). *The ethnic phenomenon*. New York: Elsevier.

Walsh, A. (1990). Becoming an American and liking it as functions of social distance and severity of initiation. *Sociological Inquiry*, 60, 177–189.

Weinberg, M. (Ed.). (1992). *The words of W. E. B. Du Bois: A quotation sourcebook*. Westport, CT: Greenwood.

West, C. (1993). *Race matters*. Boston: Beacon.

Wilson, T. C. (1986). The asymmetry of racial distance between Blacks and Whites. *Sociology and Social Research*, 70, 161–163.

REVIEW QUESTIONS

1. Explain why the "reverse" Social Distance Scale was created.
2. What were the findings from this project?
3. Explain the difference between the social distance of minorities and the social distance of majorities.

7

Sampling Made Easy

One of the goals of research is to describe or identify specific characteristics of a specific group or of the population as a whole. This isn't too difficult if the group you are studying is small, such as a group of 10 or 12 children in a day care setting. In this case, all you would need to do is observe or interview all of the children. If the group is larger, however, the process of figuring out whom to study becomes more difficult. Let's say you want to find out about the quality of life of all the female students in the United States and compare their answers to those of the male students. This project would involve many students, and it would be nearly impossible for you to interview or observe all of them.

You probably would not be able to include every student in every college and university in the United States because contacting them all would consume too much time and cost too much money. Therefore, the first step is to select a **sample** that represents the **population** you have in mind. Identifying a **representative sample** is not as simple as you might think, for your sample must *accurately* reflect the larger population so you can **generalize** about the population you are studying.

Let's say you want to conduct a study of college students. You have found that the average age of students at your particular school is 21, that 51 percent of the students are female, and that the average income of those female students is $8,000 a year. You want to collect data on the students, so you visit a computer programming class in the evening to hand out your survey to ask about their quality of life. Of the 40 students you survey, 80 percent are male, the average age is 35, and the average income is $40,000 a year. Does this sample represent your college population? No. You must decide what sampling method is appropriate for your quality of life study. In this chapter, you will learn about probability sampling and nonprobability sampling.

PROBABILITY SAMPLING

Probability sampling is the type of sampling that is used when the likelihood of selecting any one member of the population is known. The researcher decides which segment of the population will be used for the project to accurately portray the parameters of the population as a whole. The researcher makes an estimate of the extent to which the results of the sample are going to differ from the entire population. The most common way of accomplishing this is by randomization.

Randomization, or **random selection**, is a process that ensures that every subject in the population has the same chance, or probability, of being selected for a sample. As a result of randomization, the sample group should possess the same characteristics as the population as a whole.

There are a number of ways to randomly select a sample. **Simple random sampling** is a procedure that generates numbers or cases strictly on the basis of chance. Selection could result from a roll of the dice or from picking heads or tails. You could use phone numbers to create a random sample, with the help of a computer and **random-digit dialing.** Random-digit dialing is useful because if a phone number is no longer in service or no one is answers, the software program automatically replaces that number with the next random number.

Systematic random sampling is a little different from simple random sampling. In this type of sampling, every *n*th element is selected from a list after the first element is randomly selected within the first *n* cases. This type of sampling is convenient when the population elements are arranged consecutively. To use this method, you first randomly select the first element to be sampled. A few years ago, one of my students wanted to do a content analysis of crime dramas on television. Since there were so many crime shows on television, she had to limit the number she recorded and analyzed. In order to do that, she put numbers in a hat and then had a friend pull one number out. That became her first number to use in her random sampling.

After the number is picked, you must decide on your **sampling interval**, which is the total number of cases in the population divided by the number of cases required in the sample. If there are 500 students in your population and you want 50 students to be in your sample, your sampling interval will be 10. To assemble your sample, you would start with the first randomly selected element and include every 10th element until your sample population totaled 50.

Stratified random sampling uses information that is already known about the total population. When subpopulations vary considerably, it is advantageous to sample each subpopulation (stratum) independently. **Stratification** is the process of grouping members of the population into relatively homogeneous subgroups before sampling. The strata should be mutually exclusive where every element in the population must be assigned to only one stratum. The strata should also be collectively exhaustive: no population element can be excluded. Then random or systematic sampling is applied within each stratum. This often imporves the representativeness of the sample by reducing sampling error. For example, if your school is three-fourths women and one-fourth men, then your sample should look the same way. A sample is a **proportionate stratified**

sample if each stratum is represented exactly in proportion to the population. A **disproportionate stratified sample** varies from the population.

Cluster sampling is used when it is either impossible or impractical to compile an exhaustive list of elements that compose the target population. Cluster sampling requires more information before sampling than the previous methods do. Clusters are naturally occurring elements within the population. Thus, city blocks would be clusters for sampling people who live in cities, and businesses would be clusters for sampling employees. To begin, you must draw a random sample of clusters, which requires compiling a list of businesses or city blocks. You then draw a random sample of elements within each cluster. If you are interested in a cluster sample of employees, you would first record the addresses of all businesses, and then you could separate them into categories such as the following:

Category	Number	Percentage
North	469	20.8
South	738	32.8
East	653	29.0
West	392	17.4
Total	2252	100

Next, you must decide how large a sample you want. If you decide to use 100 businesses in each category, you would use a simple random selection within each category to come up with your sample.

Your project is well designed if the sample represents the population from which it has been selected. But errors can occur. A **sampling error** is the difference between the characteristics of a sample and those of the population as a whole. The less representative of a population a sample is, the larger is the room for error.

Let's say you have a probability sample from a population of 3,880 television viewers and you want to see how close the average age of the sample is to the average age of the entire population, which is 42.06 years. The average age of the first sample of 50 television viewers is 39.96, which is 2.1 years less than the average age of the population as a whole. This difference of 2.1 years is a sampling error that represents the divergence of an average in a probability sample from the average of the entire population. All samples have some degree of sampling error.

NONPROBABILITY SAMPLING

Schroer (2001) uses the Internet to study white supremacist groups. Because it would be impossible to use randomization to survey the whole population of white supremacists, Schroer uses the Internet to find his subjects. He interviews individuals he finds who are willing to talk with him. Borchard (2005) studies homeless men.

He is interested in all aspects of homelessness, but he can't study all homeless men. Instead, he studies those in Las Vegas. He dresses in jeans, an old T-shirt, and a wornout coat in order to "fit in," and he enters into an environment where he can make contact with homeless men. Not all homeless men are willing to talk with him, but many are. Both Borchard and Schroer are using nonprobability sampling.

Nonprobability sampling is a sampling technique that doesn't use randomization. As a result, the chances, or probabilities that members of the population will be selected for a sample are not equal. This type of sampling is used when probability sampling would be too expensive or would yield a precise representation that is not important to the study, or when it is not possible to obtain or define a full population. Most often, researchers use a nonprobability sample because the respondents are easy to find or they contact the researchers after finding out about a study and ask to participate.

There are four different types of nonprobability sampling. **Convenience sampling** is the use of subjects who are available but not necessarily representative, such as in Borchard's (2005) research with homeless men. Convenience sampling can happen as a result of hanging out with the people you are interested in studying. To find your subjects, you can hang out on a street corner, at your library, or in a music store.

O'Dougherty, Story, and Stang (2006) were interested in how adults purchase food when young children are present. They conducted field observations at 11 supermarkets (8 budget and 3 deluxe stores) in the Minneapolis–St. Paul metropolitan region. They observed adult-child interactions over food selections, including parental giving-in and refusal approaches toward the children's requests. They found that adults yield to children's requests for candy and snacks almost as often as they refuse them. The study supports the idea that grocery stores provide a good opportunity to teach children about nutrition.

In another example of convenience sampling, Jerome Koch and his colleagues (2005) gathered data from a convenience sample of 450 college students at a public university in the Southwest. They were interested in the correlation of having a tattoo and engaging in premarital sex. To reach a high number of participants, they distributed questionnaires on examination day. Koch and his colleagues found that tattooed men became sexually active earlier than nontattooed men. They also found no difference between tattooed and nontattooed college women.

A **quota sample** is somewhat similar to a stratified random sample. This type of sample is drawn in such a way that in pertinent characteristics the sample population resembles the larger population.

Suppose you are interested in the smoking behavior of students on your campus. The first thing to do is obtain demographic information about the students in your school. Let's say the student population is 51 percent male, 49 percent female, 87 percent white, 8 percent African American, 2 percent Native American, and 3 percent Asian. With all this information, you might create a quota sample by going to class, hanging out in the library, or attending college events and inviting students to participate in your research. Your objective is to end up with a sample population that has the same proportions of demographic characteristics as the population as a whole. The problem is that you won't know for sure whether the sample is representative of the student body in other ways as well.

A **purposive sample** is a nonprobability sample in which each element is selected by the researcher for a specific purpose. Suppose you are interested in studying women who are infected with HIV to find out about their quality of life. It would be difficult to have a random sample. Therefore, you need to find a group of women who have HIV and to select those women as your sample.

Let me give you another example. I study the quality of life of women who have a bleeding disorder that prevents their blood from clotting (Wysocki, 1999). Once I began this project, I realized that some of the women with a bleeding disorder had become HIV infected because of the blood products they had received. I wanted to interview these women. I felt obligated to allow their "voices" to be heard. I knew that some of them had only a short time to live, and I wanted to find out about their lives. In other words, I had a purpose for selecting the sample of women for my study.

Snowball sampling occurs when one member of a population is identified and that person identifies another person who could take part in the study and that person indentifies someone else, and so on. This type of nonprobability sampling is common when a researcher is interested in studying difficult-to-reach populations such as criminals, gang members, prostitutes, or people with specific diseases. In my bleeding disorder study, I had no idea which individuals in my sample were the ones living with HIV or AIDS. I had to ask a respondent, who gave me the name of one individual, and that individual gave me the name of another. Unfortunately in this case, the list of women who were living with HIV/AIDS was much smaller than the list of women who had died from the disease.

In the following selections, you will see various ways in which researchers use sampling to study the populations they are interested in.

REFERENCES

Borchard, K. 2005. *The word on the street: Homeless men in Las Vegas*. Las Vegas: University of Nevada Press.

Koch, J. R., Roberts, A. E., Armstrong, M. L., & Owen, C. D. 2005. College students, tattoos, and sexual activity. *Psychological Reports*, 97(3): 887–891.

O'Dougherty, M., Story, M., & Stang, J. 2006. Observations of parent-child co-shoppers in supermarkets: Children's involvement in food selections, parental yielding, and refusal strategies. *Journal of Nutrition Education and Behavior*, 38(3): 183–189.

Schroer, T. 2001. Social control and White racialists: The freedoms of the Internet. In *Readings in deviant behavior*, 2nd ed., A. Thio & T. Calhoun (Eds.), New York: Allyn and Bacon.

Wysocki, D. K. 1999. The psychosocial and gynecological issues of women with bleeding disorders. *Female Patient* (both the OB/GYN and Primary Care Editions), 24: 13–20.

SUGGESTED FILMS

Blocking and Sampling; Samples and Surveys (Teresa Amabile, Richard Provost, Nick Mills, 1989) (60 min.). Santa Barbara, CA: Intellimation (distributor). *Blocking and Sampling* covers further principles of design, including two or more factors and blocking. Also presents sample surveys, the danger of bias, and random sampling. *Samples and Surveys* covers more elaborate sample designs, such as stratified and multistage designs. Also discusses the practical difficulties of sampling human populations and the idea of sampling distribution.

Order from Chaos: The Surprising Consequences of Randomness (K. L. Weldon, Peter McLennan, 1985) (28 min.). Evanston, IL: Beacon Films, Altschul Group (distributors). This film covers aspects of statistical theory including variation in random samples, variation in sample averages, and the sampling distribution of an average.

Why Use Statistics? Using Samples (Steve Collier, Bob Dixon, Peter Holmes, 1996) (19 min.). Princeton, NJ: Films for the Humanities. This program begins with an explanation of the difference between a population and a sample, and the reasons why samples are so important in estimating data relating to populations too large or too impractical to be measured in their entirety. The program emphasizes the need for random samples, explains how several random samples of the same size will vary, and then looks at ways of dealing with this variability, calculating the Standard Error of the Mean, and how to estimate the 95% Confidence Interval.

Quiet Rage: The Stanford Prison Study (Philip G. Zimbardo, Ken Musen, John Polito, 1992) (50 min.). Stanford, CA: Stanford University (distributor). This film discusses a prison simulation experiment conducted in 1971 with students at Stanford University and considers the causes and effects that make prisons such an emotional issue. Documentary includes new film, flashback editing, follow-ups 20-years later, and an original music score; reveals the chronology of the transition of good into evil, of normal into the abnormal. As you watch this film, think about the way in which the researchers obtained their subjects.

Kinsey (Bill Condon, Liam Neeson, Laura Linney, Chris O'Donnell, Peter Sarsgaard, Timothy Hutton, Frederick Elmes, Carter Burwell, 2005) (118 min.). Beverly Hills, CA: Twentieth Century Fox; distributed by 20th Century Fox Home Entertainment. *Kinsey* is a portrait of a man driven to uncover the most private secrets of the nation and journey into the mystery of human behavior. Alfred Kinsey's 1948 book *Sexual Behavior in the Human Male* irrevocably changed American culture and created a media sensation. This film shows the problems that can result when a sample is less than accurate.

14

Sex in America

ROBERT T. MICHAEL, JOHN H. GAGNON, EDWARD O. LAUMANN, AND GINA KOLATA

This example of a probability sample has been called one of the most comprehensive, representative surveys of sexual behavior in the general adult population of the United States. After explaining the huge flaws in previous studies on sexuality, the authors explain how they used a stratified, multistage area probability sample of clusters of households. Within each selected household, one English-speaking adult between 18 and 59 years of age was randomly selected as the respondent. Interviews were completed with 3,342 persons, 78.6 percent of those who were eligible to participate. Watch for information about how the authors made sure they had a representative sample.

Of all the studies that purport to tell about sex in America, the vast majority are unreliable; many are worse than useless. As social scientists, we found that the well-established survey methods that can so accurately describe the nation's voting patterns or the vicissitudes of the labor force rarely were used to study sexuality. And the methods that were used in many of the popular studies had flaws so deep and so profound that they render the data and their interpretations meaningless. In fact, the field is so impoverished that experts still find themselves citing data gathered by Alfred Kinsey during the late 1930s and into the early 1950s, a time when America was very different than it is today.[1] Many of the popularized studies that came after Kinsey, like *The Hite Report* or the *Redbook* survey, are even worse, because they ignored what social scientists had learned and used methods guaranteed to yield worthless results.

Most Americans believe that the factors that determine their sex lives lie mostly or solely within themselves. Their sexual drives, their hormones, their individual desires, are all that matter. This is in large part a legacy of the long history of attempts to study and control sexuality, dating back to studies in the past century that focused on "deviants" and sex criminals.

The era of large sex surveys began with Alfred Kinsey, who felt that standard sample survey methods were a practical impossibility when it came to the subject of sex, so he compromised. And when he published his results, Kinsey shocked the nation with his findings and evoked a public response so strong that most social scientists decided to steer clear of sex research.

An evolutionary biologist from Indiana University, Kinsey was a professor of zoology, an expert on gall wasps. Using the methods he was most comfortable with, Kinsey began his study on human sexuality by first giving a questionnaire about sexual practices to the students in his classes. Finding this method unsatisfactory, he turned to face-to-face interviews and then began reaching out to different social groups. Eventually, he and his three associates interviewed nearly eighteen thousand people. It was a long and arduous task.

SOURCE: From Michael, R. T., Gagnon, J. H., Laumann, E. O., & Kolata, G. 1994. The sex survey. In *Sex in America*. Boston: Little, Brown and Company, pp. 15–32 (edited for this book).

It took him six months to persuade the first sixty-two people to be interviewed, but as he got better at interviewing it became easier to recruit respondents. The problem was not who he interviewed but how he found them.

Kinsey knew that the ideal situation would be to select people at random. That way it would be guaranteed that those he interviewed represented the general population. But Kinsey just did not think it was possible to coax a randomly selected group of Americans to answer truthfully when he asked them deeply personal questions about their sex lives.

Kinsey's compromise was to take his subjects where he could find them. He and his associates went to college sororities and fraternities, college classes and student groups, rooming houses, prisons, mental hospitals, social organizations of many kinds, and friendship groups in which one interview might lead to others. For a fourteen-year period, he even collared hitchhikers in town.

To make his data more credible, Kinsey often attempted to interview 100 percent of the members of his groups. He'd try to get every single student in a classroom or every single boarder in a rooming house to answer his questions.

It sounds impressive. After all, if he interviewed eighteen thousand people and if he got anywhere near 100 percent of the groups he approached, why would his data be unreliable?

One problem was that the people Kinsey interviewed could not stand in for all Americans. A fraternity here, a college class there, a PTA from a third place, and a group of homosexual men from somewhere else do not, taken together, reflect the population of the United States.

Instead of studying randomly selected members of the population, Kinsey interviewed what is called a sample of convenience, a sample that consisted of volunteers that he recruited or who came to him. This introduced two problems. First, the people he interviewed could not be thought of as representative of anyone in the population other than themselves. They got into the sample because they were relatively convenient for Kinsey to find and persuade to participate, or because they offered to participate on their own. Consequently, while they may have told the truth about their own sex lives, neither Kinsey nor anyone else can know how to generalize from these people to say anything useful or accurate about the whole population or about any particular subset of the population.

The second problem was that many of Kinsey's respondents volunteered to be in the study. For a sex survey, it seems likely that those who do volunteer and those who do not have different behavior, different experiences, and different attitudes about sex. If so, the data that are collected from volunteers will give an inaccurate picture of the whole population. By including the sexual histories of those who especially want to be counted in the survey, that survey gives a biased picture. This is true for any survey, not just one on sexual behavior. Many studies have suggested that people who volunteer for surveys are not like people who do not volunteer,[2] and there is some evidence that people who volunteer for sex surveys have wider sexual experience than those who do not. In addition, there is evidence that people who engage in highly stigmatized behaviors, such as incest, may refuse to be interviewed or would not volunteer to do so.

So, since Kinsey did not select his respondents in a way that permitted generalization, the data he obtained are at best interesting facts about the people he interviewed but are not useful for making statements about the population at large such as that half the husbands in America had had extramarital sex and had been improved by extramarital sex. Kinsey's data on homosexuality were most troubling for a society who thought sex between men was rare. He reported that one man in three had a sexual experience with another man at some time in his life. Ten percent of the men that Kinsey interviewed had had sex exclusively with other men for at least three years. It is this figure that may be the basis for the widely quoted "one person in ten in the United States is gay."

Even as Kinsey's studies shocked and fascinated the nation, they also elicited strong criticism from people who thought that sexuality should not be studied by scientists with questionnaires. The blistering attacks on Kinsey were so effective that surveys of sexuality were not only born with Kinsey—they almost died with him too.

Kinsey's study was followed, a decade later, by a new type of sex study, initiated by William Masters, who was a gynecologist, and Virginia Johnson, who was his research associate at Washington University in St. Louis. Masters and Johnson watched and described the sex act, performed in the laboratory by subjects that they paid. Their book, *Human Sexual Response,* was an instant bestseller, even as it disturbed many Americans. The very idea that people would agree to be volunteers in their studies (and be paid for it!) was shocking to many, who viewed the transactions as a form of prostitution.

Still, demands for facts about sexual life in America continued unabated. In the absence of systematic, scientific studies of the American population, a series of popular "reports" on sexual practices proliferated to fill the void. There was the *Playboy* report, the *Redbook report, The Hite Report,* and, most recently, *The Janus Report,* whose flaws were even more profound than those that plagued the studies by Kinsey.

In all these studies, only people who volunteered to complete the survey were included. But the people who were asked to volunteer were by no means representative of all Americans. The five million readers of *Playboy* are already a heavily selected population—they tend to be young, white men, richer than the average American, and men who are interested in sex. The nearly five million readers of *Redbook* are mostly white women in their late twenties to late thirties, married, and more affluent than the average American woman. If you asked readers of a different sort of magazine, like *Christian Century* or *Reader's Digest,* to fill out a questionnaire, you'd expect to get very different answers.

Shere Hite sent out surveys to women whose names she got from chapters of the National Organization for Women, abortion rights groups, university women's centers, and university newsletters. She also put notices in the *Village Voice,* in three magazines (*Mademoiselle, Brides,* and *Ms.*), and in church newsletters, asking readers to send to her for questionnaires. She, too, was concentrating on highly selected members of the population.

But suppose you don't care about the behavior of people not included in these surveys. Wouldn't a survey of *Playboy* readers at least tell you about sex among young, affluent white men? The problem is that very few of even those invited to answer the surveys chose to do so, which raises the question of just who these respondents are. Only 1.3 percent of the five million *Playboy* readers returned the questionnaire. In the *Redbook*[3] survey, the issue of *Redbook* magazine containing the questionnaires sold 4,700,000 copies. Barely 2 percent of the *Redbook* readers filled out and returned the survey. And of those 100,000 replies, the magazine analyzed only 2,278. Shere Hite, in her book *The Hite Report: A Nationwide Study of Female Sexuality,* said she distributed 100,000 questionnaires and got 3,000 back, a 3 percent response rate.[4]

Even though both magazines and Shere Hite trumpeted the sheer numbers of responses, large numbers in themselves do not mean anything. If too many people decline to answer your questions, you start to worry about the ones who opted out. Were they significantly different from those who participated? If, as in the *Playboy* survey, 1.3 percent of the target population answers your questions, you should be very suspicious that the people who answered are atypical for some reason and that their replies do not represent the sexual practices even of the population that received the survey.

It may sound paradoxical, but the percentage of replies is far more meaningful than the absolute number of them. If you ask 1,200 people to answer your questions, and 1,000 agree to do so, you can generalize to the target group with more accuracy than you can in 50,000 replies from a group of 1,000,000 who were asked. In the first case, 83 percent of those you asked answered your questions. In the second case, only 5 percent of those you asked replied to you, which leaves you wondering how they differed from those who did not reply.

The most recent of these "reports," *The Janus Report,*[5] by Samuel S. Janus and Cynthia L. Janus, was slightly different. The Januses said they distributed 4,550 surveys and got back 2,795 that were "satisfactorily completed." They argued that their data were credible because their respondents reflected the U.S. population. The way they got this so-called match, however, was by looking at census data on key variables, such as age, marital status, and religion, and then seeking respondents who would match the proportions found in the general population.

For example, the census said that 19 percent of the population was between eighteen and twenty-six, so the Januses sought out enough volunteers in that age group to fill in 19 percent of the slots for respondents in their survey. But it's not how many respondents are of a particular age that's so important—it's how you find them.

The Januses wanted to get enough older Americans to make their survey sample resemble the census data. So they went to sex therapy clinics and looked for older people. Does it matter where they found the old people? We have no way of knowing who these older people were, but the fact that they were at a sex therapy clinic makes it probable that they have sex partners, unlike many older Americans, and that they want to have sex. In fact, the Januses report that over 70 percent of Americans age sixty-five and older have sex once a week. A reputable national survey (the General Social Survey), which did not pre-select people, found that just 7 percent of older Americans have sex that often.

Many of these sex reports also had an additional problem—that of knowing who *had* responded. Fraudulent responses—from people who filled out the questionnaires as a lark, making up sexual adventures or pretending not to have had them—would be counted just like anyone else's. A man might have pretended to be a woman and filled in a *Redbook* questionnaire, or a woman might have said she was a man and answered the *Playboy* questions. One busy man could have filled out many questionnaires for *Playboy*.

Yet these pseudo-studies provided a picture of a very sexually active nation. And because these studies have been so widely publicized and are cited so often, many Americans walk around thinking they are among the few who do not have a lot of sex partners, thinking that even if they are satisfied, they must be missing something.

Our team, working through the National Opinion Research Center, a survey research firm associated with the University of Chicago, was awarded the contract to design this study called the National Health and Social Life Survey (NHSLS). In our original study design we wanted a sample size of 20,000, which would enable us to analyze separately data from people who are members of small subpopulations. For example, if 4 percent of the population were gay, a sample size of 20,000 men and women would yield about 400 homosexual men and 400 homosexual women, enough for us to analyze their responses separately.

In the process of designing our survey, it was clear that we would not be able to achieve this sample size with the limited resources. We received only enough money to study 3,500 adults, enough to be confident about the accuracy of the data as a whole, but the sample would not be large enough for detailed analyses of small minority groups. We knew, because we used established statistical sampling techniques, that our respondents represented the general population. In addition, we purposely included slightly more blacks and Hispanics so that we would have enough members of these minority groups to enable us to analyze their responses separately, with confidence that they made statistical sense.

We would have liked to have done the same for homosexuals, including more gay men and lesbians so that we could analyze their replies separately. However, homosexuals are not so easily identified, and for good reason, because their preferences for a partner of the same gender should be private if they want them to be. But that means we could not so easily find an expanded representative sample of homosexuals as we could find blacks or Hispanics. And that means that we could not analyze homosexual behavior separately, asking, for example, how many partners gay men and lesbians have in their lifetimes or where they met their partners. But we included homosexual sex as part of sex in general, so when we ask a question such as, "How often do you have sex?" we do not distinguish between homosexuals and heterosexuals.

The most important part of our study was the way we selected the people to be interviewed. It can be tricky, and subtle, to pick out a group that represents all Americans. For example, you might say you will go to every neighborhood and knock on the door of the corner house on each block. But that would not give you a representative sample because people who live in corner houses are different from other people—as a rule, they are richer than their neighbors on the block because corner houses tend to cost more. Or you might say you'll find married couples by taking every couple that got married in June. But then you would end up with too few Jews because there is a proscription in Judaism against marrying in certain weeks that often fall in June.

Of course, the most obvious way might be to randomly select individuals from households across the country. But finding and interviewing people scattered across the United States can be very expensive, so social scientists have found a cheaper, but equally valid, way of identifying a representative sample. Essentially, we choose at random geographic areas of the country, using the statistical equivalent of a coin toss to select them. Within these geographic regions, we randomly select cities, towns, and rural areas. Within those cities and towns we randomly select neighborhoods. Within those neighborhoods, we randomly select households.

This method gave us 9,004 addresses. Naturally, since the addresses were generated by a computer, many of the addresses either did not have a residence on them or had a residence on them that was empty. Others had a household but no one who lived there was eligible for our survey—they were not between the ages of eighteen and fifty-nine or did not speak English. We determined that 4,635 of the original 9,004 household addresses were ineligible for one of those reasons, so that left us with 4,369 households that did have someone living in them who was eligible to participate in the study. Although it may seem that our sample shrank quite a bit from the original 9,004 addresses, that is normal and to be expected. We did not say we wanted a random sample of addresses for our survey. We wanted a representative sample of Americans who were aged eighteen to fifty-nine and who spoke English,

We selected the individual in a household to interview by a random process. In effect, if there were two people living in a household who were in our age range, we flipped a coin to select which one to interview. If there were three people in the household, we did the equivalent of flipping a three-sided coin to select one of them to interview.

The difference between this method and the method used by, say, *Playboy* magazine, is profound. In the *Playboy* survey, anyone who wanted to be interviewed could be. In our survey, we did not let anyone be interviewed unless we selected them. If we selected a man who offered his wife in his stead, saying he was too busy to be interviewed, we declined to interview her. And if he adamantly refused to be interviewed, his refusal counted against us. He is a nonrespondent, even though his wife might have been eager to fill in for him.

Our method is neither unusual nor remarkable. But our method is right. There is universal agreement among all social scientists: this is the way you do it.

Of all the eligible households, our interviewers completed 3,432 interviews, so we have the remarkable outcome that nearly four out of every five persons we wanted to interview, across the nation, were willing to sit down and answer a ninety-minute questionnaire about their sexual behavior and other aspects of their sex lives. This response rate is even more remarkable because it includes as nonresponders people who simply could not be found to be interviewed.

No other fact in this study is as important as the fact that four out of five randomly selected adults were willing to give an interview and to give us honest responses, judged by all the ways we can think of to check their veracity. We had a variety of checks and crosschecks to test the honesty of the responses and the respondents passed with flying colors.

Once we had the data, we asked whether the 3,432 respondents, as a group, were representative of the population of those aged eighteen to fifty-nine in the United States. We could not do this in advance because, unlike the Januses, we were not looking for people to fit into the census niches.

Instead, we were selecting people at random, with no way of knowing ahead of time what their age, sex, race, religion, or education was.

In fact, our sample turned out to be exactly like other highly reputable and scientifically valid national samples. We compared our group to those of the Current Population Survey, the General Social Survey, and the National Survey of Families and Households, looking at such characteristics as marital status, ages, educational levels, race, and ethnicity. We found no evidence suggesting that our sample was not fully representative of the population aged eighteen to fifty-nine.

Table 1 shows a few of the comparisons we made, using our unweighted sample that excludes the extra blacks and Hispanics that we added on purpose. We compared our group to the Census Bureau's Current Population Survey of over 140,000 people for 1991 as the benchmark. It is the best information that demographers can get about the characteristics of the population.

The similarities between our sample and the Current Population Survey of the Census Bureau extend to age, education level, and marital status, as the table illustrates. This extraordinary similarity of our sample to the U.S. population, from which we randomly selected our respondents, provides assurance that the respondents who were interviewed were representative of the population of all Americans aged eighteen to fifty-nine.

We also looked at the proportions of men and women who answered our questions. We knew from the census data that 49.7 percent of Americans aged eighteen to fifty-nine are men. Among our respondents, 44.6 percent are men. Other surveys that are of high quality, like the General Social Survey and the National Survey of Family and Households, had virtually the same percentages of men and women as we have. The General Social Survey has 43.8 percent men and the National Survey of Families and Households had 43.0 percent men. So we can say with confidence that the people who agreed to participate in our survey of sexual behavior were just like the population at large in their gender. We were not disproportionately interviewing—or failing to interview—either men or women.

TABLE 1 Comparison of Social Characteristics in NHSLS and U.S. Population

	U.S. Population	NHSLS
Gender		
Men	49.7%	44.6%
Women	50.3	55.4
	100%	100%
Age		
18–24	18.2%	15.9%
25–29	14.3	14.5
30–39	29.5	31.3
40–49	22.7	22.9
50–59	15.3	15.3
	100%	100%
Education		
Less than high school	15.8%	13.9%
High school or equivalent	64.0	62.2
Any college	13.9	16.6
Advanced	6.3	7.3
	100%	100%
Marital Status		
Never married	27.7%	28.2%
Currently married	58.3	53.3
Divorced, separated	12.4	16.2
Widowed	1.6	2.3
	100%	100%
Race/Ethnicity		
White	75.9%	76.5%
Black	11.7	12.7
Hispanic	9.0	7.5
Other	3.3	3.3
	100%	100%

Notes: NHSLS unweighted cross-section sample of 3,159.
Gender: Bureau of the Census, Current Population Survey, 1991. *Age, Race/Ethnicity*: Bureau of the Census, Current Population Survey, 1991. *Education*: Bureau of the Census, Current Population Survey, 1990. *Marital Status*: Bureau of the Census, Current Population Survey, 1992.

Now there are many people in the nation who are not represented in our survey. We can speak with confidence about the behavior of the non-institutionalized, currently housed population aged eighteen to fifty-nine. We can say nothing about those who currently live in institutions like hospitals or jails or about the homeless or about those who are under age eighteen or older than fifty-nine. Our sample did not include those groups. But 97.1 percent of American adults aged eighteen to fifty-nine in the nation are represented, and this is the first large-scale study of the broad and inclusive dimensions of the sexual patterns and experiences of this large majority of Americans. All this checking of our data has convinced us that this sample is an excellent one from which we can make generalizations about sex in America and we do so with confidence.

NOTES

1. Alfred C. Kinsey, Wardell B. Pomeroy, and Clyde E. Martin, *Sexual Behavior in the Human Male* (Philadelphia: W. B. Saunders Co.,1948); Alfred C. Kinsey, Wardell B. Pomeroy, Clyde E. Martin, and Paul H. Gebhard, *Sexual Behavior in the Human Female* (Philadelphia: W. B. Saunders Co., *1953*).
2. Norman M. Bradburn and Seymour Sudman, *Pulls and Surveys: Understanding What They Tell Us* (San Francisco: Jossey-Bass Publishers, 1988).
3. Carol Tavris and Susan Sadd, *The Redbook Report on Female Sexuality* (New York: Delacorte, 1975).
4. Shere Hite, *The Hite Report* (New York: Dell, 1976)
5. Samuel S. Janus and Cynthia L. Janus, *The Janus Report on Sexual Behavior* (New York: John Wiley and Sons, 1993)

REVIEW QUESTIONS

1. Explain why the *Playboy, Redbook,* and *Hite* studies on human sexuality were not representative of people in America.
2. Was the National Health and Social Life Survey a random survey? Why or why not? What steps did the researchers take to try to make sure it was random?
3. How did the final NHSLS sample compare with the samples of Americans studied by other researchers?

15

The Eurowinter Project

The Use of Market/Social Research Methods in an International Scientific Study

COLIN MCDONALD

Colin McDonald used a standard quota sampling method to examine how cold weather is related to excess winter mortality in various parts of Europe that have different temperatures. This is one of the nonprobability sampling methods you learned about in this chapter. McDonald's results indicate that the growing death rate in colder areas is brought about by, among other factors, how people, both in the home and in the open air, protect themselves.

INTRODUCTION

The project I am about to describe involved a straightforward survey of specific age groups within a number of countries, working to a standard design and questionnaire. There is nothing novel about that, nor about the fact that the subject matter was medical. What is unusual about this project is the use of ordinary survey research data, alongside other measurements, as one of the key elements in a co-ordinated international scientific study. We (the study directors and I) believe that this is the first time that survey research has been used in this way, and on this scale, in this type of study. The purpose of this paper is to illustrate the special role of market survey data and methods in this type of project.

The Eurowinter project marks probably the first realisation in the scientific community that surveys using the methods of marketing and opinion research have become sufficiently sophisticated to provide extensive multinational data for a study of this kind, with sufficient reliability and at acceptable cost. Sampling methods of course always represent a balance between perfection and practicability, and their use in such studies requires consideration of whether they avoid biases that would disturb the results. In this case, controlled quota sampling provided Eurowinter with clear and novel data that allowed major conclusions to be drawn about the role of local customs, clothing and housing in preventing winter mortality. No such data were available from any existing source, and without quota sampling the information could not have been obtained at a cost that medical research funds could have met.

STUDY OBJECTIVES

The Eurowinter study, later followed by the two similar Russian studies, was an epidemiological investigation, designed to assess the relationship between increases in mortality during cold weather, especially

SOURCE: From McDonald, Colin, 1999. The Eurowinter project: The use of market/social research methods in an international scientific study. *Journal of the Market Research Society*, 41(3): 289–297.

from respiratory or cardiovascular diseases, and changes in winter temperature, and to discover whether this relationship differed between relatively warm and cold climates. Two specific age groups were studied: men and women aged 50–59, and 65–74. In addition to mortality and temperature data, survey research data investigating the habits of these populations in relation to protection against cold were also collected from each area studied, and analyzed together with the daily temperature and mortality statistics. The reason for this was the hypothesis, suggested by previous work by the Co-ordinating Group in Britain, that culture-related or occupation-related patterns of outdoor exposure to cold play a major role in causing excess winter deaths.

The primary objectives of the Biomed 1 Programme are stated to be:

- improvements of medical and health service in the Member States by coordination of Member States' research and development activities, and application of the results through Community co-operation and pooling of resources, and
- to encourage basic research in the field of biomedicine and health throughout the Community.

The study matched these objectives closely. Excess winter deaths in those countries participating in the Biomed Programme have been estimated at some 200,000 per year, taking July mortality as a baseline (source: *United Nations Demographic Yearbook*). But, surprisingly, the overall increase in winter mortality is generally twice as great in those countries which have milder winters (in Southern and Western Europe) as in Northern Europe where the winters are much colder. Clearly, those cultural and environmental factors which might be identified as causes of seasonal mortality were likely to vary between these areas, and the information sought could not be achieved by studying data from a single country. More detailed identification of these factors could produce major opportunities for preventive measures to reduce illness and death from respiratory and cardiovascular diseases.

There have been three stages in the project. In the first stage, covering the winter of 1994 to 1995, specific areas within eight different European temperature zones were surveyed: North Finland, South Finland, Holland, England (Greater London), Germany (Baden-Wurttemburg), Italy (Emilia Romagna), Sicily (Palermo) and Greece (Athens). Members from university departments in each of these countries were part of the Eurowinter team and helped provide the required mortality and temperature statistics. In the winter of 1995 to 1996, an extension of the grant was obtained to extend the study to Ekaterinburg in the Urals, and in the winter of 1996 to 1997 a further grant was obtained, this time from the Wellcome Foundation, to repeat the study in Yakutsk in Eastern Siberia (reputed to be the coldest town in the world). Again, local universities were involved, as well as the Russian Ministry of Health (Public Health Research Institute). Scientific papers on all three of these stages have been published (see references).

The co-ordinator of the study throughout has been Professor W. R. Keatinge of the Department of Physiology at Queen Mary & Westfield College in London; he is an international authority on the relationship between cardiovascular disease and cold exposure. His colleague at QMW, Dr G. C. Donaldson, has been responsible for the massive task of analysing and modelling the very large amount of data produced. My involvement as survey consultant was to coordinate the fieldwork for the surveys: a most interesting task, which involved me visiting both Ekaterinburg and Yakutsk, the latter (deliberately) at almost the coldest part of the year, in February, when the temperature was around −25 [degrees] C to −30 [degrees] C.

SPECIFICATION OF THE SURVEYS

In each area the study covered the winter months: November to February (1995) for Holland, England, Germany, Italy and Greece, and October to February in Finland and Russia. For these periods, daily temperature records and relevant mortality data were obtained for the precise areas covered in each country; since we were looking for the effects of variations in temperature, it was important that the data should be on a daily basis. It followed that the surveys should also represent each day during the period. Representing time in these surveys was at least as important as representing space, perhaps more so.

The samples required were 1,000 from each area: 500 aged 50–59 and 500 aged 65–74, each divided equally between men and women. Given the need to represent the whole time period, this posed its own restrictions on interviewer assignments. In order to capture all possible temperature variations it was important to interview on every day if we could, including Saturdays and Sundays when activities might well be different. This clearly meant a maximum of some eight interviews on any one day (six where the survey covered five months). For the fieldwork agencies, this meant a careful planning of assignments so that only a few interviewers would be working on any one evening, and that no part of the survey area would be unfairly bunched into a particular period of the winter which might be exposed to atypical weather.

Individual daily assignments were in any case bound to be low, because a survey requirement was that interviewing could only be done after dark, when temperatures would have reached their night-time level and heating in the house would be expected to be on. All interviews were required to take place after 5 p.m. (in Yakutsk, where winter darkness falls much earlier, this requirement was relaxed). In practice, each interviewer did a maximum of three interviews in an evening, and the norm was two.

The sampling of space was done in such a way as to represent all parts of the designated area as well as possible. Random sampling would have been unaffordable; where possible, two-stage quota sampling was used, with the primary units (blocks, streets and so on) selected with the help of whatever aids to stratification were available. Suburbs as well as city centres had to be covered: this was especially important in Russia, where the housing in the outer areas may well be of different quality and, most importantly, heated differently (for example, using wood stoves) compared with housing in the centre, which tends to be linked to a communal system. In some countries, random walk methods were used. Clustering was further avoided by a rule which stipulated that no more than two interviews could be taken in any one street or apartment block. To meet these tight requirements, agencies in all the countries found it necessary to pre-arrange interviews with eligible respondents, either by telephone or by calling in advance in daylight, which also helped to improve response by reassuring the elderly respondents.

THE INTERVIEW

The interviews lasted about 20 minutes. During each interview a temperature reading was taken: the interviewer placed a Thermax strip on a surface at table height (the instruction said 0.7 to 1.3 metres from the ground), not too near the fire or heat source, when the interview started and read it off at the end. These Thermax strips (made by Thermographic Measurements Ltd of Burton, UK) are card-mounted plastic strips, which measure temperature at 1 [degrees] C intervals. To make this measurement possible, the interview had to be conducted in the living room. The aim was, of course, to measure the ambient temperature in which people in the different countries are living when indoors during winter evenings.

The questions, identical for each country, asked respondents to think about the previous 24 hours ("since this time yesterday"). They covered:

- how many hours "this room" (the main living room) had been heated;
- how many hours the respondents had spent in any unheated parts of the house (garages, garden sheds, workrooms etc.);
- how many hours they had spent in bed the previous night, and how many hours the bedroom had been heated during that time;
- total number of hours spent at home, other than in bed;

- how many times they had been out in the open air for at least ten minutes (excluding time spent in a car, bus or train or in some other heated building, but including being outside at home, e.g. in the garden);
- for each of these times, up to three occasions (selected to represent different parts of the day whenever possible);
- what they were doing (work, traveling, recreation etc.)
- how long they were in the open
- whether they were standing/sitting still, walking or running, or equivalent levels of activity
- whether at any time during that occasion they felt cold enough to shiver, or too hot for comfort
- what they were wearing.

This last piece of information was obtained in some detail, using a self-completion sheet. This listed items of clothing in a logical order (the order in which one would get dressed), and respondents ticked the number they had worn of each item. Each shoe, sock or glove counted as 1: thus, a pair of socks would count as 2, and if two pairs were worn (quite possible in very cold weather) the code would be 4. There were separate sheets for men and women, for obvious reasons. At the end of the process, the interviewer added up the total number of items and recorded it, but the detail for each item has also been recorded.

This "total number of items worn" is of course a crude comparative measure of clothing; we miss additional detail which would have been useful but impossibly complex to collect, such as what materials overcoats, and so on, were made of, or just how much of the body is covered by an "anorak". This undoubtedly makes a difference. In Yakutsk, for example, where people are used to coping with the cold, overcoats (as we saw for ourselves) are invariably fur or leather and (at least for the women) often ground-length, hats are usually of fur and often envelope the whole head, and boots are made of fur or felt in the special Russian way; in most European countries, overcoats, boots and hats are nothing like this. Nevertheless, the total of items worn provides a proxy which works reasonably well; from it was estimated the surface area covered (for different parts of the body), which was compared in terms of fractions of the total potential surface area so as to give the average number of layers of clothing worn.

The interview ended with demographics. Great care was taken to ensure that, after translation, the questionnaires should be identical. This sometimes led to little local problems which had to be solved. In Greece, for example, we had to decide how to treat first-floor balconies, which are open to the elements even though normally considered as "inside" the house (for our purposes they had to be treated as "outside"). We learnt also that in Greece it is customary to ask for age next birthday, and that Greeks think you are trying to be funny if, as is normal in Britain, you ask for their age last birthday. In Italy we had problems arriving at an accurate translation of "long underpants," a concept Italians are evidently not used to; in both Greece and Italy we arrived at a description which worked: "pants down to the ankles." Everywhere there were the usual problems of making sure that we had identical definitions of "an occasion spent in the open air," "being in bed," the heating being on (in Russian or Finnish communal systems it is sometimes impossible for the householder to turn the heating off, and turning it down is not the same thing even if it appears to be so), the list of clothing items, and so on.

RESULTS

Data from each country were processed to a standardised data map, and the total is held on file at Queen Mary & Westfield College, where the analysis has been done. Altogether, it forms a substantial data bank. It is not possible in this paper to give more than a brief flavour of the findings. The aim of the analysis has been to assess the increases in mortality from all causes, from ischaemic heart disease (IHD), from cardiovascular disease (CVD) and from respiratory disease (RD). The increases were analysed in relation to falls in outdoor temperature after allowing for various confounding factors such as sex, age, influenza and baseline mortality, relating these increases to the usual winter climate in each country, and also relating them to the extent of personal protection against cold, indoors and outdoors, as revealed by the survey variables.

To start with, consider the range of temperatures we are dealing with. During October to March, in the areas studied, the mean temperature varies from 15.4 [degrees] C in Palermo and 12.7 [degrees] C in Athens, through between 5 [degrees] C and 8 [degrees] C for the "central" areas (North Italy, Germany, The Netherlands and England), down to −1 [degrees] C and −2.8 [degrees] C respectively for South and North Finland. In Ekaterinburg, the mean temperature is lower again, at −6.8 [degrees] C, and of course it is substantially lower than that in Yakutsk, −26.6%. These mean values represent a wide range of variation: even the relatively warm regions may sometimes have exceptionally cold days. Temperatures during the survey period ranged in Ekaterinburg, for example, from +12.5 [degrees] C to −25 [degrees] C. In Yakutsk, they ranged from +10.2 [degrees] C to −48.2 [degrees] C. Yakutsk is near the centre of the cold, high pressure weather system that forms over eastern Siberia in winter, and winter temperatures there are lower than in any other city: temperatures below −50 [degrees] C sometimes occur.

The mean temperatures in London and Emilia Romagna, during the survey period, almost exactly coincided (7.6 [degrees] C and 7.7 [degrees] C respectively). This turned out to be interesting, in view of what follows. The Netherlands and Baden-Wurttemberg were a little colder, with mean temperatures of 6.2 [degrees] C and 5.1 [degrees] C respectively. Deaths per day are related to daily temperature by regression methods (generalized linear modeling, assuming Poisson distribution of the deaths). The strongest relationships (indicated by the highest regression coefficients) occur when deaths are lagged on temperature by a few days: the number of days varies according to whether one is looking at all causes of mortality, IHD, CVD or RD. In the eight regions measured in 1994 (Palermo to Finland), it was found that all these mortality rates were at or near their lowest value when mean daily temperature was at 18 [degrees] C. As temperatures fell below this level, mortality rates rose in a broadly linear way. Taking this level of 18 [degrees] C as a baseline, it was possible to calculate the percentage increase in deaths (excess deaths) per 1 [degrees] C fall in temperature below 18 [degrees] C. After pooling age and sex, it was found that this growth of excess mortality as temperature falls below 18 [degrees] C was significant in all the eight regions (except Palermo, where there were problems with the mortality statistics), but was lower in the regions with low mean winter temperatures. The relationship was not exact, but was statistically significant, with a 2.2% increase in mortality per [degrees] C temperature decrease in Athens and, at the other extreme, a 0.3% increase in mortality per [degrees] C decrease in Finland.

The relationship was similar whether we are looking at "all cause" mortality, RD, IHD or CVD. There is one oddity: London and North Italy have almost the same mean winter temperature, but London showed a much higher increase in mortality (1.4% versus 0.5% per [degrees] C). Indeed, London is quite out of line with all the other countries.

When we come to Siberia, the pattern changes. In Ekaterinburg, there was no increase in mortality rates until temperatures fell to 0 [degrees] C, a much lower level than in any of the European zones; below that level, excess deaths increased progressively. But in Yakutsk, there was no increase at all in all-cause mortality as temperatures fell to their lowest levels; IHD and CVD mortality showed no significant increase, and the only exception was RD (respiratory disease mortality), which did show some increase at the lowest temperatures. Thus, there are significant differences in the effects of cold, and cold change, on susceptibility to these diseases, between the temperature zones, and the question that arises is why? Can we explain these variations in terms of people's lifestyle?

There are two elements to this which are both addressed in the surveys: how people protect themselves indoors, and how they protect themselves when they go outside. In interpreting the evidence there is a problem of correlation, because people who take one kind of protective measure naturally tend to also take others; it is difficult to establish independent relationships with specific factors. Linear and logit regression methods were used as appropriate to determine whether normal and binary distributed variables changed significantly with temperature and to predict the variables at any given temperature: the findings below are based on the significant changes found in this modeling process.

Indoors

The surveys gave clear evidence that warm housing was related to low winter mortality. In Europe, at a standard temperature of 7 [degrees] C outdoors, bedroom heating was much less common and living room temperatures were lower in regions with warm winters (for example, 19.2 [degrees] C in Athens, 21.7 [degrees] C in South Finland).

In Ekaterinburg, living room temperatures averaged 19.8 [degrees] C even at the lowest outside temperature. In most of the city, apart from the outlying parts, the centralized home heating could not be controlled by the occupants, and there was evidence that, on warmer days, people often found their living rooms uncomfortably hot, and chose to spend more time in unheated rooms (which often, in fact, receive indirect heating). In Yakutsk, living room temperatures were as high as 19.1 [degrees] C even at the lowest temperature of −48.2 [degrees] C. Bedroom heating also increased in both Siberian cities as temperatures fell.

Clearly, home heating is taken more seriously in cold regions. In Europe, the mortality indices (of increased deaths per 1 [degrees] C temperature fall) were significantly higher in those regions where bedrooms were seldom heated through the night, and where living room temperatures were low. We note that respondents in London were less likely than those in North Italy to heat their bedrooms at night—could this be part of the reason for the higher mortality in London, even though the mean temperature is the same?

Outdoors

The surveys also showed striking associations between outdoor cold stress and winter mortality. The mortality indices were related to the proportion who kept still (for at least two minutes) when they were outside, or who said that they shivered while they were outside, both of which were more likely in the warm-winter regions. They were inversely related to the proportion of people who wore hats, gloves or anoraks at standard outdoor temperatures.

In Ekaterinburg, as temperatures fell to 0 [degrees] C, people who went outdoors put on heavy clothing and seldom shivered, and they reported progressively spending less time standing still. Only below 0 [degrees] C did these protective measures stabilise, the tendency to shiver increased, and mortality rose.

In Yakutsk, protection by wearing heavy clothing outdoors was even more striking. Uniquely in Yakutsk, the proportion going out of doors (in the 24 hours before the interview) fell sharply at extreme low temperatures (below −20 [degrees] C) from 82% to 44% at the lowest temperature. However, when people did go out, the length and frequency of excursions did not change with temperature, nor did the time they spent standing still (for example, waiting for a bus, and so on: our observation showed that most people traveled by bus or on foot, and that cars were few). But they reported more frequent shivering. Overall, reported shivering among the population as a whole remained stable as temperature fell, because the decline in those going out was balanced by increased shivering among those who did. The hypothesis must be that people who live in this very cold place are acclimatised (more than most of us would be) to a low level of cold, but that below this level (−20 [degrees] C) they adopt strategies to avoid it, going out less often, keeping up their internal heating and, as we shall see, wearing different clothing. The fact that RD mortality alone increases with lowered temperature can probably be explained by rapid cooling of the respiratory tract when very cold air is breathed in.

Outdoor Clothing

In the European areas, there were significant differences between warm and cold countries in the clothing our sample wore when they went out. At a standardized outdoor temperature of 7 [degrees] C, people in warm-winter regions were less likely to wear a hat (13% in Athens, 72% in South Finland), an anorak, gloves or (if a woman) trousers, and they were more likely to wear a skirt (women), an overcoat or a sweater. The overall clothing area covered was similar, so the suggestion is that it is the type of clothing that is important. The indices of mortality growth were significantly higher in regions where relatively few people wore a hat, anorak, gloves, long-sleeved vests or long underpants when out at the same standard 7 [degrees] C temperature, and where more people wore sweaters or overcoats. This is likely to be because, if you wear a sweater or overcoat, you are less likely to be wearing an anorak, which is more protective. These associations were generally similar for the three disease categories, RD, IHD and CVD. There are high correlations here: those most likely to wear protective clothing (hats, anoraks) are also most likely to have warm rooms and to keep active and avoid shivering.

In London, compared with Emilia Romagna (where the mean temperature was the same), respondents claimed to wear substantially less clothing overall when they went outside, and specifically were less likely to wear an overcoat, and more likely to spend time standing still. Thus, another part of the reason why Londoners are more prone to excess death than Italians could be that they have a more Spartan attitude to going outdoors, as well as taking less trouble to keep their houses warm at night.

In Ekaterinburg, as the temperature fell to 0 [degrees] C, our samples reported wearing progressively more clothing, and also spent less time standing still; this may well explain why shivering did not increase and mortality did not grow in this temperature range. Below 0 [degrees] C, reports of shivering while outside increased (to 35% at −25 [degrees] C), but the number of items of clothing worn increased little, and stabilized at 16 items when temperatures fell below −8 [degrees] C; this included items such as hats and gloves. Qualitative evidence, from talking to people in Ekaterinburg, suggests that by the time temperatures reached this level all available clothing was being worn. In Yakutsk, the number of items of clothing, and the total area worn, increased as temperatures fell to −20 [degrees] C, by 48% and 33% respectively. Below that level, the area of clothing worn outdoors did not increase significantly any further, and the number of items worn increased by only 2%. However, the type of clothing changed. Overcoats progressively replaced anoraks at the low temperatures, and hats and gloves were always worn.

Our personal observations filled in further detail to help us understand this. An overcoat in winter Siberia usually means a ground-length coat of fur or leather. Hats and gloves are frequently fur, and it is normal to cover the ears and the sides of the face. At around −35 [degrees] C people did not put clothing or other material over the nose or mouth to warm the air breathed: when asked about this, they said that it hindered acclimatisation, although we learnt that in earlier times people in the region are recorded as having tied foxtails round their heads to screen the nose and mouth. Boots were often also of fur or the local Russian felt boot. In short, people who live in these very cold climates, even the relatively poor, have developed clothing habits to protect themselves.

DISCUSSION

The results sketched above only outline the major points emerging from this database. They underline the importance, for the health of elderly people, of both indoor and outdoor conditions. It has long been recognized that it is important to keep houses warm, and resources are applied to preserve a consistent level of interior warmth even in the coldest climates. But keeping the house warm is not sufficient: the lesson from these studies is that adequate protection out of doors is also important. Where warm winters are normal, deaths start to increase at relatively high temperature levels, and the suggestion from these data is that this may be related to inadequate concern for protection when people go outside into the cold: they are not putting on enough, or the right, clothes. In the colder regions, the need for adequate clothing is better understood, and as a result deaths from these causes do not start to increase until the temperature reaches much lower levels.

It is not that people who live in cold areas are genetically adapted to resist cold, although some such element cannot strictly be excluded. What these results seem to illustrate is that safety comes primarily from taking protective measures: heating the house adequately, and effective protection against cold stress out of doors. People accustomed to very cold winters are better prepared for this.

REFERENCES

Bucher, K., Cordioli, E., Dardanoni, L., Donaldson, G. C., Jendritsky, G., Katsouyanni, K., Keatinge, W. R., Kunst, A. E., Mackenbach, J. P., Martinelli, M., McDonald, C., Nahya S., & Vuori, I. (1997). Cold exposure and winter mortality from ischaemic heart disease, cerebrovascular disease, respiratory disease, and all-causes, in warm and cold regions of Europe. The Eurowinter project. *Lancet*, 349, pp. 1341–1346.

Donaldson, G. C., Ermakov, S. P., Komarov, Y. M., McDonald, C. D. P., & Keatinge, W. R. (1998). Cold related mortalities and protection against cold in Yakutsk, eastern Siberia: Observation and interview study. *British Medical Journal*, 317, pp. 978–982.

Donaldson, G. C., Tchernjavskii, V. E., Ermakov, S. P., Bucher, K., & Keatinge, W. R. (1998). Effective protection against moderate cold, with rise in mortality only below 0 [degrees] C, in Ekaterinburg, Russian Federation. *British Medical Journal*, 316, pp. 514–518.

Keatinge, W. R., & Donaldson, G. C. (1997). Letter replying to comments on the Lancet paper. *Lancet*, 350, pp. 591–592.

REVIEW QUESTIONS

1. How did the researchers do the quota sampling for this project?
2. Why was it important to use quota sampling?
3. What were the results? Could another kind of sampling have been used and yielded the same kind of results?

8

Experimental and Survey Research: Putting It All Together

What you have learned to this point constitutes the foundations of social science research. In the remaining chapters you will learn about various ways of gathering data. Research is of basically two types: **quantitative** and **qualitative**. In quantitative analysis, which you will be learning more about in this chapter, the observations are given some sort of numerical representation. In qualitative analysis, which you will learn more about in Chapters 9 and 10, observations are not quantified and words, pictures, descriptions, or narratives are used as data.

EXPERIMENTS

An **experiment** is a research method that allows variables to be analyzed in a controlled and systematic way. Experiments are best used when the researcher needs to control and explain the phenomenon being studied. Experimental design can be classified into three main types: true experimental design, quasi-experimental design, and double-blind procedures.

In a **true experimental design**, the researcher manipulates some variables and observes the effects of the manipulation on other variables. The **independent variable** is the variable that is manipulated.

Let's say you want to conduct an experiment to determine the effect of exercise on heart rate. You hypothesize that the more a person exercises, the higher his or her heart rate will be. This sounds reasonable, but you need to test

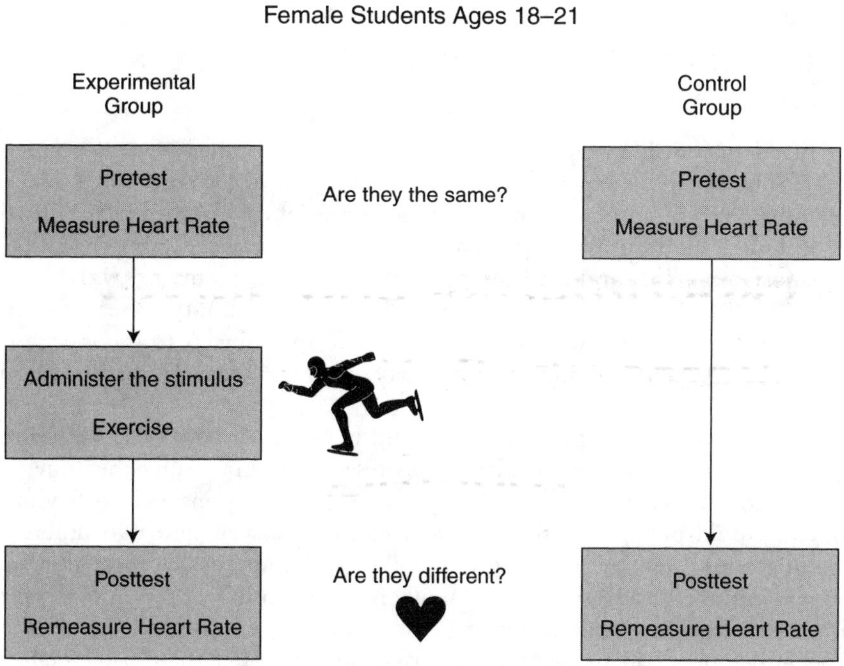

FIGURE 8.1 Diagram of a Basic Experimental Design

this hypothesis to see if it is true. You decide to use only female students who are between the ages of 18 and 21. Half of the females will receive the stimulus (the exercise) in the **experimental group**. The other half of the sample, the **control group**, will not receive the stimulus. You randomly assign the women to one group or the other by having them count off 1 and 2. Those who are designated number 1 go into the experimental group; those who are designated number 2 go into the control group.

This is a true experimental design because you randomly assign the subjects to one group or the other to reduce the variation between groups and to make sure that each subject has an equal chance of getting into either group. All true experiments have a **pretest**, which measures the outcome variable before the treatment has been given, and a **posttest** to measure the outcome of both groups after the treatment has been given, as shown in Figure 8.1.

This experiment can be illustrated by using a series of symbols commonly used to describe experimental designs:

R = random assignment to either the experimental or the control group

O = an observation or a measurement of the dependent variable

X = participants who are exposed to the experimental stimulus (i.e., the independent variable)

Therefore, this experiment would look like this:

R O1	X	O2 Experimental Group
R O1		O2 Control Group

The dependent variable (O) is the heart rate, which is measured at point 1 (pretest). Subjects in the experimental group then begin to exercise (X). Subjects in the control group do not exercise. The heart rate of each subject is measured again at point 2 (posttest) to see if there is a difference between groups.

A **quasi-experimental design** has some elements in common with a true experiment and resembles a true experiment in some ways, but the researcher has little control over the exposure or nonexposure of the subjects to the independent variable. There is no random assignment; however, there is a comparison group.

Let's say you want to investigate the effects of sex on antisocial behavior. The groups, boys and girls, would already be preset; you can't change the subjects' sex. You pretest all members of both groups to document any antisocial behaviors. Then you would put half of the boys and half of the girls into two different treatment groups. Members of one group will receive money every time they go one hour without hitting someone. Members of the other group will receive reprimands every time they hit someone. At the end you will conduct a posttest to see which treatment had an effect on the boys and which treatment had an effect on the girls.

This quasi-experiment would look like this:

Boys 01	X1	O2 Treatment A: Money
Boys 01	X2	O2 Treatment B: Reprimand
Girls 01	X1	O2 Treatment A: Money
Girls 01	X2	O2 Treatment B: Reprimand

One of the most common types of quasi-experimental design is the **time series design**, which consist of a series of repeated measures that are followed by the introduction of the experimental condition and then another series of measures. In this type of design, the experimental group might look like this:

01 02 03 04 X 05 06 07 08

It could be concluded that the independent variable produced some type of effect if the changes in the dependent variable are present after repeated observations.

A **double-blind procedure** is most often used in medical experimentation. Subjects are randomly assigned to the experimental and control groups, but neither the subjects themselves nor the researcher knows which subjects are getting the treatment and which ones are receiving a placebo. The **placebo** is an inactive substance or dummy drug used in place of the experiment stimulus. The purpose of a double blind experiment is to make all subjects believe they are receiving the experimental treatment and to observe the behaviors of all subjects.

Let me give you an example of a double-blind study. My son needed his wisdom teeth pulled. The dentist asked my son if he wanted to participate in a double-blind study of painkillers. My son agreed, and after his teeth were pulled, he was given a pill to take when he began to feel pain. Neither the dentist nor my son knew whether the pill was the real drug or a placebo. My son was asked to rate his pain for a specific amount of time. If the pill didn't relieve his pain, he told the nurses and the dentist, and he was given drugs that they knew would work.

If you live in a major city, you can often find ads in your local newspaper asking for people to participate in studies. Sometimes the researchers want you to stay overnight or for a week to participate. Guess why! So they know that you are not taking some other drug or doing something else, and so they can control for outside variables.

SURVEY RESEARCH

Survey research is the use of questionnaires to gather data about respondents' attitudes or behaviors. Surveys are probably the "most frequently used mode of observation in the social sciences and the most common method reported in the *American Sociological Review*" (Babbie, 2001: 256). Surveys are a popular way of conducting research because they are versatile, efficient, and generalizable. Although a survey is not good for testing your entire hypothesis, it certainly can enhance your understanding of a particular social issue, such as the "Sex in America" survey you read about in selection 14 in Chapter 7. Surveys are efficient because the data can be collected from a large number of people. Surveys can be mailed, sent out over the Internet, handed out at a mall, or conducted on the telephone. One of the largest surveys is conducted by the U.S. Census Bureau. The federal government tries to obtain information about every person in the United States. Because surveys are often the only way to obtain information about groups of people they are a good way to generalize about the entire population.

Basically, two types of questions are used in surveys. A **close-ended question** provides respondents with a fixed set of answers to choose from. An **open-ended question** lets respondents formulate their own responses. So, if the question asked were "What is your marital status?", a close-ended question could provide four possible answers—married, widowed, single, or divorced. If the question were "What is your race?," there could be so many possible answers that it might be best to leave a blank and allow the respondents to fill in their responses.

Designing a **questionnaire** is not as easy as you might think. To begin, you must go back to your hypothesis, and let your independent and dependent variables guide the questions you ask of your respondents. Remember that you are trying to figure out if the independent variable has some effect on the dependent variable.

Let's say you believe that the more education a person has, the higher his or her salary will be. The independent variable is education, and the dependent variable is salary. You could ask just two questions: (1) How many years have you been in school? (2) How much money do you make? However, would you get enough information, and could you be sure that education is really what had an effect on the person's salary? Other variables might have an effect on your dependent variable, and you need to make sure you are capturing **extraneous variables** which are variables that are not objects of your research. What other things can affect how much money people make in their jobs? Age, marital status, sex, and experience could all have an effect on the dependent variable, just to name a few. Therefore, you must come up with questions that address those variables.

What kind of question could you ask that would capture your dependent variable? "How much money do you receive annually from your job(s)?" would capture it. You can leave a blank for an open-ended question so respondents can write in their responses, or you can give them some choices—for example, <$10,000, $10,000–$20,000, $20,000–$30,000, and >$30,000. Would any other questions capture the dependent variable? If not, then you must go on to the independent variable. A question that would capture the independent variable would be "What is the highest grade you have completed in school?" Here are some examples of questions that would capture the extraneous variables:

1. What is your sex?
   Male ____________
   Female ____________
2. What is your age? __________
3. What is your marital status?
   Married ____________
   Divorced ____________
   Separated ____________
   Widowed ____________
   Single ____________

I'm sure you can come up with other variables that also could affect your dependent variable. The point is that you need to have survey questions that can capture all the variables you can think of that could affect the dependent variable in any way. If your questions have nothing to do with the variables, delete them from your questionnaire.

Questionnaires should be neat and well constructed. Be sure to check your grammar and spelling. If you receive a questionnaire that looks terrible, you're not likely to take the time to fill it out.

There are a few ways to distribute questionnaires. A **self-administered questionnaire** is a set of questions that the respondent is able to answer on his or her own and return to the researcher. Mail distribution and return is probably the most common type of distribution and one of the least expensive methods. You send a questionnaire through the mail and provide a self-addressed stamped envelope so respondents can return the completed questionnaires without incurring any expense. According to Babbie (2007), a response rate of 50 percent is adequate, 60 percent is good, and 70 percent is very good. The response rate can increase with follow-up mailings sent out a few weeks after the original questionnaire. One follow-up mailing can boost the response rate by an additional 20 percent, and a third follow-up mailing can add an additional 10 percent.

More and more surveys are being conducted online. According to Internet World Stats (2006), the number of individuals who have access to the Internet has grown to 1,076 million people worldwide. More and more individuals therefore have access to online surveys.

Online surveys can be set up on a Web site with a lot of fanfare to make them appealing to potential respondents. Surveys can also be distributed and retrieved via e-mail. E-mail tends to save time and money for all involved.

In the following readings, you will see examples of how researchers use the experimental and survey research.

REFERENCES

Babbie, E. 2007. *The practice of social research* (11th ed). Belmont, CA: Wadsworth.

Internet World Stats. 2006, November. *World Internet usage and population statistics.* Retrieved December 7, 2006, from www.internetworldstats.com/stats.htm

SUGGESTED FILMS

Obedience: Research Carried Out at Yale University (Stanley Milgram, 1993, 1965) (45 min.), University Park, PA: Penn State. Presents an experiment conducted by Dr. Stanley Milgram in May 1962 at Yale University on obedience to authority. Documents Milgram's early 1960s study on obedience to authority. Describes both obedient and defiant reactions of subjects who are instructed to administer electric shocks of increasing severity to another person. Milgram found subject obedience to be substantial, although obedience significantly decreased when the subject became physically closer to the victim of the shocks.

Experimental Design (Teresa Amabile, 1989) (29 min.). Washington, DC: Annenberg/CPB Collection; Santa Barbara, Ca: Intellimation (distributor). This film helps students to distinguish between observational studies and experiments and to learn basic principles of design including comparison, randomization, and replication.

Koko, a Talking Gorilla (Barbet Schroeder; Dale Djerassi, Nestor Almendros, Ned Burgess, Denise de Casabianca, Dominique Auvray, Margaret Menegoz, George Paul Csicsery, Francine Patterson, 2001, 1977) (80 min.). Home Vision Entertainment. This film gives information about Koko, a six-year-old gorilla who is the subject of a controversial Stanford University research project conducted by

Penny Patterson. A perceptive simian who communicates with humans via sign language, Koko knows more than 300 signs and can combine them to make new hybrid descriptions. Schroeder and Almendros present a visual argument exposing the contradictions that arise when scientific experiments are used to graph human behavior onto animals.

Older Voices: Interviewing Older Adults (Bonnie E Waltch, Randi Triant, 1994) (46 min.). Watertown, MA: New England Research Institutes; distributed by Terra Nova Films. The program is intended to present general principles of conducting survey interviews with older adults. It is designed to serve as one component of a study-specific interviewer training program.

16

Prepaid Monetary Incentives and Data Quality in Face-to-Face Interviews

Data from the 1996 Survey of Income and Program Participation Incentive Experiment

MICHAEL DAVERN, TODD H. ROCKWOOD, RANDY SHERROD, AND STEPHEN CAMPBELL

When respondents are asked to participate in a study, they do so for various reasons. Some do it because they have an interest in the subject and do it willingly and without payment. Many studies, however, are of no interest to respondent's, and incentives are needed to get people involved and willing to answer questions. This study is both a time series design and an experiment to see if paying people will increase the response rate in a study.

Paying people to participate in surveys, in the form of prepaid incentives, tends to increase the overall response rates for face-to-face interviews, as well as for mail and telephone surveys (Church 1993; Fox, Crask, and Kim 1989; James 1997; Kulka 1992; Singer et al. 1999; Warriner et al. 1996; Yammarino, Skinner, and Childers 1991). In addition, these prepaid monetary incentives might also affect the quality of the data being collected (Shaw et al. 2001; Shettle and Mooney 1999; Singer, Van Hoewyk, and Maher 2000). To assess the overall impact of incentives on survey

SOURCE: From Davern, M., Rockwood, T. H., Sherrod, R., & Campbell, S. 2003. Prepaid monetary incentives and data quality in face-to-face interviews: data from the 1996 survey of income and program participation incentive experiment. *Public Opinion Quarterly*, 67(1): 139–148.

data quality, this article investigates whether the use of monetary incentives affects the completeness and accuracy of information collected in face-to-face surveys.

As applied to survey methodology, social exchange theory posits greater participant willingness when incentives are used (Dillman 1991, 1999). The argument is that survey administrators who want greater cooperation (i.e., a higher response rate) should offer something of value to respondents for their participation, thereby establishing an explicit exchange relationship. Incentives can take the form of monetary payments, gifts (e.g., pens), lotteries, or summaries of survey results (Willimack et al. 1995). These incentives not only induce respondents to complete the surveys but may also encourage respondents to provide more complete and consistent information. Thus, social exchange theory yields the expectation that monetary incentives result in lower survey item nonresponse.

Others argue that monetary incentives lead to more item nonresponse through an alternative mechanism. Hansen (1980) offers a "self-perception" model in which the monetary incentive acts as an external motivator for compliance. External motivators are not as effective as internal motivators for getting people to act in desirable ways. Internal motivators increase a person's inherent interest in the subject and desire to participate, whereas external motivators succeed in gaining compliance from those who may have little interest in the subject. Overall, incentives may lower data quality because people persuaded to participate through the use of an incentive will have the least amount of internal motivation and will not fill out the survey thoroughly. Even though a higher response rate is obtained through the use of incentives, the quality of the data received may be lower because incentives convert people who are not as likely to give consistent and complete responses during the survey interview.

METHOD

The data used in this article are from the 1996 panel of U.S. Census Bureau's Survey of Income and Program Participation (SIPP). The 1996 panel was designed to produce nationally representative estimates from a sample of roughly 40,000 households. The households were sampled from clusters called primary sampling units (PSUs),[1] and interviews were obtained from 92 percent of the selected households. During the first wave of the 1996 SIPP panel, the Census Bureau gave an unconditional $10 incentive voucher to 24 percent of the sampled households, an unconditional $20 incentive voucher to 25 percent of the sampled households, and no monetary incentive to roughly 51 percent of the households. The voucher was given to a member of the household prior to beginning the core interview whether or not the household actually participated in completing it. Households receiving the monetary incentive voucher were determined randomly by designating entire PSUs into one of the three experimental groups (see table 1).[2]

All the sampled households in the SIPP are assigned to one of four rotation groups; one rotation group is interviewed every month. During the life of the panel, a particular rotation group is interviewed once every 4 months (SIPP Quality Profile 1998). As table 1 shows, a randomization control feature was added to the experiment to take advantage of the rotation group design of SIPP. The first rotation group in each of the $10- or $20-dollar-incentive PSUs did not receive an incentive. This experimental design allows researchers to control for the fact that,

1 There are 322 PSUs in the SIPP sample (SIPP Quality Profile 1998).

2 Other analyses of the 1996 SIPP experiment found overall response-rate differences between the control and experimental groups. James (1997) found that the $20 group had 7.5 percent nonresponse rate and both the $10 and $0 dollar group had a 9.1 percent nonresponse rate. Subsequent research on the 1996 SIPP panel, which examined incentives, response rates, and panel attrition, was conducted by Mack et al. (1998), and Martin, Abreu, and Winters (2000).

TABLE 1 Layout of the Incentive Experiment and the SIPP Sample

	SIPP Rotation Groups Are Randomly Assigned Cases Within a PSU			
Primary Sampling Units Were Randomized into Three Groups	**Group 1**	**Group 2**	**Group 3**	**Group 4**
Control group (no incentive)	No incentive	No incentive	No incentive	No incentive
Group 1 ($10 incentive)	No incentive	$10 incentive	$10 incentive	$10 incentive
Group 2 ($20 incentive)	No incentive	$20 incentive	$20 incentive	$20 incentive

NOTE: SIPP = Survey of Income and Program Participation; PSU = Primary Sampling Units.

although the PSUs were assigned to an incentive group randomly, people do not randomly assign themselves to a PSU. Roughly 25 percent of the households in the incentive-designated PSUs did not receive an incentive.[3]

The SIPP uses a computer-assisted personal interview (CAPI) instrument. The core content of the survey covers labor force participation, household characteristics, transfer program participation, basic demographics, and sources of income. Topical modules are added to the core survey during each wave of the panel. The topical modules include health care, education, household net worth, disabilities, and work history.

ANALYSIS

Data quality is measured using three indicators of the degree of respondent cooperation and the accuracy of a particular respondent's record: (1) edit occurrences, (2) imputation occurrences, and (3) overall completeness of the household reference person's record. We limit our analysis to the household reference person's record because we assume that the reference people are the most likely to have received or know that the household did receive the incentive voucher. The first two dependent variables consist of counts of the number of edited and "hotdeck" imputed values of variables drawn from the household reference person's record during the first wave of the SIPP 1996 panel.[4] The number of edits and imputations are counted and tabulated for 40 survey items.[5] The 40 items were chosen because they are asked of all the adults in the household and are nonbranched items. They include questions on race, age, gender, employment, military service, and asset ownership. The completeness measure is coded by the staff at the U.S. Census Bureau. The measure of completeness used in the analysis compares "mostly complete interviews" to partially incomplete and "type Z interviews." A mostly complete interview is defined as an interview that is not terminated prior to the first asset income question. A "type Z interview" occurs when there is a missing interview for one person inside an otherwise participating household (SIPP Quality Profile 1998). In general, the greater the number of edit or imputation occurrences on a person's record, the poorer

3 Although individual household randomization would have been better from an experimental design point of view, for operational reasons PSUs were chosen, and the first rotation was not given an incentive. This allowed for easier control over the experimental condition in the groups because specific interviewers were assigned always to hand out the incentive or never to hand out the incentive. For all four dependent variables examined in this article, there is no effect of rotation group on the dependent variable among the nonincentive PSUs (for the three continuous measures, the overall F-test was not significant, much less any one of the contrasts).

4 The household reference person is usually an owner or renter of the household.

5 One wave of SIPP data contains four records for each person. The first record for each person represents the first reference month of data, the second record represents the second reference month for each person, etc. For the analyses contained within this article, only data from the first reference month are used to construct the indexes.

the data quality. Edits and imputations are modeled separately and together because they can be caused by separate types of measurement problems. Hotdeck imputations address instances of "item nonresponse." Item nonresponse occurs when a respondent refuses to answer a particular question or responds that she or he does not know the answer to a question. Hotdeck imputation is used to replace the missing information with a response from a similar person's record, and the variable is flagged as imputed. Edits occur when the data on the respondent's record seem to be inconsistent or problematic. Although SIPP is a computerized survey instrument that allows for built-in consistency checks, there are still many opportunities for people to give answers that are inconsistent with answers given earlier in the interview. The 1996 core SIPP instrument does not include follow-up consistency checks to clear up problematic or inconsistent information provided earlier in an interview. For example, a person may report participating in the food stamp program or in Temporary Assistance for Needy Families, and also report significant earned income and assets (e.g., $100,000). In this case, an edit may be made to the data, depending on the specific edit process that is in place.

Three Poisson regression models are estimated using the SIPP data. The first model counts the number of edit and hotdeck imputation flags on the respondent's record for the 40 variables, the second model only counts the number of hotdeck imputations, and the third model only counts the number of edits.[6] A Poisson model is appropriate for modeling "count" data, such as counting the number of edits or imputations on a household reference person's record (Ott 1992). As seen in table 2, the mean number of edits and imputations is 0.86 per record, the mean number of hotdeck imputations is 0.44, and the mean number of edits per record is 0.44.

The fourth model uses logistic regression to predict the probability of the household reference person's survey responses being mostly complete versus having significant amounts of missing data. In wave 1 of the SIPP 1996 panel, 94 percent of the households in the public use data file had a mostly complete data record.

The independent variable in these analyses is the type of incentive that the household received. In the Poisson regression results reported in table 3, the people who did not receive any incentive are used as the reference category. Respondents who are asked more questions have a greater opportunity to give inconsistent answers or to terminate an interview before some of the questions are administered. Several variables are used in the model to control for survey length. Respondents are asked more questions during an interview if (1) they participate in transfer programs, (2) they have children present in the household, (3) they have other adults present in the household, (4) they are self-employed, or (5) they are employed by someone other than themselves.

Demographic control variables are used in this analysis as well.[7] The variables sex, race, Hispanic ethnicity, monthly earnings, marital status, New York City PSU, Los Angeles city PSU,[8] age, age squared,[9] and highest educational degree attained are in the Poisson regression models reported in tables 2 and 3. Table 2 presents the descriptive statistics of the variables used in the analyses.

The following analyses do not use the survey weights or adjust the variances for the complex sampling design of SIPP. We did not use the weights or adjustments in our analyses for three reasons: (1) the

6 Poisson regression models assume that the variance of the dependent variable is equal to its mean. This assumption is not the case with the number of imputations and edits (see table 2 for details). Thus, a scale parameter is added to the model that makes the analysis robust to this key assumption.

7 The control variables in the model are fully edited and imputed, and there are not any missing data.

8 New York City and Los Angeles are the two largest PSUs. Each accounted for a little over 3 percent of the entire sample.

9 We included both age and the square of age in the model; there is a curvilinear relationship between age and data quality. In our analyses middle-aged people tend to have less items missing and edited data than younger people. By contrast, older people are more likely to have significant amounts of missing data or to be a "type Z" interview than middle-aged people.

TABLE 2 Descriptive Statistics

Variable	Mean	Standard Deviation	Minimum	Maximum
Age	48.01	17.27	15	99
Survey mostly complete	.94	24	0	1
Imputations and edits	.86	2.34	0	30
Imputations	.44	2.15	0	27
Edits	.44	.72	0	7
Male	.54	.50	0	1
White	.83	.38	0	1
Hispanic	.09	.29	0	1
Monthly earnings (ln)	−1.35	2.64	−6.91	5.89
Transfer program	.24	.43	0	1
Senior (age 65+)	.21	.41	0	1
Married	.52	.50	0	1
No. of children	.72	1.12	0	10
No. of adults	1.87	.82	1	9
Highest degree	1.95	1.62	0	6
No. of jobs	.64	.59	0	3
Self-employed jobs	.11	.34	0	5
New York City	.03	.17	0	1
Los Angeles	.03	.17	0	1
Metro resident	.70	.46	0	1
$10 incentive	.24	.43	0	1
$20 incentive	.25	.43	0	1
No incentive	.51	.50	0	1

SOURCE: Wave 1 of the Survey of Income and Program Participation 1996 panel.
NOTE: N = 36,370 for all variables.

experimental design and randomization controls for selection bias, (2) we are making inferences to a generalized population and not the target population of the survey, and (3) other control variables are used in the multivariate models to control for additional selection bias. The unweighted parameter estimates should be far more sensitive and more likely to reject a true null hypothesis (i.e., are more likely to support the alternative hypothesis that incentives affect data quality). As seen in the tables summarized in the following section, this methodology did not result in the rejection of the null hypothesis and, therefore, makes a stronger statement that the incentives did not affect the number of imputations.[10] Because the weights were not used and the standard errors were not adjusted, care should be exercised in inferences regarding the parameter estimates of the control variables.

10 Weighted analyses are available from the authors on request. The weighted models do not change the conclusions drawn in this article regarding the effect of incentives on data quality.

TABLE 3 Regression Models of the Number of Edited and Imputed Variables from the Household Reference Person's Record or Whether the Household's Record Was Mainly Complete Regressed on Incentive Receipt and Control Variables

	Regression Model Estimates			
Variable Name	**Model 1 (a)**	**Model 2 (b)**	**Model 3 (c)**	**Model 4 (d)**
Intercept	−.1085	−1.9553	−.84	3.806***
Male	−.0019	−.1522**	.159***	.02
White	.0149	.3146***	−.2042***	.3376***
Hispanic	.0438	−.6007***	.3734***	.1161
Monthly earnings (ln)	−.0469***	−.0346*	−.0505***	−.0964***
Transfer program	.4017***	−.1438	.8115***	−.2878***
Age	.0244***	.0387***	.0156***	.0386***
Married	−.0632	.0874	−.2249***	.4471***
No. of children	−.0399***	−.0056	−.074***	−.1305***
No. of adults	.0673***	.1132**	.0299**	−.7078***
Highest degree	−.0686***	−.0049	−.158***	.0304
No. of jobs	−.3557***	−.0431	−.6233***	−.0302
Self-employed jobs	−.0848	.0419	−.179***	−.1858**
Metro resident	−.1551***	−.2709***	−.039****	−.2479***
New York City	.3487***	.6246***	.1002****	−.3461***
Los Angeles	.1484	.081	.1402***	−.2972***
$10 incentive	.034	.731	−.007	−.0826
$20 incentive	−.0512	−.0721	−.0299	.0061
Scale (e)	2.6074	3.1989	1.0394	NA

*p <.05.
**p <.01
***p <.001.
(a) Poisson regression of the number of edited and imputed variables.
(b) Poisson regression of the number of imputed variables.
(c) Poisson regression of the number of edited variables.
(d) Logistic regression of a household record being mostly complete.
(e) The scale parameter was estimated by the square root of Pearson's [chi square]/df.
SOURCE: Wave 1 of the Survey of Income and Program Participation 1996 panel.
NOTE: N = 36,370.

RESULTS AND DISCUSSION

Table 3 contains the fitted Poisson regression models predicting the number of the imputations or edits (models 1–3) and the logistic regression model of whether the respondent's data were mostly complete (model 4). These analyses show no significant relationship between the receipt of a $10 or $20 incentive and the data quality measures. Receiving a $10 or $20 incentive is not related to the number of edits or imputations per household reference person's record, nor is it related to the probability of having a mostly complete reference person's record.

Two theories predicted opposite effects from receiving an incentive on the quality of the data. One theory predicted poorer data quality (Hansen 1980), and the other theory predicted better data quality (Dillman 1991, 1999). Our analysis supports neither theory because a relationship was not found between incentive receipt and (1) whether the reference person's record was mostly complete, and (2) the number of edits or imputations on the household reference person's record. Our finding is similar to that found by Shettle and Mooney (1999) in their analysis of data quality. They found no effect on item nonresponse in four out of five data quality indexes that they examined.

Unlike Singer, Van Hoewyk, and Maher (2000), we did not find that incentives decreased the number of times a respondent failed to answer a question (item nonresponse measured in our article by the number of imputations). The discrepancy between our findings and those of Singer, Van Hoewyk, and Maher (2000) could be attributable to several different factors. A plausible explanation is that the difference results from question type. The Survey of Consumer Attitudes contains many opinion questions that are included in the work of Singer, Van Hoewyk, and Maher (2000) on item nonresponse. When the respondent answered "don't know" or "not applicable/appropriate" to these attitude questions, it was considered to be nonresponse. The SIPP survey items reviewed here are more factual questions (such as race, age, sex, earnings, and asset ownership). For example, there may be some respondents who do not know what an "interest bearing savings account" is, and giving the respondents an incentive does not change their likelihood of answering a question about it. It is possible that incentives encourage respondents to give an opinion but not to reveal economic or demographic facts about themselves.

REFERENCES

Church, Allan H. 1993. "Estimating the Effect of Incentives on Mail Survey Response Rates: A Meta-Analysis." *Public Opinion Quarterly* 57: 62–79.

Dillman, Don. 1991. "The Design and Administration of Mail Surveys." *Annual Review of Sociology* 17: 225–49.

———. 1999. *Mail and Electronic Surveys: The Tailored Design Method.* New York: Wiley.

Fox, Richard J., Melvin Crask, and Jonghoon Kim. 1989. "Mail Survey Response Rate: A Meta-Analysis of Selected Techniques for Inducing Response." *Public Opinion Quarterly* 52: 467–91.

Hansen, Robert A. 1980. "A Self-Perception Interpretation of the Effect of Monetary and Non-monetary Incentives on Mail Survey Response Behavior." *Journal of Marketing Research* 17: 77–83.

James, Tracey. 1997. "Results of the Wave 1 Incentive Experiment in the 1996 Survey of Income and Program Participation." In *Proceedings of the Survey Research Section of the American Statistical Association.* pp. 834–39. Baltimore: American Statistical Association.

Kulka, Richard A. 1992. "A Brief Review of the Use of Monetary Incentives in Federal Statistical Surveys." Paper prepared for the Symposium on Providing Incentives to Survey Respondents, convened by the Council of Professional Associations on Federal Statistics for the Office of Management and Budget, Harvard University, John F. Kennedy School of Government, Cambridge, MA.

Mack, Stephen, V. Huggins, D. Keathley, and M. Sundukchi. 1998. "Do Monthly Incentives Improve Response Rates, in the Survey of Income and Program Participation?" In *Proceedings of the Section on Survey Research Methods of the American Statistical Association*, pp. 529–34. Baltimore: American Statistical Association.

Martin, Elizabeth, Denise Abreu, and Franklin Winters. 2000. "Money and Motive: Effects of Incentives on Panel Attrition in the Survey of Income and Program Participation." *Journal of Official Statistics* 17(2): 276–84.

Ott, Lyman. 1992. *An Introduction to Statistical Methods and Data Analysis.* Belmont, CA: Wadsworth.

Shaw, M. J., T. J. Beebe, H. L. Jensen, and S. A. Adlis. 2001. "The Use of Monetary Incentives in a Community Survey: Impact on Response Rates, Data Quality, and Cost." *Health Services Research* 35: 1339–46.

Shettle, Carolyn, and Geraldine Mooney. 1999. "Monetary Incentives in U.S. Government Surveys." *Journal of Official Statistics* 15(2): 231–50.

Singer, Eleanor, John Van Hoewyk, N. Gerbler, T. Raghunathan, and K. McGonagle. 1999. "The Effect of Incentives on Response Rates in Interviewer-Mediated Surveys." *Journal of Official Statistics* 15(2): 217–30.

Singer, Eleanor, John Van Hoewyk, and Mary Maher. 2000. "Experiments with Incentives in Telephone Surveys." *Public Opinion Quarterly* 64(2): 171–88.

Survey of Income and Program Participation Quality Profile. 1998. Washington, DC: U.S. Census Bureau.

Warriner, Keith, John Goyder, Heidi Gjertsen, Paula Hohner, and Kathleen McSpurren. 1996. "Charities, No; Lotteries, No; Cash, Yes: Main Effects and Interactions in a Canadian Incentives Experiment." *Public Opinion Quarterly* 60(4): 542–62.

Willimack, Diane, Howard Schuman, Beth-Ellen Pennell, and James Lepkowski. 1995. "Effects of a Prepaid Nonmonetary Incentive on Response Rates and Response Quality in a Face-to-Face Survey." *Public Opinion Quarterly* 59: 78–92.

Yammarino, Francis, Steven Skinner, and Terry Childers. 1991. "Understanding Mail Survey Response Behavior: A Meta-Analysis." *Public Opinion Quarterly* 55: 613–39.

REVIEW QUESTIONS

1. Why is this study considered a time series design?
2. Explain what the independent and dependent variables are in this study.
3. What is the control group in this study?

17

Sex in America—The Sex Survey

ROBERT T. MICHAEL, JOHN H. GAGNON, EDWARD O. LAUMANN, AND GINA KOLATA

The portion of the National Health and Social Life Study that you read in Chapter 7 (selection 14) is devoted to the issue of sampling in sexuality research. The portion of the study in this chapter describes how the researchers became interested in the study of sex, how they designed and administered the survey, and how the survey questions compare with the questions in other big national surveys. Notice how much thought and planning must go into a survey to make sure it provides valid and reliable information.

SOURCE: From Michael, R. T., Gagnon, J. H., Laumann, E. O., & Kolata, G. 1994. The sex survey. In *Sex in America*. Boston: Little, Brown and Company, pp. 15–32 (edited for this book).

The long history of attempts to study sexuality had as a dominant theme this idea that sexuality comes from within, that it is a feature of the individual, and that to understand sexual behavior we have to understand the individual's sex drives and hormonal surges and even genetic predispositions. As a consequence, the popular explanations of sexual behavior, the belief that the individual is the sole actor on the sexual stage, are an echo and a legacy of previous sex studies.

Our viewpoint is very different. We are convinced that sexual behavior is shaped by our social surroundings. We behave the way we do, we even desire what we do, under the strong influence of the particular social groups we belong to. We do not have all the latitude we may imagine when we look for a partner, nor do we have all the choices in the world when we decide what to do in bed. The choices we make about our sex lives are dramatically affected by our social circumstances.

Previous surveys, however, fed Americans' thirst for information on sexual practices and their results were often cited uncritically and the pseudo-studies of Kinsey (1948), Masters and Johnson (1966), Hite (1976), and Janus (1993) provided a picture of a very sexually active nation. Because these studies have been so widely publicized and are cited so often, many Americans walk around thinking they are among the few who do not have a lot of sex partners, thinking that even if they are satisfied, they must be missing something. Our study, called the National Health and Social Life Survey, or NHSLS, has findings that often directly contradict what has become the conventional wisdom about sex. They are counterrevolutionary findings, showing a country with very diverse sexual practices but one that, on the whole, is much less sexually active than we have come to believe.

Our survey, in contrast to the "reports" that preceded it, was a truly scientific endeavor, using advanced and sophisticated methods of social science research. Although these methods had been developed and used in the past for investigations of such things as political opinions, labor force participation and hours of work, expenditure patterns, or migration behavior, they work equally well in studying sexual behavior. Like studies of less emotionally charged subjects, studies of sex can succeed if respondents are convinced that there is a legitimate reason for doing the research, that their answers will be treated nonjudgmentally, and that their confidentiality will be protected.

Our study was completed only after a long and difficult struggle that shows, if nothing else, why it has been so enormously difficult for any social scientists to get any reliable data on sexual practices. The fact that it succeeded in the end was more a matter of our research team's stubbornness and determination than it was a mandate for this information to emerge.

The survey was conceived in 1987, as a response to the AIDS crisis. The human immunodeficiency virus, which causes AIDS, had been identified in 1984. By 1987, it was abundantly clear that it was not going to be easy or quick to find a vaccine or a cure for the disease. As the AIDS epidemic spread across the land, medical scientists began to focus on how to prevent the disease, and which groups of people were most at risk. The disease was infectious, scientists' realized, and one of the ways it was spread was through sex. This understanding immediately gave rise to three questions: How quickly was the disease going to spread? Who was most at risk for getting AIDS through sexual contact? How can people be persuaded to change risky behaviors?

But to answer those questions and to contain the epidemic, scientists needed to know about sexual practices in America and they needed to know about people's attitudes toward sex. Yet after years during which sexual research was treated as somehow beyond the pale, public health officials and some policy workers realized that they had almost no data that would enable them to answer these pressing questions. They were left with the forty-year-old Kinsey data, which everyone recognized to be highly problematical. Those findings were out of date and, moreover, were not even an accurate reflection of the population of Kinsey's era. Although it seemed useless to rely on Kinsey to try to analyze the spread of HIV and staunch the epidemic, in the absence of other data, scientists had to turn to his data to estimate, for example, the numbers of men who had sex with men.

Faced with the national emergency of the AIDS epidemic and the dearth of needed data, scientists and administrators at several agencies of the federal government, including the National Institute of Child Health and Human Development, the Centers for Disease Control and Prevention, the National Institute on Aging, and the National Institute of Mental Health, supported the idea of doing a national survey of sexual practices. Leading scientists in these agencies had wanted more general studies of sexuality to examine such issues as teen pregnancy, sexual dysfunction, and child abuse, and they realized that the AIDS crisis finally made such a study politically feasible as well as crucially important.

After scientific blue-ribbon panels, such as one established by the Institute of Medicine, spoke out strongly in favor of a national sex study, the government took the first step toward conducting one. In July of 1987, the National Institute of Child Health and Human Development invited researchers to apply for a grant to design such a study, with the understanding that the best design would be used to conduct the survey. The institute also asked for proposals for designs of a parallel study on adolescent sexual practices.

But our national squeamishness about asking questions about sex and our collective ambivalence about knowing the answers surfaced right away. Even the name of the request for proposals—"Social and Behavioral Aspects of Fertility Related Behavior"—illustrated this simultaneous inching forward and pulling back. Nowhere in that title was there any hint that this was supposed to be a sex survey. And even though such a survey was intended, the original funding was to be only for a year, to determine whether the survey was feasible. Then, after a design was established, the government would issue another request for proposals on actually carrying out the study.

Our team, working through the National Opinion Research Center, a survey research firm associated with the University of Chicago, was awarded the contract to design the study. But even with this support from the federal health establishment, there was still much resistance to such a study elsewhere in the government. In the months that followed, there was a constant pressure to compromise, to pare down a sex survey into an AIDS study.

Many government officials wanted to steer clear of topics that might be important to an understanding of sex but that were not obviously related to the spread of AIDS. For example, they did not want the survey to ask about masturbation, reasoning that masturbation was a private matter and unlikely to have anything to do with the transmission of the AIDS virus. As researchers, facing the problem of limited knowledge, we wished to cast our net widely. Nothing was known about masturbation in relation to sexual practices. Do people masturbate as a substitute for sexual intercourse? Is it used to enhance sexual arousal? Do men use it to prevent premature ejaculation?

Another consequence of the focus on disease and health problems was an argument that if a couple was monogamous, the questioning should cease then and there. The attitude was that we should not be asking these sex questions of "respectable" Americans. In short, some officials assumed they already knew what the answers would be and they knew what behaviors were acceptable and innocuous and which people to leave alone.

Eventually, even this narrow inventory of AIDS-related questions turned out to be too controversial for the government. In September 1991, Senator Jesse Helms introduced an amendment to a bill on funding for the National Institutes of Health that specifically prohibited the government from paying for such a study. The amendment passed, by a vote of 66 to 34, dooming the effort.

Nonetheless, we had been able to work on interview questions and methodology during the period when it looked as if the government might go ahead with the project. Part of the feasibility study that we conducted allowed us to test questions, conduct focus groups, do pilot interviews, and to design the sample. This work laid the groundwork for a full-scale study of sexuality.

When the Senate refused funding to continue the study, we turned to private philanthropic organizations for support. Freed of political constraints, we decided to make this a sex survey that would go far beyond the original purpose of helping to fight AIDS. We would treat sexual behavior like any other social behavior, using established methods to study it. Our hope was to glean data that would help not only with the fight against AIDS, sexually transmitted diseases, and unwanted pregnancies, but that also would help us understand what enabled some sexual partners to stay together for years while others break apart after only one or a few encounters. We also hoped to learn what were the key features of sexual relationships that were both emotionally and physically satisfying.

A much trickier problem arose when we wrote our questionnaire. We had to decide how, and with what language, to ask people about their sex lives. We did not want to confuse people by using technical language. Even words like *vaginal* and *heterosexual* were not well understood by many people, we found. Yet we did not want subtly to make the interview itself sexy or provocative or offensive by using slang terms. We wanted to create a neutral, nonjudgmental atmosphere in which people would feel comfortable telling us about one of the most private aspects of their lives.

We also needed to make the questions flow naturally from one topic to another and without prejudicing people's replies because of the order of the questions. We began by asking people about their backgrounds, their race, education, and religion, for example, and moved on to marriages and fertility. Then we gradually moved on to ask about sex. We asked for many details about recent sexual events and we asked for fewer specifics about events further in the past, reasoning that inability to recall details from long ago could result in erroneous, if well-intentioned, answers.

We decided to administer the questions during face-to-face interviews, which lasted an average of an hour and a half. By asking people directly, we could be sure that the respondents understood the questions and that the person who was supposed to be answering really did answer. These were to be questions that would gently lead people through their entire sexual history without making them anxious or bored, and without antagonizing them. At the same time, we wanted the questions to be neutral, so that there was no "right" answer. And we wanted a certain covert redundancy that would allow us to check answers for consistency.

Once we had the questions, we needed trained and experienced interviewers who could put people at their ease and gain their trust. To help us select interviewers whom people would talk to, we used focus groups, asking people of different races and backgrounds whom they would feel most comfortable with. To our surprise, almost everyone, including blacks, Hispanics, and men, preferred middle-aged white women. In the end, we selected 220 interviewers, mainly women in their thirties and forties. These interviewers were for the most part veterans of several other survey projects and all had a professional attitude and commitment to working on this particular survey under the careful management of the National Opinion Research Center.

After selecting the interviewers, we flew them to Chicago for further training, instructing them about how to conduct our survey and suggesting the kinds of difficulties they might encounter. For example, they might hear vernacular terms that might, in ordinary circumstances, embarrass them. As professionals, they could not let their own reactions become apparent to the respondents. We also encouraged the interviewers to tell us their own ideas about how to interview people about sexuality. The interviewers had a very high morale because they saw this study as stretching the limits of what is possible in a scientific survey. It was a professional challenge for them to make this study a success, and they had a shared sense of collective purpose.

In order to be sure that people who were identified as part of the study would agree to participate, the interviewers used all their powers of persuasion, returning again and again to the homes of people who declined, in some cases even paying the most recalcitrant to encourage them to agree to be interviewed. The participants were guaranteed anonymity. We have destroyed all identifiers from our completed interviews; thus, we could not name or find these people again if we wanted to. We also checked our data and found those reluctant respondents answered no differently than the others.

The interviewers began work on Valentine's Day, February 14, 1992, and continued until September of that year, which enabled them to spend as long as seven months in their attempts to find people and persuade them to participate in the study. In most surveys, interviewers spend two to three months tracking down and questioning respondents.

The survey was an expensive proposition, far different from mailing out questionnaires and tallying those that came back, as others have done. But we could be assured that the designated person answered our questions and not someone else. Each interview cost, in the end, an average of about $450, including the interviewer training, the several trips to the residence when necessary to do the interview, and entering the data into a computer for analysis.

Our interviewers clearly persuaded the prospective respondents of two key things. First, that the information they gave would be of value in understanding sexual behavior in America and in informing public health officials, counselors, and policymakers about the sexual matters we were addressing. And second, that the information they provided would be obtained in privacy, held in confidence, and not be associated with them personally. The success of this survey is a testament to the skill of the professional interviewers and the goodwill of the public.

The first question, of course, is: Were the respondents telling us the truth about their sex lives? Why should we believe that anyone, sitting in a face-to-face interview with a stranger, would answer honestly when questioned about his or her most intimate, personal behavior, including behavior that might be embarrassing to admit?

Survey researchers have several ways to check on the veracity of their data, and we used many of them. First, we had several questions that were redundant, but because they were asked in different ways at different times in the long interview, it would be difficult for a subject to dissemble convincingly. For example, we asked people twice how many sex partners they had had. The first time was as a simple question early in the interview, and the respondent was asked to write down the answer privately and place it into an envelope that was then sealed; the interviewer sent this envelope into the office without opening it. The second time was about an hour later, when the respondent was reviewing a lifetime sexual history. In this case, the number of partners was summed over various periods in the respondent's life. We found that the numbers came out essentially the same both ways, increasing our confidence that people were telling the truth.

We also inserted eleven sex questions from another survey into our survey to see if our respondents gave replies that corresponded to the results of that survey. That other survey, the General Social Survey (also conducted by NORC), did not mention to the respondents when the interview began that there were any sex questions and the sex questions only constituted about two minutes of a ninety-minute interview. Our survey, in contrast, stressed that sexual behavior was the primary focus of the whole study. So this comparison lets us see if the emphasis on sex had any influence on the type of people who answered our questions or on the type of answers they gave. This is one of the only ways we know of to see if there is any indication that our respondents did not tell us the truth about their sex lives or did not have sexual histories that were similar to those of the population at large. The comparison of our results to those of the 1991 General Social Survey is displayed in Table 1.

The table shows our respondents' replies to two of the eleven questions as compared to the replies of respondents in the General Social Survey. The answers were remarkably similar. For example, about 11 percent of the men in both surveys said they had no sex partner within the past twelve months, while 68 percent or 69 percent said they had one sex partner in the past twelve months. The women's replies were just as similar in the two studies. The match between the responses in both surveys was extraordinary. We could not expect to get more corroboration or similarity if we asked about any other behavior.

The top panel of the table assures us of an important fact: that our respondents appear to have taken the interview seriously and responded honestly.

TABLE 1 Comparison of Sex Partner Data in NHSLS and GSS

Q: "How many sex partners have you had in the past twelve months?"

Response	Men		Women	
	GSS	NHSLS	GSS	NHSLS
0	11.6%	11.1%	13.4%	13.7%
1	69.4	67.6	76.4	75.5
2	9.2	9.6	6.7	6.3
3	2.4	4.8	3.6*	4.5*
4	2.4	2.8	—	—
5–10	3.9	3.1	—	—
11+	1.2	1.0	—	—
	100%	100%	100%	100%

*Three or more partners.

Q: "Have your sex partners in the past twelve months been exclusively male, both male and female, or exclusively female?"

Response	Men		Women	
	GSS	NHSLS	GSS	NHSLS
Exclusively male	2.8%	2.6%	99.4%	98.3%
Both male and female	0.6	1.0	0.2	0.5
Exclusively female	96.6	96.3	0.4	1.2
	100%	100%	100%	100%

Or, at least, they responded with remarkable consistency with those in that other survey conducted in quite a different context. There is no indication in the distribution of the number of sex partners in the past twelve months that people thought the question was a joke and wrote down some funny numbers. There may well be some error in our data, as in all measurements, but the respondents here seem to be trying to answer the questions we asked.

The lower panel of the table is one of several pieces of information we have about homosexuality in the population, a topic we discuss at length [later]. Looking at the information here, it is striking how similar the answers are in the two surveys: a little more than 2.5 percent of the men in both samples who had sex partners in the previous twelve months said their partners were exclusively men during that period and another 0.5 percent to 1 percent said they had sex with both men and women. This leaves 96 percent of men who had sexual intercourse in the past year reporting that they had sex only with women during that time. For women, around 1 percent said they had sex exclusively with other women, another half of 1 percent or less said they had sex with both men and women. This leaves nearly 99 percent of women reporting that they had sex exclusively with men in the past twelve months.

Finally, we checked our data on sexual behavior against several other very recent and well-conducted studies that each looked at a part of the general picture we were assembling. Our study, and all of these others, came to the same basic conclusions, greatly strengthening the argument that our data can be trusted.

A final reason we trusted our data was the reports of our seasoned interviewers. They reported back to us that the participants enjoyed the interview, that they found it a rewarding and often illuminating experience to be gently led through their sex lives and attitudes about sex. In fact, they said it was an affirming event to talk about their sexuality and their sexual history in a nonjudgmental way. The interviewers reported that they had the sense that the respondents were telling the truth.

REFERENCES

Shere Hite, *The Hite Report* (New York: Dell, 1976).

Samuel S. Janus and Cynthia L. Janus, *The Janus Report on Sexual Behavior* (New York: John Wiley and Sons, 1993).

Alfred C. Kinsey, Wardell B. Pomeroy, and Clyde E. Martin, *Sexual Behavior in the Human Male* (Philadelphia: W. B. Saunders Co., 1948).

William H. Masters and Virginia E. Johnson, *Human Sexual Response* (Boston: Little, Brown, 1966).

REVIEW QUESTIONS

1. How was the questionnaire administered in this study? Would there have been a better way?
2. How did the researchers make sure that respondents were telling the truth? What did they find?
3. Do you think that the answers would be more accurate or less accurate if this type of survey was done over the Internet rather than face-to-face? Why?

18

The Internet and Opinion Measurement

Surveying Marginalized Populations

NADINE S. KOCH AND JOLLY A. EMREY

Using the Internet as a means to obtain survey data has increased in the last few years. However, the validity of online surveys is often questioned. This study addresses the issues of self-selection, selection bias, and response rates by examining population data for a group of Internet users who responded to a series of online surveys posted on a gay and lesbian Web site. The demographic data collected from the online study sample were compared with

SOURCE: From Koch, N. S., and Emrey, J. A. 2001. The Internet and opinion measurement: Surveying marginalized populations. *Social Science Quarterly*, 82(1): 131–138.

national data on gays and lesbians to determine if differences existed between participants and nonparticipants. Watch for the different ways in which the researchers went about making sure that their sample was reflective of other samples.

Social scientists are increasingly interested in studying the attitudes of subgroups whose members are not easily identified. The use of standard survey research methods is not always feasible, especially when reliable sampling frames of certain subgroups are difficult or impossible to acquire. In such situations, purposive samples have been relied upon. It is clear that self-selected samples pose problems of statistical inference and generalizability. However, such samples allow research on rare and marginalized populations that would otherwise not be conducted. Nonprobability sampling techniques have been used to study such subgroups as Vietnam veterans (Rothbart, Fine, and Sudman, 1982), members of Alcoholics Anonymous (Fortney et al., 1998), Mexican American gang members (Valdez and Kaplan, 1999), and fundamentalist and rural Christian congregations (Jelen, 1992, 1993; Wald, Owen, and Hill, 1988). Presumably, most social scientists would agree that it is preferable to conduct research with admitted limitations rather than to ignore certain topics altogether because of methodological difficulties.

The Internet has not been considered a good source of survey respondents because of selection effects. However, Internet surveys are an extension of survey research techniques (i.e., purposive samples) that, although not optimal in the classic textbook sense, are used quite frequently in sampling populations where adequate sampling frames are not available. Although online surveys have been in use for a number of years, problems of self-selection have precluded the calculation of response rates and degree of selection bias. To date, no self-selected, easily accessible online survey has reported response rates and degree of selection bias. This study addresses those problems by examining population data for a group of Internet users who responded to online surveys, enabling us to provide a calculation of both response rate and selection bias. We find that participants in the online survey are nearly indistinguishable from nonparticipants and are demographically comparable to their nationwide cohort. The overall response was slightly more than 16 percent, similar to response rates for nontargeted, mass mail surveys. In short, we argue that online surveys should not be dismissed outright as a research tool for difficult-to-reach populations.

SAMPLE SELECTION BIAS

Sample selection bias is a serious concern for researchers, and attention has focused on the causes of, diagnosis of, and corrections for sample selection bias (Berk, 1983; Groves, 1987; and Winship and Mare, 1992). Researchers are often confronted with a dilemma when researching populations that are difficult to find. How does one study a particular subgroup without compromising the validity of the data, especially when employing nontraditional sampling methods? As Rothbart, Fine, and Sudman (1982: 408) argue, "The problems involved in sampling rare populations, and therefore the methods for their solutions, are becoming increasingly important in survey research . . . social researchers are increasingly being asked to conduct studies of persons with special characteristics—such as laid-off workers or people with certain categories of illness—so as to provide policy-relevant data." Winship and Mare (1992: 327) in their research on sample selection bias also acknowledge this research dilemma by pointing out that "nonrandom selection is both a source of bias in empirical research and a fundamental aspect of many social processes."

The three general questions of concern for this paper are: (1) How do those accessing the Internet Web site where the survey(s) are posted differ demographically from their cohorts in the general population? (2) How do those who participated in the online survey differ demographically from those who visited the site but elected not to participate? and (3) What is the overall response rate to online surveys?

METHODOLOGY

A series of three surveys were posted on a gay/lesbian Web site (http://www.qcc.org). In addition, a Computer Center was established at a community gay/lesbian center to provide computer access to those without home computers. As of June 1997, there had been over 10,000 visits to this Web site. In order to use the Web site, users were required to complete an online demographic profile. The demographic data collected on the over 10,000 gay/lesbian users of this Web site will be compared to demographic information on gays/lesbians in the general population.

To evaluate survey response rates, we compare the response rates to the general demographic questionnaire of all users with the response rates to the three online attitudinal surveys posted on the Web site beginning in May 1996 and ending in June 1997. The first survey posted on the site was voluntary. The second online survey was "semimandatory." The importance of participating in this second survey was stressed, yet an option was given where the user could continue to access the site if (s)he "promised" (s)he would complete the survey at a later time. Since no oversight mechanism was installed to make certain a user kept his/her promise, participating "at a later time" was more or less optional. The third survey was mandatory. The Web site could be accessed only upon the user's completion of the survey.

In addition to calculating an overall response rate to the online surveys for those accessing the Web site, we categorized users as participants or nonparticipants. Analysis was performed to discern any differences between those who elected to respond to online surveys and those who chose not to participate.

RESULTS

Internet Sample Versus National Cohort

Because online surveys are subject to selection bias, there is an increased likelihood of obtaining a skewed sample. Therefore, it is necessary to investigate the characteristics of those initially self-selecting. Gays/lesbians accessing the gay/lesbian Web site at www.qcc.org were compared with gays/lesbians in the general population. The 1992 Voter Research and Surveys (VRS) exit poll (Edelman, 1993) sample of national voters included a sexual orientation variable, providing a useful comparison.

This study's sample and VRS's gay/lesbian sample were compared across six demographic variables: education, income, age, race, party identification, and ideology. The two samples are similar with regard to education. The difference in education categories between the two samples makes sense when we incorporate the results of the income variable in the analysis. Differences between the groups can be found on the basis of age, with the Internet sample being younger. From these data, it appears that the Internet sample is somewhat more racially diverse, with more Hispanics, Asians, and members of other racial/ethnic backgrounds represented.

The Internet sample is distinct in terms of political party identification. Over 25 percent of the Internet sample indicated "no party affiliation." Those indicating some party identification did so at a lower rate in each category than those participating in the national sample. With regard to political ideology, the two samples are similar. Although Table 1 illustrates some differences, overall the distribution of responses on the six demographic variables across the two samples tends to be similar, with only slight under- and overrepresentation in some categories.

Statistical Analysis of the QCC Data: A Logistic Regression Model

The literature and our initial analyses suggested that important explanatory variables in differentiating gay/lesbian participation in online surveys were income, age, education, gender, and access to the Internet. A logistic regression model was constructed to further assess what differences existed between those participating in the attitudinal surveys and those answering only the required demographic questions.

TABLE 1 Internet And National (VRS) Samples Of Gays And Lesbians

	Internet Sample N = 10,633	National (VRS) Sample N = 466
Education		
<H.S.	4%	4%
H.S.	11%	21%
Some coll.	34%	31%
College	28%	21%
Postgrad.	23%	23%
Income		
<$30,000	39%	48%
$30–50,000	27%	29%
>$50,000	34%	23%
Age		
<45 years	88%	70%
45 years +	12%	30%
Race		
White	72%	84%
Black	4%	10%
Hispanic	8%	4%
Asian	6%	*
Other	10%	2%
Party Identification		
Dem.	43%	50%
Repub.	12%	18%
Indep.	14%	23%
Other	4%	10%
No Affil.	28%	*
Ideology		
Lib.	48%	51%
Mod.	36%	42%
Conserv.	9%	8%
Rad.	7%	*

*Indicates data unavailable. "Asian" and "radical" were not included as response categories in the VRS survey.

Our initial analysis also led us to conclude that any differences among those who participated in the attitudinal surveys were most likely due to greater familiarity with the Internet and greater ease of access to the technology (Walsh et al., 1992). Therefore, our hypothesis for the logistic regression model is that users who participated in the attitudinal surveys are more familiar with the Internet and have greater ease of access to this technology than users who chose not to participate.

To measure familiarity with the Internet, all Web site registrants were asked if this was their first use of the Internet and how many hours per week each spent on the Internet. Registrants were also asked how they accessed the QCC Web site. For purposes of model specification we collapsed all responses into two categories: home and other (included accessing the site from the Gay and Lesbian Community Center (QCCSITE). The dependent variable in this model is participation, a dichotomous dummy variable with 1 = participating in an online survey and 0 = not participating in an online survey.

The ten independent variables included in this model are first time use of the Internet (NETUSE); hours spent per week on the Internet (HOURS); access to the Internet (ACCESS); (QCCSITE); (OWN); (PREVIOUS); and income, education, gender, and age. NETUSE and HOURS are included in the model to attempt to ascertain users' expertise and level of comfort with the Internet. PREVIOUS indicates whether or not a user had visited the Web site before. As with familiarity of the technology, familiarity with the Web site may affect future participation in an attitudinal survey. ACCESS, QCCSITE, and OWN tap into the availability and accessibility of the Internet.

Our analysis of this model indicates that those persons participating in the surveys differ somewhat from the nonparticipating population, but not in any substantive manner. Although six of our ten independent variables did perform at statistically significant levels, each reported only slight (less than 3.5 percent) changes in the predicted probabilities. The variables ACCESS and GENDER appear to have the greatest effects at 3.49 percent and −3.54 percent respectively. Income appears to have a negative effect on this model. Those making the most money were 2 percent less likely to have participated in a survey.

Participants in Voluntary, Semivoluntary, and Mandatory Online Surveys Versus Nonparticipants

Three additional logistic regression models were run to assess differences between those respondents who participated in each of the three (voluntary, semivoluntary, mandatory) online surveys and those who did not participate. The differences between those participating in the voluntary survey and those who did not participate in any of the surveys are not particularly substantive. The most meaningful differences appear to be with regard to age. Older persons were more likely to voluntarily participate in the survey. The QCC site variable was statistically significant in this model, indicating that participants in the voluntary survey were 2 percent less likely to have participated in the survey if they were accessing the Web site from the computer facilities at the Gay and Lesbian Community Center. This may be due to limited access to equipment and time limitations imposed. Although the effect was statistically significant at the 0.05 level for this variable (QCCSITE), its substantive impact is very small.

Those who participated in Survey 2 or the "semimandatory" survey also differed little from those who participated in the voluntary survey and those who did not participate in any of the three surveys. Two variables were shown to be statistically significant in the Survey 2 model. The QCCSITE variable indicated that those registering from the computer facilities at the Gay and Lesbian Community Center were almost 9 percent less likely to participate in the semimandatory survey than those who registered from other sites. INCOME was also shown to be significant in this model, with those of higher income less likely to participate.

Our third survey was mandatory. When we compare the two groups in this model (those who participated in the mandatory survey versus nonparticipants) we find that fewer variables produced statistically significant results in our model. These findings are expected, since one would anticipate that the participants in a mandatory survey (which had the greatest number of survey participants overall) should most closely resemble our population. The two variables, which performed at a statistically significant level in this model, were ACCESS and QCCSITE. Although each was statistically significant, they did not predict at levels that would indicate to us that our participants in the mandatory surveys differed much from the nonparticipants.

CONCLUSION

The independent variables yielded little explanatory power as to differences between participants and nonparticipants in our study. We believe that we can walk away from this exercise with cautious optimism and some interesting conclusions regarding the use of online surveys. First, selection bias appears to have occurred prior to respondents' participating in the surveys. Although this is somewhat reassuring, selection bias remains a problem with this new methodology. Second, the demographic characteristics of the participants and nonparticipants are practically indistinguishable. In fact, the demographic characteristics of our study of gays/lesbians comported well with the VRS national sample of gays/lesbians. Hence, we can generalize from our nonrandom sample to our population with a modicum of confidence. Finally, we can compare the response rate for our online surveys with those of more traditional mail-in surveys. Our overall response rate was approximately 16.4 percent. Although this is not an exceptionally high response race, it is well within the range of reported response rates for more well established mail survey techniques.

REFERENCES

Berk, R. 1983. "An Introduction to Sample Selection Bias in Sociological Data." *American Sociological Review* 48: 386–397.

Edelman, M. 1993. "Understanding the Gay and Lesbian Vote in 1992." *Public Perspective* 4: 32–33.

Fortney, J., B. Booth, M. Zhang, J. Humphrey, and E. Wiseman. 1998. "Controlling for Selection Bias in the Evaluation of Alcoholics Anonymous as Aftercare Treatment." *Journal of Studies on Alcohol* 59: 690–697.

Groves, R. 1987. "Research on Survey Data Quality." *Public Opinion Quarterly* 51 (Suppl.): S156–72.

Jelen, T. 1992. "Political Christianity; A Contextual Analysis." *American Journal of Political Science* 36: 692–714.

———. 1993. "The Political Consequences of Religious Group Attitudes." *Journal of Politics* 55: 178–190

Rothbart, G., M. Fine, and S. Sudman. 1982. "On Finding and Interviewing the Needles in the Haystack: The Use of Multiplicity Sampling." *Public Opinion Quarterly* 46: 408–421.

Valdez, A., and C. Kaplan. 1999. "Reducing Selection Bias in the Use of Focus Groups to Investigate Hidden Populations: The Case of Mexican-American Gang Members from South Texas." *Drugs and Society* 14: 209–224.

Wald, K., D. Owen, and S. Hill. 1988. "Churches as Political Communities." *American Political Science Review* 82: 531–548.

Walsh, J., S. Kielser, L. Sproull, and B. Hesse. 1992. "Self-Selected and Randomly Selected Respondents in a Computer Network Survey." *Public Opinion Quarterly* 56: 241–244.

Winship, C., and R. Mare. 1992. "Models for Sample Selection Bias." *Annual Review of Sociology* 18: 327–350.

REVIEW QUESTIONS

1. What were the independent variables used in this study?
2. How did the researchers compare their survey data? What did they use? What were the results?
3. Do you believe that using the Internet is a good way to gather data? Why or why not? What type of study would you like to do online?

9

Field Research and Unobtrusive Measures: Fun in the Field

ANALYSIS AND INTERVIEWING

The first thing you need to do before conducting most research is to look at the world around you. What do you see? I bet if you think about it, you have been a researcher for a long time without even realizing it. You might have even made some observations and come to some conclusions about the various things you see around you. We all do.

Let me give you an example. When I first moved to Nebraska, I needed furniture. Friends told me about an auction where I would find really great deals. So every Wednesday night I went to the auction wearing my backpack, and I watched what was going on around me while I graded my students' papers. I had never been to an auction before and found that many things were happening. Auctions aren't just about buying furniture and other items. I saw that people in the audience socialized and appeared to know each other. The "ringmen" working the front tables, who held up the merchandise so prospective bidders could see it, had different ways of holding and talking about the items, depending on what the item was and how high they thought the bidding was likely to go. They put on a show for the audience. Buyers had different ways of placing a bid. Some scratched their noses, others lifted their hats, and some pulled on their ears. The gestures of some were so subtle that it was impossible for me, at least, to spot them. By watching and paying attention, I soon realized that many things were happening at the auction that I never would have known about without observing the behaviors for months.

Fieldwork can also be called **ethnography** or **participant observation.** This type of observation amounts to "let's hang out" and watch what happens around us, which can be fun. But watching and participating in the auction also helped me develop questions about auctions—about the rituals, socialization, and economic exchanges that take place.

Field researchers can explore all kinds of situations. Let me give you some examples. Tamotsu Shibutani (1978), a research assistant for the University of California's Evacuation and Resettlement Study, observed the evacuation of Japanese living in the United States into resettlement communities. Shibutani became part of Company K, a unit in the U.S. military during World War II. Company K had problems such as rampant absenteeism, insubordination, violence, and protests, along with very bizarre behavior portrayed to other military personal in other units. Because Shibutani (1978: vii) was on the inside, he was able to view the behaviors through the "eyes of the participant" and was able to chronicle "one of the more disorderly units in United States military history and form a sociological generalization concerning the process of demoralization" among the members of Company K. Collecting data in this type of environment isn't easy. Shibutani wrote his notes and sent them through the mail almost daily to friends and relatives, who kept them for him until after his term in Company K ended.

Mitch Duneier (1992), a young white man, spent time in the Valois "See Your Food" Cafeteria on Chicago's South Side for four years while he was a graduate student at the University of Chicago. Duneier began to notice a group of poor, working-class black men who congregated at a table that became known as "Slim's table." Over the years, he got to know the men, observed their behaviors, found out about their lives, and listened to their troubles. He was able to refute stereotypes by spending time with Slim, an elderly white car mechanic who was more or less the respected master of the table where the diners met for a meal once or twice a day. Duneier observed Slim, who treated Bart, an African American, as a father figure and cared for him. The diners formed a close-knit community that transcended the roles and images commonly associated with black men. In *Slim's Table: Race, Respectability, and Masculinity* (1992), Duneier was able to discredit many previous studies on black men that generalized about working-class blacks but from essentially middle-class researchers' points of view. *Slim's Table* helped to confirm the unfairness of black stereotypes appearing in the popular media. Duneier was able to accomplish this by spending time in the field with these men.

Being a participant observer has some drawbacks. How much will your participation influence the activities and behaviors of the people you are studying? True, observing is an important aspect of field research, but you must also take notes. How will you do it? Your field notes must provide extensive descriptive detail about the situation you are observing. **Jotted notes,** which are written in the field, are short and meant to trigger your memory at a later time. **Direct observation notes** are written soon after the researcher leaves the field. These notes should be detailed, with concrete information and comments from respondents. Maps and diagrams should also be included in direct observation notes.

Let's return to the auction example. Suppose you want to see what goes on at the auction. You find a seat in the bleachers and take out your notebook and pen so it looks as though you are taking part by keeping track of your bids and purchases. You have a bid card and are ready to embrace your role as a participant observer. One of the first things you can do is jot down what you see and where

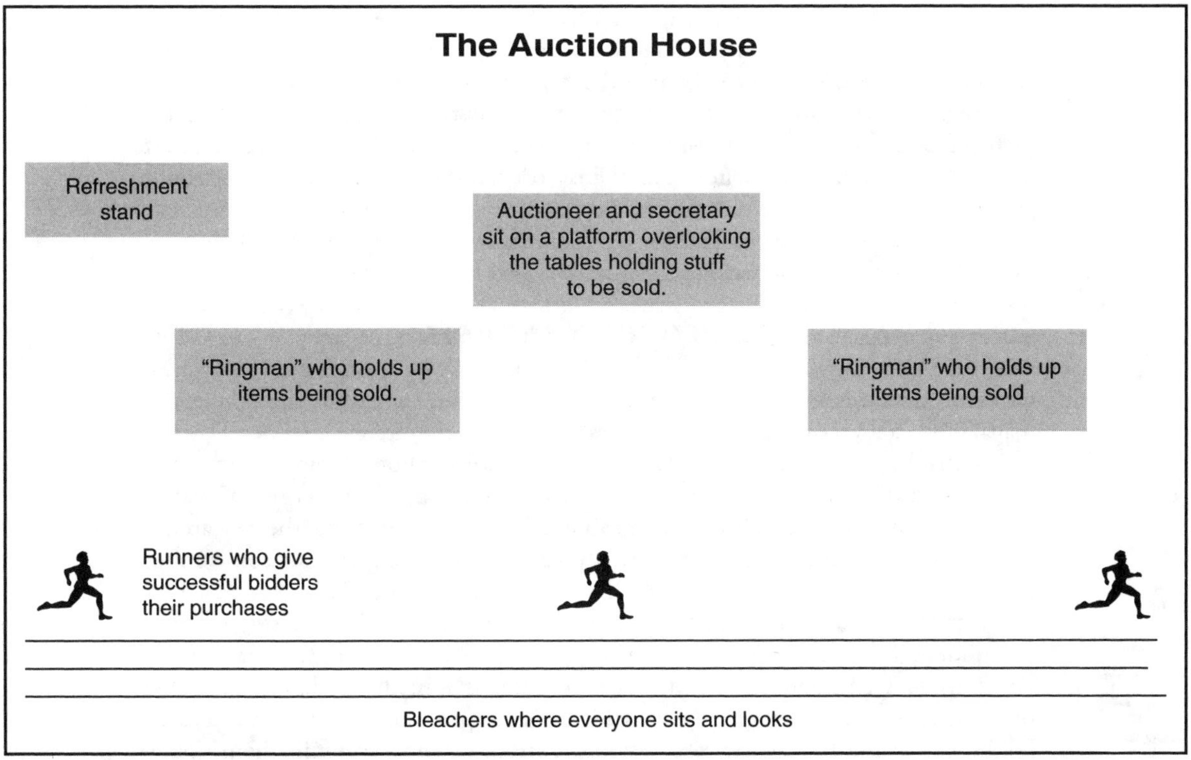

FIGURE 9.1 Diagram of Activity at an Auction House. The auctioneer calls the bids while the ringman shows the items to the people in the bleachers. This happens pretty fast and the ringmen alternate tables to keep the auction going at a fast pace.

people are standing. Later, you can diagram the scene to show who is involved (see Figure 9.1). Your direct observation notes are terribly important. They need to contain very specific information and as much detail as you can remember, and to be as accurate as possible.

INTERVIEWING

Observing will help you determine what types of questions to ask respondents during an **interview**—a data collection method in which a researcher questions a subject face-to-face or by phone and records respondents' answers. When you go into the field to collect data and observe what is going on, you have the opportunity to gather a rich set of data and ask questions of the people you are studying. Interviews in the field are usually unstructured, as in-depth as possible, and informal. Interviewing is interactive and differs from survey research by means of questionnaires. It is more intensive because of the thoroughness of the questioning. Effective interviewing relies heavily on open-ended questions to develop a comprehensive understanding of respondents' behaviors, attitudes, and actions. **Follow-up questions** allow the researcher to ask for clarification or for additional information. What happens if you question a subject regarding his or her feelings about a new homeless shelter and the subject responds, "I don't like the new homeless shelter"? A follow-up question might be "Why don't you like it?"

CONTENT ANALYSIS

Content analysis is a quantitative research technique applied to the content of magazines, television, and other types of media. Content analysis allows a researcher to study cultural artifacts such as books, films, fashion, textbooks, and billboards to look for trends, patterns, and themes. The content that is analyzed was not created for the purpose of the study; instead, the researcher systematically studies comics, or television shows, or song lyrics, or some other media of communication that she or he is interested in (Reinharz, 1992).

Anderson and Hamilton (2005) were interested in gender-role stereotyping in children's picture books. They believed that even though women's social positions had changed during the last decades, the media had not addressed that social change enough. They selected 200 prominent children's picture books and examined the representations of mothers and fathers in them. They found the following: Fathers were underrepresented in those books; the mothers had much more contact than fathers with the children; and the fathers were portrayed as unaffectionate and uninterested in feeding, carrying babies, and talking to their children. Anderson and Hamilton's research supported their general hypothesis that the media reinforce gender-role stereotyping of parents.

Bissell and Holt (2005) examined three news and sports Web sites covering the 2004 Olympic Games in Athens, Greece. They hypothesized that there is gender bias in sports reporting and in sports photography. Their findings supported their hypothesis. On those Web sites, male athletes received greater print and visual coverage than female athletes.

Content analysis provides interesting information about the way people, ideas, or behaviors are portrayed to the general public.

HISTORICAL RESEARCH

Historical researchers look at past and present articles which can include diaries, graduation records, maps, religious artifacts, books, court transcripts, clothing, and photographs. You might think that historical research is mainly about gathering facts about a significant event, such as a war, to document it. But it is more than just gathering information. **Historical research** is about interpreting information about the past. Without the interpretation, there would be no research.

The historical researcher makes an effort to go back as far as possible to primary sources. A **primary source** is a participant's or an observer's firsthand account of events that she or he experienced or witnessed. If you want to research the life of women in the 1920s in a specific state, primary sources would include newspaper articles, diaries, letters, and photographs. The use of primary sources would ensure the integrity of your study.

Secondary sources provide important information about primary sources and are just as valuable as firsthand accounts. Secondary sources include bystanders who were not involved in an incident but were told about it by someone who was there. One problem with secondary sources is knowing how much to trust a secondary source's understanding of the primary sources.

A researcher who conducts historical research must be concerned about the authenticity and accuracy of the data. **Authenticity** is the genuineness of historical data sources. It isn't always easy to tell if a document is a fake or truly a primary source. Authenticity can be established from indicators such as printing techniques, language, and writing styles. **Accuracy** is a measure of the trustworthiness of a source. Suppose you are investigating teen behavior in the 1940s and one secondary source suggests that teens back then were much more promiscuous than teens today. Would you consider that source trust accurate, given what you know about events during that period?

NARRATIVE

Few mainstream research methods books mention narrative and oral history as ways of collecting data, and in most research methods classes there is little training in or discussion about using them to collect data. According to Reinharz (1992), the reason for this oversight appears to be mainstream social scientists' tendency to find little of value in studies that are subjective.

An **oral history** is a recording or a transcript of a person's own account of events that she or he witnessed or experienced. Oral histories are primary sources.

A **narrative** is an account of events that is told either by the person who experienced them or by someone, such as a researcher, who wants to give a voice to individuals who otherwise might not be heard. Narrative provides a way to listen to the voices of those who are being studied and a way to uncover "hidden histories, [to contest] academic androcentrism, and [to reinstate] the marginalized and dispossessed as makers of their own past" (Miles & Crush, 1993: 84). Narrative research is also used to analyze documents, to reanalyze previously published oral histories from a different perspective, to identify empirical patterns, and to examine groups quantitatively (Reinharz, 1992). According to Reinharz (1992: 133), "The researcher's purpose is to create a written record of the interviewee's life from his/her perspective in his/her own words."

Boetcher Joeres and Laslett (1993) state that personal narratives are a way of studying the problems of women (and men) from all cultures and walks of life. Telling their histories is a way to pay tribute to the people being studied, as you will see in the readings that follow.

REFERENCES

Anderson, D.A., & Hamilton, M. 2005. Gender role stereotyping of parents in children's picture books: The invisible father. *Sex Roles*, 52 (3–4): 145–152.

Bissell, K., & Holt, A. 2005. Who's got game? Gender bias in coverage of the 2004 Olympic Games on the Web. *Conference Papers: International Communication Association*, New York, 1–30.

Boetcher Joeres, R. E., & Laslett, B. 1993. Personal narratives: A selection of recent works. *Signs*, 18(2): 389–392.

Duneier, M. 1992. *Slim's table: Race, respectability, and masculinity*. Chicago: University of Chicago Press.

Miles, M., & Crush, J. 1993. Personal narratives as interactive texts: Collecting and interpreting migrant life-histories. *Professional Geographer*, 45(1): 84–95.

Reinharz, S. 1992. *Feminist methods in social research*. New York: Oxford University Press.

Shibutani, T. 1978. *The derelicts of company K*. Berkeley: University of California Press.

SUGGESTED FILMS

Tearoom Trade (Johnson et al., 1994) (12 min.). Amherst, Ma: Ballerino Productions. An interview with two young gay men who discuss the politics of public restroom cruising, punctuated by film clips from various motion pictures (in particular Jean Genet's *Un chant d'amour*), images of blooming flowers, and scenes from commercial gay male video pornography.

Magical Curing (Mitchell, 1989) (27 min.). Prospect Heights, Il: Waveland Press. Filmed between 1970 and 1972 during fieldwork with the Wape people of West Sepik Province in Papua New Guinea.

Fieldwork (Singer et al., 1990) (52 min.). Princeton, NJ: Films for the Humanities. Sir Walter Baldwin Spencer (1860–1929), along with Frank Gillen, studied Australian aborigines, who up until then had been regarded as a step in the evolutionary ladder between the Neolithic period and the "civilized" Victorian Age. The approach that the two men used to study the aborigines strongly influenced the way other cultures have been studied.

Taking Notes (Craft et al., 2000) (28 min.). New York: Insight Media. This video explains the advantages, processes, and appropriate uses of mind maps, standard outlines, and free-form paragraphs.

Slim Hopes: Advertising and the Obsession with Thinness (Jean Kilbourne, Sut Jhally, 1995) (30 min.). Northampton, Ma: The Foundation. In this film Jean Kilbourne uses examples of over 120 ads from magazines and TV in a content analysis that offers a new way to think about demoralizing and life-threatening eating disorders such as anorexia and bulimia.

Auschwitz: Inside the Nazi State (Linda Hunt, Dominic Sutherland, Martina Balazova, Detlef Siebert, Laurence Rees, Linda Ellerbee, Megan Callaway, 2005) (300 min.). Burbank, CA: Warner Home Video. This film about Auschwitz is the result of three years of research, drawing on the close involvement of world experts, recently discovered documents, and nearly 100 interviews with camp survivors and perpetrators, many of them speaking on the record for the first time.

19

Comparisons Between Thai Adolescent Voices and Thai Adolescent Health Literature

VIPAVEE THONGPRIWAN AND BEVERLY J. MCELMURRY

Thongpriwan and McElmurry believe that because Thai adolescents are hesitant to talk openly to adults, they are avid users of the Internet. In 2002, the faculty of the Boromarajonani College of Nursing in Nopparat Vajira, Thailand, established a Web-board where adolescents could pose health questions that would be answered by nursing faculty and students. A total of 106 questions were selected for content analysis. Physiological development, sexuality, and risky behaviors were common themes as well as concerns about love and dating relationships. As you are reading this article, pay attention to how the authors coded what the adolescents said on the Web in order to come up with their conclusions.

The Internet is a powerful means of communication widely used by adolescents. Research has shown that 66% of secondary school students in Bangkok (capital of Thailand) were exposed to sexually explicit content via the Internet, and 58% of the students used the Internet to view

SOURCE: From Thongpriwan, V., & McElmurry, B. J. 2006. Comparisons between Thai adolescent voices and Thai adolescent health literature. *Journal of School Health*, 76(2): 47–52.

pornography. (1) Cultural factors influencing adolescents vary from country to country and result in different adolescent problem behaviors. Thai adolescents showed more behavioral problems than did American adolescents. These behaviors included shyness, fearfulness, inhibition of talking, and constipation. (2) Use of the Internet as a means to address sensitive topics of concern to Thai adolescents is a reasonable outreach strategy.

In a comparison of South Asian countries, Thai adolescents ranked third in the number of participants and messages posted to an online forum. (3) It is important to understand the cultural context for adolescents as well as their concerns when providing healthcare services that are responsive to their needs. Thai adolescent characteristics, such as use of the Internet and hesitancy to openly communicate with adults, were considered by the faculty of Boromarajonani Nursing College, Nopparat Vajira, Thailand, when they established a webboard in 2002 for students in 5 partnership urban high schools to post their health concern questions. Student nurses enrolled in child and adolescent health courses passed the webboard information to high school students when they gave them health education, and they assumed the primary responsibility for answering these questions. By 2003, over 124 questions and answers were posted.

Adolescent health concerns are beginning to receive increased attention from Thai healthcare researchers. A systematic review of research articles is an important method for gaining an in-depth understanding of a phenomenon. In 1978, there was a research article listed in MEDLINE under the keywords, Thai Adolescents. In 1990, that number grew to 6, in 2000 there were 10, and at this writing (2005) 11 articles are listed on the topic. The purpose of this study is to (a) analyze the webboard content to determine issues of concern to Thai adolescents, (b) identify existing research on the health of Thai adolescents, and (c) compare the expressed concerns of Thai adolescents posted on the webboard with published research on Thai adolescents.

METHODS

Selection and Analysis of Questions

The first author analyzed the webboard content as a means to determine the importance of an issue to Thai adolescents. The content from this webboard was selected for analysis because the webboard was established and directly promoted to urban high school students, while other Thai popular Websites, such as Sanook or Pantip, target general populations. However, it was not certain to verify that the users of this webboard were only Thai adolescents. Therefore, established inclusion criteria for judging whether questions were presumably posted by Thai adolescents were the use of indigenous terms such as Nong, Phii, Pheuuan, Rohng Riian, and Ma Haa Wit Tha Yaa Lai in the questions, discussions, and usernames. Thai language uses gender- and age-specific pronouns. The terms Nong and Phii are kinship terms between younger and older siblings but are normally used when addressing each other in conversations and informal writing. For example, if the username on the webboard was Nong Toon, it was assumed that the person who posted the question was a younger female speaking to university students who answer and discuss the questions on the webboard. The terms Pheuuan, Rohng Riian, and Ma Haa Wit Tha Yaa Lai literally mean "friend," "school," and "college," respectively. In some cases, questions that might not have been posted by an adolescent were included in the analysis because they focused on adolescent health.

For the 124 questions posted on the webboard, the first step in the analytic strategy was to verify that all selected questions met the inclusion criteria. Overall, a total of 106 questions were retained for analysis. Of the 106 questions, a few questions were posted by the same username. Descriptive statistics were used to analyze the webboard content. The first author used a code sheet for examining 1 primary keyword in each question. The primary keyword was judged the direct focus of a question. All questions were written and answered in Thai language. Content validity of coding was determined through discussion with the second author. Then, all primary keywords were systematically categorized for core concepts and ranked from the highest to the lowest frequency. Emerging themes for the content analysis were identified based on the clustering of keywords.

Selection and Analysis of Existing Literature

A systemic review of research articles was conducted to compare the expressed concerns of Thai adolescents with the focus of research. To locate the studies included in this review, the authors searched 4 electronic health publication databases (CINAHL, ERIC, MEDLINE, and PsycINFO) by combining the keywords of Thai, Adolescents, and Health. After performing searches of 4 databases, 28 articles were found. The authors have expanded the searching method by combining the keywords Thai and Health with the keywords Youth, Young Adults, Boys, Girls, College Students, and University Students. Within the combination of the several searching methods, 68 references were found. Studies were selected for inclusion if they met the following criteria: (a) All keywords appeared in the title and/or abstract of the study reports; (b) The participants of the study were Thai early adolescents, adolescents, and young adults, aged 10–25 years; (c) The focus of the study was primarily the health and health-related issues of the participants; and (d) The studies were written in English and retrievable during the period 1992–2004. Studies were excluded if one of the following criteria was present: (a) the studies related to laws and the rights of Thai adolescents, (b) the references were books or book chapters; and (c) the studies were dissertation reports and written in Thai that were difficult to obtain in full texts. Finally, to achieve the third objective of this study, the author compared the results of the webboard content with the research focus identified in the systematic review of Thai adolescent health.

The first analytic strategy for the integrative review was to ascertain that all selected studies met the inclusion criteria. Of the 68 references, the authors eliminated 16 duplicate studies, 12 dissertation reports, and 1 book chapter reference. The authors also eliminated references that were not research based. A final total of 23 studies were retained for review. The analysis of the studies was organized into descriptive information of methodological characteristics and the primary focus of the studies. A code sheet was designed to identify all key information, including publication date, journal types, number of authors, research designs, sampling methods, settings, and the common constructs found in the literature. The literature constructs were categorized according to themes found on the webboard. To enhance the validity of the code sheet, coders discussed all variables to reach consensus concerning data.

RESULTS

The Webboard Content Analysis

The authors tracked the gender of participants who posted questions on the webboard. Gender is identified from the basic use of sentence-final particles for username, politeness, and first-person pronouns such as Phom for males, Dichan or Chan for females, and Nuu for young females. The sentence-final particles for politeness also differ between genders, for example Khrap for males and Kha for females. Examples of usernames, such as PeChia, KidJa, Akom, and Marut, were classified as males; Kavalin, Runi, Ravida, and Onn were classified as females. Of the 106 questions, the authors found that females posted 48 queries and males posted 41 queries. The remaining questions (n = 17) could not be specified by gender. Three themes emerged from the analysis of the webboard content: general health, relationships, and physiological and sexual development.

Theme 1: General Health The majority of the questions posed on the Thai webboard were primarily related to general health and included physical diseases/health problems (20/106), mental health and illness (18/106), reproductive health (10/106), risky behaviors (11/106), and health promotion and maintenance (7/106). The topic of allergies was a physical health question of primary interest, and questions about heart disease ranked second. The other questions included shortsightedness, gastritis, migraine headaches, hemorrhoids, chicken pox, and poor school performance. The mental health and illness questions were primarily about body image, followed respectively by conflicts and satisfaction of friendships, emotional expressions, and the need for emotional support. For example, "I'm so worried about active acne on my face. I like to have clear facial skin." "I want to know how to smooth things over with my friend." "I get angry easily. How do you control it?" "I'm feeling down today. I have nobody to talk to." The questions about the reproductive health were in the area of pregnancy and birth control (7/10) and HIV/STD (3/10). For example, "Do we have birth control pills for men?" "I'd like to know how to do a pregnancy test." "How can we know that we have AIDS?" Behaviors leading to physical violence among male students in high school were the major interest in the risky behavior questions (4/11). The other concerns were smoking (3/11), substance use (2/11), suicide ideation (1/11), and multiple sexual partners (1/11). Health promotion and maintenance was the last interest. Health promotion questions focused on nutrition and exercise in relation to health and healthy bodies. For example, "What kind of exercise makes me taller?" "Do I still have constipation if I eat bananas everyday?"

Theme 2: Relationships The second focus of the questions posted on the webboard was a relationship-based theme. The majority of the questions in this area were about love and dating relationships (25/106) with the remainder pertaining to parenting and parent-child relationships (5/106). Love and dating relationship questions were seen in Thai adolescent discussion about the idealization of dating partners and relationship conflicts. "What is the most favorite type of guys that the girls like?" "I have seen guys mostly like a light skin girl. Why?" "My girlfriend dumped me. What should I do?" Remaining questions related to age at first date, online dating, same-sex relationships, and general dating tips. For example, "Do you trust a guy on cyber?" "I will have a first date soon. I don't know how to impress a girl." "I'm in love with a same sex person. Is it OK?" Questions in the area of parenting were primarily about sex education, and parent-child relationship questions focused on relationship conflicts and communications. For example, "My kid is becoming a teenager girl. How do I talk to her about sex education?" "I want to be a musician but my parents do not agree with me."

Theme 3: Physiological and Sexual Development The third theme that emerged from the webboard content analysis was concern about physiological and sexual development (10/106). This theme included the areas of physiology, menstrual cycle, hormones (6/11), and sexuality (4/11). Sexuality was categorized into the physiological and sexual development because the focus of questions concerned anatomy, physiology, and pathology in relation to sex and sex organs. Results revealed that all questions pertaining to sexuality were posted by males. Examples of the questions asked were "How do I know whether she is a virgin?" "Why do women have pain while having the first sexual intercourse?" "What is a wet dream?" "What is the sex hormone?" Only 1 question posted on the webboard concerned academics: "My grade is poor. I did badly in class. Do you have any suggestions?"

SYSTEMATIC REVIEW OF EXISTING LITERATURE

Methodological Characteristics of the Studies

The methodological characteristics of the systematic review of 23 research articles are shown in Table 1. Approximately 75% of the articles were published since 1998, and 80% of the articles were conducted and written by 2 or more persons. Of the 21 articles with multiple authors, 11 were collaborative efforts of Thai and Western researchers. Publications were categorized within 2 types of

TABLE 1 Methodological Characteristics of Selected Thai Adolescent Health Articles Published from 1992 to 2004 (N = 23)

Methodological Characteristics	Total (%)
Date of publication	
1992–1997	6 (26)
1998–2004	17 (74)
Number of authors	
1	2 (8)
2–5	10 (44)
6–9	11 (48)
Journal type	
Specialty	10 (44)
General	13 (56)
Research designs	
Experimental	1 (4)
Quasi experimental	9 (39)
Nonexperimental/descriptive	9 (39)
Qualitative	3 (13)
Mixed methods	1 (5)
Sampling methods	
Nonprobability	16 (70)
Probability	
Simple random sampling	1 (4)
Cluster random sampling	1 (4)
Proportional quota	5 (22)
Setting	
School	10 (43)
Clinic/laboratory/hospital	5 (22)
Temple	1 (4)
Factory	2 (9)
Community	5 (22)

journals—general and specialty. Specialty refers to a journal focus on a particular disease, care, or treatment such as addictions, AIDS care, contraception, and sexually transmitted disease. Of the 13 articles published in a general journal, 6 (46%) were retrievable from the *Journal of the Medical Association of Thailand*. Only 2 articles were retrievable from nursing journals, one from the United States and the other from Asia. While the available studies (N = 23) reviewed might not be a comprehensive representation of Thai adolescent health research, it is important to note that 5 of the 23 manuscripts presented a repeat of the same project with selected outcomes presented in different journals by different first authors.

Empirical Characteristics of the Studies

As shown in Table 2, the primary focus of the 23 studies was risky behaviors (5/23) and physiological and sexual development (5/23), followed by health promotion and maintenance (3/23). The other foci included reproductive health (2/23), mental health and illness (2/23), physical disease and health problems (2/23), and sexuality (1/23). No study focused on a relationship construct. In the multiple focus studies, researchers measured the sexuality domain in contrast to other categories such as reproductive health and risky behaviors. Topics included assessment of sexual behaviors related to substance abuse, HIV infection, and condom use.

DISCUSSION

It is important to note that Thai health care researchers focused on an area different from the Thai adolescents who expressed concerns about relationships, especially love and dating relationships. Dating is part of the developmental tasks of adolescents and young adults. Thai parents believe that a romantic relationship between adolescents is inappropriate, and the best age to develop a romantic relationship is 18 to 20 years of age. (4) However, empirical evidence has shown that by age 14 or 15, many girls had already had their first boyfriend, and there is a trend for urban young couples to live together without parental approval.

TABLE 2 Comparisons of Questions Posted on the Webboard and Focus of Thai Adolescent Health Articles

	Number (Percent)	
Primary Focus	**Posted Questions, N = 106**	**Selected Article, N = 23**
General health		
Physical diseases/health problems	20 (18)	2 (9)
Mental health/illness	18 (17)	2 (9)
Reproductive health	10 (9)	2 (9)
Risky behaviors	11 (10)	5 (22)
Health promotion and maintenance	7 (7)	3 (13)
Relationships		
Love and dating relationship	25 (24)	0 (0)
Parenting/parent-child relationships	5 (5)	0 (0)
Physiological/sexual development	6 (6)	5 (22)
Physiology/menstrual cycle/hormone	6 (6)	5 (22)
Sexuality	4 (4)	1 (4)
Multiple foci	0 (0)	3 (12)

(5) Furthermore, research has shown that the most stressful problems of Thai adolescents in a slum community included dating relationship problems. (6) Thai adolescents were taught to respect elders and authority figures from an early age, and the distinction between elders (Phy-Yai) and juniors or subordinates (Phu-Noi) is critical. (7) Because Thai parents qualify as Phu-Yai, Thai adolescents might be inclined to avoid discussion of stressful interactions, such as dating relationship problems, with adults. Understandably, the characteristics of Thai adolescents lead to the lack of relationship advice from trusted adults, which in turn encourage them to seek information in cyber communities.

Risky behaviors and sexuality were the main focus of the studies for the growth and physiological development domain and yet were not the main concerns expressed by Thai adolescents. Approximately half of the retrievable studies came from the *Journal of the Medical Association of Thailand,* where a focus on physiology and a disease model could be expected. Thai parents train girls more strictly than boys about the gender roles of sexuality, and sexual expressions such as talking or kissing are not socially acceptable in public spheres. (8) Empirical evidence supported beliefs that Thai young men had open-mind, positive attitudes about sexual feelings compared to Thai young women. (9) Furthermore, research has shown that friends have been the main source for information about sexual education, sex organs, and sexual relationships among Thai adolescents in a slum community. (6) Thai cyber communities still preserve the cultural identity of sexual expressions on the Internet. For example, the most popular Thai webboard (http://www.pantip.com) has rules that do not allow comments, discussions, or pictures with sexually explicit content to be posted, and webmasters reserve the right to eliminate questions on these matters. Even though Thai girls were more active than Thai boys on the webboard, Thai boys predominantly posted the questions about sexuality since Thai girls are supposedly not predisposed to express their sexual concerns.

Thai adolescents expressed their concerns about mental health as a priority, whereas the literature has not emphasized this area. In Thailand, mental health problems are a growing problem. Thai adolescents in secondary schools in the Songkla province, the south of Thailand, had moderate levels of susceptibility and responded that stress was the highest level of emotions. (10) Thai cultural mores promote the concealment of anger, doubt, anxiety, or grief. (7) Cyber communities are therefore a safe place for Thai adolescents to express their feelings. School performance was mentioned in both the webboard and the literature. Six years of primary school education is compulsory in Thailand, and a grading system is used to score student performance. (11) Fowle contends that Thai students do not read enough. (12) Poor school performance was one of the most stressful problems for Thai adolescents in a slum community. (6)

The use of an anonymous username to post questions on the forum is innovative to encourage high school students to be active in expressing their feelings, especially in asking questions about undesirable social behaviors, and it can be widely used in global settings. The analysis of the webboard content is an alternative tool for qualitative approaches. Several limitations should be noted. First, because urban high school students knew that student nurses and faculty had the main responsibility to answer their questions, this might lead to an overall finding bias with a focus on general health questions. In addition, even though the webboard was promoted to 5 urban high schools, it was uncertain whether only students posed the questions. In a future study, allowing high school students to create a login name and password could be beneficial to target adolescent population. Lastly, only 1 webboard was selected for analysis, and urban high school students were presumably the major users. These were the major limitations of the study.

REFERENCES

(1) O-Prasertsawat P, Petchum S. Sexual behavior of secondary school students in Bangkok metropolis. *J Med Assoc Thai.* 2004;87(7):755–759.

(2) Weisz JR, Suwanlert S, Chaiyasit W, Weiss B, Achenbach TM, Eastman K. Behavioral and emotional problems among Thai and American adolescents: parent report for age 12–16. *J Abnorm Psychol.* 1993;102(3):395–403.

(3) Cassell J, Tversky D. The language of online intercultural community formation. *JCMC.* [serial online]. 2005;10:1–31. Available at: http://jcmc.indiana.edu/vol10/issue2/cassell.html. Accessed November 30, 2005.

(4) Poomsuwan P, Yamarat K, Chompootaweep S, Dusitsin N. A study of reproductive health in adolescence of secondary school students and teachers in Bangkok I: general characteristics and knowledge on reproductive health. *Thai J Health Res.* 1990;4(2):85–108.

(5) Cash K, Anasuchatkul B, Busayawong W. Understanding the psychosocial aspects of HIV/AIDS prevention for northern Thailand single adolescent migratory women workers. *Appl Psychol.* 1999;48(2):125–137.

(6) Somrongthong R, Sitthi-amorn C. Existing health needs and related health services for adolescents in a slum community in Thailand. *Int J Adolesc Med Health.* 2000;12(2–3): 191–203.

(7) McCarty CA, Weisz JR, Wanitromanee K. Culture, coping, and context: primary and secondary control among Thai and American youth. *J Child Psychiatry.* 1999;40(5): 809–818.

(8) Taywaditep KJ, Coleman E, Dumronggittigule P. *The International Encyclopedia of Sexuality: Thailand.* Available at: http://www.2.hu-berlin.de/sexology/IES/Thailand.html. Accessed October 23,2005.

(9) Ford NJ, Kittisuksathit S. Destinations unknown: the gender construction and changing nature of the sexual expressions of Thai youth. *AIDS Care.* 1994;6(5):517–531.

(10) Petcharat B. Mental health self-care behaviors of adolescents in secondary schools, Songkla province, Thailand. *J Ment Health Thai.* 2003;11:21–28.

(11) Mo-suwan L, Lebel L, Puetpaiboon A, Junjana C. School performance and weight status of children and young adolescents in a transitional society in Thailand. *Int J Obes Relat Metab Disord.* 1999;23(3): 272–277.

(12) Fowle C. Developing a reading habit with Thai young learners. *English Teacher: Int J.* 2001;5(1):18–26.

REVIEW QUESTIONS

1. Why did the authors use the Internet to collect data for this project?
2. Explain the themes that were used in this project. What were the findings?
3. What kind of methodology did the authors use?

20

Amateur Stripping and Gaming Encounters

Fun in Games or Gaming as Fun?

JULIE ANN HARMS CANNON, THOMAS C. CALHOUN, AND RHONDA FISHER

For this observational study the researchers used Erving Goffman's (1961) theories on games and gaming encounters to investigate the involvement of the audience and the staff at a club's weekly amateur stripping competitions. The study authors also used Goffman's (1959) discussion of "front stage" and "back stage" interactions. Unlike the literature on professional stripping, this study highlights the importance of the meanings that both the audience and the staff members attribute to the entertainment. The researchers used

SOURCE: From Cannon, J. A. Harms, Calhoun, T. C., & Fisher, R. 1998. Amateur stripping and gaming encounters: Fun in games or gaming as fun? *Deviant Behavior: An Interdisciplinary Journal*, 19: 317–337.

fieldwork and interviewing to gather data. As you read this article, think about the ways in which the researchers managed to participate in the setting while at the same time obtaining the information they wanted.

The research on professional stripping has been extensive. Research on amateur stripping, however, is a relatively recent development. Currently, studies of amateur stripping have focused on observational analyses (Calhoun, Cannon, and Fisher 1996), gender differences in male and female amateur stripping competitions occurring within a heterosocial setting [(Calhoun, Fisher, and Cannon, 1998)], and the motivational accounts of amateur strippers (Calhoun, Cannon, and Fisher 1998).

Unlike professional stripping, which can be considered an occupation, amateur strippers voluntarily remove their clothing in public, in hopes of securing limited prize monies and/or other gifts (e.g., compact disks, swimwear, clothing). However, and most important for our research, amateur strippers perform without guarantee of any financial compensation. As it turns out, money is not the primary motivating factor for amateur performers (Calhoun et al. 1998). Amateurs engage in the competition because they find it fun.

Interestingly, most research on professional and amateur stripping has focused on the strippers themselves, yet no studies, to our knowledge, have adequately addressed the interactions between the staff and the audience members. This is understandable given that professional stripping differs dramatically from the amateur stripping competition.

The purpose of the present study is to discuss the ways in which the staff and audience of an amateur stripping club, Kato's, manipulate the dancers to keep the competition fun and profitable. Using the work of Erving Goffman (1961), we discuss the "gaming encounter" of the amateur stripping competition, which necessarily includes the audience and staff. Given that these groups ultimately work together and most determine the "winners" of the amateur stripping competition, it is crucial to understand the implicit rules of the amateur stripping competition. Although the explicit rules are fairly simple in that the participants (a) must not expose buttocks or genitalia (i.e., strippers cannot be nude or wear underwear that is too revealing, such as G-strings), (b) cannot touch audience members, and (c) have three minutes to perform their routine, the implicit rules (discussed in greater detail later) of the amateur stripping competition are much more revealing. Viewing the competition from this perspective de-centers the dancers, allowing us to view them as mere pawns in a more complex competition occurring between the audience and staff. In this study we use Goffman's (1961) work on games and gaming encounters to investigate the sociological imperative of untangling the "front stage" and "back stage" interactions of the amateur stripping competition (Goffman 1959).

The amateur stripping contest offers us the opportunity to assess the applicability of Goffman's (1961) game theoretical perspective to the study of a relatively new social behavior, amateur stripping in a heterosocial setting. We examine how the manipulations of the dancers by the audience and staff constitute a gaming encounter quite different from the interactions described in the literature on professional stripping behavior. As noted previously, amateur stripping involves much more than the game rules of the competition. More specifically, a dancer cannot win the competition without assistance—this is true whether or not she or he follows the explicit or implicit contest rules. To understand the outcome and goal of the competition, it is essential to talk with two key players in this gaming encounter—the staff and audience members.

METHOD

Subjects and Setting

Amateur strip night occurs each Thursday at a bar known as Kato's.[1] Thursday is the main night out for college students in this large midwestern city with a population of just over 200,000. At Kato's, there are two contests taking place. The men's competition begins at approximately 10:30 p.m., and the women's competition begins shortly thereafter.

During our eight-month investigation we were able to observe, on an average evening, 5 male and 5 female participants in the weekly dance contest. Some nights the number of participants in each contest was as high as 11. Only on one occasion did the number of participants fall below 3 per contest.

We interviewed 6 staff members (5 men, 1 woman), 9 audience members (4 men, 5 women), and 19 dance contestants (10 men, 9 women). The racial-ethnic composition of each of the categories was representative of Kato's (primarily White, with some African American, Asian, and Hispanic participants). For the purposes of this research, our findings are based solely on the responses of the audience members and staff.

Anyone who pays the $2 cover charge on entry can participate in the competition. Each contest carries a cash prize—$100 for first, $50 for second, and $25 for third place. The atmosphere at Kato's is quite similar to that of a typical nightclub or disco. The lighting is dim, the music is loud, and the dance floor is the main attraction. Alcohol is available from the beer stand at the main entrance and from bars on the first and second levels. Customers may be seated at tables or booths located on both levels. The dance floor, however, is on the first level, and this is where most customers seek seating. The second floor has a balcony overlooking the dance floor, and those who prefer it, or who cannot find seating on the first floor, sit or stand and look on from above. The activity on the second level is less specifically focused on the contest. It is often difficult to obtain a good view of the competition from this location. Dancing occurs before and immediately following the stripping contests. Finally, customers may play pool at any time during the evening on either floor even while the dance contest is in progress.

The heterosocial setting provides patrons with the sense that they are at a "typical" dance club. Thus, Kato's is not seen as a seedy men's stripper bar or an all-women's night club where stripping is the only focus. The environment is supportive and friendly in that there is a core of patrons who regularly socialize. Most of these patrons arrive at Kato's at least one hour before the contest as seating is limited. During the wait, individuals may dance alone or in groups of two or three; they may even participate in a very large group dance called the Electric Slide. The atmosphere is one that creates the sense that men and women are on an equal playing field (Calhoun et al. 1996).[2]

However, there are actually two separate contests occurring at Kato's on amateur night, with men always performing first and women second. During each contest, the participants dance by themselves or with a partner to the music of their choice. After each contestant has had the opportunity to dance for at least three minutes, the dancers are brought back out on the floor as a group for the final "cheer-off." The announcer for the competition encourages the audience to cheer for their favorite dancers, and those receiving the loudest applause win. The announcer and staff subjectively determine which dancer received the best response.

The atmosphere during the contests is generally speaking quite rowdy or chaotic. As previously noted, the men's competition is always the first of the evening. At this time, women circle the dance floor, often jockeying for the best location. There is some pushing and shoving between the women, but seldom does it result in physical confrontation. As soon as the men's competition is over, there is a very aggressive readjustment of floor space and atmosphere as men advance to the inside perimeter of the dance floor to view the women who will participate in the main event. Because many women do not retreat, the dance floor becomes extremely congested. The security staff repeatedly ask the men to move back. Consequently, the women are pushed farther away from the dance floor. During the observation period, it was not unusual for men to literally crawl over the top of female researchers to gain a strategic spot on the inside of the perimeter. Not surprisingly, fights were common occurrences on amateur night at Kato's (Calhoun et al. 1996).[3]

Data Collection and Techniques

As noted earlier, the data for this study were collected over an eight-month time period from the population of male and female dancers, staff, and audience members observed at Kato's. During the beginning stages of the project, we engaged solely in observational research. It was essential for us to become regulars at Kato's. Although note-taking during the competition was somewhat difficult and often focused a great deal of attention on our work, we took this as an opportunity to let customers and staff know about the project. Additionally, once audience members, staff, and participants realized what we were doing at Kato's they were eager to offer suggestions and observational responses that would prove quite helpful later in our research efforts.

Each of the participants agreed to participate by written consent.[4] The participants were given information regarding the nature of the project during the initial contact and at the time of the interview. Participants were also informed that a copy of the research findings would be available at Kato's on completion of the project.

Because this study was of a potentially sensitive nature, steps were taken to protect the identities of the participants. Participants were notified that real names would not be used in the final report of the research findings, that they could refuse to answer any question, and that the interview could be terminated at any time during the conversation.

Typically, participants were contacted at Kato's after the amateur stripping competition; however, some contacts were made by means of snowball sampling techniques. Interviews were conducted at a variety of locations, including our offices, participants' and investigators' residences, restaurants, and professional and amateur stripping establishments. Additionally, a few interviews were conducted over the telephone. Data were collected by using a semistructured interview format. Although all interviews were directed by the interview schedule, conversations were not limited only to the scheduled questions. Participants were encouraged to discuss all aspects of amateur stripping that had the potential for the development of future research. All interviews were audiotaped and completely transcribed for future analyses.

FINDINGS

Games and Gaming

Again, Goffman (1961) argued that games and gaming encounters involve very different types of interaction strategies. Whereas games involve very formal and explicit rules, gaming encounters are generally more spontaneous and depend on implicit rules or expectations. Amateur stripping, we argue, can be viewed as a game in that it has formally and explicitly stated rules. However, and more important in terms of stripping behavior in general, amateur stripping can also be viewed as a gaming encounter between the audience and staff. It is this dynamic that is the most compelling component of the amateur dance contest.

More specifically, the strippers themselves, although central to the fun, do not control the gaming encounter. Jay, the disc jockey, in discussing this aspect of the competition, stated,

> *In everyday life they [the dancers] can be very good-looking people, very tight if you will, be very strong, and have one percent body fat, and nobody will talk to them because they're just that way. But once they get on stage and people look at them and see how tight they are, then it's a different story because now they're just an object, whereas before they were a person.*

Thus, the dancers themselves may only manipulate the audience through the presentation of self (i.e., having a good body or dressing in sexy or provocative clothing). However, a positive outcome cannot be ensured by an attractive physique or costume. Ultimately, the audience determines the outcome of the competition, and this decision may not be based on appearance or any other component of self-presentation the dancer may use.

In addition to addressing the nature of the stripper's role in the competition, Jay also discussed the importance of creating an alternative reality—a reality in which the body takes precedence over internal attributes or personality. As Goffman (1961) noted, this alternative reality is critical to the maintenance and creation of fun in any gaming encounter. In the world of amateur stripping, individuals become merely objects of desire subject to the evaluation of audience members and staff—evaluations based solely on physical attributes or entertainment value.

Socially Creating and Manipulating Fun

First, it is important to reiterate the primary goals of the amateur stripping competition—fun and profit. Although these goals are unique, ultimately the two are intrinsically linked. Fun for the audience typically equals profit for Kato's. The staff at Kato's work hard to make sure that the audience members are having fun, as this is ultimately more profitable for Kato's. Paul, the manager of Kato's and announcer for the competition, spoke to this directly:

> *Lately, I've been having to cut it [the amateur contest] off at a certain amount of people [performers] because a lot of people, they like to come down for strip night, but they also want to dance too. And so I try to get it over as close or before midnight as possible. . .a lot of people brought it to my attention that they are bothered by the fact that they don't get a chance to dance.*

This balance between the contest and the socializing is very important at Kato's. Although the competition itself is generally considered to be central to the creation of a fun experience, people also come to Kato's to dance and socialize.

Ultimately, the entire staff works to get the customers excited about the competition. However, the bulk of this responsibility falls on the manager's shoulders as he is ultimately accountable for success of Kato's. Paul had this to say in reference to the competition and the creation of fun and profit at Kato's:

> *I would say that it's more important to get a lot of good-looking guys out there dancing and get the girls all fired up because hopefully it will carry over to Friday and Saturday night. They'll say, boy, I was down there Thursday night and I had a really good time. . .Let's go check it out Friday and Saturday night and see what's going on.*

It is essential that the fun of amateur night be extended to the weekend at Kato's. The amateur contest is a way to bring patrons to the establishment on weekends and thus to ensure the club's profitability.

Interestingly, as the previous quotation suggests, men and women do not necessarily have the same definition of fun. Ron, an audience member, stated,

> *I think women tend to see it [the men's competition] more as a fun thing. This is the stereotype of even watching it [male stripping] on TV and stuff where women will be like, "This is fun." And, it's more of a social fun event. But the men will go there themselves to get a jolly, just to play out the fantasies in their heads. But I think women do it in a big group of friends.*

More specifically, women attend the amateur contest as form of entertainment and social solidarity with other women, whereas men attend to achieve a type of sexual stimulation or gratification.

However, the disc jockey also takes responsibility for pumping up the crowd. Jay described his work:

> *Well, basically you welcome people down. You don't usually do a lot of speaking over the mike, but when we do it's usually for a drink special. While you're doing a drink special, you're saying "Hey, you know [Kato's] Thursday night, it's amateur strip night. You know why you're here.". . .I think in the future, as I'm there a little longer, I'm sure it's gonna turn into me pumping the crowd up a little more. I think we're [the staff] going to be having more talks about that because I think it's a good thing.*

Again, fun equals profit. While the customers wait for the contest to begin, Jay keeps them entertained and works to build enthusiasm about the competition. Simultaneously, he encourages the audience members to buy drinks. Alcohol is used for profit in two ways. First, the more drinks the customers buy, the more money the bar makes. Second, the more people drink, the more likely they are to lose their inhibitions and strip—this is critical in terms of the spontaneity of the competition and the creation of fun.

Implicit Rules of the Amateur Contest

As noted above, anyone who pays the $2 cover charge to attend the amateur contest is eligible to participate as a performer. Yet, there are also implicit rules about men's and women's performances and about who is actually supposed to perform at Kato's.

Audience members have very different views about what makes a winning male-female performance. Ron, in speaking about the performances, stated,

> *I think you have to be self-confident but not arrogant. Like, I think it's always good to have some kind of gimmick. . .don't be like a plain Jane dude. [You should] always [be] working on a little dance. Have a routine to catch people's attention.*

However, the requirements are very different for women, according to Ron: "I think it is important to look timid, [yet] look confident. [You should] look like you don't do this all the time." Jay (the disc jockey) offered a similar opinion:

> I found that women that almost have a playful, midwestern kind of look to them have done well. You know whether they're professional or not, but they kind of come out there and they just kind of tease the audience. And they're good at it. However, the bottom line seems to be the same for both men and women.

He continued by saying, "I guess. . .the main thing is that whether you've stripped [or] danced before, if you can get out in front of people, and you're comfortable with your body, you [are] probably going to do pretty well."

There are definite beauty standards at Kato's. However, Paul, the manager of Kato's, described the variety of women who perform during the dance competition:

> *I like the fact that we have a lot of different types of girls. Sure, in a perfect world they'd all look like supermodels. But we get a lot of different types of people. I'm sure a lot of guys like heavier girls. A lot of guys like perfect girls. A lot of guys like flat-chested girls. . .I have no problem with anybody dancing.*

Although Paul extolled the virtues of diversity in the female form, he acknowledged the ideal type of female performer.

Interestingly, those who participate in the competition should be "natural" beauties. Kim, a regular audience member, addressed the issue of dancers with breast implants: "I don't think it's fair to the other girls. Because some of the girls, they're good and they [the audience] usually are not used to the ones that aren't professionals." These sentiments call into question the nature of the implicit rules at Kato's. Although technically anyone who follows the explicit rules regarding time limits, degree of nudity, and physical contact can participate in the competition, compliance with these rules is not enough to ensure success. The participants must be aware of the implicit rules, or "beauty codes" (Calhoun et al. 1996), if they are to win the competition. However, as noted previously, these rules are gender based.

The Rules Change for Fun's Sake

Although there are explicit rules as well as implicit rules operating during the amateur contest, the rules are almost always subject to change (except for those that are legally sanctioned, such as the degree of nudity and the prohibition against dancers and audience members touching one another). Jay (the disc jockey) spoke of the time limit per performance: "Well, that three-minute rule is basically just a minimum. We say 'We're going to let you out there for at least three minutes.' Most people are out there for about three and one-half."

During our observations of the amateur stripping contest, we repeatedly viewed extended performances. When the audience is having fun, it is profitable for Kato's to allow the dancers to continue past the three-minute time limit.

Additionally, the staff at Kato's is known to be inflexible regarding the nudity and contact restrictions. However, although there appears to be a show of enforcement by the security staff, many violations of these explicit rules occur while the staff is preoccupied with another facet of the contest. Specifically, dancers have been known to reveal more clothing than explicitly allowed (i.e., to have removed underwear or worn G-strings) and also to touch audience members. In fact, breaking the explicit nudity and contact rules is often an implicit rule of the competition. Audience members encourage this type of activity and are quite enthusiastic when it occurs. Again, controlled spontaneity or fun takes precedence over the explicit rules. The audience has more fun if some rules are violated, thus potentially creating a more profitable evening for Kato's.

Spontaneous Involvement

As noted previously, spontaneity is essential to fulfilling the goals of amateur strip night (i.e., fun for the audience and profit for the staff). The audience and staff must work together to facilitate the desired effects or outcomes—the transformation of the mundane or everyday into a fun and profitable evening. This involves the complete involvement of these two groups. However, in amateur stripping, spontaneity is actually socially created and subject to manipulation.

Again, it is important to note that the game of amateur stripping is very different than stripping as a gaming encounter. People have definite expectations about Thursday night at Kato's that do not actually correspond to the rules of the competition. Paul (the manager) discusses the atmosphere on amateur strip night versus an off-night at Kato's:

> *Thursday nights about 10:15 or so, people start gathering around the dance floor. Thursday nights they're geared for kind of one thing, the strip contest. . . You can feel it in the air. You feel the difference in the air down here. It's a lot more tense down here on Thursday nights. I don't mean tense in a physical way, like there's going to be a fight breaking out or anything, but people are expecting something on Thursday nights. They are expecting to see the girl of their dreams out there dancing. Girls are expecting to see the hunk from the Playgirl calendar out there dancing. There's a lot of expectations, I guess, on Thursday nights. Fridays and Saturdays there are no expectations. They want to come down, have drinks, have some fun, and dance.*

Part of the fun of the amateur night is the chaos, as Paul describes it. The audience seems to enjoy that element of uncertainty and spontaneity.

Tension, like spontaneity, is also an essential dynamic of the amateur stripping competition. The tension is used to manipulate the dancers and to stimulate the audience. As Goffman (1961) noted, tension in gaming encounters results from the interaction of the formal and implicit rules or the mixing of the real world with the socially created fantasy of the gaming encounter. It is precisely the stress of these interactions that sets the tone for the amateur stripping contest and contributes to the fun and profit.

In her discussion of the order of the competition, Sonya speaks directly to the tension component of the amateur gaming encounter: "They're building excitement, like a warm-up band before a concert."

Incidents, Integrations, and Flooding Out

It is a constant effort and necessity to maintain the socially constructed world of the gaming encounter. "The dynamics of an encounter [are] tied to the functioning of the boundary-maintaining mechanisms that cut the encounter off selectively from wider worlds" (Goffman 1961: 66). This is particularly true of the amateur stripping competition. The audience members and staff must constantly work together to keep incidents from interrupting the flow of events. However, this is not always possible or desired, as discussed below.

Amy, a waitress at Kato's, described the following incident in which a dancer violated one of the implicit appearance rules of the competition:

> *A month or two ago a real old lady stripped. I think she was about 50 or so, and the whole crowd just . . . I never sell beer usually too much during the strippers because everyone just doesn't want to lose their place. And I've had tons of people come up to me and they're like, "This is disgusting."*

This incident was disturbing to the patrons of Kato's, but the disruption was useful in terms of profit—Amy was able to sell more beer. Also, the woman provided the audience with an opportunity to articulate the implicit rules—knowing who is not supposed to strip also provides individuals with information about who should participate in the competition.

Another incident occurred when a seemingly intoxicated woman proceeded to take her turn in the competition. She was clearly in a world of her own, which violated the expectations of a shared experience between audience members and dancers. Further, she attempted to remove more clothing than was legal. Normally, this behavior would not disturb the audience members, but the woman did not meet the beauty norms at Kato's. In this way she broke the interaction frame, and the bouncers were forced to remove her from the floor.

Again, as Goffman (1961) noted, it is critical to integrate these incidents into the proper frame of the encounter in some way. The most obvious way is to remove the participant and explain the regulations of the competition. However, it is also possible for the announcer to make a joke about the performance and allude to the "proper participant."

DISCUSSION AND CONCLUSIONS

This study sought to assess the importance of Goffman's (1961) concepts of the game and gaming encounters in an investigation of amateur stripping competitions. We found that although technically amateur stripping can be viewed as a game with explicit rules, it is better viewed as a gaming encounter whereby both explicit and implicit rules operate simultaneously. Additionally, we discovered that the staff and audience members are influential in determining the outcome of the competition. Although explicit sanctions can be applied to norm violators, the actual application of sanctions depends on the mood of the audience and the needs of the staff (i.e., fun and profit).

The implicit rules are determined primarily by the audience and staff, with the dancers being manipulated for fun and profit. We do not argue that the dancers cannot manipulate both the audience and staff, for this is indeed the case. However, we argue that this is not the primary reason for the event. Specifically, the event exists to meet the needs of the management. This translates into profit for the management, fun for the audience, and potential monetary gain for the participants.

It is up to the audience and staff to keep the environment spontaneous and fun. This is accomplished through the implementation of beauty codes, allowing specific rules to be violated by some participants in varying degrees, and ensuring that the fantasy of amateur strip night is maintained. We also found that some violations by the dancers could not be integrated into the interaction frame, thus creating a break in the fantasy-constructed reality—which is critical to attracting a large crowd weekly.

The significance of this study is that amateur stripping, we argue, is a demonstration of the larger social norms governing interactions. As with most encounters, there are norms, implicit and explicit, that dictate the interactional patterns between the participants. Amateur stripping also illustrates the impact that rules have on framing situations and, more important, on dictating the nature of the interaction. Fun is not an inherent component of stripping behavior. Rather, in the case of amateur stripping, fun is socially constructed from week to week and from participant to participant on the basis of the needs of the management and the mood of the audience.

Although this study highlights the complex interactions of audience and staff at an amateur stripping competition, additional research is needed.

In the future, research should consider the racial and ethnic composition of those who participate in this behavior. Given the diversity of audience members and participants at Kato's and other urban establishments, it is likely that key differences may be identified in terms of identity formation, beauty standards, motivations, and so on. In addition, class may be a significant factor and should be investigated. Although Kato's is situated in a college town, the patrons and participants may be quite different from the college population in terms of socioeconomic status. For this reason, attention must be given to the regional characteristics of the community and patrons. Finally, given the nature of this behavior and the methods currently used to study it, it would be beneficial to assess the impact of researcher as insider versus researcher as outsider. For example, the researcher as insider might become privy to additional knowledge about the participants and their involvement in other types of behavior, including those that are clearly deviant.

NOTES

1. All names referred to in this work are pseudonyms.
2. This information is abstracted from the article cited.
3. See previous footnote.
4. One of the male participants agreed to participate over the phone. His verbal consent was audiotaped at this time. Although we sent him a consent form, it was never returned.

REFERENCES

Calhoun, Thomas C., Julie Ann Harms Cannon, and Rhonda Fisher. 1996. "Amateur Stripping: Sexualized Entertainment and Gendered Fun." *Sociological Focus* 29(2): 155–166.

———. 1998. "Explorations in Youth Culture and Amateur Stripping: What We Know and What We Don't." Pp. 302–326 in *Youth, Youth Culture and Identity*, edited by Jon Epstein. Malden, MA: Blackwell Publishers.

Calhoun, Thomas C., Fisher, Rhonda, and Julie Ann Harms Cannon. 1998. "The Case of Amateur Stripping: Sex Codes and Egalitarianism in a Heterosocial Setting." Pp. 47–62 in *The American Ritual Tapestry: Social Rules and Cultural Meanings*, edited by Mary Jo Deegan. Westport, CT: Greenwood Press.

Goffman, Erving. 1959. *The Presentation of the Self in Everyday Life*. New York: Anchor Books.

———. 1961. *Encounters: Two Studies in the Sociology of Interaction*. Indianapolis: Bobbs-Merrill.

REVIEW QUESTIONS

1. Earlier in this book we pointed out that data without theory and theory without data are often empty and without purpose. What theory was used in this project? How did this particular theory drive the research question?
2. What did the researchers need to do so they could conduct fieldwork in a strip club? How did they manage to blend in?
3. If this study had been conducted using the conflict theory, what types of research questions could have been asked?

21

Thinking Through the Heart

ANN GOETTING

As you read this article, think about how Ann Goetting uses narrative to find out about women who have successfully left abusive relationships. Because she listened to the women's stories, Goetting was able to describe some very clear symptoms of and patterns that take place in abusive relationships. It isn't enough simply to listen to the voices of respondents. It is important to learn from their experiences.

THE PROJECT IN DEVELOPMENT

This book is the product of an idea long in incubation, with antecedents reaching back into my youth. My father's unpredictable episodes of rage followed by fits of hollow kindness, in the daily context of condescension, trepidation, and humiliation, introduced me to battering before it had a name. No one in the household was spared my father's wrath, which continues to affect every member of my family today. The hardest part, as I see it now, was my inability to understand what it was all about. It was that ignorance that victimized me and rendered me powerless all those years. Later, as a family studies scholar and criminologist, I was drawn to the notion of studying and teaching about family violence. The knowledge and insights gained by that work provided the framework necessary to free me, to a great extent at least, from that childhood legacy of battering. It is that sense of liberation that inspired this book. Battering thrives on ignorance and is snuffed out by understanding. I want everyone to understand battering because I want it to stop.

The project called for biographical accounts of American women that described the battering process from inception through exit. Diversity in terms of ethnicity, age, social class, religion, geographical region, sexual orientation, and general experience was a critical consideration. There was no intention to create a representative sample, because the goal was to demonstrate patterns and provide instructive cases rather than to generalize. Armed with this vision, I set out to find the women.

A nationwide call for participants to abuse shelters and other organizations and agencies sympathetic to battered women elicited a substantial response. Additionally, a personal search concentrating on my university and community yielded several participants. I first gathered basic background information from each woman and then shifted my attention to her battering and exit processes. My work was theory driven, always focused on the patriarchy and established patterns of battering and getting out. The texts I have created to tell women's stories combine information supplied by them—from autobiographical essays, diaries, newspaper and magazine articles, letters, and interviews—with my own interpretations. Their stories

SOURCE: From Goetting, A. 1999. Thinking through the heart. In *Getting out: Life stories of women who left abusive men*. New York: Columbia University Press, pp. 1–23.

are filtered through me. I met with all except two of the participants, Lucretia and Raquelle, and in all cases I was invited into their homes. I wrote a story only when I was certain that I "knew" the woman well enough.

Early on, as I approached the third or fourth essay, the original concept of the project underwent dramatic revision. It was when I was preparing Colette's story that I knew for certain that I could not sterilize women's biographies by excluding critical dimensions that may at first blush seem unrelated to the subject at hand—battering.

I had read and heard Colette's heart-rending account of her treacherous childhood that culminated in the blood-drenched suicide of her clinically depressed mother. My image of Colette in the telling is frozen in time: visiting her on a cool summer afternoon in shaded, open sunroom, her clear-eyed candor and her serene style. A small framed black-and-white photo of her fashionably suited mother as a young Frenchwoman rested on a shelf nearby. Then, as Colette concluded the story of her own battering, I heard the tale of the death by car accident of Colette's only child at age six—with whom Colette had endured and escaped years of abuse. There were more framed photos on display to relay the significance of Michelle's life and death. Here was a woman's life story whose integrity should not be violated in the name of research on battering (Riessman, 1993: 4). It is only in the context of Colette's story of her youth that her account of her battering rings true.

At that point the book in progress became a collection of life stories of women who had endured and safely left abusive men—not just stories of abuse and escape. The stories are more honest this way. They are stories packed full of women's issues and human issues: contextual knowledge at its best. The thematic link is the abuse and the getting out. I revised the biographies completed before Colette's, then went on to construct the rest contextually. So now the book teaches about childhood, good and bad alike; eating disorders; homelessness; clinical depression culminating in suicide; alcoholism; sibling relationships; baby smuggling; drug trafficking; homosexuality; motherhood; and adult child-parent issues. And it provides glimpses into Puerto Rico; Israel; Star Lake, New York; Wind River Indian Reservation; professional baseball; a Michigan outlaw militia; and the dreadful personal toll exacted by the United States involvement in the Vietnam War. When placed in context, issues surrounding battering seem neutralized and perhaps even dwarfed by the other life processes and events experienced by some of these women.

The construction of the biographies progressed at a brisk and even pace and without a hitch for one year beginning in February 1995. Each essay was a joint endeavor for me and the storyteller. I sent her my first draft, and from there we revised and refined together until we were both satisfied with the product. The women were allowed choice in revealing or suppressing first names and other identifying features. Some participated in the project as a gesture of liberation—a "coming out" of sorts. Their disclosure of their identity symbolizes their pride in having escaped a life of fear and oppression. Other women chose pseudonyms and withheld other specifics in order to protect family members. Using first names only, and leaving the real undifferentiated from the contrived, was my decision.

The stories are uneven. Some are eloquently expressed and nuanced exposés, while others are stilted by comparison. The variation in tone and texture reflects the uniqueness of the teller. Some women found comfort and even elation in the reflection process from their now safe spot, while others could barely tolerate remembering. Additionally, some women were basically more verbally expressive, articulate, and uninhibited than others. These variations produced detectable differences in the biographies, making an important contribution to understanding women's diversity. That women's lives cannot be packaged in some standard way is clearly evidenced by this collection. Nevertheless, every story is worth the telling, and each makes a unique contribution to the product of our combined efforts: a better understanding of battering and getting out and their consequences.

Ethnic diversity is an important part of this collection of life stories of battered women. A small but telling research literature apprises us of the enhanced problems that battered women of color face because of their minority status (Hendrickson, 1996; Mousseau & Artichoker, 1993; Bachman, 1992; White, 1995; Zambrano, 1985, 1994; Moss et al., 1997). Six women in this book—Sharon, Lucretia, Freda, Rebecca, Annette, and Blanca—are women of color, and their life experiences, when compared with those of White women, reflect reported differences between minority and White battered women. Themes of racism as well as sexism permeate the stories of these six women in predictable ways.

I have no war stories related to the production of this book; without exception, the women were generous, gracious, and patient teachers. This feminist project has made my journey to feminism well worth the trouble (see my autobiographical essay: Goetting, 1996).

THE TRUTH ABOUT BIOGRAPHY

Concerns with accuracy have surrounded the literary form of narrative or lifetelling, including biography, for a couple of decades (Goetting, 1995). Do people tell the truth about their lives? The answer to that question is succinctly articulated by the legendary Cree hunter who traveled to Montreal to offer court testimony regarding the effect of the new James Bay hydroelectric scheme on his hunting lands. He would describe the way of life of his people. But when administered the oath he hesitated: "I'm not sure I can tell the truth. . .I can tell only what I know" (Clifford, 1986: 8). We tell the truth pretty much as we know it, but that may not be someone else's "truth."

Some scholars of narrative speak of lifetelling as fiction. They claim that memory is faulty and leaves but a quiver of recognition of times past, which we then adjust into story. In that sense biography is "something made," "something fashioned"—the original meaning of fiction. The claim is not that life stories are false but rather that they are interpretations constructed around a string of imperfect recollections. These scholars point out additionally that lived experience is mediated by language, which is also imperfect. Often there are not words to accurately describe what has happened to us. Lived experience is further mediated by the context in which it is told. The version offered by Colette that day in her sunroom may be different in tone and texture from the version she told her current husband during their courtship years earlier. Biography, as a special form of narrative, further "distorts" the lived experience by adding the biographer's layer of interpretation to those of the storyteller. The perspective of the biographer can add a critical dimension to a story. My biography of Colette is surely different than would be, for example, O. J. Simpson's version of that same life. In sum, biography is not simply a "true" representation of an objective "reality"; instead, memory, language, the context of the telling, and the interpretations of both storyteller and biographer combine to create a particular view of reality. The counterpoint to lifetelling as fiction rather than truth is that it is truth if truth is properly defined. It is argued that in spite of inherent distortions, lifetelling does reveal truths. These truths do not disclose the past "as it actually was" by some arbitrary standard of objectivity; instead, they are reconstructed and, therefore, superior truths. We continue through our lifetime to interpret old events from new positions. Each time, we tell the story differently, and with each telling the story matures and gains depth. My story as a ten year-old of my father's rages was different than the story I tell today of the same times and incidents. From this perspective on truth, biography is better than having been there because it adds the element of seasoned consciousness to the original experience. In the words of Georges Gusdorf (1980):

> In the immediate moment, the agitation of things ordinarily surrounds me too much for me to be able to see it in its entirety. Memory gives me a certain remove and allows me to take into consideration all the ins and outs of

> the matter, its context in time and space. As an aerial view sometimes reveals to an archaeologist the direction of a road or a fortification or a map of a city invisible to someone on the ground, so the reconstruction in spirit of my destiny bares the major lines that I have failed to notice, the demands of the deepest values I hold that, without my being clearly aware or it, have determined my most decisive choices. (38)

Our real concern with biography is not whether it is "truth" or "fiction" but what it can teach us about human feelings, motives, and thought processes. For example, in this book we are far less interested in knowing who hit or slapped whom how often than we are with knowing how a woman feels about being hurt by her partner, how she reacts and why. Biography does not supply us with verifiable truths; rather, it offers a special kind of impassioned knowing. A final note on truth as it applies specifically to these biographies: certainly a curiosity about "his side of the story" is reasonable. Would these women's abusers tell the same stories about the relationship? Would they minimize or deny what they are accused of in these pages? First, it must be emphasized that we live in a gendered universe, where men and women are considered to be two distinct types of people and are treated accordingly. In that sense men and women occupy two different worlds and, in so doing, define and understand little, if anything, similarly (Tannen, 1990; Szinovacz, 1983). It is no surprise, therefore, that when researchers separate couples and inquire about shared activities and the dynamics of their relationship, those couples seem to describe two different relationships altogether (Szinovacz, 1983). It is that phenomenon that inspired sociologist Jessie Bernard (1972) to title her now classic essay of American marriage "Marriage: Hers and His." Battering is no exception to the rule. Two sound studies of couples in relationships where the woman is physically abused (one, from the United States [Szinovacz, 1983]; the other, Scottish [Dobash et al., 1998]) inform us that women report more types of violent victimization and in greater frequency than their male partners admit to. Furthermore, more women than men report injuries from the abuse and, again, women report higher frequencies. All in all, women perceive more violence in these relationships and tend to judge it as more serious. I suspect that the abusers of the women in this collection would tell very different stories and that they would minimize and deny the abuse of which they are accused.

WINNING WITH BIOGRAPHY

Biography enjoys popularity among readers of every stripe. It offers privileged access to understandings of the human condition in all of its complexity. The life of the emotions, the life of the mind, the physical life, and the social life are told in context to produce a comprehensive whole. It is all there within easy grasp: the obscurities, the reasonings, the motivations, the passions. German sociologist Wilhelm Dilthey touts biography as the highest and most instructive form of knowledge about humanity (translated by Kohli, 1981). From that perspective the best way to truly understand a category of human experience, such as escape from battering, would be through examination of a diverse assemblage of biographies focusing on that experience—in this case life stories of battered women who got out.

In addition to providing a superior method of understanding the human experience, reading biography helps us make sense of our own lives by connecting us with others. It activates us to construct a benchmark against which to compare our own existence, thereby prompting us to rethink that existence. We continually test our own realities against such stories and modify our perceptions accordingly. In that way biography transforms us. In the process of this personal transformation, this reconceptualization of our life, we typically are comforted and sometimes elated by the newfound connections that inspired the journey. Finding people in situations comparable to ours who have discovered similar truths fortifies us with consensus and affirmation. We are no longer alone and vulnerable. Jane Tompkins (1989) tells it best:

> I love writers who write about their own experience. I feel I'm being nourished by them, and that I'm being allowed to enter into a personal relationship with them, that I can match my own experiences with theirs, feel cousin to them, and say, yes, that's how it is. (170)

By delivering sensitive insight and inspiring a reinterpretation of life through human connectedness, reading biography can forge informed life change. The sociologist C. Wright Mills's promise of "the sociological imagination" (1959) instructs us that insights into social context can supply the resources necessary not only to understand one's own life but to at least partially control its outcomes. Similarly, social theorist Max Weber insists that humans can succeed only if "each finds. . .the demon who holds the fibers of his very life" (Gerth & Mills, 1946: 156).

It becomes apparent that reading biography can be personally rewarding and a joy to experience. It has the potential to nourish and fortify us and to propel us into a constructive path of personal renewal. Biography represents reason informed by passion, arguably the most powerful form of knowledge production. Robbie Pfeufer Kahn (1995) refers to that process as "thinking through the heart." The women whose stories grace these pages have generously and bravely embraced this process to one point of completion, many specifically in hopes that their stories would find, inform, soothe, and intelligently activate battered women. This book personifies "thinking through the heart."

REFERENCES

Bachman, R. 1992. *Death and violence on the reservation: Homicide, family violence, and suicide in American Indian populations*. New York: Auburn House.

Bernard, Jessie. 1972. Marriage: Hers and his. *Ms*. December: 46–49, 110–111.

Clifford, James. 1986. Introduction: Partial truths. Pp. 1–26 in *Writing culture: The poetics and politics of ethnography*, James Clifford & George E. Marcus (eds.). Berkeley: University of California Press.

Dobash, Russell, Rebecca Dobash, Kate Cavanagh, & Ruth Lewis. 1998. Separate and intersecting realities: A comparison of men's and women's accounts of violence against women. *Violence Against Women* 4(4): 382–414.

Gerth, H. H., & C. Wright Mills (eds. & trans.). 1946. *From Max Weber: Essays in sociology*. New York: Oxford University Press.

Goetting, Ann. 1995. Fictions of the self. Pp. 3–19 in *Individual voices, collective visions: Fifty years of women in sociology*, Ann Goetting & Sarah Fenstermaker (eds.). Philadelphia: Temple University Press.

Goetting, Ann. 1996. Ecofeminism found: One woman's journal to liberation. Pp. 174–179 in *Private sociology: Unsparing reflections, uncommon gains*, Arthur B. Shostak (ed.). Dix Hills, NY: General Hall.

Gusdorf, Georges. 1980. Conditions and limits of autobiography. Pp. 28–48 in *Autobiography: Essays theoretical and critical*, James Olney (ed. & trans.). Princeton, NJ: Princeton University Press.

Hendrickson, Roberta M. 1996. Victims and survivors: Native American Womenwriters, violence against women, and child abuse. *Studies in American Indian Literatures* 8(1): 13–24.

Kohli, Martin. 1981. Biography: Account, text, method. Pp. 61–75 in *Biography and society: The life history approach in the social sciences*, Daniel Bertaux (ed.). Thousand Oaks, CA: Sage.

Mills, C. Wright. 1959. *The sociological imagination*. New York: Oxford University Press.

Moss, Vicki A., Carol Rogers Pitua, Jacquelyn C. Campbell, & Lois Halstead. 1997. The experience of terminating an abusive relationship from an

Anglo and African American perspective: A qualitative descriptive study. *Issues in Mental Health Nursing* 18: 433–454.

Mousseau, Marlin, & Karen Artichoker. 1993. *Domestic violence is not Lakota/Dakota tradition*. Sisseton, SD: South Dakota Coalition Against Domestic Violence and Sexual Assault. To obtain free copy, call 1-800-572-9196, or write P.O. Box 141, Pierre, SD 57501.

Pfeufer Kahn, Robbie. 1995. *Interviewing the midwife's apprentice: The question of voice in writing a cultural ethnography of patriarchy*. Paper presented at annual meetings of the American Sociological Association, Washington, DC.

Riessman, Catherine Kohler. 1993. *Narrative analysis*. Thousand Oaks, CA: Sage.

Szinovacz, Maximiliane E. 1983. Using couple data as a methodological tool: The case of marital violence. *Journal of Marriage and the Family 45*: 633–644.

Tannen, Deborah. 1990. *You just don't understand*. New York: William Morrow.

Tompkins, Jane. 1989. Me and my shadow. Pp. 169–178 in *Gender and theory: Dialogues on feminist criticism*, Linda Kauffman (ed.). Oxford: Basil Blackwell.

White, Evelyn C. 1995. *Chain chain change: For Black women in abusive relationships*. Seattle: Seal.

Zambrano, Myra M. 1985. *Mejor sola que mal acompanada: Para Ia Mujer Golpeada/For the Latina in an abusive relationship*. Seattle: Seal.

———. 1994. *No Mas! Guia Para la Mujer Colpeada*. Seattle: Seal.

REVIEW QUESTIONS

1. How did the researcher gather her respondents?
2. Why does Goetting believe that narratives are "more honest" than surveys?
3. What is the "truth about biography"?

10

Existing Data and Evaluation Research: Let's Find Out What Works

In the previous chapters, you learned about the various ways to collect data and conduct social science research. In this chapter, you will learn about using data collected not by youself but by someone, and you will learn about evaluating a research program or study.

EXISTING STATISTICS

Many large organizations gather data for policy decisions or as a public service. You can use **existing statistics** as data for any topic you are interested in. Suppose you are writing a report about the positive aspects of private education. You may look for statistics gathered by the U.S. Department of Education and find differences in the SAT and ACT scores of private and public high school students. For many research projects, it would not make sense for you to collect data from scratch. Using existing data can save you time, money, and energy. Also, existing statistics give you a place to begin figuring out what you will be studying.

Using existing statistics is most appropriate when you are interested in testing a hypothesis that involves variables that can be found in reports by official agencies such as those that address economical, political, and social conditions. The amount of data available for you to look at can be mind-boggling. Much of it is free and can be found either on the Internet or in your library. Here are some sources of **primary existing data:**

- *Statistical Abstract of the United States,* first published in 1878 and published annually since then, is a compilation of official reports produced by more than 200 U.S. government and private agencies. Many other national governments publish similar reports. For instance, Canada produces the *Canada Yearbook* and New Zealand publishes *New Zealand Official Yearbook.*
- *Standard and Poor's Register of Corporations, Directors and Executives* lists more than 37,000 U.S. and Canadian companies and provides information on the corporations, their products, officers, and sales figures.
- *Dictionary of American Biography* was first published in 1928 and updates information regularly. It details the careers, travels, and publications of prominent Americans.
- *Vital Statistics on American Politics* provides information about the campaign spending practices of every candidate for Congress. It describes legislators' voting records, their ratings by various political organizations, and voter registration regulations by state.
- *The General Social Survey,* conducted by the National Opinion Research Center at the University of Chicago, is an ongoing study based on personal interviews of U.S. households. Sample sizes for this project have been around 1,500 for each of the 19 years of the survey. Each interview lasts about 90 minutes. Data from *The General Social Survey* would be helpful if your project is in any of these areas: economics, education, epidemiology and public health, health services, statistics and methodology, and substance abuse, mental health, and disability.

Let's say you want to compare the rates of AIDS in various countries. To begin, you go to the U.S. Census Bureau Web site, at http://www.census.gov. Using the subject A–Z listing, you look under A, find the section called AIDS, then AIDS Surveillance, where you can find the AIDS Surveillance Data Base. From here, you can find AIDS prevalence rates in various countries and compare them (U.S. Census Bureau, 2003). You then can incorporate the U.S. **census data** into own your research project and draw your own conclusions about the differences you find.

When existing statistics come from a **secondary source**, such as a previously published survey, you can reanalyze the data. Your main focus when using secondary data is on the analysis rather than on data collection. This type of data is used so frequently because it is inexpensive, it permits comparisons between individuals, groups, and nations, and it allows for replication. It also provides opportunities for new research questions to be asked that were not asked in the previous study.

EVALUATION

Evaluation research is widely used to measure the effectiveness of a program, policy, or a specific way of doing something. Evaluating is common; we all do it. Think back to the last test you took. After the test was completed, did you think, "I should have studied more," or "Multiple choice tests really make me nervous," or "I think I passed, but just barely"? You were evaluating yourself. The goal of evaluation research is to evaluate the effectiveness of various types of social programs to measure whether or not they are working.

Social programs tend to address social problems such as homelessness, drinking and driving, and HIV/AIDS prevention. Because public policy and funding for social programs tend to depend on the need for the program and its success in helping users of the program, it is important to be able to evaluate social programs. Many federal granting agencies require social agencies to have an evaluative researcher involved in a project from the outset to make sure that the effectiveness of the program is well documented.

Suppose you are interested in reducing the rate of teen automobile fatalities and you believe that developing a program to encourage teens not to drink and drive would be effective. You obtain information about fatalities in your area. Then after spending many months putting the program together and presenting it to high school students in the area, you decide to try to find out whether it reduces the number of fatalities. You develop a survey asking students about their drinking and driving patterns before the program and retest them after they complete the program to see whether their behaviors changed.

In the following articles, you will see how researchers use data from large studies to investigate the phenomena they are studying.

REFERENCES

General Social Survey. 2006. http://www.norc.uchicago.edu/projects/gensoc.asp

U.S. Census Bureau. 2003. *Estimates of HIV-1 Seroprevalence.* Retrieved December 9, 2006, from www.census.gov/ipc/www/hiv1.html

SUGGESTED FILMS

Evaluating Social Work Practice: A User-Friendly Approach (Yoshio Saito, Pauline Collins, Karen Kayser, Jerry Dunklee, Arleen Fins, MaryAnne VanBuren, Fred Groskind, 1992) (35min.). This film discusses the Single System Evaluation model used by the School of Social Work to teach students to systematically assess interventions and apply integrated research and practice methods to clinical work in the field.

Research Skills for Students (Andrew Schlessinger, Devin Haaq, 2004) (138 min.). Wynnewood, PA: Schlessinger Media, a division of Library Video Co. Throughout their lives, successful people use information to make decisions, solve problems, and communicate more effectively. Based on information literacy standards, this six-part series helps students learn to navigate our complex, information-rich world through the development of critical research skills and the ability to access, evaluate, and use information.

Effectiveness Measurement Tools and Techniques (Magnet Media; Films for the Humanities, 2000) (13 min.). Princeton, NJ: Films for the Humanities. Dispelling the belief that click-through rate is the ultimate online benchmark, this program identifies the cyber-factors that e-tailers need to measure, how they should go about quantifying them, and how they should interpret and apply the resulting data. The interrelationship of impressions, click-through, and conversions is clearly explained by e-commerce experts, along with the use of Internet research analyst services, ad servers, and path-tracking software to assist in gauging the success of an online ad campaign or to optimize a Web site.

22

What Sociologists Do and Where They Do It

The NSF Survey on Sociologists' Work Activities and Workplaces

ROBERT J. DOTZLER AND ROSS KOPPEL

Dotzler and Koppel used data from the National Science Foundation Survey of Doctoral Recipients to investigate what sociologists do besides working in an academic setting. The researchers found that only 45.8 percent of Ph.D. sociologists actually teach sociology and that other jobs that a sociologist could have, besides teaching, are either ignored or dismissed. Rather than sending out a survey and asking sociologists what sorts of work they do, the researchers were able to use existing data collected by the National Science Foundation, which saved not only time but money. As you read this article, watch for the questions that the researchers "asked" the data and the techniques they used to find their answers.

INTRODUCTION

Sociologists' self-perceptions are inconsistent with the reality of their professional activities. The discipline *as taken for granted* sees itself primarily as professors teaching sociology. Recent data from the NSF survey of Ph.D. sociologists, however, reveal that this view is anachronistic and more wrong than right. Less than one-half of all sociologists—45.8%—teach sociology. The majority of our colleagues spend their days managing and administrating, conducting applied or basic research, teaching in areas other than sociology, and engaging in a wide range of tasks that are divergent from the traditional image.

We do not know why sociologists persist with a traditional, classroom-based image, but we do know that this image is profoundly consequential to the way sociologists interact with each other and with the larger society. As a discipline, we tend to ignore or dismiss the *doing* of sociology in favor of the

SOURCE: From Dotzler, R. J., & Koppel, Ross. 1999. What sociologists do and where they do it: The NSF survey on sociologists' work activities and workplaces. *Sociological Practice: A Journal of Clinical and Applied Sociology*, 1(1): 71–83.

teaching of sociology or of theoretically focused research. As a discipline, we usually view sociology's use in society as something teachers do on the side—a perception that these data show to be false. Moreover, we argue that the perception is detrimental to the influence and role of sociology. Consider the role of the other sciences, both the social and the physical. Are their statuses and strengths *eroded or enhanced* by their practitioners? Are economists, biologists, psychologists, physicists, or anthropologists perceived as working primarily within the classroom? Sociology appears to be special in its adherence to a traditional image, despite its distorting and ultimately disempowering effects.

This report on sociologist's activities and types of employment is based on the 1995 Survey of Doctorate Recipients, which is produced every 2 years by the National Research Council under contract with the National Science Foundation. The survey was conducted the week of April 15, 1995, of all individuals with an earned doctorate. We were fortunate to obtain support and encouragement from NSF staff and contractors who devised many tables for this research.

We envision this article as the first of several that provide insight into our profession, our work lives, and our labor supply and demand. In future publications, we expand our analysis to include information on cohort effects (e.g., the great job dearth of the 1970s; see Koppel, 1993), quality and the status of the Ph.D. granting institutions, pay differences by employer type, gender, and region.

In this first analysis of the data we ask:

- What do sociologists do? What are the principal tasks and job descriptions?
- Where do sociologists work? What is the proportion in academic institutions, in practice settings, in private industry, and in not-for-profits?
- How do academic and practicing (applied) sociologists differ in their principal tasks?

A general caveat: It is probable that those in applied fields and in noneducation institutions were more difficult to find and less likely to respond than sociologists in academe. Thus, we suspect, but cannot document, systematic underrepresentation of applied/nonacademic sociologists in all of the data presented here.

TABLE 1 Type of Employer[a]

	Number	Percent
Educational institution	8,901	72.9
Noneducational institution	3,310	27.1
Total	12,211	100

[a]All data for Ph.D. sociologists employed during week of April 15, 1995; weighted 1995 SDR data. Actual sample size, 1300.

TABLE 2 Type of Educational Employer

	Number	Percent
Precollege education	63.1	0.08
College		
2-year	406.2	4.6
4-year	7451.3	83.7
Medical school	313.9	3.5
University research	579.9	6.5
Other	87.1	0.9
Total	8901.6	100

Most sociologists work in educational employment settings. However, as we shall see, many of those in educational institutions do not teach and, even of those who teach, sociology is not always the subject.

Table 1 gives us a sense of the size of the profession as well as the distribution between educational and noneducational employers for those with earned Ph.D.s up to age 76—a figure of 12,221. Of these, approximately five-sevenths (72.9%) work in educational institutions; about two-sevenths (27.1%) do not. The latter figure of 27.1% represents some 3300 Ph.D. sociologists working outside of educational institutions. Note that the data are weighted to reflect the actual number of sociologists in the profession. The actual sample size is 1300.

Table 2 reflects the distribution for those employed by educational institutions. We can see that fully 83.7% of the almost 9000 Ph.D. sociologists

TABLE 3 Type of Noneducational Employer

	Number	Percent
Private for profit	823.8	24.9
Private not-for-profit	835.8	25.3
Self-employed	614.2	18.6
Government		
State and local	459.8	13.9
Federal and military	512.7	15.5
Other	63.6	1.9
Total	3,309.9	100

TABLE 4 Type of Employer for Those in Educational and Noneducational Settings

	Number	Percent
Private for profit	823.8	6.7
Private not-for-profit	835.8	7.0
Self-employed	614.2	5.0
Government		
State and local	459.8	3.8
Federal and military	512.7	4.2
Other noneducation	63.6	0.5
Precollege education	63.1	0.5
College		
2-year	406.2	3.3
4-year	7451.3	61.0
Medical school	313.9	2.6
University research	579.9	4.7
Other	87.1	0.7
Total	12,211.4	100

working in educational institutions work in the traditional four-year college setting. Note that 6.5% of those in educational institutions work at "university research" jobs; medical schools represent another 3.5%. Precollege education occupies less than 1% of sociology's teachers.

Of the 3300 or so working in noneducational institutions (see Table 3), we see that about one-quarter (24.9%) are in private for-profit institutions; another one-quarter (25.3%) are in private not-for-profit institutions. Almost one-fifth (18.6%) are self-employed, and almost 30% work in government: state, local, military, and federal.

By combining Tables 2 and 3 (see Table 4), we get a sense of the great diversity of employment settings. Although educational institutions still predominate, a notable percentage of sociologists work in private, private not-for-profit, government, and self-employment settings.

We now shift focus from employer category to the more central question of principal job codes. Moreover, we examine these data for all sociologists (Table 5). We present the information for sociologists in education (left-hand column); sociologists in noneducational settings (middle column), and all sociologists combined (last column). These data are among the most powerful to emerge from this recent NSF survey of sociologists. They are based on the respondent's own classification of "best principal job code."

Look first at the left column, which comprises principal tasks for those employed by educational institutions: The leading category, not surprisingly, is teaching sociology (62.7%). This is followed by management (15%) and by sociologists teaching subjects other than sociology (16.3%). Sociologists as sociologists—presumably research and practice—is next at 4.6%. (We are obliged to use categories employed by the National Science Foundation's questionnaire and data reduction structure (cf. National Science Foundation 1995a, 1995b, 1996a, 1996b)).

Look next at the middle column, which comprises principal tasks for those employed by noneducational institutions. We see that management and administration is the modal category, at 38%—almost two-fifths of the group. Sociologists (as researchers, policy experts, etc.) are another 17.1%. These are followed by "other social sciences," 8.6%; computer systems experts, programmers, and analysts, total 5.2%; clergy, 4.5%; entertainment, TV, and the arts, 3.9%; and judges/lawyers, 3.4%.

Now, we move to the data and column that we find most revealing—the combined or "both"

TABLE 5 Best Principal Job Code for Sociology with Education Employers, Noneducation Employers, and Both Types of Employers[a]

	Education Employer (%)	Noneducation Employer (%)	Both
Clergy and other religious		4.5	1.2
Computer science programmers, analysts	0.2	5.2	1.8
Health workers	0.2	5.2	1.9
Artists, TV, public relations		3.9	1.0
Lawyers, judges	0.2	3.4	1.1
Management and administration	15.0*	38.0	20.3
Statisticians	0.2	3.3	1.0
Sales and service		4.2	1.5
Economists	0.02	1.0	0.4
Psychologist and clinical		2.4	0.7
Sociologists	4.6	17.1	8.0
Other social scientist	1.0	8.6	3.1
Elementary education	0.2		0.1
Secondary-social sciences	0.2		0.1
Postsecondary teaching			
Sociology	62.7		45.8
Assorted, not sociology	16.3		11.7
Social workers		1.8	0.5
Other occupations	0.2	1.5	0.4
Totals	100	100	100
(wt. N)	8,901.6	3,309.7	12,211

[a]Numbers do not equal 100% because of rounding, which is exacerbated by collapsing of cells.

column, on the right. The most significant finding is the fact that, when examined as a discipline, less than one-half—45.8%—of sociologists teach sociology. This is, we argue, a noteworthy and oft-ignored reality of our profession. Other notable findings in this right-hand column include:

- It is striking that 20.3% of all sociologists work in management and administration. That is, slightly over one-fifth of all Ph.D. sociologists concern themselves primarily with coordination, administration, or management of organizations, government agencies, educational institutions, policy, etc.
- As we saw in the other columns, sociologists as "sociologists" comprise another 8% of the profession.
- Teaching other social sciences in postsecondary educational settings totals 11.7% of all sociologists. This includes teaching of psychology, social work, health specialties, law, computer science, marketing and business, math, and education.
- Work in computer systems and programming occupies less than 2% of the profession.
- Note that very few are working as statisticians (1%), social workers (0.5%), and psychologists (0.7%).

TABLE 6 Primary Work Activity of Sociology Ph.D.s Employed in Noneducational Institutions

	Number	Percent
Accounting, finance, contracts	170	5.1
Applied research	1,116	33.7
Basic research	74	2.2
Computer applications, programming, systems development	253	7.6
Development	120	3.6
Design	88	2.7
Employee relations	41	1.2
Managing and supervising	575	17.4
Production, operations, maintenance	3	0.1
Professional services	354	10.7
Sales, purchasing, marketing, customer service, public relations	217	6.6
Quality or productivity management	27	0.8
Teaching	94	2.8
Other	177	5.3
Total	3,309	100

These new NSF data allow us to extend the analysis of what sociologists do (Table 6). Specifically, the survey asked respondents about their primary work activity—a question that allows more nuanced responses than the previous question on "best principal job code." We present these findings for sociologists in noneducational institutions. These data manifest the work of practicing sociologists, who apparently are occupied with conducting applied research, running institutions or agencies, advising clients or colleagues, building computer systems, and making money (for the institutions, if not themselves).

- Fully one-third, 33.7%, are engaged in applied research as their *primary* activity.
- Managing, leading, planning, coordinating, developing, designing, and supervising occupies almost one-half of the work of non-academic sociologists (48.1%), if we add: managing and supervising (17.4%); employee relations (1.2%); sales, purchasing, marketing, customer service, and public relations (6.6%); quality or productivity management (0.8%); professional service (10.7%); production, operations, and maintenance (0.1%); design (2.6%); development (3.6%); and accounting, finance, and contracts (5.1%).

We emphasize that the exact meaning of some of these categories has not been defined entirely to our satisfaction. As noted previously, we are dependent on the classifications established by the NSF survey. We understand, for example, that "professional service" refers to dealing with clients or performing professional sociological work. Thus, this category could easily be considered "applied research."

The questions reflected in the previous two tables required sociologists to select one major category to define their "primary work" or "best job code." Of course, our work lives often defy a single definition or single category. Often our work days or work weeks are too diverse to be reflected in one designation. The next table and set of comparisons address that reality. Table 7 reflects the work at which the respondents spend 10 hours or more per week. As might be expected, the question, from which it is derived, allows multiple responses—reflecting the fact that there is more than one 10-hour period in a week.

Moreover, just as in the format for Table 5, we provide these data for sociologists: (1) employed in educational institutions, (2) employed in noneducational institutions, and (3) all sociologists (both groups combined). Thus, the left column shows the breakdown of major work activities for sociologists in education; the middle column shows the breakdown for sociologists employed by noneducational institutions; and the last column is for the combined population.

This table contains several powerful discoveries:

- The first row reveals that over 50% of those employed by both educational and noneducational institutions spend at least 10 hours or more per week of their time on applied

TABLE 7 Major Work Activities (10 Hours or More Per Week) of Sociology Ph.D.s in Educational Institutions, Noneducational Institutions, and Both

Work Activity	Education Employer (%)	Noneducation Employer (%)	Both (all, %)
Applied research	52.8	59.1	54.5
Management and administration	37.7	55.2	42.4
Employee relations	26.2	41.9	30.4
Computer applications	18.2	35.8	23.0
Accounting, finance, contracts	9.0	32.0	15.2
Sales, purchasing, marketing	7.1	31.3	13.7
Development	10.5	28.5	15.4
Professional services	17.3	26.8	19.9
Quality and productivity management	6.2	24.4	11.1
Design	5.9	23.5	10.6
Basic research	58.3	16.8	47.1
Teaching	90.5	15.2	70.1
Production, operations	0.6	3.5	1.3

research. Almost 53% of those employed by educational institutions spend at least 10 hours per week on applied research; the comparable figure for those with noneducational employers is 59.1%. This is a finding of signal importance. It reflects a central reality (versus the current image) of sociology as something other than pedagogy and supports the need for greater attention to sociological practice and the use of sociology in society.

- The second row illustrates the large role that management and administration occupies for *both* those employed by educational institutions and those who are not in educational institutions. "Management and administration" is a major job for almost two-fifths of academic and for four-sevenths of the nonacademic samples. Moreover, as we have seen in the previous analyses, if we add the time spent on accounting, employee relations, productivity management, development, etc., it appears that most sociologists are involved in several forms of management and supervision. This finding is consistent with the earlier tables and reflects a theme we have seen before.
- We are surprised by the differences in basic research. Almost three-fifths of those employed by educational institutions state that this is an important time allocation, whereas less than one-fifth of those who are not in educational institutions make similar claims. Frankly, we thought there would be more similarities between the two groups. Perhaps there is some normative pressure or ambiguity in definitions. Similarly, we were very surprised to see the noneducational institution employees spending almost twice as much time with computer applications as the educational employees. Perhaps academe is less digital than we thought or the nonacademic world is more high-tech than we supposed.
- Of course, teaching predominates among the educational employees, but we note that almost one in six noneducational institution employees is involved in teaching.

Implicit in several of the tables reviewed above is the question: why are some people in academe and others in practice? We do not have as complete an answer as we would wish, but we can address some elements of that question.

TABLE 8 Is Work Related to Doctorate for Those Employed in Noneducational Institutions?

	Number	Percent
Closely related	1361.7	41.2
Somewhat related	1356.8	41.0
Not related	591.3	17.9
Total	3309	100

The NSF survey asked if one's current work is related to one's doctorate (Table 8). This is a question that must be examined in light of a heavy dose of cognitive dissonance. Nevertheless, the results are of interest. Note that, at this point, we have data only for those *not* in educational institutions. (Was the assumption that all those in educational settings are working in areas related to their doctorates?)

We find that even for those employed in nonacademic institutions, slightly over two-fifths (41.1%) state their work is closely related to their doctorates, while another two-fifths (41%) report that their work is somewhat related. Thus, less than one-fifth (17.9%) state that their work is not related to their doctorates.

As we suggested above, there is much room for individual conceptual wiggling about what "related" means and the interpretations of both doctorate and current work. Nevertheless, over 82% of those not in educational settings claim their work is related to their doctorates. We await data on those in educational settings.

We are able to examine the reasons *why* work is not related to doctorate for those with noneducation employers. In the first of two tables (Table 9) more than one answer is possible: The major response is "job not available," although "pay/promotion" and "location" are also frequently noted. This is not a surprising finding.

The next table (Table 10) presents the findings where only the *most important* reason is allowed. We see the importance of nonavailability of a job in one's field. Note that "family," which was given in the earlier table, is not listed here.

TABLE 9 If Work Not Related to Doctorate, Why?

	Number	Percent
Pay and promotion	265	44.9
Working conditions	227	38.4
Location	264	44.7
Career change	205	34.7
Family	50	8.5
Job not available	332	56.3
Other	137	23.2

Note: More than one answer is possible.

TABLE 10 If Work Not Related to Doctorate, Most Important Reason for Those With Noneducational Employment

	Number	Percent
Pay and promotion	115	19.5
Working conditions	64	10.8
Location	14	2.4
Career change	54	9.1
Job not available	280	47.4
Other	64	10.8
Total	591	100

SUMMARY AND CONCLUSIONS

Our major findings confront what we argue is a false and anachronistic image of what sociologists do. The data reported here, tabulated for this study by the National Science Foundation, reveal that most sociologists are not primarily classroom teachers of sociology. Moreover, even if we include all classroom-based sociologists in the analysis, most of the members of the profession spend most of their time working on applied research, administering and managing, advising on policy or programs, and dealing with computers, contracts, or clients.

What we find is that a lot of sociologists are out in society practicing sociology. We suggest that this is a valuable activity both for our discipline and for society. Our concern is that our failure to reflect this reality within the discipline undermines our strength as a profession. How we understand what we do and how we present ourselves to others is consequential. (Need we recite W. I. Thomas's dictum?) Until very recently, however, the American Sociological Association (ASA) devoted limited attention to the practice of sociology. We argue that the ASA and sociologists, for the long-term health and integration of the discipline, should devote more resources to the practice sector.

Our data address the reality and the image of sociology as a strictly university-based profession. We argue that the "use-value" of sociology is as meaningful as its "knowledge value." Any reasonable understanding of the role of social sciences in society suggests that neither will flourish without the flowering of both. The rise of the "market" perspective and of the focus on a discipline's role in society, even within the walls of academe, calls for a better balance between "use-value" and "knowledge-value" within the discipline.

Contrary to the views of many (e.g., Halliday & Janowitz, 1992), these data indicate that a large number of Ph.D. sociologists work in roles very different from those of the college-based teacher/scholar. Our objective, however, is not to challenge academic sociology. We want to see it grow and flourish. Our argument is that it will grow and flourish best if the practice side of sociology is better cultivated and understood by sociologists across the board. The creation and expansion of jobs in the sociological practice sector depend in no small way on the university-based sociologist's understanding of and involvement with this sector. Equally important, the perceived and actual utility of sociology as a discipline is enhanced by sociological practice. Both academe and practice will benefit if sociologists are equipped technically and intellectually for work in practice. This will require a transformation of our current graduate programs.

We envision this article as the first of several that examines the NSF sociology Ph.D. dataset. We hope to provide insight into our work lives and into our labor supply and demand, cohort effects, pay differentials, quality/status of Ph.D.-granting institutions, gender, part- and full-time status, and region. We are negotiating with the NSF to obtain the dataset so that we can run multivariate analyses and can free the NSF staffers from their roles as intermediaries—although they have been both kind and helpful. We hope that better information about what sociologists do will help all of us better understand, guide, and use our discipline in society.

REFERENCES

Halliday, Terence, & Morris Janowitz (eds.). 1992. *Sociology and its publics: The forms and fates of disciplinary organization*. Chicago: University of Chicago Press.

Koppel, Ross. 1993. Looking for the "lost generation" in the wrong places. *ASA Footnotes,* May 1993.

National Science Foundation. 1995a. *Guide to NSF Science and Engineering Resources Data*. NSF 95–318, Arlington, VA.

———. 1995b. *NSF Survey Instruments Used in Collecting Science and Engineering Resources Data*. NSF 95–317, Arlington, VA.

———. 1996a. *Selected Data on Science and Engineering Doctorate Awards, 1995*. NSF 96–303, Arlington, VA.

———. 1996b. *Characteristics of Doctoral Scientists and Engineers in the United States, 1993*. NSF 96–302, Arlington, VA.

———. 1997. *Characteristics of Doctoral Scientists and Engineers in the United States, 1995*. NSF 97–319, R. Keith Wilkinson. Arlington, VA.

REVIEW QUESTIONS

1. How are data for the National Science Foundation Survey of Doctoral Recipients collected and how often?
2. What did the researchers find out from the survey they used?
3. Do you think Dotzler and Koppel should have sent out their own survey, instead of using the existing data? Why or why not?

23

Professors Who Make the Grade

(Factors That Affect Students' Grades of Professors)

VICKY L. SEILER AND MICHAEL J. SEILER

Evaluation research can take many forms, such as the evaluation of a program, of a drug, or of a research project. This study, evaluates the factors that affect professors' scores on student teaching evaluations. It shows how faculty evaluation scores are related to how much students learn and what happens when students grade their teachers. The study demonstrates that the professors' and the courses' characteristics significantly affect professors' evaluation scores and students' learning. While reading this article, watch for the way in which the researchers used evaluation and any problem that you think you see with the way this study was done. Does it tell the complete story?

INTRODUCTION

The Accounting Education Change Commission (AECC) states that the first objective of accounting educators is to teach students effectively (1993). The AECC also says that the best way to ensure continuous improvement in the classroom and in all areas of teaching is to develop measurement and evaluation systems that encourage these improvements. In short, the AECC maintains that teaching should be the primary consideration for universities when promoting and granting tenure. Indeed, the importance of teaching is directly emphasized by colleges and universities [7, 13, 15, 18, 24, 26, 27, 28].

Because so much time and importance are associated with teaching, these institutions of higher learning should make sure they are able to evaluate a professor's teaching effectiveness as accurately as possible. There are several ways: self-assessment; peer review; supervisor ratings; and, alumni, outside consultant and student evaluations.

SOURCE: From Seiler, V. L., & Seiler, M. J. 2002. Professors who make the grade (factors that affect students' grades of professors). *Review of Business,* 23(2): 39–44.

Not surprisingly, the primary method used by colleges and universities is the student evaluation. According to Hooper and Page [11], there are several reasons:

First, students are the customers of the university. Hence, their satisfaction with how they are taught is what really matters. Second, compared to other groups, students can be argued to be the best qualified to evaluate faculty members since they have the unique opportunity to continually observe their professors throughout the semester. As such, their evaluation is not biased by "a bad day" or "a good day," as can be the case with a one-time external reviewer. Third, students provide an inexpensive way to collect data. And fourth, student evaluations are anonymous. Conversely, with a peer review, professors know exactly who is evaluating them. For professional reasons—such as not wanting to make enemies, black-balling yourself in the eyes of the reviewed member, etc.—faculty members are much less likely to objectively review their peers.

In spite of these advantages, there are some potential problems with student evaluations, however. For example, students have enough time with their professor, but do they possess the skills to know how the professor should teach? A classic example is given by Naflulin, Ware and Donnelly [16], where an actor who knew nothing about the subject being taught posed as a professor. This "teacher" made jokes, smiled a lot and was a great communicator—receiving excellent student evaluations even though his performance had little or no educational content.

These potential drawbacks notwithstanding, student evaluations continue to be the primary and, in some cases, the only method used to evaluate teaching performance in the classroom [29]. In its seven sections, this study examines which factors affect professors' scores on student teaching evaluations and how these factors influence students' learning. This article also determines whether professors' evaluation scores are related to students' learning—using "Structural Equation Modeling (SEM)," a methodology not used in previous articles examining teacher evaluations. SEM is a statistical method that combines features of multiple regression, and factor and path analyses to examine both observed and latent variables.

And finally, we will discuss the potential benefits and implications of our study, as well as why we think others should employ SEM in future research on teaching evaluations.

DATA

We obtained teaching evaluations from a mid-sized American Assembly of Collegiate Schools in Business (AACSB) accredited university in the Midwest. Students from this school's accounting department completed a total of 520 evaluations.

The university's department of accounting offers 17 classes at the undergraduate and Master of Business Administration (MBA) levels. Of these 17, eight are undergraduate, nine are MBA, seven are required, 10 are elective; and, six are given during the day, 11 at night. Most importantly, we found no difference in response rates between the graduates and undergraduates.

Various combinations of tenured and part-time professors teach the accounting classes, and 10 instructors were involved in this study.

The Evaluation

Exhibit 1 provides the actual teaching evaluation survey this university uses. The surveying instrument is a standard, 34-item questionnaire, employing a seven-point semantic differential scale (1 = lowest possible score; 7 = highest). Often if a student likes a professor, he/she will circle all answers to the right, thus grading on a global basis (halo effect or yea/saying), rather than item-by-item. The converse is also true (nay/saying). Professors and administrators do not like this practice because it prevents them from determining where improvements can be made. To reduce this bias, the survey states approximately one-third of the questions in reverse order.

EXHIBIT 1 Student Evaluation Survey

Part I: Background Information

Q1 Year in School
Q2 Undergraduate Major
Q3 Undergraduate G.P.A. (Graduate Students ONLY)
Q4 Graduate G.P.A.
Q5 Where Is Undergraduate Degree From?
Q6 If Graduate, Number of Courses Taken

Part II: Descriptive Items on Professors

Listed below are 12 sets of items. Mark the box on the answer sheet that corresponds to the letter on the scale which best describes your feelings about the instructor of each of the 12 sets. Please indicate only one letter for each set.

Q7 Fair	A	B	C	D	E	F	G	Unfair
Q8 Muddled Thinking	A	B	C	D	E	F	G	Clear Thinking
Q9 Irresponsible	A	B	C	D	E	F	G	Responsible
Q10 Thoroughly Knowledgeable	A	B	C	D	E	F	G	Unknowledgeable About the Subject Matter
Q11 Helpful	A	B	C	D	E	F	G	Not Helpful
Q12 Unoriginal	A	B	C	D	E	F	G	Original
Q13 Enthusiastic	A	B	C	D	E	F	G	Unenthusiastic
Q14 Encourages Critical Thinking	A	B	C	D	E	F	G	Discourages Critical Thinking
Q15 Poor Listener	A	B	C	D	E	F	G	Good Listener
Q16 Humorless	A	B	C	D	E	F	G	Humorous
Q17 Likes Teaching	A	B	C	D	E	F	G	Doesn't Like Teaching
Q18 Lacks Confidence	A	B	C	D	E	F	G	Highly Confident

Q19 In comparison to faculty members *outside* the College of Business Administration, how would you rate this professor?

A	B	C	D	E	F	G
One of the Worst	Very Poor	Below Average	Average	Above Average	Very Good	One of the Best

The first six survey questions are asked to obtain background information on the responding student. Questions 1 through 3 are to be filled out by both undergraduates and MBA students, while only graduate students complete questions 4 through 6. All students answer questions 7 through 34, which are the focus of our analysis.

Items describing overall professor characteristics are listed in questions 7 through 18. Question 19 and 20 ask for professor comparison ratings. Course-specific items are asked in questions 21 through 33. Finally, question 34 asks the student to rate how much he/she has learned in the course.

METHODOLOGY

According to the university, there are many questions that ask almost the same thing. Twenty-five of the 34 questions, for example, are aimed at answering only two general questions: "How good

Q20 In comparison to faculty members *within* the College of Business Administration, how would you rate this professor?

A	B	C	D	E	F	G
One of the Worst	Very Poor	Below Average	Average	Above Average	Very Good	One of the Best

Part III: Descriptive Items Concerning the Course
Listed below are 14 sets of items. Mark the box on the answer sheet that corresponds to the letter on the scale which best describes your feelings about the course for each of the 14 sets. Please indicate only one letter for each set.

Q21 Standards Undemanding	A	B	C	D	E	F	G	Standards Extremely Demanding
Q22 Course Materials Stimulating	A	B	C	D	E	F	G	Course Materials Boring
Q23 Course Materials Very Relevant	A	B	C	D	E	F	G	Course Materials Irrelevant
Q24 Written Assignments Very Valuable	A	B	C	D	E	F	G	Written Assignments of No Value
Q25 Magnitude of Work Very Heavy	A	B	C	D	E	F	G	Magnitude of Work Extremely Light
Q26 Course Is of High Value	A	B	C	D	E	F	G	Course Is of Little Value
Q27 Content Too Much for One Term	A	B	C	D	E	F	G	Content Too Little for One Term
Q28 Syllabus Highly Useful	A	B	C	D	E	F	G	Syllabus of No use
Q29 Course Very Challenging	A	B	C	D	E	F	G	Course Offered No Challenge
Q30 Teach. Methods Highly Appropriate	A	B	C	D	E	F	G	Teach. Methods Highly Inappropriate
Q31 Course Objectives Clear	A	B	C	D	E	F	G	Course Objectives Unclear
Q32 Class Well Organized	A	B	C	D	E	F	G	Class Poorly Organized
Q33 Content Exceeded Expectations	A	B	C	D	E	F	G	Content Did Not Exceed Expectations

Q34 All in all, how much to you feel you learned from this course?

A Great Deal	A	B	C	D	E	F	G	Nothing at All

is the professor?" and "How good is the course/class?"

This particular university reports each question's rating to its professors individually, but only ranks the professors based on their average score on three summary measures.

The first category measures the instructor's characteristics as a teacher and consists of questions 7 through 18. The second measures the relative rank of the instructor in the business school and the university, and consists of only questions 19 and 20. The third measure examines course content and consists of questions 21 through 34.

Our analysis focused on the first and third categories. As just mentioned, the first measure attempts to answer the question, "How good is the professor?" while the third measure attempts to answer, "How good is the course/class?"

We performed an exploratory factor analysis to determine if these categories were accurate. We used the statistical package, LISREL VII, to determine the causal relationships between the independent and

EXHIBIT 2 Hypothesized Model

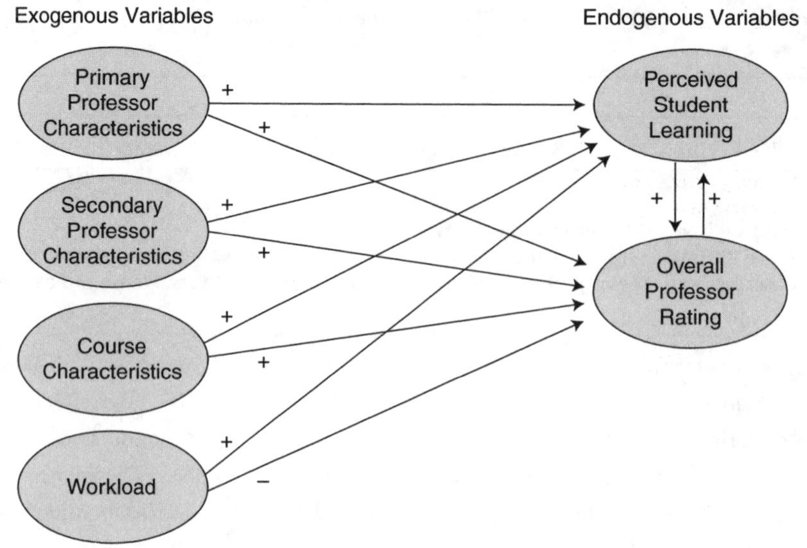

All exogenous variables are latent, while all endogenous variables are single indicator variables.

dependent variables. The factors produced in the analysis became the latent exogenous variables used in SEM. Also in the model were two endogenous variables: question 20, "professor's rating," and question 34, "amount students learned." Exhibit 2 shows the hypothesized relationships among the variables.

RESULTS

To evaluate the underlying dimensions of the surveying instrument, we conducted a factor analysis on responses to items 7 through 18 and 21 through 33. We used oblique rotation due to correlations among the factors, an eigenvalue cutoff of 1.0 and factor loadings over 0.30 [9] to assess the dimensionality of the instrument. The resulting four factors explained 60.3 percent of the overall variation in the model.

Cronbach alphas were utilized to determine reliability estimates of latent constructs. Exhibit 3 shows which variables compose each latent construct, the name of each construct and the corresponding Cronbach alpha values.

Our analysis yields several interesting results. For one, the university's contention that survey questions 7 through 18 ask the same general question, "How good is the professor?" is itself questionable. While it seems these questions seek to answer the same general question, the factor analysis yielded strong results indicating the presence of two distinct factors. Along the same lines, questions 21 through 33 share two factors, not one. Specifically, we found that four questions (21, 25, 27 and 29) break out of the second category, "How good is the course/class?" These questions form their own factor, which measures the amount of work required in the class. . . .

EXHIBIT 3 Factor Analysis for Survey Questions 7–18 and 21–33

Pattern matrix coefficients greater than 0.30 are shown for each variable.

		Factor					
	s	1	2	3	4	Cronbach Alphas	Percentage of Explained Variation
Factor 1	**Primary Professor Characteristic**					**0.9124**	**41.8%**
Q7	Fairness	0.7830					
Q 8	Thinking	0.6869					
Q 9	Responsible	0.7554					
Q 10	Knowledgeable	0.7470					
Q 11	Helpful	0.5117					
Q 15	Listener	0.5100					
Q 17	Likes Teaching	0.5374					
Q 18	Confidence	0.4372					
Q 30	Teaching Methods	0.5279					
Q 32	Class Organization	0.6597					
Factor 2	**Secondary Professor Characteristics**					**0.7371**	**5.5%**
Q 12	Original		0.6689				
Q 13	Enthusiasm		0.5804				
Q 14	Encouragement of Critical Thinking		0.5518				
Q 16	Humorous		0.6938				
Factor 3	**Course Characteristics**					**0.8001**	**4.5%**
Q 22	Course Materials Stimulating			0.7911			
Q 23	Course Materials Relevant			0.5832			
Q 24	Value of Written Assignments			0.6126			
Q 26	Value of Course			0.6424			
Q 28	Syllabus			0.4028			
Q 31	Course Objectives			0.3019			
Q 33	Course Expectations			0.3907			
Factor 4	**Work Load**					**0.8406**	**8.4%**
Q21	Demanding Standards				0.6472		
Q25	Magnitude of Work				0.8571		
Q27	Course Content				0.8378		
Q29	Challenging				0.5742		

EXHIBIT 4 Goodness-Of-Fit Measures for the Final Structural Equation

Goodness-of-Fit Measures	Value
Chi-Square Value	2.87
Degrees of Freedom	3
p-value	0.412
Chi-Square Value/D.F.	0.957
Goodness-of-Fit Index	0.998
Adjusted Goodness-of-Fit Index	0.985
Root Mean Square Residual	0.013

Exhibit 4 shows the goodness-of-fit measures for the final model. The first measure, a chi-square test, indicates the model's overall fit. The hypotheses are as follows:

[H.sub.o]: The fitted model is the same as the perfect model.

[H.sub.a]: The fitted model is not the same as the perfect model.[1]

Since the chi-square's corresponding p-value (0.412) is greater than the alpha value of 0.05, we do not reject H_o and conclude that the model is not significantly different from the perfect model. A second indicator of the model's fit is the ratio, chi-square/degrees of freedom. If the ratio is below 5.0 ($n > 200$), the model's fit is good [12]. At 0.957, the ratio for our model is exceptional.

A third and fourth measure of fit criteria are the goodness-of-fit index and the adjusted goodness-of-fit index. The perfect model has a measure of 1.0. Any value greater than 0.9 is considered to be a good fit [25]. Our goodness-of-fit equals 0.998 and the adjusted goodness-of-fit equals 0.985—both extremely good measures.

And a fifth measure of fit is the root mean square residual, in which a value closer to zero indicates a better fit (the closer to zero, the better the fit). Our root mean square residual equals 0.013, again indicating a good fit [21].[2]

Exhibit 5 presents the effects of the exogenous variables on the endogenous variables (gamma paths) for the final model. Maximum likelihood estimates (unstandardized solutions), standardized solutions, standard errors and T-statistics are given for each of the effects. We found that the factor "work load" did not have a significant relationship with either of the endogenous variables and was thus eliminated from the final model. Also, secondary professor characteristics do not significantly affect overall professor rating. Hence, this path was also eliminated in the final model. . . .

Significant Causal Relationships

There were significant positive causal relationships between professor and course characteristics, and professor summary evaluation scores and student perceptions of how much they learned overall. There was also a positive causal relationship between professor summary evaluation scores and perceived student learning. These paths were statistically significant at the 99 percent confidence level. The final model is shown in Exhibit 6.*

* Original Exhibit numbers have been changed to reflect the deletion of an exhibit.

EXHIBIT 5 Maximum Likelihood Estimates of the Effects of the Exogenous Variables on the Endogenous Variables for the Final Lisrel Model

	Endogenous Variables					
	Perceived Student Learning			Overall Professor Rating		
Exogenous Variables	*ML-Est.*	SE	T-Test	*ML-Est.*	SE	T-Test
Primary Professor Characteristics	0.34 (0.24)	0.06	5.55*	0.67 (0.49)	0.05	13.72*
Secondary Professor Characteristics	0.50 (0.37)	0.05	11.22*			
Course Characteristics	0.68 (0.40)	0.05	14.03*	0.17 (0.13)	0.05	3.79*

* Statistically significant at the 99% confidence level.

Note: Standardized solutions are in parentheses.

In addition to verifying statistically significant relationships, the factor analysis of the evaluation data (Exhibit 1) revealed that four variables form an additional factor, which is inconsistent with the university's position. However, upon running SEM, the factor consisting of these variables did not prove to be statistically significant. Thus, we believe these four questions are of no use in the evaluation and should be eliminated.

Implications

The SEM analysis provides clear empirical results that can easily translate into policy implications and decisions for colleges and universities. The 14 professor and seven course characteristic variables provide a good measure of the latent constructs.

These constructs affect both the level of perceived learning and the overall professor rating. Professor rating affects perceived learning, but the converse is not true. Finally, the latent construct, "workload," does not affect either professor rating or perceived learning. Therefore, it should be removed from the evaluation survey entirely.

The bottom line is that administrators can use the evaluation instrument in Exhibit 1—incorporating the adjustments we've just recommended—to more accurately measure professor performance in the classroom. Administrators should test their current evaluating instrument, which is most likely different from the one we've set forth. They can use our SEM methodology to determine if they are measuring what they are attempting to measure. In doing so, they will be able to make more accurate tenure/promotion decisions, and professors will be able to teach more effectively.

CONCLUSION

We examined 520 student evaluations from accounting students at a mid-sized AACSB-accredited university in the Midwest. We used Structural Equation Modeling to determine the significant relationships between professor and course characteristics, and professors' ratings and students' perceived learning.

A word of caution should be noted. The data in this study were gathered from just one department in one university—so we are not generalizing our results to other departments or universities across the country, nor should you. Instead, we

EXHIBIT 6 Final Model

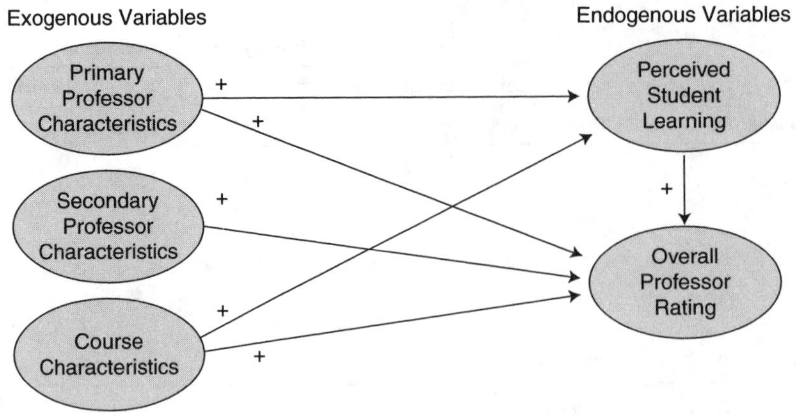

All arrows shown here represent statistically significant relationships at the 99% level of confidence.

believe we provide a solid foundation on which future research can, and should, be directed.

Important questions for further research might include whether it's necessary to develop department-specific and/or university-specific models describing the relationships among professor and course characteristics and teaching evaluations, or whether general models would be more appropriate.

In any case, we believe colleges and universities can benefit from using the results of this study and any subsequent studies using SEM. It's a sophisticated technique that can be used very effectively in the area of teacher evaluations.

NOTES

1. The perfect model is defined as the (unobtainable) benchmark that fully and completely represents all relationships among all relevant variables. Since it is virtually impossible to quantify any relationship exactly, we measure a model relative to the perfect model.
2. Several papers in various research fields discuss acceptable levels of measurable indicators of model quality. See, for example. Herting and Costner (1985); Anderson, Jay, Sehweer, and Anderson (1986); Biddle and Marlin (1987); Anderson (1987); Lavee (1988); Anderson and Gerbing (1988); Rodgers (1991); Segars and Grover (1993); Saunders and Jones (1992); and Kettlinger and Lee (1995).

REFERENCES

1. Accounting Education Change Commission. "AKCC Urges Priority for Teaching in Higher Education." *Issues in Accounting Education*, 5, 1993, 330–331.
2. Anderson, J. "Structural Equation Models in the Social and Behavioral Sciences: Model Building." *Child Development*, 58, 1987, 49–64.
3. Anderson, J., S. Jay, H. Schweer, and M. Anderson. "Physician Utilization of Computers in Medical Practice: Policy Implications Based on a Structural Model." *Social Sciences Medicine*, 233, 1986, 259–267.
4. Andersen, J. and D. Gerbing. "Structural Equation Modeling in Practice: A Review and Recommended Two-Step Approach." *Psychological Bulletin*, 103:3, 1988, 441–423.
5. Raison, J. *Managing Services Marketing*. London: Dryden Press , 1989.
6. Biddle, B. and M. Marlin. "Causality, Confirmation. Credulity, and Structural Equation Modeling." *Child Development*, 58, 1987, 1–17.
7. Cornwell, K. "The Evaluation of Family Performance." *Collegiate News and Views*, 1984, 9–13.
8. Deberg, C., and J. Wilson. "An Empirical Investigation of the Potential Confounding Variables in Student Evaluation of Teaching," *Journal of Accounting Education*, 8, 1990, 37–42.
9. Hair, J., R. Anderson, R. Tathani, and W. Black. *Multivariate Data Analysis*, Fourth Edition. NY: Prentice Hall. 1995.
10. I. Herting, J., and H. Costner. "Causal Models in the Social Sciences," *Respecification in Multiple Indicator Models*, Ed. H. Blalock Jr. NY: Alfine, Second Edition. 15, 1985, 321–393.
11. Hooper, P. and J. Page. "Measuring Teaching Effectiveness by Student Evaluation." *Issues in Accounting Education*, 1986, 56–64.
12. Kettinger, W. and C. Lee. "Perceived Service Quality and User Satisfaction with the information Services Function. *Decision Sciences*, 25, 1995, 737–766.
13. Kreuze, J. and G. Newell. "Student Ratings of Accounting Instructors: A Search for Important Determinants," *Journal of Accounting Education*, 5, 1987, 87–98.
14. Lavee, Y. "Linear Structural Relationships (LISREL) in Family Research," *Journal of Marriage and Family*, 50, 1988, 937–948.
15. McKeachie, W. "Student Ratings of Faculty; A Research Review," *Improving College and University Teaching*, 1967, 4–8.
16. Nafulin, D., J. Ware and F. Donnelly. "The Dr. Fox Lecture: A Paradigm of Educational Seduction." *Journal of Medical Education*. 48, 1973, 630–635.
17. Ostrowski. P., T. O'Brien and G. Gordon. "Service Quality and Customer Loyalty in the Commercial Airline Industry," *Journal of Travel Research*, Fall 1993, 16–24.
18. Porcano, T. "An Empirical Analysis of Some Factors Affecting Student Performance." *Journal of Accounting Education*, 2, 1984, 111–126.
19. Quinn, J. "Technology in Services: Past Myths and Future Challenges." *Technological Forecasting and Social Change*, 34, 1988, 327–350.
20. Rodgers, W. "Evaluating Accounting Information with Causal Models: Classification of Methods and Implications for Accounting Research." *Journal of Accounting Literature*, 10, 1991, 151–180.
21. Rupp, M. and R. Segal. "Confirmatory Factor Analysis of a Professionalism Scale in Pharmacy," *Journal of Social and Administrative Pharmacy*, 6:1, 1989, 31–38.
22. Saunders, C. and J. Jones. "Measuring Performance of the Information Systems Function, *Journal of Management Information Systems*, 8:4, 1992, 63–82.
23. Segars, A. and V. Grover. "Re-examining Perceived Ease of Use and Usefulness: A Confirmatory Factor Analysis." *MIS Quarterly*, 17:4, 1993, 517–527.
24. Street, D., C. Baril and R. Benke. "Research, Teaching, and Service in Promotion and Tenure Decisions of Accounting Faculty." *Journal of Accounting Education*, 12, 1993, 43–60.
25. Taylor, S., A. Sharland, J. Cronin and W. Bullard. "Recreational Service Quality in the International Setting." *International Journal of Service Industry Management*, 4:4, 1993, 68–86.

26. Tompkins, J., H. Hermanson and D. Hermanson, "Expectations and Resources Associated with New Finance Faculty Positions," *Financial Practice and Education*, 6, Spring/Fall, 1996, 54–64.

27. Tripathy, N. and G. Ganesh. "Evaluation, Promotion, and Tenure of Finance Faculty: The Evaluators' Perspective," *Financial Practice and Education*, 6, Spring/Fall 1996, 46–53.

28. Wright, P., R. Whittington and G. Whittenburg. "Student Ratings of Teaching Effectiveness: What the Research Reveals." *Journal of Accounting Education* 2, 1984, 5–30.

29. Yunker, P. and J. Sterner. "A Survey of Faculty Performance Evaluation in Accounting," *The Accounting Educator's Journal*, 1988, 63–71.

REVIEW QUESTIONS

1. What were the hypotheses in this study?
2. What methodology did the researchers use? Why did they use it?
3. List three findings of this project.

Appendix

Writing and Reading a Research Paper

No one can read what has never been put on paper.
HOWARD BECKER, 1986: 5

Students often find the thought of a research assignment daunting. They do not always know how to read the papers they find in the library or how to use the sources they gather for their papers. Writing is important in the social sciences, and reluctance to start the process is common. According to Howard Becker (1986), who has been teaching graduate students to write for years, each of us has writing habits that we don't want to share with others because they seem so silly. Becker says the time-wasting writing habits that his students describe are "a common disease. Just as people feel relieved to discover that some frightening physical symptoms they've been hiding are just something that is 'going around,' knowing that others had crazy writing habits should have been, and clearly was, a good thing" (Becker, 1986: 3).

AN ACADEMIC RESEARCH PAPER

The very first thing you need to know is some basic terminology. I find that it is best that students in research methods classes use mainly **primary sources**. A primary source is the original article that describes and reports **empirical research** and **theoretical articles** that have been published in a **peer-reviewed journal**. An empirical research paper is a description of a systematic observation or study, whereas a theoretical article explains a theory and how it relates to the variables being investigated. *Peer-reviewed* means that the research paper has been blindly reviewed, usually by three other scholars in the same field, who decide if the research meets the standards of the journal. We discuss primary sources in this appendix, but you should know that **secondary sources** are summaries of original research that you find in newspapers and magazines and hear about on the news. Secondary sources are good because they give us ideas for studies and also give us clues about where to look for the original study. However, it is difficult to know for sure that the reporter interpreted and then reported the original research correctly. Therefore, your professor might not want you to use secondary sources.

Let me give you an example of why using secondary sources might not be a good idea, even though it is something we often do. Recently, an article that appeared in a number of newspapers and was covered by television news channels said that a Pentagon report claimed that homosexuality is a mental illness (Shoffman, 2006). In a document called a "Defense Department Instruction," homosexuality was placed alongside mental retardation, personality disorders, and physical disabilities. How many people who read the article or saw the news reports would think that homosexuality really is a mental illness and then act negatively toward homosexuals because of the Pentagon and TV news (secondary sources) reports? If you go to the American Psychological Association Web site (a primary source), you will find that in 1973 the American Psychiatric Association's Board of Trustees passed a resolution stating that "Homosexuality, per se implies no impairment in judgment, stability, reliability, or general social or vocational capabilities. Further, (we) urge all mental health professionals to take the lead in removing the stigma of mental illness associated with homosexual orientation" (APA, 2006). These changes began in the 1950s when Dr. Evelyn Hooker studied 30 homosexual males and 30 heterosexual males who were recruited through various community organizations and matched for age, IQ, and education. After administering a number of tests, Hooker found that homosexuals were as psychologically normal as heterosexuals (primary source)(Hooker, 1957).

READING A JOURNAL ARTICLE

Now let's get back to learning how to read a journal article. If you go back to a few of the articles you have been asked to read in your course, you will notice that they have the same basic format. There are usually six parts to an empirical research article: (1) abstract, (2) literature review or introduction, (3) methods, (4) results, (5) discussion or conclusion, and (6) references. If you are a visual person, you might look at the various parts of a paper as an hourglass where you begin broadly with the abstract, then go to the introduction or literature review, which gets more and more narrow as you focus in on your hypothesis (see Figure A1.) Then you begin once again to broaden out as you talk about the specifics in your methods section, explaining the results and getting broader still with your conclusion. You end with the references.

Now let's consider each section in detail, referring to an article called "Construction of Masculinity: A Look into the Lives of Heterosexual Male Transvestites," which I wrote while in graduate school (Wysocki, 1993). The complete article appears on pages 222–226.

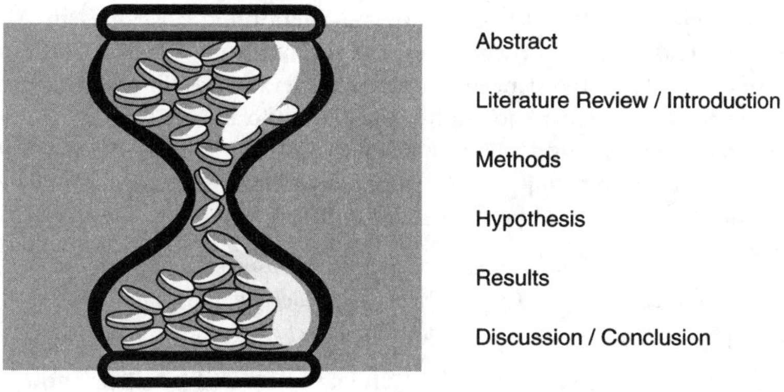

FIGURE A.1 Parts of an Empirical Research Article

Abstracts

An abstract is usually the first thing you see when you read an academic research article. An **abstract** begins with a brief statement about the research hypothesis, the purposes of the research, or questions that the researcher is trying to answer. After that, a sentence or two describes the methodology used in the project, such as whether a survey or face-to-face interviews were conducted or all the data were collected over the Internet. The abstract also includes information about the participants or the sample. The results are mentioned in the next-to-last sentence, which provides a very brief description of the findings. The last sentence often draws a conclusion for the reader.

Abstracts are very short. The goal of an abstract is to provide just enough information to help readers decide whether the article is something they are interested in and something that will help with their projects. Many researchers, including me, write the abstract after writing the paper, because it is easier to summarize results and conclusions then. Since almost all research papers begin with an abstract, you should be able to pick one and follow its format in your own paper.

Literature Review/Introduction

A **literature review** introduces the problem, develops the background by providing a history of scholarly work on the subject, and ends with the purpose and the rationale of the study. Some of my students think that the literature review is the only part of a published research paper that they need to read and cite, but they are mistaken. The literature review is difficult to cite and often gets cited incorrectly, if at all.

Remember the hourglass? We went from broad to narrow, or general to specific. That is how a literature review goes. Referring to my article on transvestites (see pages 222–226), you can see that I start broadly by introducing the differences between sex and gender. Then because the journal that I sent this article to focuses on feminism and psychology, I mention those issues in my literature review so readers will know where I am coming from. Then I go on to talk about transvestites. I felt that I needed to define them and differentiate them from other individuals who wear the clothing of the opposite sex.

Then I get more specific and mention the reasons that adolescents were at risk, using empirical research to support my ideas along the way and getting more specific as I go until I get to my hypothesis, saying that

> *The aim of this study is to look at transvestism as a way of investigating gender roles, the continuum of masculinity, and the problems some men may develop when they deviate from what society dictates is acceptable gender behavior.*

Because a literature review reflects someone else's understanding of previously published empirical studies that she or he mentioned in the literature review—the author's "story" leading up to the rationale or hypothesis of the project you are currently reading about. Let's say you liked what I wrote in my article (Wysocki, 1993) and in your paper you quote from my literature review, writing that "transvestites are probably one of the most misunderstood groups of people. Sometimes they are thought of as 'gay,' 'drag queens,' 'transsexuals,' or, sometimes just 'degenerative perverts' (Wysocki, 1993)." Is that citation to Wysocki 1993 correct? No, it isn't, because the quoted terms appeared in Ellis and Arbarbanel (1961).[1]

Why do we use literature reviews in articles? It's a great way to find out where the primary sources can be located by matching the citation in the literature review to the full reference in the bibliography section.

Methods

This section describes in detail how the study was conducted. The methods section allows readers to evaluate the research. It should be so detailed that another researcher could replicate the research exactly.

Let's say that you want to study eating disorders on your campus, which is in the Midwest. You don't need to figure out how to do the methods all by yourself. If you do a literature search and read other articles on eating disorders on college campuses, you are likely to find the methods used by other researchers who already conducted this type of study. You can use their methods and conduct your own research. You don't have to reinvent the wheel!

Within the methods section there are often subsections labeled "Participants," "Materials," and "Procedure," depending on the organization and detail of the study. Here is the methods section of my study of heterosexual male transvestities (Wysocki, 1993):

---

1 For a complete citation, see the list of references on pages 225–226. To see the quotation from Wysocki (1993) in content, see page 222.

Procedure

I made contact with my participants after seeing an advertisement for their support group in a Phoenix newspaper during the summer of 1987. I was invited to attend their gatherings after meeting with the "first lady" of the group. The preliminary ethnographic field research consisted of observations, informal interviews and written correspondence that originated at those gatherings.

Participants

Letters written to me have been used for this paper, and were from white males ages 35–71. There were ten participants. Three were married, and one was single but has been married twice. Three of them have children who ranged from 5 to 43 years, with only the older children (ages 41 and 43) knowing that their father cross-dresses. They all had completed high school, two have Bachelor of Science degrees and one has a Master's in Computer Science. All of the participants' feminine names have been changed with the exception of "Nancy Ann," who specifically asked me to let "hers" remain as it is.

Methodology

Goffman argues that a biography is a special way of defining a person (Watson, 1990: 190). Writing one's history provides the author with a way of ordering his or her life, constructing a coherent self-description. The letters that I have collected helped me accomplish this by revealing insight into the history of the heterosexual male transvestite's life, providing an outlet for the person who is writing to express his feelings, and talk about his life.

The letters are highly emotional, and intense. Almost all of them were written on feminine stationery. Some had little bears or hearts, similar to what adolescent girls might use. Others were written on pastel or colored paper with pink or purple ink. It became clear to me as I reread the letters that the men were, for the most part, into their "female" role while writing.

Results

The results section summarizes the data that have been collected and explains the findings in enough detail to justify the conclusions. This section often includes tables, figures, and statistics. Sometimes this is a difficult section to read, especially if you haven't taken a few statistics courses—or don't remember them. Summarizing data in tables and figures is always helpful and easy to do in either your word-processing program or Excel. If you want to be creative, you can also use SPSS and PowerPoint—they are both pretty user-friendly. Remember to refer to the tables and figures in the text.

Discussion or Conclusion

Here, the information in the results section is evaluated and interpreted. Usually the section begins with a clear statement about whether or not the hypothesis was supported. Also using the literature review (remember, it gives information on other scholarly work to set up the current project), the author can compare and contrast the findings in this study with the studies presented in the literature review. This section also discusses what this project contributes to the current base of knowledge on the topic, what conclusions can be drawn from the study, and suggestions for future research possibilities.

So, now you might be thinking, "Oh, that's easy for Dr. Wysocki to say. But how am I supposed to do this for the paper that is due in the morning?" Well, the answer to that is . . . you can't. You must start writing a research paper very early. You can't do it in one night. And now you know you have to read the entire article beyond the literature review when citing an article in your paper.

WRITING FOR THE SOCIAL SCIENCES

I always suggest that students find a topic that interests them. Suppose you are interested in some aspect of domestic violence. Many interesting topics fall under the "domestic violence" heading—family issues, economic issues, drug and alcohol use, the criminal justice system. But let's say you are interested in the media and you believe that the media play some part in domestic violence because you know that everyone is socialized by the media somehow. You also know, because of Court TV and news reports, that although domestic violence was once a private trouble it now is a public issue. You believe that as media coverage increases so do acts of domestic violence—this is your hypothesis. What will your independent variable and dependent variables be?

Independent variable	→	Dependent variable
Media coverage		Increase in domestic violence

You have an idea for your topic, so now would be a great time to sit down and write out an outline for a literature review to locate scholarly work on the subject. Should you head for the library right away? You could, but you might end up with a lot of stuff you don't need. You don't go to the grocery store without a shopping list (because if you do, you bring home lots of things you don't need), so you shouldn't go to the library without two outlines—one for the dependent variable, which is domestic violence (DV) this case, and one for the independent variable (media).

Let's start with domestic violence (DV). Remember to start broadly.

1. Definition of DV
   a. National statistics
   b. Incidents of DV to police departments
   c. Problems with reporting
   d. Comparison of DV to other crimes
      i. Murder
      ii. Theft

2. Reasons for DV
   a. Control
   b. Power
   c. Gender Differences
3. Reasons women stay in DV relationships
   a. Financial
   b. Fear
   c. Children
4. Misconceptions about DV
   a. Women could leave if they wanted to
   b. Women need the violence
   c. Women deserve the violence

Now for Media, the independent variable:

1. Kinds of media
   a. Music
   b. Television
   c. Movies
   d. Newspapers
2. Socialization
   a. Socialization theory
   b. How the media socialize us (Don't forget, you need a theory because research without theory is pretty empty. So if you believe that the news is socially constructed, you might want to use that as your theory.)
   c. How the media construct our reality
3. The media's portrayal of DV

This is a very rough outline (shopping list), but it is enough to take to the library as a guide. Next you look up scholarly work to plug into the various parts of the outline to support what you think you want to write about.

So, is that the final outline? No, it's just a beginning. When you get into the literature, you might find that someone else talks about something that you hadn't thought of. You can put that topic in your outline. Similarly, you might find that something in your outline simply doesn't fit and you don't need it . . . so out it goes. Also, after getting into the literature, you might find that you need to reorganize your outline.

PLAGIARISM

Citing properly seems to be one of the most difficult tasks in writing a research paper. However, it is also one of the most important things to learn, because failure to cite properly could put you in danger of being charged with **plagiarism**—using someone else's writing without crediting the author. Each discipline has its own "ethical standards for the reporting and publishing of scientific information." Plagiarism is often grounds for failing your class or for expulsion from school. It wreaks havoc with your reputation.

I believe that sometimes students don't realize they are plagiarizing. A few years ago, I gave an assignment and as I was grading the papers, I found I was very impressed by one student's paper. This student had been pretty quiet in class, so I was pleasantly surprised to see her do such good work on a subject I was really interested in. As I kept reading, I realized that the information sounded really familiar, and a few pages later I realized that the student had used a chapter out of my dissertation, which was available on the Internet. When I asked her why she had copied my work, she said she thought what I wrote was good, believed I would like it if she used my work, and didn't know she was cheating. It appears that this one young student is not an isolated case and that many students don't intentionally plagiarize but, rather, don't know how to cite their sources properly.

According to Donald McCabe (2001), 74 per cent of the 4,500 high school students who answered a written survey reported at least one or more instances of serious cheating on tests, 72 percent reported cheating on written work, and 30 percent reported more serious, repetitive cheating. In study of 2,100 students on 21 different college campuses, one-third admitted to serious test cheating and one-half admitted to one or more instances of serious cheating on written assignments (McCabe & Trevino, 1996). To some students, cheating is just part of student life (McCabe, 1999). More males than females cheat, members of fraternities and sororities are more likely to cheat than are students who are not members, and individuals who believe their peers strongly disapprove of cheating are less likely to cheat (McCabe & Bowers, 1996).

Although the Internet is a wonderful tool for research, it provides new opportunities for plagiarizism. As you probably know, there are plenty of places on the Internet to buy a paper if you are willing to pay $10 per page. Many students seem be willing, and some professors belive that Internet plagiarism is becoming more dangerous and more common than we might realize (Laird, 2001; McCabe, 1999). In fact, teachers and librarians publish articles, lists of Web sites, and other information to help professors catch those who plagiarize from the Internet (Lincoln, 2002). Although only 15 percent of high school students have purchased a paper from an Internet paper mill, 52 percent have reported lifting a few sentences directly from the Internet without citing the source (McCabe, 2001). School policies vary on this subject, and it's best to learn how to keep yourself out of trouble.

There are different types of plagiarism. Most serious is **intentional plagiarism**, cheating of any kind—from copying directly from an article or a book to buying an article off the Internet. Intentional plagiarism is becoming increasingly common. **Unintentional plagiarism**, however, is even more common. It results when you paraphrase or summarize another author's ideas but do not give credit to the author. One of the problems I encounter most often in an undergraduate research methods class occurs when a student uses an academic article, reads only the literature review, and then uses information out of the literature review as her or his own literature review.

Suppose, for example, that in 1990 Smith wrote an article on child abuse. The student goes to Smith's article and finds in Smith's literature review that Smith used articles from Jones (1984), from Kelley (1989), and from Rodney and Roe (1987) to describe various reasons for child abuse in our country. The student decides to talk about the reasons for child abuse and uses what Smith's literature review says about the findings of Jones (1984), Kelley (1989), and Rodney and Roe (1987). Then the student cites Smith (1990). What's wrong with this scenario? The student should have hunted up the three articles that Smith cited to make sure that Smith cited them accurately; the student should have cited the studies of the other researchers, rather than Smith's literature review.

The best way to make sure you do not plagiarize unintentionally is to consult a book on how to write and use citations both in the body of your paper and in your reference list or bibliography. The American Psychological Association's *Publication Manual* (5th ed., 2001), the American Sociological Association's *Style Guide* (2nd ed., 1997), or the *Chicago Manual of Style* (15th ed., 2003) will help you with any papers you write.

One more way in which students plagiarize unintentionally is by using for one class a paper that was used and graded in another class.

REFERENCES

American Psychiatric Association. 2006. Resolutions related to lesbian, gay and bisexual issues: DSM III and homosexuality. Retrieved from http://www.apa.org/pi/reslgbc.html.

Becker, H. 1986. *Writing for social scientists: How to start and finish your thesis, book or article.* University of Chicago Press: Chicago.

Hooker, E. 1957. The adjustment of the male overt homosexual. *Journal of Projective Techniques*, 21, 18–31.

Laird, E. 2001, July 13. Internet plagiarism: We all pay the price. *Chronicle Review*, p.5.

Lincoln, M. 2002. Internet plagiarism. *Multimedia Schools*, 9(1): 46–49.

McCabe, D. L. 1999. Academic dishonesty among high school students. *Adolescence*, 34(136): 681–687.

McCabe, D. L. 2001. Student cheating in American high schools. Retrieved from http://www.academicintegrity.org/

McCabe, D. L., & Bowers, W. J. 1996. The relationship between student cheating and college fraternity or sorority membership. *NASPA Journal*, 33, 280–291.

McCabe, D. L., & Trevino, L. K. 1996. What we know about cheating in college. *Change*, 28: 28–33.

Shoffman, M. 2006. Pentagon lists homosexuality as a mental disorder. Retrieved from http://www.pinknews.co.uk/news/articles/2006-1771.html.

Wysocki, D. K. 1993. Construction of masculinity: A look into the lives of heterosexual male transvestites. *Feminism and Psychology*, 3(3): 374–330.

24

Construction of Masculinity

A Look into the Lives of Heterosexual Male Transvestites

DIANE KHOLOS WYSOCKI

This is an article that I wrote in graduate school based on my master's thesis. If you read this and refer back to what you have previously read, you will find the different parts of an academic research paper. Read the literature review and see if you can come up with another outline I might have used when writing this paper. Remember to start broadly and become narrower and more focused as you go along.

The sex of the new-born child, in the United States, is the biological criterion used to classify a baby as either female or male (West and Zimmerman, 1987; Martin and Voorhies, 1975). This pattern of mapping out gender roles is started at birth and continues throughout the life cycle, demonstrating social norms, and creating differences between both sexes that are not "natural, essential or biological" (West and Zimmerman, 1987: 137), but socially constructed (Oakley, 1972; Benjamin, 1966).

Psychology has usually studied sex and gender with the male experience as its norm. Feminist scholars (Squire, 1989; Harding, 1989; Griffin, 1986) are moving away from what they consider an androcentric way of doing science to develop a perspective which will enable researchers to analyze sex and gender in order to bring about a more egalitarian discipline (Squire, 1989; Condor, 1986). Squire (1989) states that "feminism and psychology are important for each other," and that research in the area of gender difference will prove to be an important step in looking at the development of identity (Squire, 1989), personality (Williamson et al., 1982) and sexuality (Freud, 1962). Studying transvestism can reveal that gender is not dichotomous but constitutes a spectrum for both men and women.

Transvestites are probably one of the most misunderstood groups of people. Sometimes they are thought of as "gay," "drag queens", "transsexuals," or, sometimes just "degenerative perverts" (Ellis and Arbarbanel, 1961). Some might even think they fall into the category of "nuts, sluts and perverts" (Liazos, 1972). Many researchers, for example, Benjamin (1966), Brierley (1979), Docter (1988), Talamini (1982a, 1982b) and Woodhouse (1989) have investigated different aspects of transvestism; further, different modes of describing transvestism have also been utilized, such as medical (Benjamin, 1966; Masters et al., 1986), psychological (Brierley, 1979) and sociological (Devor, 1989; Woodhouse, 1989).

SOURCE: From *Feminism and Psychology*, © 1993 Sage (London, Newbury Park, and New Delhi), Vol. 3(3): 374–380.

The aim of this study is to look at transvestism as a way of investigating gender roles, the continuum of masculinity, and the problems some men may develop when they deviate from what society dictates is acceptable gender behavior.

METHODS

Procedure

I made contact with my participants after seeing an advertisement for their support group in a Phoenix newspaper during the summer of 1987. I was invited to attend their gatherings after meeting with the "first lady" of the group. The preliminary ethnographic field research consisted of observations, informal interviews and written correspondence that originated at those gatherings.

Participants

Letters written to me have been used for this paper, and were from white males ages 35–71. There were ten participants. Three were married, and one was single but has been married twice. Three of them have children who ranged from 5 to 43 years, with only the older children (ages 41 and 43) knowing that their father cross-dresses. They all had completed high school, two have Bachelor of Science degrees and one has a Master's in Computer Science. All of the participants' feminine names have been changed with the exception of "Nancy Ann," who specifically asked me to let "hers" remain as it is.

Methodology

Goffman argues that a biography is a special way of defining a person (Watson, 1990: 190). Writing one's history provides the author with a way of ordering his or her life, constructing a coherent self-description. The letters that I have collected helped me accomplish this by revealing insight into the history of the heterosexual male transvestite's life, providing an outlet for the person who is writing to express his feelings, and talk about his life.

The letters are highly emotional, and intense. Almost all of them were written on feminine stationery. Some had little bears or hearts, similar to what adolescent girls might use. Others were written on pastel or colored paper with pink or purple ink. It became clear to me as I reread the letters that the men were, for the most part, into their "female" role while writing.

RESULTS

The life of a transvestite is not easy. It is filled with the pain of living a double life. Sometimes it is one where the man lets very few, if any, know of his secret. His childhood has often times been very rough, because of the guilt and confusion that stems from knowing his activities were outside the realm of acceptable male behavior. "Nancy Ann" states:

> *I had one brother and one sister. The joy and pleasure of dressing up was greater than the teasing, pain, and ridicule resulting from those actions. Thus I was driven into the closet to continue enjoying what I now call my fantasy.*

And "Kate" says:

> *I do not feel it is acceptable to society for me to do what I like to do . . . I carry a sense of guilt and shame for doing what I like to do . . . Those of us blessed with the desire (compulsion) to dress, act, and feel the way we do carry a big burden for fulfilling those desires.*

For many transvestites, the contact with cross-dressing started very early in life. It usually began quite innocently, by finding their mother's or sister's clothes, wondering how it would feel, and trying them on. "Nancy Ann" writes:

> *I can remember even as a youngster (around 4 or 5) the pleasure and excitement involved with dressing up in whatever I could get my hands on. As a young boy, I was bashful and never thought I was good enough to be friends with girls although I admired them from a distance. So I made my own girlfriend, which was my other inner self. At the age of 6 or 7*

I just had to try on my sister's yellow one piece swim-suit. I was caught and punished for doing it. I don't remember the spanking that I got, but still to this day remember that swim-suit and how natural it felt.

For others, the precipitating event could have been dressing as a girl in a school play or Halloween and liking the way it made them feel.

In general two types of transvestite evolve from the childhood experience. One derives emotional or sexual relief from dressing as a woman. This type, a fetish cross-dresser (Feinbloom, 1976; American Psychiatric Association, 1987; Docter, 1988) has an emotional attachment to women's clothing and can derive sexual excitement from holding, touching or wearing women's items of clothing. Another kind of transvestite is one who becomes very attached to and involved in the feminine way of life. It feels nice emotionally, sensually and perhaps spiritually. Whatever the feeling, it has an alluring effect, that draws the cross-dresser back time and time again.

Often at the beginning it is enough for a transvestite to see himself in women's clothing. Yet, the combination of the excitement and the guilt are what sometimes makes him dress again and again. After awhile he might not be satisfied any more with just dressing at home. A strong desire to go out dressed up can develop. "Nancy Ann" talks about his first time out:

I couldn't believe how much I enjoyed it. I slipped out of the house, it was late at night and walked around our neighborhood. It was a cool breezy evening and my skirts were really caressing my legs. The cold didn't bother me, all I could think of was the delicious feeling of being like a girl. When I got back home I wanted to wake everyone up and show them what I was doing. I was so excited. I was hooked for life.

And although "Nicki" does not really believe he is out completely, he writes:

I came out one night in the deep and dark back roads of this town. I was scared to death, I packed into a plastic bag my wig and shoes and left my apartment for my trip. I had on underneath my male clothing, my hose, bra and the necessities that my heart required. I drove to the darkest place that I could find and I removed my male clothing, put on my wig, Levi skirt and blouse within the darkness of the car. I stepped out of the car and left that safe zone, walking along that dirt road for about 300 feet and loving the sense of freedom that I had and the feeling that it was so right.

"Passing," going out in public as a woman, is usually the next step a transvestite will take. Docter (1988: 12) states that "passing is highly valued" by the transvestite and something that he wants to do. Yet, transvestites have different degrees in which they want to pass. For some, it is a walk around the block at three in the morning. For "Tracy," it started by going to church as a woman. He felt no one would look at him closely there and he would be safe. "Denise" went to the shopping malls and looked forward to being approached by the market research lady,

If the lady put an X into the female box without asking me the question, that meant I passed for sure. I was in ecstasy!

Although a few male cross-dressers are gay or bisexual, the majority are heterosexually oriented (Stoller, 1985; Talamini, 1982a, 1982b; Docter, 1988). If the man is single and has actively been cross-dressing for some time, the secret can be a heavy burden to bear. "Nicki" reveals:

Because I am orientated as a "normal" male, I continued having relations with women. I never did confide in any of them my innermost feelings and desires. I feel this puts a huge road block in our potential for true intimacy. Two or three discovered my "cache" and were quite disturbed—eventually leading to the demise of our relationship. Being found out, lack of communication, or fear of rejection always led to the break up.

Many of these men state that they are happily married. Telling their wives their secret can be very difficult. Some never tell, others do and end up paying a price, while others are able to incorporate their desires into their total marital lives. Once the husband has "come out of the closet" a surprising number of wives prove to be understanding and sympathetic. "Katie" says:

After 18 years of marriage, I figured that our relationship could stand it. In fact I owed it to her—the emotional strain in keeping an important part of me hidden was affecting our lives. Our relationship is stronger than ever. She still has problems dealing with my dressing, but she accepts that is part of my Me-ness . . . yet she is still not comfortable with my dressing and much prefers not to be involved or even to be reminded of it.

Some wives do not see this as a healthy situation, but go along with it for the sake of the marriage. The transvestite feels that the ideal wife should love her husband and stick by him no matter what he does. He wants a woman who believes in partnership without reservation and who will become knowledgeable about transvestism. "Nancy Ann" states:

My wife at least accepts my feelings, but does not really understand. She is cooperative and even buys items for me to wear as little surprises and gifts. I have dressed in her clothes, but usually do it in private. . .As a concession to my wife she has her husband during the day, but not at night and I have promised her I would not go out dressed.

All of the men I spoke with or who wrote to me were very willing to tell their stories. Some felt it was a relief to finally be able to talk about it with someone and believed that explaining to others was important and worth it for them if it took away the pain for someone else. When I asked them for permission to use their letters, their response was unanimous that I could use their information and they would help me with more as I needed it. They all believe that it is necessary information that could even help others. "Bev" says:

It is mandatory for a better understanding of TVs in society. I have carried the burden of guilt, shame, non-acceptance and personal non-understanding my whole life. Through efforts, strength, and unity of the community (TV) now maybe the lives and desires of the others and those to follow will be a little easier.

DISCUSSION

The data that I have analyzed in this paper are just the beginning of my project. Currently I am sending out questionnaires to transvestites around the country. If you are working in these areas, I would be very interested in hearing from you.

NOTE: This discussion section is shorter than some of the others you have seen, because the journal was publishing a special issue of work-in-progress and in this case a full discussion wasn't needed. However, in other articles reprinted in this book, the discussion ties everything together for you.

REFERENCES

American Psychiatric Association (1987) *Diagnostic and Statistical Manual of Mental Disorders*. Washington, DC: American Psychiatric Press.

Benjamin, H. (1966) *The Transsexual Phenomenon*. New York: Julian Press.

Brierley, H. (1979) *Transvestism: A Handbook with Case Studies for Psychologists, Psychiatrists, and Counselors*. Oxford: Pergamon.

Condor, S. (1986) "Sex Role Beliefs and Traditional Women: Feminist and Intergroup Perspectives," in S. Wilkinson (ed.) *Feminist Social Psychology Developing Theory and Practice*, pp. 97–118. Philadephia, PA: Open University Press.

Devor, H. (1989) *Gender Blending: Confronting the Limits of Duality*. Bloomington, IN: Indiana University Press.

Docter, R. F. (1988) *Transvestites and Transsexuals: Toward a Theory of Cross-Gender Behavior*. New York: Plenum.

Ellis, A. and Abarbanel, A. (1961) *The Encyclopedia of Sexual Behavior*. New York: Hawthorn Books.

Feinbloom, D. H. (1976) *Transvestites and Transsexuals, Mixed Views*. Los Angeles: Delacorte.

Freud, S. 1962, *Beyond the pleasure principle*, translated by James Strachey. New York: Liveright.

Garfinkel, H. (1967) *Studies in Ethnomethodology*. Englewood Cliff, NJ: Prentice-Hall.

Griffin, C. (1986) "Qualitative Methods and Female Experience: Young Women from School to the Job Market," in S. Wilkinson (ed.) *Feminist Social Psychology Developing Theory and Practice*, pp. 97–U8. Milton Keynes: Open University Press.

Harding, S. (1989) "Is There a Feminist Method?," in N. Tuana (ed.) *Feminism and Science*. Bloomington, IN: Indiana University Press.

Liazos, A. (1972) "The Poverty of the Sociology of Deviance: Nuts, Sluts, and Perverts," *Social Problems* 20: 103–20.

Martin, M. K. and Voorheis, B. (1975) *Female of the Species*. New York: Columbia University Press.

Masters, W. H., Johnson, V. E. and Kolodny, R. C. (1986) *Masters and Johnson on Sex and Human Loving*. Boston: Little, Brown.

Oakley, A. (1972) *Sex, Gender, and Society*. New York: Harper & Row.

Perkins, R. (1983) *The Drag Queen Scene: Transsexuals in Kings Cross*. Sydney: George Allen and Unwin.

Squire, C. (1989) *Significant Differences: Feminism in Psychology*. London: Routledge.

Stoller, R. (1985) *Presentations of Gender*. London: Yale University Press.

Talamini, J. T. (1982a) "Transvestites as a Minority Group," *International Review of History and Political Science* 19(2): 1–11.

Talamini, J. T. (1982b) "Transvestites: Deviant or Minority?," *International Review of History and Political Science* 19(1): 50–67.

Watson, C. M. (1990) "The Presentation of Self and the New Institutional Inmate: An Analysis of Prisoners' Response to Assessment for Release," in D. Brissett and C. Edgley (eds.) *Life as a Theater*. New York: Aldine de Gruyter.

West, C. and Zimmerman, D. (1987) "Doing Gender," *Gender and Society*, 1(2): 125–51.

Williamson, R. C, Swingle, P. G. and Sargent, S. S. (1982) *Social Psychology*. Itasca IL: F. E. Peacock.

Woodhouse, A. (1989) *Fantastic Women: Sex, Gender and Transvestism*. Basingstoke: Macmillan.

REVIEW QUESTIONS

1. If you were going to do a study on transvestites, what type of methodology would you use? How would you set the study up?
2. What variables were used in this study? Can you think of any that were left out?
3. Make your own outline of this literature review. After you have done that, find more current literature to support your outline.

Glossary

Abstract a brief summary of a research hypothesis, methods, results, and conclusions.

Accuracy a measure of how trustworthy a historical data source is.

Agreement reality things you consider real because other people seem to believe they are real and have told you they are real.

Anonymity keeping respondents' identities unknown, even to a researcher. Anonymity is ensured if no identifying information is recorded that could be used to link respondents to their responses.

Attributes characteristics of people or things.

Authenticity the genuineness of historical data sources.

Authority a person whom we believe because we think he or she truly knows about a subject.

Bogardus Social Distance Scale a measurement technique that indicates the willingness of the respondents to participate in social relations with other kinds of people in varying degrees of closeness.

Census data data, collected by the government, detailing the characteristics of the population.

Close-ended question a question that has a clear and apparent focus and a clearly defined answer. A close-ended question may provide a fixed set of answers for the respondent to choose from.

Cluster sampling a probability sampling method used when it is impossible or impractical to compile an exhaustive list of elements that compose the target population.

Code of ethics guidelines set up by a professional organization to guide research endeavors and protect respondents from harm.

Concept a mental image that summarizes a set of similar observations, feelings, or ideas explaining exactly what is meant by the term used.

Conceptualization the process of specifying what is meant by a term.

Confidentiality making identifying information that could be used to link respondents to their responses available only to designated personnel.

Conflict theory a Marxist theory that claims that people are always competing for power.

Content analysis a quantitative method used to study communications processes in magazines, television, and other types of media.

Control group the group of research participants who do not receive the treatment that members of the experimental group receive.

Convenience sampling a nonprobability sampling method in which subjects are selected because they are available.

Cross-sectional study research that examines age differences in subjects rather than age changes.

Dependent variable a variable, or factor, causally influenced by the independent variable. See also *independent variable.*

Descriptive research research in which the researcher describes a phenomenon without making any attempt to determine what causes it.

Dimension a specific aspect of a concept.

Direct observation notes detailed notes that the researcher writes soon after leaving the field; they include concrete information, respondents' comments, maps, and drawings.

Disproportionate stratified sample a sample in which a subpopulation is disproportionate to ensure there are sufficient numbers of cases from each stratum for analysis.

Double-barreled question a single survey item that asks two questions but allows only one answer.

Double-blind procedure an experiment in which neither subjects nor staff who are delivering the experimental treatments know which subjects are getting the treatment and which subjects are getting the placebo.

Double negative question a question in which the presence of two negative words, such as *never* and *not*, paves the way for misinterpretation.

Ecological fallacy the fallacy that occurs when a conclusion about individuals is based on data drawn from the observation of groups.

Empirical research a statement or theory that can be tested by some kind of evidence drawn from experience.

Ethics guidelines for research that enable a researcher to ensure that all respondents participate voluntarily and are not harmed.

Ethnocentrism the tendency to look at other cultures through the eyes of one's own culture and thereby misinterpret the other cultures.

Ethnography the study of people firsthand using participant observation or interviewing. See also *participant observation*.

Evaluation research research that evaluates social programs or interventions.

Exhaustive attributes values in which every case can be classified as having one attribute.

Existing statistics someone else's data that a researcher uses to undertake her or his own statistical analyses. See also *secondary sources*.

Experiment a research method in which variables can be analyzed in a controlled and systematic way, either in an artificial situation constructed by the researcher or in naturally occurring settings.

Experimental group the group of research participants who receive the treatment in an experiment.

Experimental reality things you know as real because you have had your own direct experience with them.

Explanatory research research that seeks to identify causes or effects of the phenomenon being studied.

Exploratory research research in which social phenomena are investigated without prior expectations so researchers can develop explanations.

Extraneous variables variables that represent an alternative explanation for the relationship observed between the independent and dependent variables.

Feminist theory theory that looks at inequality in race, gender, sex, and sexuality.

Fieldwork the activity of collecting data in empirical research. See also *ethnography; participant observation*.

Follow-up questions interview questions intended to clarify an interviewee's response or to generate new information.

Functionalist theory a theoretical perspective based on the notion that social events can best be explained by the functions they perform and the contributions they make to the equilibrium of society.

Generalize to draw inferences and conclusions from sample data and apply them to a whole population.

Historical research a methodology for examining how past events affect the present and might affect the future.

Hypothesis an idea or a guess about a given state of affairs, put forward as a basis for empirical testing.

Independent variable a variable, or factor, that causally affects the dependent variable. See also *dependent variable*.

Index a composite measure that summarizes several specific observations and represents some more general dimension.

Indicator the end product of the conceptualization process: a specific set of characteristics that signal the presence or absence of the concept being studied.

Informed consent consent that a person grants after he or she understands what a research project involves and who is conducting it.

Institutional review board (IRB) a group required by federal law to review the ethical issues in all proposed research that is federally funded and involves human subjects or has the potential to harm subjects.

Intentional plagiarism cheating of any kind, including copying directly from an article or a book or buying an article off the Internet.

Interrater reliability the extent of consistency in the findings of at least two different, independent observers.

Interview a data collection method in which a researcher questions a subject face-to-face or by phone.

Jotted notes brief notes written by a researcher during fieldwork and intended to jog his or her memory later. See also *direct observation notes.*

Likert Scale an attitude scale that requires the respondent to agree or disagree with a statement.

Literature review the section of a research paper that introduces the problem, develops the background in a history of the scholarly work on the subject, and ends with the purpose and the rationale of the study.

Longitudinal study research that assesses changes in behavior in one group of subjects at more than one point in time.

Macrolevel analysis analysis and theories that examine broad areas of society such as the political system or the economy.

Measurement techniques methods of collecting data, such as surveys, interviews, and focus groups.

Mesolevel analysis analysis and theories that examine social groups or organizations such as classrooms and offices.

Microlevel analysis analysis and theories that examine narrow or small aspects of social life such as differences in play between boys and girls.

Mutually exclusive attributes a variable's attributes or values are mutually exclusive if every case can have only one attribute.

Narrative an account of events told either by the person who experienced them or by someone else.

Nonprobability sampling a sampling technique that doesn't use randomization; as a result, the likelihood of selecting any one member of a population is unknown.

Open-ended question a question that provides an opportunity for respondents to respond in any way they want.

Operationalize to specify the operations that will indicate the value of cases on a variable.

Oral history a recording or a transcript of a person's own account of events that she or he witnessed or experienced.

Paradigm a fundamental model or framework that organizes our view of something and tells us where to look for answers.

Participant observation a method of research, widely used in the social sciences, in which the researcher takes part in the activities of the group or community being studied. See also *ethnography; fieldwork.*

Peer-reviewed journal a journal in which research papers are published only after they have been blindly reviewed, usually by three other scholars in the same field who decide if the research meets the journal's standards.

Personal troubles problems that individuals think are a reflection of only themselves.

Placebo something that is used in place of an experimental stimulus to make the subject think he or she is receiving the stimulus.

Plagiarism using someone else's writing without crediting the author. See also *intentional plagiarism; unintentional plagiarism.*

Population people who are the focus of social research.

Posttest a test given to subjects in a randomly assigned group after the end of an experiment.

Pretest a test given to subjects in a randomly assigned group before an experiment begins.

Primary existing data original sources of information that is used in a research study.

Primary sources firsthand accounts.

Probability sampling a sampling technique that uses randomization; as a result, the likelihood of selecting any one member of a population is known.

Proportionate stratified sample a sample in which a uniform proportion of cases is drawn from each homogeneous group.

Public issues social issues that individuals have no control over.

Purposive sample a nonprobability sample created by a researcher for a specific purpose.

Qualitative research research that emphasizes depth of understanding and the deeper meanings of the human experience and that aims to generate theoretically rich observations.

Quantitative research research based on precise, objective, and generalizable findings.

Quasi-experimental design an experiment in which subjects are preassigned to treatments.

Questionnaire a set of structured, focused questions in a self-reporting format.

Quota sample a nonprobability sample created by the researcher to match the proportions of specific characteristics in the larger population.

Random-digit dialing a sampling method in which a computer automatically dials telephone numbers at random.

Randomization a probability sampling method in which every member of a population has the same chance of being selected for a sample. Also called *random selection*.

Reductionism A problem that arises when a strict limitation (reduction) of the kinds of concepts is considered relevant to the phenomenon under study.

Reliability the extent to which the same data are collected each time in repeated observations of the same phenomenon.

Representative sample a sample that resembles the population from which it was selected in all respects that are potentially relevant to the study.

Research a way of answering a hypothetical question.

Research methods diverse methods of investigation used to gather empirical or factual material.

Sample a proportion of individuals or cases from a larger population, judged to be representative of the larger population.

Sampling error the difference between the characteristics of a sample and the charactecistics of the population as a whole.

Sampling interval the standard distance between elements selected in systematic random sampling.

Scale a composite measure composed of several items that have a logical or empirical structure among them, such as the Likert Scale or the Bogardus Social Distance Scale.

Secondary sources data collected by someone other than the researcher doing an analysis; information provided by someone other than a participant or observer of the event.

Self-administered questionnaire a collection of questions that the respondent is able to answer on his or her own.

Semantic differential scale a scale in which respondents are asked to chose between two opposites on a questionnaire.

Simple random sampling a probability sampling method in which every sample element is selected on the basis of chance.

Snowball sampling a nonprobability sampling method in which the sample elements are selected as they are identified by successive informants or interviewees.

Social desirability the appeal of the question being asked of the respondent.

Stratification the process of grouping members of a population into relatively homogeneous subgroups before sampling.

Stratified random sampling a probability sampling method in which the sample elements are selected separately from population strata identified in advance by the researcher.

Survey research a research method in which questionnaires are administered to the population being studied.

Symbolic interactionism a theoretical approach that emphasizes the role of symbols in all human interaction.

Systematic random sampling a probability sampling method in which every *n*th element in a list is systematically chosen after the first element is randomly selected.

Theoretical articles articles that explain a theory and how it relates to the variables being investigated.

Theory an attempt to identify general properties that may explain observed events. Theories form an essential element of all scientific works. Theories tend to be linked to broader theoretical approaches, but they are strongly influenced by the research results they help to generate.

Time series design a quasi-experimental design that consists of many pretest and posttest observations of the same group. See also *posttest; pretest*.

Tradition the way things have always been and always will be done.

True experimental design an experiment in which the subjects are randomly assigned to an experimental group that receives a treatment or other manipulation of the independent variable or to a comparison group that does not receive the treatment and whose outcomes are measured in a posttest. See also *double-blind procedure*.

Unintentional plagiarism paraphrasing or summarizing another author's ideas without giving credit to the author.

Unit of analysis the level of social life on which a research question is focused.

Validity the truthfulness or accuracy of the score of a test or the interpretation of an experiment.

Variable a dimension along which an object, individual, or group may be categorized, such as weight or sex.

Voluntary participation knowing about a research study and freely agreeing to take part in it.

Index

A
Abstract of article, 215
Accuracy in historical research, 167
Advertisement claims
  doctors/drug recommendations, 3-4
  judging, 3
AFDC aid/study, 67-72
Aggregates
  family as, 67, 69, 70, 71
  family household as, 67, 69, 70, 71
  household as, 67, 69, 70, 71
  minimal household unit as, 67-68, 69, 70, 71
  as unit of analysis/example study, 66-72
Agreement reality
  definition/description, 4
  research and, 5
AIDS. *See* HIV/AIDS
Amateur stripping/gaming study, 176-184
American Sociological Association (ASA)
  Code of Ethics, 58-60
  functions, 201
  Style Guide, 221
Analysis of Variance. *See* ANOVA
Anonymity
  amateur stripping/gaming study, 176-184
  definition/description, 44
  domestic abuse study, 185-189
  STDs and, 49
  Thai adolescent health concerns study, 169-175
ANOVA
  business ethics study example, 105-107
  Reverse Social Distance Scale study, 114
Anti-achievement culture, 28
Articles. *See also* Reading a journal article
  writing for social sciences (overview), 218-221
ASA. *See* American Sociological Association (ASA)
Authenticity in historical research, 167
Authority effects, 5
Autonomy
  indirect recruitment and, 51, 52, 53
  Internet research and, 56

B
Bell, Anthony, murders, 3
Beneficence, 49
Bias
  with indirect recruitment, 50, 52
  self-selection and, 124, 125, 159-161
Biographies. *See also* Narratives
  domestic abuse study, 185-189
  significance of, 188-189
  in transvestites research example, 217, 223-225
  truth and, 187-188
Biomed Programme, 131
Blumer, H., 24
Bogardus Social Distance Scale
  definition/description, 100-101, 111, 113
  Reverse Social Distance Scale/ study, 111-115
  use of, 112, 115

C
Canada Yearbook, 192
Castes
  overview, 25
  school tracking and, 25, 30
Census data, 192. *See also* U.S. Census Bureau/data
Chicago Manual of Style, 221
Clinton, Bill, 43
Close-ended questions, 85, 141
Cluster sampling
  definition/description, 119
  sexual behavior (U.S.) study, 123-129
Code of Ethics, 41, 58-60

Columbine High School shootings, 23
Commonsense ideas
phenomenological analysis and, 12
social reality vs., 11-16
Communications Decency Act, 45
Competence of professionals (ASA Code of Ethics), 59-60
Comprehensive Quality of Life Scale, 100
Computer programs/data analysis. *See also specific programs*
overview, 101
resources on, 101-102
Comte, Auguste, 19
Concept of research
definition/description, 83
dimensions of, 83
Concepts, 20
Conceptualization
definition/description, 83
Nigeria toxic chemicals study, 86-90
Conceptualization of terrorism
article excerpts, 91-96
definition of terrorism, 92-95
research and, 91-92, 96
Conclusion/discussion section of article, 217-218
Confidentiality
definition/description, 44
indirect recruitment and, 49-50, 52-53
Internet research, 56
privacy and, 49-50
Conflict theory
definition/description, 19
domestic abuse study and, 185-189
Consciousness
as intentional, 12
multiple realities and, 12
reality of everyday life and, 13-16
temporality of, 15-16
Consent. *See* Informed consent
Content analysis
definition/description, 166
Thai adolescent health concerns study, 169-175
Control group, 139
Convenience sampling
definition/description, 120
example, 124
Cooley, C. H., 24
Cosmetics/soaps use study, 86-90
Cross-sectional study, 64

D

Data. *See also* Existing statistics; Primary existing data
computer programs for analyzing, 101-102
raw data, 92
Debriefing information, 55-56
Deception and research, 44
Dependent variable, 21, 83
Descriptive research, 17, 62
Dictionary of American Biography, 192
Dimensions
concept of research, 83
scales and, 100
Direct observation notes, 164
Disclaimers, 56
Discussion/conclusion section of article, 217-218
Disproportionate stratified sample, 119
Distributive justice, 51-52
Domestic abuse study, 185-189
Double-barreled questions, 85
Double-blind procedures, 140-141
Double negative questions, 85
Drug use example studies, 1

E

Ecological fallacy, 64
Empirical research, 213
Escalante, Jaime, 24-25
Ethics in research. *See also* Non-maleficence
analysis and, 44-45
ASA Code of Ethics, 58-60
conducting research on Internet, 55-58
deception and, 44
definition/description, 41
indirect recruitment and, 47-53
individuals who harm, 53
issues overview, 43-45
"Prison Experiment,", 44
reporting and, 44-45
unethical examples, 42-43
Ethnocentrism, 6
Ethnography, 163. *See also* Fieldwork
Eurowinter research project, 130-137
Evaluation research, 192-193
Existing statistics. *See also* Primary existing data
definition/description, 191
professors' student evaluations study, 202-210
sociologists' work activities/workplaces study, 194-201
Experimental group, 139
Experimental reality
definition/description, 5
research and, 5
Experiments
definition/description, 138
types overview, 138-141
Explanatory research, 62
Exploratory research
definition/description, 61-62
questionnaires use with, 61

F

Factor analysis, 206, 207
Family as aggregate, 67, 69, 70, 71
Family household as aggregate, 67, 69, 70, 71
Feminist theory
definition/description, 20
domestic abuse study, 185-189
murder-suicide study, 33-39
transvestites research example, 222-225
Fieldwork
amateur stripping/gaming study, 176-184
auction example, 163, 164-165
examples, 163-165
note taking/diagrams, 164-165
overview, 163-165
researcher's effects, 164
Follow-up questions, 166
Functionalist theory, 19

G
Gaming/amateur stripping study, 176-184
Gaming theory, 176-184
Generalizing from sampling, 117
General Social Survey, The, 192
Goodness-of-fit measures, 208
"Green Run Study," 42
Group as unit of analysis, 63

H
Harm. *See* Non-maleficence
Helms, Jesse, 153
Helsinki Declaration, 49, 52
Historical research, 166-167
Hite Report, The, 123, 125
HIV/AIDS studies
  examples, 1, 48, 121, 152-154
  indirect recruitment and, 48
Homeless men study, 119-120
Household as aggregate, 67, 69, 70, 71
Human papilloma virus (HPV), 1
Human Sexual Response (Masters and Johnson), 125
Hydroquinone/use study, 86-90
Hypothesis, 20-21, 83

I
Immigrants/natives study. *See* Public assistance for natives/immigrants study
Incentives study, 144-150
Independent variable, 21, 83, 138
Index
  definition/description, 99
  example, 99
Indicator of variable, 83
Indirect recruitment
  AIDS studies and, 48
  autonomy and, 51, 52, 53
  bias with, 50, 52
  confidentiality and, 49-50, 52-53
  consent and, 48, 52
  description, 47-48
  distributive justice and, 51-52
  harm and, 49-53
  privacy and, 49-50, 52, 53
  sexual networks, 48-53
  trust and, 50-51
Individual as unit of analysis, 62-63, 69, 70, 71
Informed consent
  definition/description, 43
  indirect recruitment and, 48, 52
  Internet research, 55
Institutional review boards (IRBs)
  definition/description, 45
  importance of, 47
  Internet research and, 56-57
  privacy and, 50
  risk/benefit ratio, 47, 48-53
Integrity of professionals (ASA Code of Ethics), 60
Intentional plagiarism, 220
Internet
  plagiarism, 220
  purchasing papers from, 220
Internet research
  autonomy and, 56
  commercial data-collection sites and, 57
  computer hackers' risk, 56
  confidentiality and, 56
  credibility of, 57
  debriefing information, 55-56
  disclaimers, 56
  ethics overview, 55-58
  guidelines, 57-58
  identifying information, 56
  increase in, 55
  informed consent and, 55
  institutional review boards and, 56-57
  response rate and, 158-161
  sampling and, 158-161
  Thai adolescent health concerns study, 169-175
  unethical analysis/reporting example, 45
Interviewing, 165-166
IRBs. *See* Institutional review boards (IRBs)
Israel community study, 18-19
Ivy, A. C., 42

J
Janus, S.S./C.L., 125-126, 127
Janus Report, The, 125-126, 127
Johnson, V., 125
Jotted notes, 164
Journal articles. *See also* Reading a journal article
  writing for social sciences (overview), 218-221

K
Kinsey, A., 123-125, 152-153
Kuhn, T., 18

L
Likert Scale
  business ethics study example, 103-110
  definition/description, 100
LISREL VII statistical package, 205-206
Literature review section of article, 215-216
Longitudinal studies
  business ethics study example, 103-110
  definition/description, 64
  effects of study, 74-79
  marriage study example, 74-79

M
Macrolevel analysis, 18, 19
Marriage study example
  effects of study, 74-79
  as longitudinal study, 74-79
  measurements, 78
Marx, K., 19
Masters, W., 125
Mead, G. H., 19, 25
Mercuric iodide/use study, 86-90
Mesolevel analysis, 19
Methods section of article, 216-217
MicroCase, 101
Microlevel analysis, 18-19
Milgram shock studies, 44
Mills, C. W.
  author's reality/research, 7-8, 41
  personal troubles vs. public issues, 6, 10
  Sociological Imagination, 6, 8-10
Minimal household unit as aggregate, 67-68, 69, 70, 71
Minorities and Reverse Social Distance Scale study, 111-115

Monetary incentives study, 144-150
Movies and agreement realty, 4
Murders by Anthony Bell, 3
Murder-suicide study
  alcohol and, 37
  cases, 38-39
  child victims/parent gender, 38-39
  feminist theory perspective, 33-39
  gender/method, 36
  gender roles, 34, 37-39
  male possessiveness and, 37-38
  perspective overview, 33-34
  statistics, 35-37
Mutually exclusive attributes, 98

N

Narratives. *See also* Biographies
  definition/description, 167-168
  domestic abuse study and, 185-189
  truth and, 187-188
National Health and Social Life Survey. *See* NHSLS sexual behavior study
National Science Foundation statistics/use, 194-201
Natives/immigrants study. *See* Public assistance for natives/immigrants study
Nazi experiments on people, 42
New Zealand Official Yearbook, 192
NHSLS sexual behavior study
  questionnaire design, 154-157
  sampling, 123-129
  survey design, 151-157
  validity and, 155-157
Nigeria toxic chemicals study, 86-90
Non-maleficence
  classification of harm, 49
  overview, 49-53
  physical harm, 47
  psychological harm, 44, 49
Nonprobability sampling
  definition/description, 119-120
  Eurowinter project, 130-137
  types, 120-121
Note taking/diagrams, 164-165
Nuremberg Code, 49, 51-52
Nuremberg war crimes, 42

O

Objectivations of subjective processes/meanings, 11
Observation study example, 176-184
Office for Protection of Research Risks (OPRR)
  harm classification, 49
  privacy and, 50, 52
  risk/benefit ratio, 48
Online questionnaires, 142-143
Open-ended questions, 85, 141
Operationalizing a variable
  definition/description, 84
  example, 99
OPRR. *See* Office for Protection of Research Risks (OPRR)
Oral history, 167
Organization as unit of analysis, 63

P

Paradigms
  definition/description, 18
  replacement of, 18
Participant observation, 163. *See also* Fieldwork
Peer-reviewed journal, 213-214
Personal narratives, 167-168
Personal troubles
  definition/description, 6
  public issues vs., 6, 10
Placebo, 140
Plagiarism
  Internet and, 220
  literature review and, 216, 220-221
  overview, 219-221
  statistics on, 220
Playboy sexual behavior study, 125
Plutonium experiments on people, 42
Poisson regression models, 147, 149
Population, 117
Pornography on Internet study, 45
Posttest, 139
PowerPoint, 217
Premarital sex/tattoo study, 120
Prepaid monetary incentives study, 144-150
Pretest, 139
Primary existing data
  professors' student evaluations study, 202-210
  sociologists' work activities/workplaces study, 194-201
  sources, 191-192
Primary sampling units (PSUs), 145-146, 147
Primary sources, 167, 213, 214
Privacy
  confidentiality and, 49-50
  definition/description, 49
  indirect recruitment and, 49-50, 52, 53
Probability sampling
  definition/description, 118
  overview, 118-119
  sexual behavior (U.S.) study, 123-129
Professors' student evaluations study, 202-210
Proportionate stratified sample, 118-119
Protection of Human Subjects Act, 48
PSUs (primary sampling units), 145-146, 147
Psychological harm
  dimensions of, 49
  overview, 49-53
Public assistance for natives/immigrants study
  overview, 66-72
  unit of analysis importance, 68-72
  unit of analysis selection, 66-68
Publication Manual (American Psychological Association), 221
Public identity and school tracking, 26
Public issues
  definition/description, 6
  personal troubles vs., 6, 10
Purposive sample, 121

Q

Qualitative research, 83
Quantitative research
  definition/description, 82-83, 98
  Nigeria toxic chemicals study, 86-90
Quasi-experimental design, 140
Questionnaires
  designing, 141-142
  distributing, 142-143
  with exploratory research, 61
  NHSLS sexual behavior study, 154-157
  self-administered questionnaires, 142-143
  in toxic chemicals study, 88
Questions
  constructing (overview), 84-85
  recommendations on, 85
  in toxic chemicals study, 88
  types overview, 85
Quota sample
  definition/description, 120-121
  Eurowinter research project, 130-137

R

Radioactive gas experiments on people, 42
Random-digit dialing, 118
Randomization/random selection, 118
Reading a journal article
  abstract, 215
  discussion/conclusion section, 217-218
  hourglass organization, 214, 215
  literature review section, 215-216
  methods section, 216-217
  organization of article, 214, 215
  overview, 214-218
  results section, 217
  transvestite study example, 214-218
Reality of everyday life. *See also* Social reality
  distortion and, 15
  routines and, 14
  shifts and, 14-15
  spatial structure, 15
  subjectivity of, 13
  temporal structure, 15-16
  verification and, 13
Redbook sexual behavior study, 123, 125
Reductionism, 64
Reliability
  definition/description, 84
  scales and, 99
  sexual behavior studies and, 123-126
Reporting and ethics, 44-45
Representative sample, 117
Research. *See also specific types*
  agreement/experimental reality and, 5
  definition/description, 3
  main question types, 9
  prevalence of reports/results, 1, 2
  unethical research on humans, 42-43
Research methods
  definition/description, 4
  importance of, 4
Research reasons
  curiosity and, 3
  judging advertisement claims, 3
  overview, 17, 61-62
Respect shown by professionals (ASA Code of Ethics), 60
Responsibility of professionals (ASA Code of Ethics), 60
Reverse Social Distance Scale study, 111-115
Rimm, M., 45
Risk/benefit ratio, 47, 48-53

S

Sample definition/description, 117
Sampling. *See also specific types*
  generalizing from, 117
  Internet/opinion measurement study, 157-161
  Internet research and, 158-161
  NHSLS sexual behavior study, 123, 127-129
  overview, 117
  percentage of response, 125, 127
  self-selection and, 124, 125, 159-161
  sexual behavior studies/problems, 123-126, 127
Sampling error, 119
Sampling interval, 118
SAS, 101
Scales. *See also specific scales*
  definition/description, 100
  examples, 100-101
School tracking
  bonding and, 26, 27
  castes and, 25, 30
  education quality and, 27
  school violence and, 23-30
  socializing into model citizens vs., 29, 30
  teacher expectations and, 24, 26-27
  variables used for, 37
  violence and, 23-30
School violence
  bonding and, 26
  recent history, 23
  school tracking and, 23-30
  social control theory and, 26
Secondary sources
  data from, 12
  definition/description, 167, 214
  problems with, 214
Self-administered questionnaires, 142-143
Self-esteem
  racism/prejudice and, 28
  school tracking and, 28-29
Self-identity and school tracking, 26
Self-image and school tracking, 26
SEM (Structural Equation Modeling), 203, 206, 208-209
Semantic differential scale, 101
Sexual behavior studies
  fraudulent responses, 126
  NHSLS study, 123-129
  reliability and, 123-126
  sampling problems, 123-126, 127
Sexual networks and indirect recruitment, 48-53
Shock (Milgram) studies, 44
Simple random sampling, 118
SIPP (Survey of Income and Program Participation), 68-69, 145-150

Snowball sampling, 121
Soaps/cosmetics use study, 86-90
Social artifacts
  definition/description, 63
  as unit of analysis, 63
Social control theory and school violence, 26
Social desirability (of questions), 85
Social reality
  commonsense ideas vs., 11-16
  every day life reality and, 12-16
  question types on, 9
Sociological imagination, 8-10
Sociological Imagination (Mills)
  excerpts from, 8-10
  personal troubles vs. public issues, 6, 10
Sociologists' work activities/workplaces study, 194-201
Spatial structure, 15
SPSS (Statistical Package for the Social Sciences), 101, 102, 217
SSI aid/study, 67-72
Stand and Deliver, 24
Standard and Poor's Register of Corporations, 192
STATA, 101
Statistical Abstract of the United States, 192
Statistical Package for the Social Sciences (SPSS), 101, 102, 217
Stratification, 118
Stratified random sampling, 118
Stress as psychological harm, 49
Structural Equation Modeling (SEM), 203, 206, 208-209
Student evaluations of professors study
  overview, 202-210
  problems with student evaluations, 203
Student-teacher interactions
  as critical, 30
  factors affecting, 25
  symbolic interactionism, 24-29
  tracking and, 25-26
Style Guide (ASA), 221
Survey of Doctoral Recipients statistics/use, 194-201
Survey of Income and Program Participation (SIPP), 68-69, 145-150
Survey research
  definition/description, 141
  overview, 141-143
Symbolic interactionism
  definition/description, 19-20
  premises of, 24
  school tracking/school violence and, 23-30
  student-teacher interactions and, 24-29
Symbols and communication, 19-20, 25
Syphilis, "Tuskegee Syphilis Study," 42-43
Systematic random sampling, 118

T

Tattoo/premarital sex study, 120
Teachers. *See also* Student-teacher interactions
  professors' student evaluations study, 202-210
  school tracking/student violence study, 23-30
Temporal structure
  of consciousness, 15-16
  finiteness and, 15
  sequences and, 16
Terrorism. *See* Conceptualization of terrorism
Thai adolescent health concerns study, 169-175
Theoretical articles, 213
Theory
  definition/description, 17
  types, 19-20
Time dimension of research, 64-65
Time series design
  definition/description, 140
  prepaid monetary incentives study, 144-150
Toxic chemicals study, 86-90
Tradition effects, 5
Transvestites research example
  article, 222-225
  biographies use, 217, 223-225
  feminist theory and, 222-225
  perspectives, 17-18
  reading a journal article, 214-218
True experimental design, 138-140
Trust and indirect recruitment, 50-51
"Tuskegee Syphilis Study,", 42-43

U

Unethical research examples, 42-43
Unintentional plagiarism, 220
Units of analysis
  aggregates as, 66-68
  definition/description, 62
  examples/overview, 62-64
  importance of, 64, 66-68
  problem example, 66-72
  problems with, 63-64
  public assistance for natives/immigrants study example, 66-72
U.S. Census Bureau/data, 68, 141, 145, 146, 192
U.S. News and World Report index example, 99
Uterine (unethical) cancer studies, 43

V

Validity
  definition/description, 84
  NHSLS sexual behavior study, 155-157
  scales and, 99
Value changes over time, 8-9
Variables
  definition/description, 20-21, 83
  indicators of, 83
  in research design, 98
Vital Statistics on American Politics, 192
Vitamin use example studies, 1
Voluntary participation, 43

W

White supremacist groups study, 119, 120
Writing for social sciences
  overview, 218-221
  plagiarism, 219-221
  writing resources, 221